MASTERING THE ART OF
OILS, ACRYLICS
AND GOUACHE

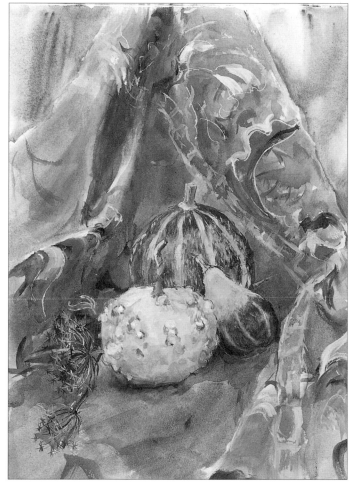

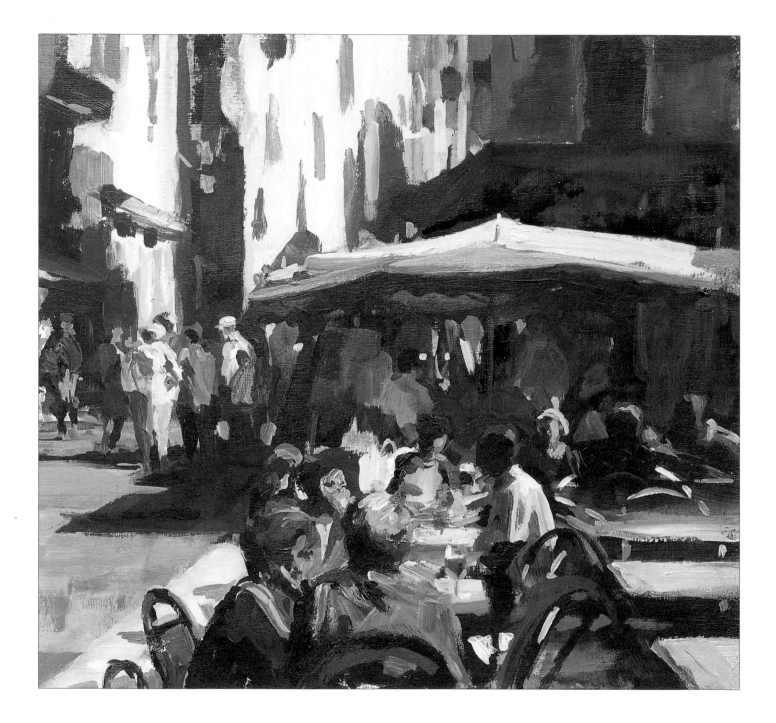

MASTERING THE ART OF
OILS, ACRYLICS
AND GOUACHE

mixing paint • brushstrokes •blending • underpainting • working alla prima
glazing • scumbling • painting with knives • impasto work • drybrush work

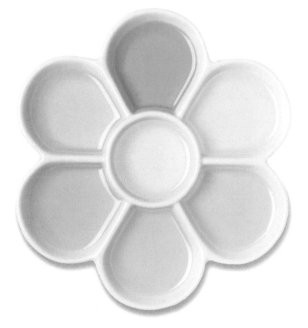

IAN SIDAWAY

HERMES HOUSE

This edition is published by Hermes House

Hermes House is an imprint of Anness Publishing Ltd
Hermes House, 88–89 Blackfriars Road, London SE1 8HA
tel. 020 7401 2077; fax 020 7633 9499; info@anness.com

A CIP catalogue record for this book is available from the British Library.

Publisher: Joanna Lorenz
Editorial Director: Helen Sudell
Consultant Editor: Sarah Hoggett
Photographers: George Taylor
Designer: Nigel Partridge
Illustrator: Ian Sidaway
Project Contributors: Martin Decent, Paul Dyson, Timothy Easton, Abigail Edgar,
Wendy Jelbert, John Raynes, Ian Sidaway
Editorial Readers: Rosanna Fairhead and Lindsay Zamponi
Production Controller: Pedro Nelson

1 3 5 7 9 10 8 6 4 2

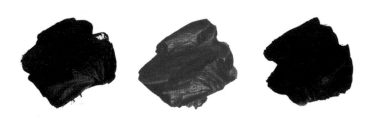

Contents

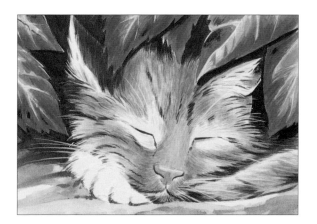

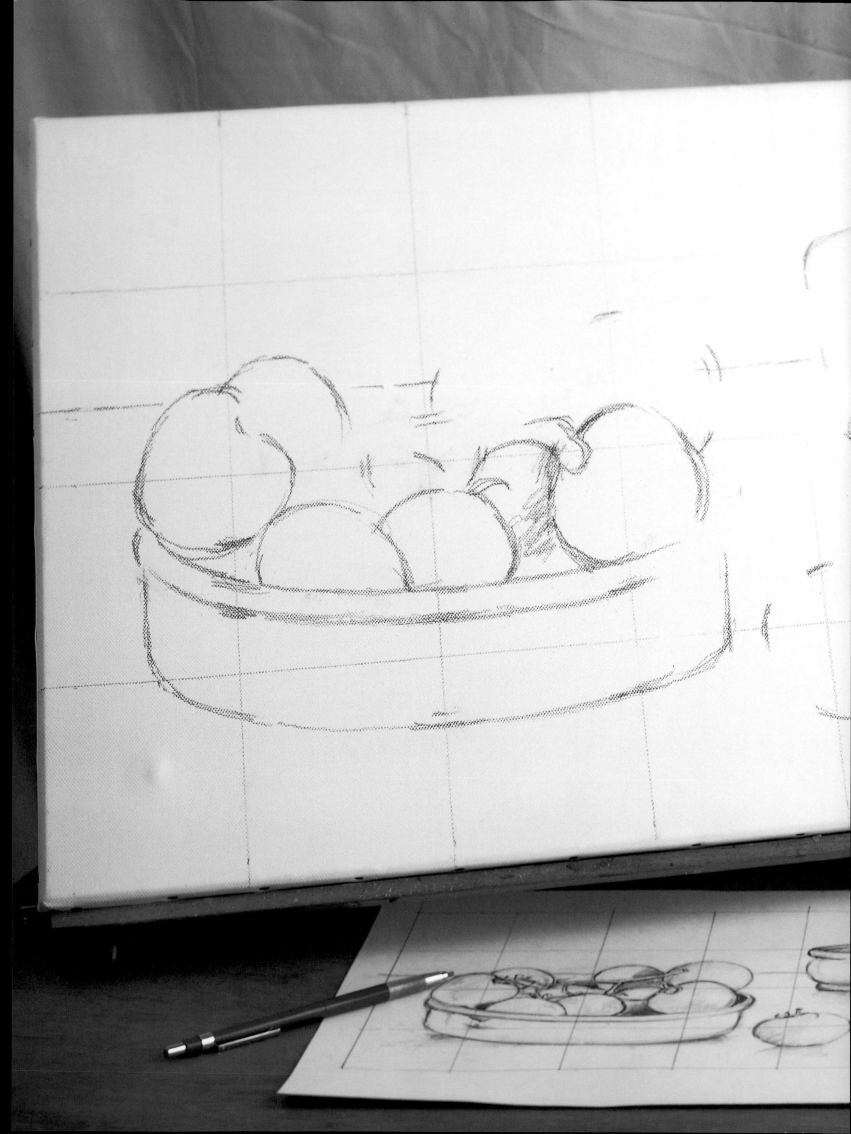

Getting started

Oil paint

There are two types of traditional oil paint – professional, or artists', quality and the less expensive students' quality. The essential difference is that artists' quality paint uses finely ground, high-quality pigments, which are bound in the best oils and contain very little filler, while students' paints use less expensive pigments and contain greater quantities of filler to bulk out the paint and give it more body. The filler usually consists of *blanc fixe* or aluminium hydrate, both of which are white pigments with a very low tinting strength.

Students' quality paint is often very good and is, in fact, used by students, amateur painters and professionals alike. The range of colours is more limited but still comprehensive, and each tube of paint in the range, irrespective of its colour, costs the same. Artists' quality paint is sold according to the quality and cost of the pigment used to make it. Each colour in the range is given a series number or letter; the higher the number or letter, the more expensive the paint. Various oils are used to bind the paint and make it workable; linseed, poppy and safflower oil are the most common. The choice of oil depends on the characteristics and drying properties of the pigment being mixed.

Tubes or tubs? ▷
Oil paint is sold in tubes containing anything from 15 to 275ml (1 tbsp to 9fl oz). If you tend to use a large quantity of a particular colour – for toning grounds, for example – you can buy paint in cans containing up to 5 litres (8¾ pints).

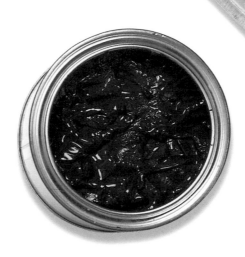

Oil bars

Like "tube" paint, oil bars can be used to draw on to the support and the paint can be thinned and manipulated in exactly the same way as one would use traditional paint. They can be used in conjunction with traditional oil paint but, because of the added wax content, they are not recommended for heavy or extensive underpainting use.

Drawing with oils ▼
Oil bars consist of paint with added wax and drying agents. The wax stiffens the paint, enabling it to be rolled into what resembles a giant pastel.

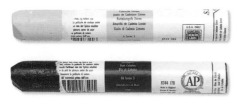

Alkyd oil paints

A synthetic resin, which is made by combining acid and alcohol, is used in the manufacture of alkyd oil paints. The paints are used in exactly the same way as traditional oil paints and can be mixed with all the traditional mediums and thinners.

The range of colours is not as extensive as that for traditional oil paint, but it is wide enough for most purposes. The largest tube size available is 200ml (7fl oz).

Alkyd-based paint dries much faster than oil-based paint. This makes it very useful for underpainting prior to using traditional oils and for work incorporating glazes or thin layers.

However, you should not use alkyd paint over traditional oil paint, as its fast drying time can cause problems with the stability of the oil paint.

Water-mixable oil paint

One of the most recent developments in paint technology is water-mixable oil paint. Although it sounds like a contradiction in terms, it was conceived so that people who are allergic to mineral and vegetable solvents could still have access to paint with the handling characteristics of traditional oil paint.

Water-mixable oil paint is made using linseed and safflower oils that have been modified to be soluble in water. Once the paint has dried and the oils have oxidized, it is as permanent and stable as conventional oil paint. Some water-mixable paint can also be used with conventional oil paint, although its mixability is gradually compromised the more traditional paint is added. Water-mixable oil paint is available in tube sizes up to 275ml (9fl oz).

Oil starter palette

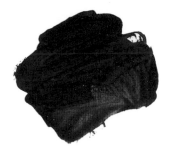

Ultramarine blue

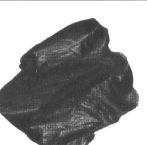

Cerulean blue

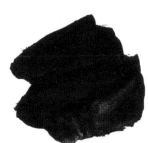

Cadmium red

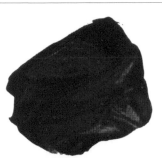

Alizarin crimson

Cadmium lemon yellow

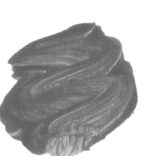

Yellow ochre

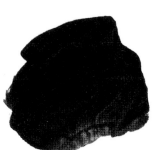

Raw umber

Burnt sienna

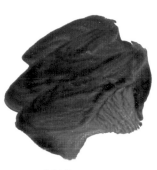

Viridian green

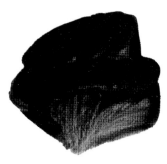

Ivory black

The starter palette shown here is based on readily available colours and should cover most eventualities.

Ultramarine blue: originally made from lapis lazuli, it is now more commonly made from an artificial and less expensive pigment that is stable in mixes, although it is relatively slow to dry. The synthetic colour is often sold as French ultramarine. Ultramarine blue is a transparent blue. It has good tinting strength and is the classic "warm" blue.

Cerulean blue: a "cool", semi-transparent blue. The artificial pigment is mixed with either linseed or poppy oil and dries relatively fast. Phthalocyanine blue is often used in place of cerulean.

Cadmium red: made from an artificial mineral pigment, this is the classic "warm" red. Slow to dry but stable, it is opaque and has good tinting strength.

Alizarin crimson: a transparent colour with a high tinting strength. Once made from madder root but now produced synthetically, alizarin is a "cool", slow-drying red. The colour can fade when used in light mixes. Quinacridone red is often used as an alternative.

Cadmium lemon yellow: made from an artificial mineral, the colour has a relatively high tinting strength and opacity and is slow to dry. Mixed with cadmium red, it makes a deep cadmium yellow or cadmium orange.

Yellow ochre: a natural, relatively opaque earth colour with medium tinting strength, yellow ochre dries moderately slowly and mixes well with most colours.

Raw umber: a natural pigment with good tinting strength, raw umber is relatively transparent. It mixes well to create a range of browns. It dries quickly, which makes it ideal for underpainting.

Burnt sienna: a fast-drying, bright red-brown with good tinting strength, burnt sienna is relatively transparent.

Viridian green: a strong, bright, transparent green with high tinting strength. Viridian mixes well with other colours to create a range of greens. It dries relatively slowly.

Ivory black: a natural pigment with a slight brown bias. It has good tinting strength but is slow to dry. It creates a range of interesting greens when mixed with yellow.

You will also need a good white.

Titanium white (not shown here): a very bright, opaque white that is not prone to yellowing. The pigment is usually bound in safflower oil and so is slow drying.

Characteristics of oil paint

Oil paint has been the favoured painting medium of artists for many centuries since its development during the early Renaissance. It is a tried and tested material that, given its relatively long drying time, is astonishingly adaptable and versatile. Works created using oil paint possess a depth and richness of colour that is difficult to achieve with any other type of paint.

Oil paint has a reputation for being difficult to use, but nothing could be further from the truth. The secret lies in efficient preparation and good working practice. Because oil paint takes a long time to dry, you can easily rectify mistakes by simply wiping or scraping off the wet paint and repainting. Alternatively, you can paint over the area in question once the first layer of paint is dry. The long drying time,

together with the smooth, creamy consistency of the paint, also allows you to blend colours and tones seamlessly. It also means that expressive brush work and vibrant colour combinations can be achieved by working paint wet into wet. However, this same drying characteristic can lead to areas being overworked, and without discipline can result in jumbled and muddy colours. Unlike fast-drying acrylics, unused paint can be left for a limited time on the palette between painting sessions without the danger of it drying out.

Oil paint can be used thick or thin and mixed with various oils and additives to increase and improve its handling. Paint used straight from the tube is the consistency of toothpaste and unless it is brushed smooth it will hold the brush mark. The paint can

easily be thickened further by mixing in an additive that increases the volume or amount of paint without altering the depth of colour. These types of additives also contain drying agents, without which thick impasto applications of paint might take months, if not years, to harden and dry.

The paint is thinned using thinners or diluents. These can be used alone or mixed with various oils to create painting mediums. Many ready-prepared mediums can be purchased from art stores, including mediums that enable the paint to be thinned and used as transparent glazes. If the smell of white spirit and turpentine is unpleasant, low-odour thinners are available that do the same job as traditional thinners without their associated smell.

Good working practice

However you use and apply oil paint and whatever techniques you elect to use, the most important rules are to work on correctly prepared supports and always to work "fat over lean".

"Fat" paint, or paint that contains oils, is flexible and slow to dry, while

"lean" paint contains little or no oil, is inflexible and dries quickly. Oil paintings are often painted in layers and can be unstable and prone to cracking if lean (inflexible, quick to dry) paint is placed over fat (flexible, slow to dry) paint. For this reason, any

underpainting and initial blocking in of colour should always be done using paint that has been thinned with a solvent and to which no extra oil has been added. Oil can be added to the paint in increasing amounts in subsequent layers.

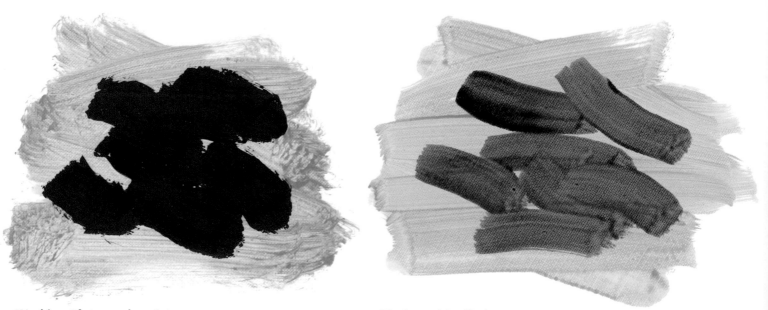

Working "fat over lean" ▲
The golden rule when using oil paint is to work "fat" (or oily, flexible paint) over "lean", inflexible paint that contains little or no oil.

Glazing with oils ▲
Oils are perfect for glazes (transparent applications of paint over another colour). The process is slow, but quick-drying glazing mediums can speed things up.

Thick and thin paint ▶
Oil paint can be used straight from the tube (left) or
thinned using a medium or solvent (right).

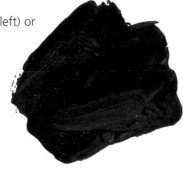
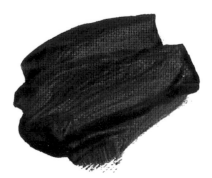

Working wet into wet ▼
The slow drying time of oil paint gives you the chance to
work at your leisure and blend colours and tones together on
the canvas.

Paint straight from the tube ▼
Paint applied straight from the tube holds its shape and the
mark of the brush. For heavy impasto work, the paint can be
thickened further by using an additive.

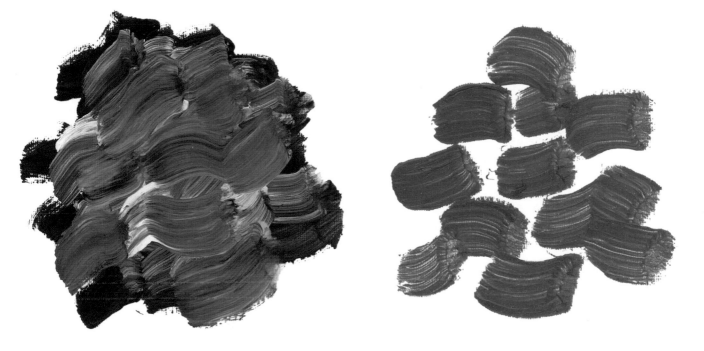

Mixing colours with oils

Colour mixing with oils is relatively
straightforward, as there is no colour
shift as the paint dries: the colour that
you apply wet to the canvas will look
exactly the same in intensity when it
has dried, so (unlike acrylics, gouache
or watercolour) you do not need to
make allowances for colour changes as
you paint. However, colour that looks
bright when it is applied sometimes
begins to look dull as it dries. This is
due to the oil in the paint sinking into a
previously applied absorbent layer of
paint below. You can revive the colour
in sunken patches by "oiling out" –
that is, by brushing an oil-and-spirit
mixture or applying a little retouching
varnish over the affected area.

No change in colour when dry ▼
Unlike acrylic and watercolour paints, the depth and intensity of oil colours remains
the same even when the paint has dried.

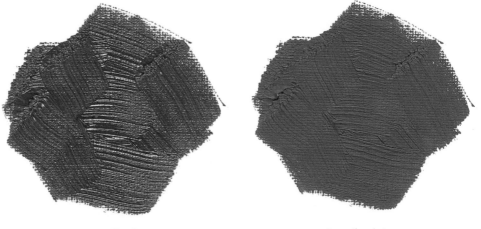

Wet oil paint   Dry oil paint

Acrylic paint

Perhaps the most important and far-reaching advance in artists' materials in the last 100 years has been the formulation of water-mixable acrylic paint. Acrylic resins were formulated in the 1920s and 1930s, although it took several years before a liquid acrylic emulsion that dried to a clear film was used to carry and bind together pigment. The first commercially available paint based on these emulsions was made available in the 1950s.

Acrylic paint can be mixed with a wide range of acrylic mediums and additives and is thinned with water. Unlike oil paint, it dries quickly and the paint film remains extremely flexible and will not crack. The paint can be used with a wide range of techniques, from thick impasto, as with oil paint, to thin, semi-transparent washes, as with watercolour. Indeed, most if not all of the techniques used in both oil and watercolour painting can be used with acrylic paint. Acrylic paint should not be thought of as an alternative to either, however, but as a very adaptable and unique painting material in its own right.

Acrylic paint is made by suspending pigment in an acrylic emulsion; in some paint formulations, several slightly different emulsions are combined. The paint may also contain various dispersants to ensure the uniform distribution of the pigments, defoamers, preservatives and thickeners.

Both students' and artists' quality acrylic paint is made. As with oil paint, artists' quality paint is available in a wide range of colours, with the cost depending on the pigments used. A less extensive range of colours is available in the students' range and the cost is the same across the whole range.

Acrylic paints come in three different consistencies. Tube paint tends to be of a buttery consistency and holds its shape when squeezed from the tube. Tub paint is thinner and more creamy in consistency, which makes it easier to brush out and cover large areas. There are also liquid acrylic colours that are the consistency of ink and are often sold as acrylic inks.

◄ **Liquid acrylics**
Liquid acrylics are the consistency of ink.

It has been suggested that, because they are made using slightly different formulations, you should not use or mix together paint from different manufacturers. You may experience no problems in mixing different brands or consistencies of paint, but it is always good practice to follow the manufacturers' instructions.

▲ **Tubes and jars**
Acrylic paint is available in tubes and jars of various sizes.

Characteristics of acrylic paint

The pigments in acrylic paints are bound with an acrylic resin that is water soluble and virtually odour free. Because it is water soluble, the paint is very easy to use, requiring only the addition of clean water. Water is also all that is needed to clean up wet paint after a work session. Once it has dried, however, acrylic paint creates a permanent hard but flexible film that will not fade or crack and is impervious to further applications of acrylic or oil paint and any of their associated mediums or solvents.

Acrylic paint dries relatively quickly: a thin film will be touch dry in a few minutes and even thicker applications dry in a matter of hours. Unlike oil

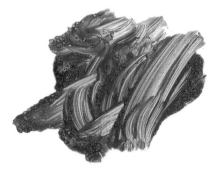

Texture gels ▲
Various gels can be mixed into acrylic paint to give a range of textural effects. These can be worked into while the paint is still wet.

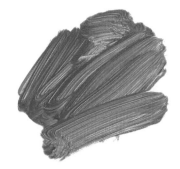

Mediums and additives ▲
A wide range of mediums and additives can be mixed into acrylic paint to alter and enhance its handling characteristics.

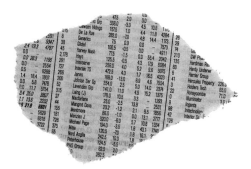

Adhesive qualities ▲
Many acrylic mediums have very good adhesive qualities, making them ideal for collage work.

paints all acrylic colours, depending on the thickness of paint used, dry at the same rate.

Athough hardened paint can be removed with strong paint strippers, this will quickly ruin your brushes. Wet paint, however, can easily be removed by rinsing in water. Try to get into the habit of rinsing your brushes regularly as you work.

Paint can also quickly dry on the palette, although you can avoid this by laying out and mixing only small quantities of paint and by spraying your palette periodically with clean water or using a special "stay-wet" palette.

The unique qualities of acrylic paint mean that many of the techniques that are commonly used with both oil paint and watercolour can be used. Acrylic paint is also excellent when used for underpainting prior to completing a work in oils, but it should not be used over oil paint.

However, it would be a mistake to see acrylic paint as a substitute for any of these traditional materials. It is, in fact, very different from other media and needs to be treated as such. Thinned with water and used on paper, acrylic paint behaves like watercolour paint – the big difference being that once it is dry, acrylic paint is no longer re-soluble. It also behaves like oil paint and can be used thickly, straight from the tube, to build up heavily textured areas of paint. Unlike oil paint, it dries in a matter of minutes – and this can make blending colours together, even over a small area, somewhat difficult.

Manufacturers have thought of many of these problems, and over the years since acrylics were first invented, they have steadily introduced a long list of mediums and additives. Perhaps one of the main advantages of acrylic paint, especially for abstract painters or for artists who like to work on a large scale, is the use of additives that extend or bulk out the amount of paint without altering its handling characteristics or depth of colour. Needless to say, using these extenders in large works makes economic sense, as you can make a relatively small amount of paint go much further.

Acrylic paint and acrylic painting mediums also have good adhesive qualities, which are useful if you are making mixed-media works that include collaged materials.

Extending drying time ▲
The drying time of acrylic paint can be extended by using a retarding medium, which gives you longer to work into the paint and blend colours.

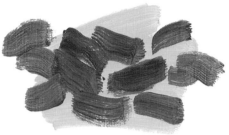

Glazing with acrylics ▲
Acrylic colours can be glazed by thinning the paint with water, although a better result is achieved by adding an acrylic medium.

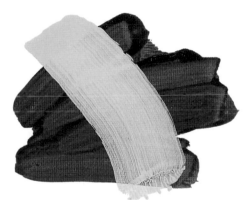

Covering power ▲
Acrylic paint that is applied straight from the tube has good covering power, even when you apply a light colour over a dark one.

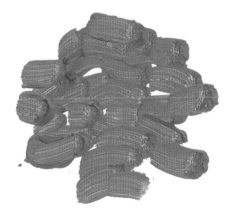

Shape-holding ability ▲
Like oil paint, acrylic paint that is applied thickly, straight from the tube, holds its shape and the mark of the brush as it dries.

Lightening acrylic colours ▼
Acrylic colours can be made lighter by adding white paint, which maintains opacity (below top), or by adding water, which increases transparency (bottom).

Acrylics starter palette

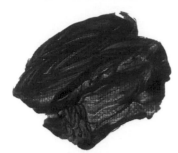

Ultramarine blue

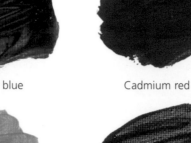

Phthalocyanine blue

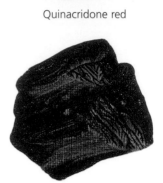

Cadmium red

Quinacridone red

Cadmium yellow light

Yellow ochre

Raw umber

Burnt umber

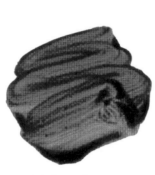

Phthalocyanine green

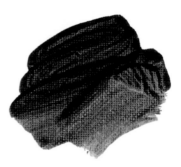

Payne's grey

As always, this range is only a suggestion and can be extended if a particular subject demands it.

Titanium white (not shown): this is the only white available in acrylic. It is a bright, opaque white with a high tinting strength.

Ultramarine blue: a deep, warm, transparent blue that is permanent and has a high tinting strength.

Phthalocyanine blue: a strong, deep, vivid blue available with either a red or a green undertone. Use sparingly, as it has an incredibly high tinting strength.

Cadmium red: a warm, opaque red with good tinting strength.

Quinacridone red: a very bright red with high tinting strength. Cooler than cadmium red, it makes very good purples when mixed with phthalocyanine blue.

Cadmium yellow light: a relatively opaque yellow that mixes well with red to create a range of orange hues and with blue to create a range of intense greens.

Yellow ochre: a semi-opaque earth colour with relatively low tinting strength. It is good for modifying other colours.

Raw umber: a useful transparent earth colour with low tinting strength.

Burnt umber: a rich, deep, warm brown, which is a good starting point for mixing a range of other browns.

Phthalocyanine green: a brilliant strong green with a high tinting strength. This is a good "base" from which to mix a wide range of greens.

Payne's grey: a transparent blue-grey with relatively low tinting strength that is useful for modifying other colours.

Change in colour when dry ▼
One of the fundamental differences between oil and acrylic paint is the slight darkening of colour as acrylic paint dries. This is due to the milky appearance of the wet acrylic emulsion binder: as the emulsion dries it becomes clear and transparent, allowing the pigment it is carrying to be seen more clearly. It can be difficult to judge the exact tone or intensity of your mixes.

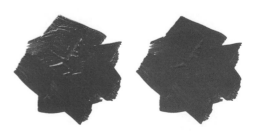

Wet acrylic paint   Dry acrylic paint

Gouache paint

Made using the same pigments and binders found in transparent watercolour, gouache is a water-soluble paint. The addition of *blanc fixe* – a precipitated chalk – gives the paint its opacity. Because gouache is opaque you can paint light colours over darker ones – unlike traditional watercolour, where the paint's inherent transparency means that light colours will not cover any darker shades that lie underneath.

Recently some manufacturers have begun to introduce paint made from acrylic emulsions and starch. The best-quality gouache contains a high proportion of coloured pigment. Artists' gouache tends to be made using permanent pigments that are light fast. The so-called "designers" range of colours uses less permanent pigments, as the work produced by designers is intended to last for only a short time.

Gouache paint is available in tubes and jars. Some brands are sold in series, with the price reflecting the varying cost of the raw materials, while other brands cost the same across the range. Different brands can be mixed, and the range of colours available is relatively wide. Tube and jar colours have much the same consistency.

What to purchase

Tubes of gouache are large enough for most purposes, although you might like to consider buying a larger jar for colours that you use a lot of, such as permanent white (good for highlights) or zinc white (good for mixing with other colours to lighten them).

All of the equipment and techniques used with watercolour can be used with gouache. Like watercolour, gouache can be painted on white paper or board; due to its opacity and covering power, it can also be used on a coloured or toned ground and over gesso-primed board or canvas. Gouache is typically used on smoother surfaces that might be advised for traditional watercolour, as the texture of the support is less of a creative or aesthetic consideration.

If they are not used, certain gouache colours are prone to drying up over time. Gouache does remain soluble when dry, but dried-up tubes can be a problem to use.

Certain dye-based colours are very strong and, if used beneath other layers of paint, can have a tendency to bleed through. These colours should be avoided or used only in overlying layers.

Gouache paint

Characteristics of gouache

Gouache paint is water based and remains water-soluble when dry. This allows you to remove paint easily – but it also means that you need to take care when working over previously applied paint layers. If the brushwork is anything but direct and sure, it can pick up previously applied paint, resulting in muddy and confused colour.

Gouache can be used as thin, dilute, semi-transparent washes like watercolour or, due to its innate density, applied to form a thicker, opaque film. As with traditional watercolour, you can

Work confidently ▲
Gouache remains soluble when it is dry, so if you are applying one colour over another, your brushwork needs to be confident and direct: a clean, single stroke, as here, will not pick up paint from the first layer.

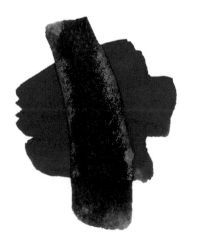

Muddied colours ▲
If you scrub paint over an underlying colour, you will pick up paint from the first layer and muddy the colour of the second layer, as here.

Blending colours ▲
Gouache colours can be blended together wet into wet on the support, so that colours merge together almost imperceptibly.

lighten the colour simply by thinning it with water: this increases its transparency and allows more of the support of a previously applied layer of paint to show through. Alternatively, you can add white paint, which increases the opacity and enables you to paint light colours over darker ones.

The paint film shrinks as it dries: if you apply gouache too thickly, therefore, you run the risk of the paint cracking. You can overcome this simply by re-wetting a cracked area: this makes the paint soluble again, allowing you to brush or clean off some paint. Once it is dry, the area can be repainted if required.

Due to the high chalk content of the paint, there is a slight colour shift as the paint dries: gouache generally looks a little lighter when it is dry than it does when it is wet. As with acrylics, it will not take you long to get used to this and to compensate by making your wet mixes slightly stronger or more intense. Always test any mixes on a piece of scrap paper and wait for them to dry before you apply them to your actual painting.

It can sometimes be difficult to obtain dark, deep rich colour with gouache so, although it is often necessary to add white paint to mixtures, this should be done with care.

Wet into wet ▲
Like transparent watercolour paint, gouache paint can be worked wet into wet (as here) or wet on dry.

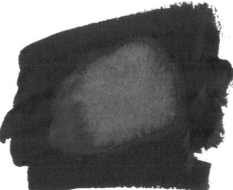

Removing dry paint ▲
Dry paint can be re-wetted and removed by blotting with an absorbent paper towel.

Change in colour when dry
Gouache paint looks slightly darker when dry than it does when wet, so it is good practice to test your mixes on a piece of scrap paper – although, with practice, you will quickly learn to make allowances for this.

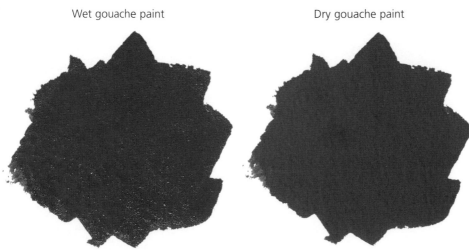

Wet gouache paint

Dry gouache paint

Lightening gouache colours ▲
Gouache colours can be made lighter either by adding water, which increases transparency (above left), or by adding white paint, which maintains opacity (above right).

Gouache starter palette

Cadmium red

Quinacridone red

Cadmium yellow light

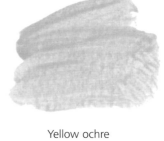
Yellow ochre

Ultramarine blue

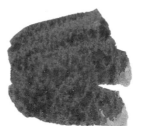
Phthalocyanine blue

Phthalocyanine green

Raw umber

Payne's grey

Burnt umber

The colours suggested here will provide you with a good, multi-purpose palette of gouache paints from which you will be able to mix virtually any colour that you need. However, you may want to adapt or extend the list if you tend to paint a particular type of subject frequently – portraits or figures, for example, or landscapes. The benefit of using a limited palette such as this is that it will force you to mix your colours carefully, learning as you go. Experiment to see what colours you can create – and get into the habit of making a note of any particularly useful mixes, so that you can recreate them easily the next time you need to use them. You will soon begin to see how different colours can be combined to make new ones.

Cadmium red: a warm, opaque red with good tinting strength.

Quinacridone red: a very bright red with high tinting strength. Cooler than cadmium red, it makes very good purples when mixed with phthalocyanine blue.

Cadmium yellow light: a relatively opaque yellow that mixes well with red to create a range of orange hues and with blue to create a range of intense greens.

Yellow ochre: a semi-opaque earth colour with relatively low tinting strength. It is good for modifying other colours.

Ultramarine blue: a deep, warm, transparent blue that is permanent and has a high tinting strength.

Phthalocyanine blue: a strong, deep, vivid blue available with either a red or green undertone. Use it sparingly, as it has an incredibly high tinting strength.

Phthalocyanine green: a brilliant strong green with a high tinting strength. This is a good "base" green from which to mix a wide range of other greens.

Raw umber: a useful transparent earth colour with low tinting strength.

Payne's grey: a transparent blue-grey, with relatively low tinting strength that is useful for modifying other colours.

Burnt umber: a rich, deep, warm brown, which is a good starting point for mixing a range of other browns. As with other media, you will also need a white paint in your palette.

Titanium white (not shown) is a bright, opaque white with a high tinting strength and is particularly good for painting bright highlights such as sunlight sparkling on water. Zinc white tends to be better for mixing with other colours in order to lighten them.

Paintbrushes

Brushes are available in a wide range of shapes and sizes, from tiny brushes that consist of just a few hairs or fibres that are used to paint very fine detail to large, flat brushes several inches (centimetres) across. Most brushes are sold in series, with each brush being given a number depending on its size: the higher the number, the larger the brush.

The cost of a brush depends on the quality of the materials from which it is made and on its size. Good-quality brushes are worth their initial high cost as, provided you look after them, they will last longer than cheaper alternatives. Having said that, however, certain types of paint application and painting techniques can be very rough and this, coupled with the corrosive nature of some solvents, means that the bristles or fibres used to make a brush do wear out. In these cases, it can be more economical to use a cheaper alternative.

Regardless of cost, when you are buying brushes discard any that do not hold their shape, lack spring, or have loose fibres or bristles.

Brush materials

The materials used to make brush fibres may be either natural or synthetic, hard or soft. The type you choose depends on the medium in which you are working.

Oil-painting brushes are traditionally made from bristle from the back of a hog. Today, most bristle is obtained from China, with the best coming from an area known as Chungking. The bristles hold their shape well and the fibres are thick, which means they can hold a substantial amount of paint. In the very best bristle brushes, the end of each bristle is split; this is known as "flagging", and it allows the bristle to hold more paint and distribute it evenly.

Synthetic brushes are good quality and hard wearing. They are also less expensive than either bristle or natural-hair brushes. However, they can quickly lose their shape if they are not looked after and cleaned well. Synthetic brushes can be used with oil, acrylic and gouache.

Natural hair brushes can be made from sable, goat, squirrel, ox and even mongoose hair. Traditionally, natural hair brushes are more often associated with watercolour painting, and so they are ideal for using with gouache. They can also be used with acrylics; in fact, as painting in acrylics draws on techniques that are used in both watercolour and oil painting, it is best to have a selection of hard and soft brushes for acrylics.

There is also a tradition of using sable- and mongoose-hair brushes with oils; the fine-tipped hairs are good for fine detail, although it is not easy to move oil paint around on the canvas with natural-hair brushes. If you do use natural hair brushes with oils or acrylics, however, you must clean them scrupulously after use. Given the availability of good-quality synthetic brushes, it is perhaps better to reserve natural-hair brushes for working in water-soluble media.

Cleaning brushes

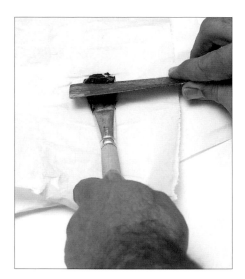

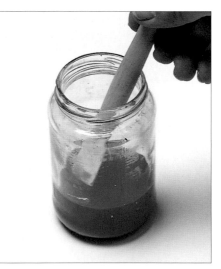

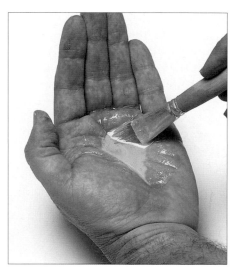

1 Cleaning your brushes thoroughly will make them last longer. Wipe off any excess wet paint on a rag or a piece of newspaper. Take a palette knife and place it as close to the metal ferrule as possible. Working away from the ferrule towards the bristles, scrape off as much paint as you can.

2 Pour a small amount of household white spirit (paint thinner) (or water, if you are using a water-based paint such as acrylic or gouache) into a jar; you will need enough to cover the bristles of the brush. Agitate the brush in the jar, pressing it against the sides to dislodge any dried-on paint.

3 Rub household detergent into the bristles of the brush with your fingers. Rinse the brush thoroughly in clean water until the water runs clear. Reshape the bristles or fibres with your fingertips and store the brush in a jar with the bristles pointing upwards, so that they hold their shape.

Brush shapes

Several brush shapes are available in bristle, synthetic fibres and natural hair. Although the choice might seem bewildering at first glance, some of the more "specialist" brushes are of limited use, and you would probably do better to experiment with a small range and find out what kind of marks you can make with each one. Finally, do not overlook the range of brushes available from home improvement stores: decorators' brushes can be very useful for laying in large areas of colour – when toning a ground, for example. These are often of a very high quality and cost far less than similar brushes sold in art supply stores.

Regardless of the medium in which you are working, you will need a range of different brush sizes. The shapes that you select are often very much a matter of personal preference, but the following are all useful.

Flat brushes ▼
These brushes have square ends. They hold a lot of paint, which can be applied as short impasto strokes or brushed out flat. Large flat brushes are useful for blocking in and covering large areas quickly. Short flats, known as "brights", hold less paint and are stiffer. They make precise, short strokes, ideal for impasto work and detail.

Brushes for fine detail ▶
A rigger brush (top right) is very long and thin. It was originally invented for painting the straight lines of the ropes and rigging on ships in marine painting – hence the rather odd-sounding name. A liner (bottom right) is a flat brush which has the end cut away at an angle. Both of these brushes may be made from natural or synthetic fibres.

Wash brushes ▶
The wash brush has a wide body, which holds a large quantity of paint. It is used for covering large areas with a uniform or flat wash of paint. There are two types of wash brush: rounded or "mop" brushes (top right), which are commonly used with watercolour and gouache, and flat wash brushes (bottom right), which are more suited for use with oils and acrylics.

Round brushes ▼
These are round-headed brushes that are used for detail and for single-stroke marks. Larger round brushes hold a lot of paint and are useful for the initial blocking-in. The point on round brushes can quickly disappear, as it becomes worn down by the abrasive action of the rough support. The brushes shown here are made of natural hair.

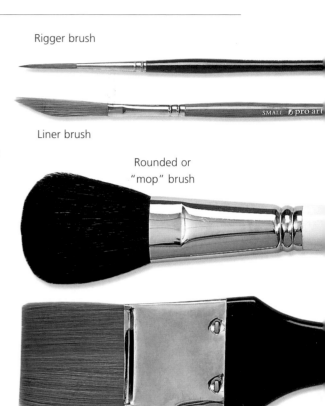

Rigger brush

Liner brush

Rounded or "mop" brush

Flat wash brush

Unusually shaped brushes ▼
Fan blenders (below left) are intended for blending together colours on the support. They are also useful for special effects such as drybrush work. A filbert (below right) combines some of the qualities of a flat and a round brush.

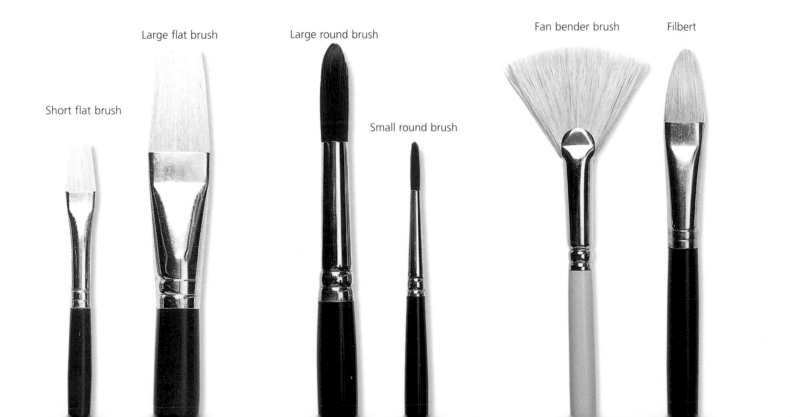

Large flat brush

Short flat brush

Large round brush

Small round brush

Fan bender brush

Filbert

Alternative paint applicators

Although brushes are the most usual means of applying paint to the support, there are a number of other tools that you can use. Some, such as palette and painting knives, are intended specifically for painting, but you can also improvise using virtually anything that comes to hand, including old rags, cardboard and even your fingertips.

Artist's palette and painting knives

Palette knives are intended for mixing paint with additives on the palette, scraping up unwanted paint from the palette or support, and general cleaning. Palette knives are available with either plastic or stainless steel blades. The steel blades are more durable and can be found in several different shapes. With plastic blades, there is a more limited range of shapes. The blade of most palette knives extends straight out from the wooden handle, although some have a cranked handle. This raises the hand holding the knife clear of the surface being worked on.

Strong knives can also be found in DIY or home improvement stores. Although they are intended for stripping wallpaper or applying quick-drying filler to cracks and holes, they made very good palette knives.

All painting knives have cranked handles. Made from flexible stainless steel, the knives – like brushes – come in different shapes and sizes. You can create a wide range of marks using painting knives. In general, the body of the blade is used to spread paint, the point for detail, and the edge for making crisp linear marks. The knife is not as adaptable as the brush and you will need a range of painting knives in order to create a range of different marks and effects.

Plastic painting knives are also available, but they are not recommended for use with oils or acrylics. They can, however, be used with the more liquid gouache; the gouache seems to be "held" more by the blade, while it is difficult to pick up thin paint using knives with steel blades.

Regardless of the type of knife you use, it is important to clean it thoroughly after use. Paint that has dried on the blade will prevent fresh paint from flowing evenly off the blade. If paint dries on to a steel blade, remove it using paint stripper, the caustic action of which will not damage the blade. Do not use caustic paint strippers on plastic blades, as they will dissolve; instead, peel the paint away. Ideally, you should clean the paint from plastic knives while it is still wet.

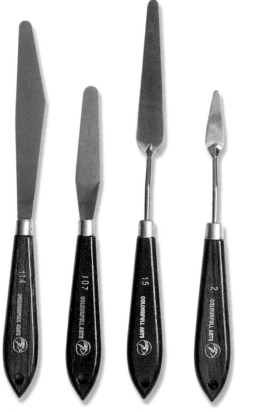

Steel knives
Painting and palette knives made of steel are available in a range of shapes and sizes. In order to work successfully with this method of paint application, you will require several.

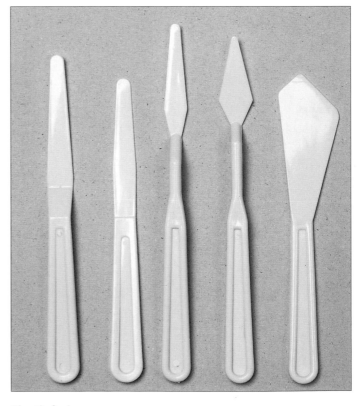

Plastic knives
Less expensive and less durable than steel knives, plastic knives manipulate watercolour and gouache paints better than their steel counterparts.

Paint shapers

A relatively new addition to the artist's range of tools are paint shapers. They closely resemble brushes, but are used to move paint around in a way similar to that used when painting with a knife. Instead of bristle, fibre or hair, the shaper is made of a non-absorbent silicone rubber. Various tip shapes are available in several different sizes and degrees of firmness. They are used in a number of ways to apply and push paint around the support, as well as to remove paint and blend different-coloured areas together. Although they are not as versatile as the brush, they bring a different quality to the work.

Shapers can be used with all types of paint, mediums and adhesives. They are easy to clean, as wet paint can be washed off and dry paint can be peeled off the rubber tip without the use of solvents. Another advantage is that the rubber tip will not harden or wear with use.

Foam and sponge applicators

Nylon foam is used to make both foam brushes and foam rollers. Both of these are available in a range of sizes and, while they are not intended as substitutes for the brush, they are used to bring a different quality to the marks they make.

Natural sponges have always found a place in the watercolourist's work box and, together with man-made sponges, can be used to good effect with acrylics and gouache. They are invaluable for spreading thin paint over large areas and for making textural marks. They are also useful for mopping up spilt paint and for wiping paint from the support in order to make corrections.

Foam and sponge applicators are better used with water-based mediums than with oil-based ones, as cleaning the applicators first in solvent and then in soap and water can be a long and messy process. With water-based mediums, however, all you need to do is rinse the paint from the applicator by holding it under a running tap.

Alternative applicators

Paint can be applied and manipulated using almost anything. Artists are, by and large, thoughtful and inventive people, and the only limitations are set by practicality and imagination. The cutlery drawer and tool box are perhaps a good starting point, but you will no doubt discover plenty of other items around the home that you can use. Cardboard, pieces of rag, wood, wire wool and many other seemingly unlikely objects can all be – quite literally – pressed into service.

Sponge applicators and paint shapers ▼
Shapers (below left) can be used to apply paint and create textures, and to remove wet paint. Foam rollers (below centre) are useful for covering large areas quickly. Sponge applicators (below right) are useful for initial blocking in.

Natural and man-made sponges ▼
With their pleasing irregular texture, natural sponges (below top) are used to apply washes and textures. They are especially useful to landscape artists. Man-made sponges (below bottom) can be cut to the desired shape and size and used in a similar fashion.

Everyday household items ▼
Although they might not seem like the obvious choice, everyday household items, such as an old rag, wire wool and piece of cardboard shown here, can also be used to apply paint to a support.

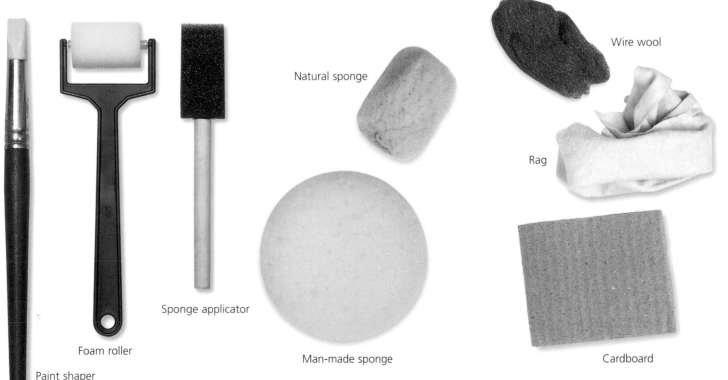

Natural sponge

Wire wool

Rag

Sponge applicator

Foam roller

Paint shaper

Man-made sponge

Cardboard

Palettes

The surface on which an artist arranges colours prior to mixing them and applying them to the support is known as the palette. Somewhat confusingly, the same word is also used to describe the range of colours used by a particular artist, or the range of colours found in a particular painting. The type of palette that you use depends on the medium in which you are working, but you will undoubtedly find that you need more space for mixing colours than you might imagine. A small palette gets filled with colour mixes very quickly and it is a false economy to clean the mixing area too often: you may be cleaning away not only usable paint, but also mixed colours that you might want to use again. Always buy the largest palette practical.

Wooden palettes

Flat wooden palettes in the traditional kidney or rectangular shapes with a thumb hole are intended for use with oil paints. They are made from hardwood, or from the more economical plywood.

Before you use a wooden palette with oil paint for the first time, rub linseed oil into the surface of both sides. Allow it to permeate the surface. This will prevent oil from the paint from being absorbed into the surface of the palette and will make it easier to clean. Reapply linseed oil periodically and a good wooden palette will last for ever.

Wooden palettes are not recommended for acrylic paint, as hardened acrylic paint can be difficult to remove from the surface.

Holding and using the palette ▼
Place your thumb through the thumb hole and balance the palette on your arm. Arrange pure colour around the edge. Position the dipper(s) at a convenient point, leaving the centre of the palette free for mixing colours.

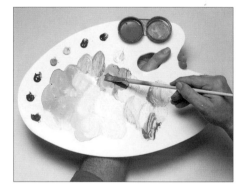

White palettes

Plastic palettes are uniformly white. They are made in both the traditional flat kidney and rectangular shapes. The surface is impervious, which makes them ideal for use with either oil or acrylic paint. They are easy to clean, but the surface can become stained after using very strong colours such as viridian or phthalocyanine blue.

There are also plastic palettes with wells and recesses, intended for use with watercolour and gouache. The choice of shape is entirely subjective, but it should be of a reasonable size.

White porcelain palettes offer limited space for mixing. Intended for use with watercolour and gouache, they are aesthetically pleasing but can easily be chipped and broken.

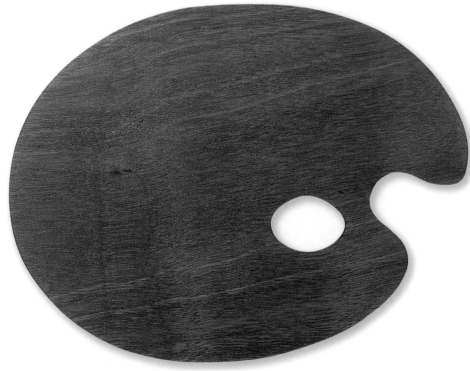

Wooden palette ▲
These wooden palettes are generally used for oils. Always buy one that is large enough to hold all the paint and mixes that you intend to use.

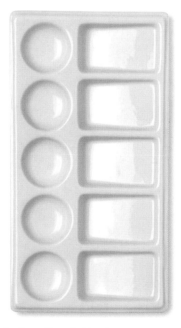

Slanted-well palette ▲
This type of porcelain palette is used for mixing gouache or watercolour. The individual colours are placed in the round wells and mixed in the rectangular sections.

Disposable palettes

A relatively recent innovation is the disposable paper palette, which can be used with both oils and acrylics. These come in a block and are made from an impervious parchment-like paper. A thumb hole punched through the block enables it to be held in the same way as a traditional palette; alternatively, it can be placed flat on a surface. Once the work is finished, the used sheet is torn off and thrown away.

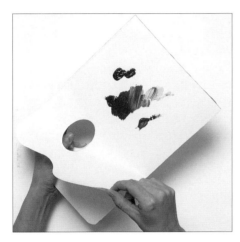

Paper palette ▲
Disposable palettes are convenient and make cleaning up after a painting session an easy task.

Stay-wet palette

Intended for use with acrylic paints, the stay-wet palette will stop paints from drying out and becoming unworkable if left exposed to the air for any length of time. The palette consists of a shallow, recessed tray into which a water-impregnated membrane is placed. The paint is placed and mixed on this membrane, which prevents the paint from drying out. If you want to leave a painting halfway through and come back to it later, you can place a plastic cover over the tray, sealing the moist paint in the palette. This prevents the water from evaporating and the paint from becoming hard and unusable. The entire palette can be stored in a cool place or even in the refrigerator. If the membrane does dry out, simply re-wet it.

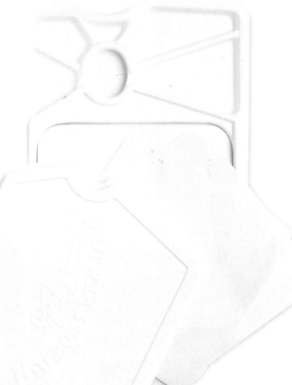

Stay-wet palette ▶
This type of palette, in which the paint is mixed on a water-impregnated membrane, prevents acrylic paint from drying out. If you like, you can simply spray acrylic paint with water to keep it moist while you work.

Containers for water, solvents and oil

Although a regular supply of containers such as empty jam jars, can be recycled from household waste, several types of specially designed containers are available from art supply stores.

Among the most useful are dippers – small, open containers for oil and solvent that clip on to the edge of the traditional palette. Some have screw or clip-on lids to prevent the solvent from evaporating when it is not in use. You can buy both single and double dippers, like the one shown on the right.

Dipper ▼
Used in oil painting, dippers are clipped on to the side of the palette and contain small amounts of oil or medium and thinner.

Improvized palettes

For work in the studio, any number of impermeable surfaces and containers can be used as palettes. Perhaps the most adaptable is a sheet of thick counter glass, which you can buy from a glazier; the glass should be at least ¼ in (5 mm) thick and the edges should be polished smooth. Glass is easy to clean and any type of paint can be mixed on it. To see if your colours will work on the support you have chosen to use, slip a sheet of paper the same colour as the support beneath the glass.

Aluminium-foil food containers, tin cans, glass jars, paper and polystyrene cups also make useful and inexpensive containers for mixing large quantities of paint and for holding water or solvents. Take care not to put oil solvents in plastic or polystyrene containers, as the containers may dissolve.

Oil additives

Although oil paint can be used straight from the tube, it is usual to alter the paint's consistency by adding a mixture of oil or thinner (solvent). Simply transfer the oil or thinner to the palette a little at a time and mix it with the paint. Most oil painters attach dippers to the edge of the palette so that the oil and thinner are readily at hand, but any small container will do. There are a great many oils and thinners on the market. Some of the more common ones are shown below.

Oils and mediums

Oils and mediums are used to alter the consistency of the paint, allowing it to be brushed out smoothly to increase its transparency or to make it dry more quickly. Once exposed to air, the oils dry by oxidization, leaving behind a tough, leathery film that contains the pigment. Different oils dry at a different rate. Because some oils (linseed, for example, which dries relatively quickly) tend to yellow slightly with age, they are used only in the manufacture of darker colours. Delicate colours and white are often manufactured using safflower or poppy oil, both of which dry more slowly. Many oils are made from plant extracts, but more recent additions are made from synthetic resins that also speed up drying.

A painting medium is simply a ready-mixed painting solution that may contain various oils, waxes and drying agents. The oils available are simply used as a self-mixed medium. Your choice of oil or medium will depend on several factors, including cost, the type of finish required, the thickness of the paint being used, and the range of colours.

All oils take several days to dry. The exact drying time, however, depends on the amount used and on atmospheric temperature and humidity.

There are several alkyd-based mediums on the market. They all accelerate the drying time of the paint. Some alkyd mediums are thixotropic; this means that they are initially stiff and gel-like but, once worked, they become clear and loose. Other alkyd mediums contain inert silica and add body to the paint, which is useful for impasto techniques where a thicker mix of paint is required.

Oils and thinners

There are a great many oils and thinners on the market. The more common ones are listed below.

Cold-pressed linseed oil
Cold-pressed oil is slightly yellow in colour and, when mixed with paint, increases gloss and transparency. It is reasonably slow to dry.

Poppy oil
Poppy oil is slow drying. It is very pale and is traditionally used with pale colours to ensure that they do not yellow over time. Paint mixed with poppy oil has a beautiful buttery consistency.

Safflower oil
Safflower oil is pale and, like poppy oil, traditionally used with light colours. It also slows down the drying time of the paint.

Stand linseed oil
A pale oil that is slightly thicker than other linseeds. It is very slow to dry but leaves the paint with a tough, flexible finish.

Refined linseed oil
Refined linseed oil is slow to dry, pale yellow in colour. It increases gloss and flow.

Thinner
There are several thinners on the market. Turpentine, shown here, is widely used but smells strong. Some people become allergic to it.

Bleached linseed oil
This is a refined, pale oil. It flows very easily, and so increases the viscosity of the paint. It dries slightly faster than other linseeds.

Thinners

If you dilute oil paints using only oil, the paint may wrinkle or take too long too dry. As the name suggests, a thinner (also known as a diluent) thins the paint, making it easier to brush out. It does not remain in the paint, but evaporates from the surface.

The amount of thinner that you use depends on how loose or fluid you want the paint to be. Do not use too much, however, or you may find that the paint film becomes weak and prone to cracking.

Ideally, any thinner that you use should be clear and should evaporate easily from the surface of the painting without leaving any residue. There are several thinners suitable for use with oil paints. There is very little, if any, difference in appearance between them – but they do have different characteristics.

Turpentine

Distilled from the thick, resinous sap or oleoresin of several different species of pine tree, turpentine is colourless, with a distinct odour. Many people develop an allergy to it, so use it with care and make sure that the room in which you are working is well ventilated.

Turpentine is the strongest and best of all the various thinners used in oil painting. Use only fresh turpentine, as old turpentine can become discoloured with a gummy residue if it is exposed to air and light. To minimize the risk of this happening, store your turpentine in closed metal cans or dark glass bottles.

Good-quality turpentine is expensive, so use it only for painting; for cleaning your brushes, use cheaper white spirit.

White spirit

Paint thinner or white spirit, which is also known as mineral spirit, is a petroleum by-product. It is clear, has a less pronounced smell than turpentine, does not deteriorate over time and dries faster than turpentine. It is inexpensive and can therefore be used both for painting and for cleaning brushes, although ideally it is best used for cleaning brushes. However, it is not as strong a solvent as turpentine and can leave the paint surface matt.

Oil of spike lavender

This exotic-sounding solvent is made from lavender oil and smells wonderful. Unlike other solvents, which speed up the drying time of oil paint, oil of spike lavender slows the drying time. It is very expensive. Like turpentine and white spirit, it is colourless.

Low-odour thinners

For those who dislike the smell of traditional thinners, are allergic to them, or are simply concerned about the health implications of breathing in the fumes, various low-odour thinners such as sansador have come on to the market in recent years and are now a popular choice. However, the drawback of low-odour thinners is that they are relatively expensive and dry slowly.

Citrus solvents

You may be able to find citrus thinners. They are thicker than turpentine or white spirit but, like spike lavender oil, smell wonderful. They are more expensive than traditional thinners and slow to evaporate.

Liquin ▼

Liquin is just one of a number of alkyd painting mediums that speed up drying time considerably – often to just a few hours. It also improves flow and increases the flexibility of the paint film. It is excellent for use in glazes.

Warning

• Always follow any instructions and warning advice carried on containers.
• All solvents are flammable and should be used in a well-ventilated environment, away from naked flames.
• Avoid contact with the skin and eyes and avoid breathing the fumes.
• Do not use solvents when handling food and drink.
• If you experience any adverse effects when using solvents, switch to a low-odour variety.
• All oil-painting mediums and varnishes can be an irritant and should be used following the same procedures as for solvents.
• Keep a suitable empty container available into which you can pour used solvent. When the container is full, dispose of it at your local refuse or waste disposal centre.

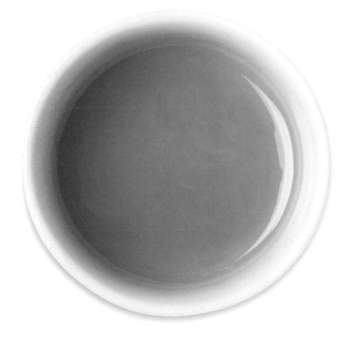

Acrylic additives

Although acrylic paint can be used straight from the tube or jar, or thinned with water, manufacturers have steadily introduced a wide range of mediums and additives that enable the real potential of the paint to be exploited to its maximum. Scour the shelves of any good art supply store and you will find additives that make the paint finish gloss or matt, thick or thin, textured or smooth.

There are additives that slow down the drying time of the paint, giving you longer to work into it. There are even additives that make colours glow in the dark or turn acrylic into a fabric paint that can withstand being put through a washing machine. The chances are that if you want to do something creative with acrylic paint, there is an additive to enable you to do it.

Types of finish

Acrylic paints dry to leave a matt or slightly glossy surface. The finish depends entirely on the brand being used. Gloss or matt mediums can be added to leave the surface with the desired finish. Gloss and matt mediums can also be mixed together to give the dry paint varying degrees of sheen. The choice is a personal one. As a general rule, colours on a gloss surface tend to look brighter. It is also preferable to use gloss mediums when glazing colours.

Gloss and matt mediums ▼
It is impossible to tell simply by looking at it whether a medium will give a matt or a gloss finish. Both gloss (below) and matt (bottom) mediums are relatively thin white liquids that dry clear if applied to a support without being mixed with paint.

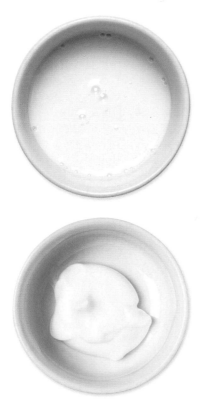

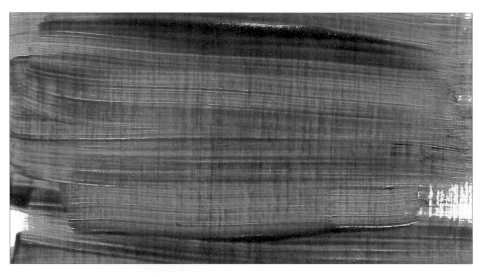

The effect of gloss medium ▲
Adding gloss medium to the paint increases its transparency. This allows you to build up several thin glazes relatively quickly, leaving the dry paint with a slight gloss sheen. Gloss medium also enhances the depth of colour, improves adhesion to the support and increases the flexibility of the paint. It can be used as an adhesive for collage work. Some manufacturers also advise using gloss medium as a varnish.

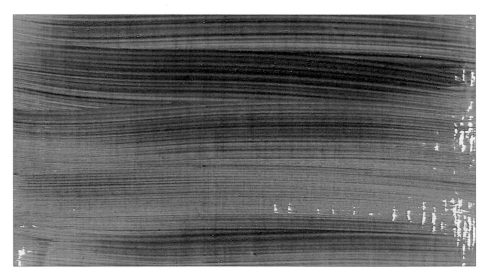

The effect of matt medium ▲
Matt medium also increases transparency and can be used to make matt glazes. Matt medium has good adhesive properties. It can be thinned with water and used to size canvas, or diluted 50:50 with water and used as a fixative for drawings. Matt mediums are not generally used as varnish, as they can deaden colour and look slightly cloudy.

Adding flow-improving mediums

Flow-improving mediums reduce the water tension, increasing the flow of the paint and its absorption into the surface of the support.

One of the most useful applications for flow-improving medium is to add a few drops to very thin paint, which can tend to puddle rather than brush out evenly across the surface of the support. This is ideal when you want to tone the ground with a thin layer of acrylic before you begin painting.

When flow-improving medium is used with slightly thicker paint, a level surface will result, with little or no evidence of brushstrokes.

The medium can also be mixed with paint that is to be sprayed, as it assists the flow of paint and helps to prevent blockages within the spraying mechanism.

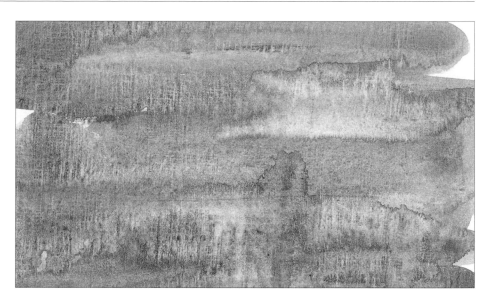

Without flow-improving medium ▲
Very thin acrylic paint tends to puddle rather than brush out evenly.

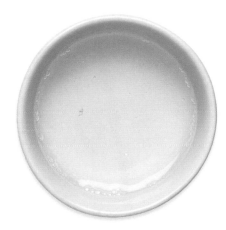

Flow-improving medium ▲
This medium is a colourless liquid and therefore does not affect the colour of the paint.

With flow-improving medium ▲
Adding flow-improving medium to thicker paint results in a level surface in which no brushstrokes can be seen.

Adding retarding mediums

Acrylic paints dry quickly. Although this is generally considered to be an advantage, there are occasions when you might want to take your time over a particular technique or a specific area of a painting – when you are blending colours together or working wet paint into wet, for example. Adding a little retarding medium slows down the drying time of the paint considerably, keeping it workable for longer.

Always follow the manufacturer's instructions regarding how much medium to add to your mixes. Beware of adding too much medium as this can result in the paint becoming sticky and leaving a soft, easily damaged paint film.

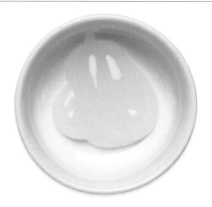

Retarding medium ▶
Retarding mediums are available as gels (shown here) and as fluids.

Adding gel mediums

Gel mediums are the same consistency as tube colour. Available as matt or gloss finishes, they are added to the paint in the same way as fluid mediums. They increase the brilliance and transparency of the paint, while maintaining its thicker consistency. Gel medium is an excellent adhesive and extends drying time. Gel mediums can be mixed with various textural substances such as sand or sawdust to create textural effects.

There are also thicker versions of gel mediums, which (not surprisingly) are known as heavy gel mediums. They hold brush or knife marks well, making them ideal for impasto work. Another effect of heavy gel mediums is to extend the working time of the paint. Some brands dry to a translucent finish and others to an opaque one.

Heavy gel mediums have very good adhesive properties and can be mixed with sand or sawdust. It is better to

build up very thick applications in several thin layers than in one thick one, as this reduces the chance of any splitting in the paint film due to water evaporation and shrinkage. Very thick applications can be heavy and are best made on non-flexible surfaces such as board, rather than on canvas, which may sag.

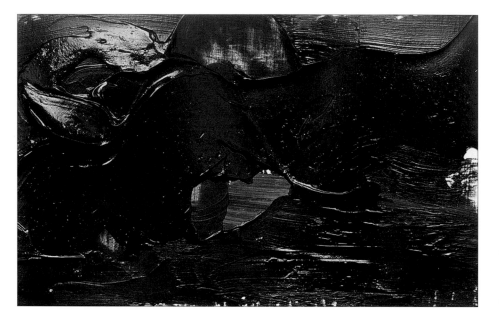

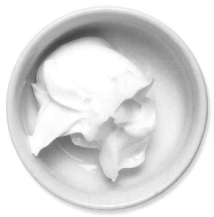

Heavy gel medium ▲
Heavy gel medium is a thick paste.

◄ **The effect of heavy gel medium**
Mixed with acrylic paint, heavy gel medium forms a thick paint that is used for impasto work.

Adding modelling paste

Modelling pastes can be mixed with acrylic paint and dry to give a hard finish, which can be sanded or carved into using a sharp knife. They are best used on non-flexible substrates, as thick applications can be heavy, although there is a modelling paste with a lighter structure, which is ideal for use on canvas. If you are using modelling pastes on flexible supports, add a gel medium to maximize flexibility.

In order to aid drying, it is better to build up several thin coats, allowing each layer to dry before adding the next, rather than apply one thick layer. Although heavy applications may crack, they do not affect the structural strength of the application and any cracks can be filled using more paste once the area is dry.

Modelling paste ▼
White or light grey in colour, modelling pastes are either smooth to the touch or very slightly granular in texture. As with other acrylic mediums, there are several reputable brands on the market.

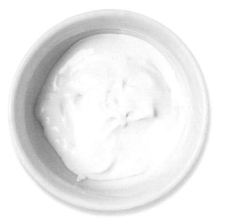

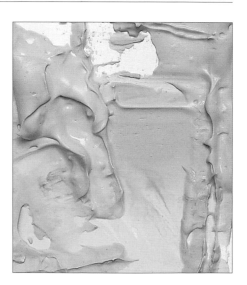

The effect of modelling paste ▲
Modelling pastes dry to give a hard finish, which can be sanded or carved into using a sharp knife.

Adding texture pastes and gels

While sand, gravel, sawdust and various other materials can be added to texture paste and other acrylic gel mediums, there are several proprietary texture gels with different textural characteristics. These pastes have fine, medium or coarse textures and resemble sand, stucco, plaster, lava, flakes or fibres. Paint can be mixed into the paste, or the paste can be applied and painted over when dry. To avoid damaging your brushes, it is best to apply texture paste with a knife.

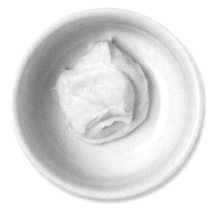

Natural sand texture gel ▲
The natural sand texture gel shown here is fine in texture.

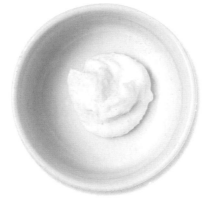

Glass beads texture gel ▲
Glass beads are embedded in the gel. It looks grainy, like medium-textured sand.

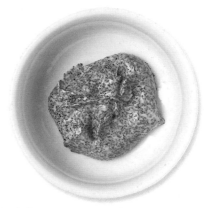

Black lava texture gel ▲
Black lava texture gel is speckled grey in appearance.

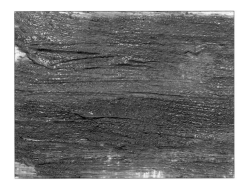

Natural sand texture gel ▲
This gel creates the texture of sand. The colour is more even than real sand.

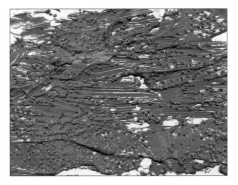

Glass beads texture gel ▲
Glass beads texture gel creates an effect like medium-textured sand.

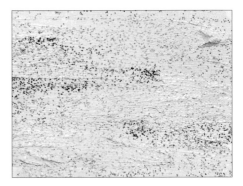

Black lava texture gel ▲
Mixed with a pale colour, as here, the colour of the gel remains visible.

Pearlescent, iridescent and phosphorescent mediums

These mediums are intended primarily for decorative works. Pearlescent mediums create a shimmering effect. Iridescent mediums contain tiny flakes of mica that, when mixed with paint, appear to change colour depending on the direction of the light. The mediums are particularly effective with transparent colours. Phosphorescent medium is green and glows in the dark. It can be mixed with other colours but the glow effect is gradually reduced.

The effect of iridescent medium ▶
Tiny flakes of mica in the medium appear to change colour.

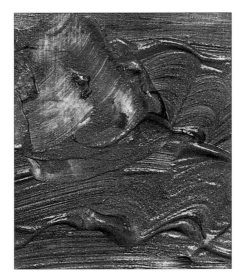

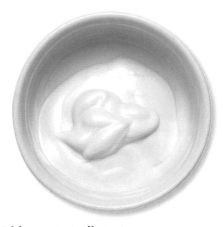

Iridescent medium ▲
Iridescent medium looks very similar to some of the other acrylic additives.

Supports

A "support" is the name for the surface on which a painting is made. It needs to be physically stable and resistant to deterioration from both the corrosive nature of any of the materials being used and the surrounding atmosphere. It needs to be light enough to be transported from one place to another. It also needs to have a sympathetic surface texture, as this will have a direct effect on the marks and techniques that you use. Your choice of support depends on the medium in which you are working.

Canvas

Without doubt, canvas is the most widely used support for both oil and acrylic work. Several types of canvas are available, made from different fibres. The most common are made from either cotton or linen, both of which can be purchased ready stretched and primed to a range of standard sizes (although there are suppliers who will prepare supports to any size) or on the roll by the yard (metre) either primed or unprimed. Unprimed canvas is easier to stretch.

Linen canvas is made from the fibres of the flax plant, *Linum usitatissimum*. The seeds of this plant are also pressed to make linseed oil, used by artists. Linen is the finest type of canvas available. It is light brown in colour, very strong, and gives a pleasingly receptive surface on which to work. Depending on the gauge or weight of the thread used, linen canvas can be found in a wide variety of weave textures and weights. Linen canvas is often described as being fine, medium or coarse. As a general rule, lighter weights (200–225g/ 7–8oz) with a fine tooth are used for smaller works, while heavier grades (375–450g/12–15oz) are best for larger works. Because of the way linen is woven, the surface texture never looks too even or mechanical.

Cotton canvas is known as cotton duck. It is light cream in colour and has a more regular or mechanical weave than linen. Stretched cotton duck is more stable than linen and is less prone to becoming slack on its stretcher if the air becomes damp. Seen as inferior to linen, it is nonetheless a popular and widely used support. It is substantially cheaper than linen and is also easier to stretch. Cotton duck is available in a range of weights from 200–450g/ 7–15oz; for larger works, use weights over 250g/10oz.

Linen canvas ▲
Linen canvas is available in a number of different textures and weights, from very fine to coarse. The fibres are stronger than cotton fibres, which means that the fabric is less likely to sag and stretch over time.

Cotton duck ▶
Cotton duck has a more regular (some people might say more mechanical) weave than linen. It is also less expensive than linen.

Stretching canvas

Canvas must be stretched taut over a rectangular wooden frame before use. For this you will need stretcher bars and wooden wedges.

Stretcher bars are usually made of pine and are sold in pairs of various standard lengths. They are pre-mitred and each end has a slot-in tenon joint. Longer bars are morticed to receive a cross bar (recommended for large supports of 75 x 100cm/30 x 40in or more).

The wooden wedges are tapped lightly into the inside of each corner and can be hammered in further to allow you to increase the tension of the stretched canvas a little if necessary.

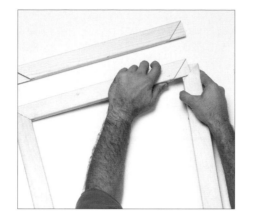

1 Press or tap the stretcher bars together to make a frame. They should slot together easily, without you having to exert much pressure.

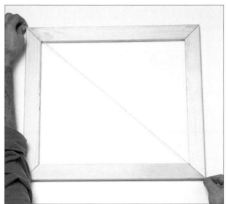

2 Using a tape measure or piece of string, measure diagonally from corner to corner in both directions to check that the corners are square.

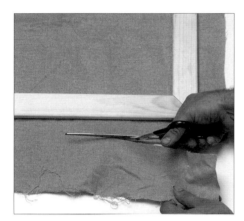

3 Arrange the canvas flat on a work surface. Place the frame on top, bevelled side down. Cut out allowing an overlap of approximately the width of the stretcher bars on all sides.

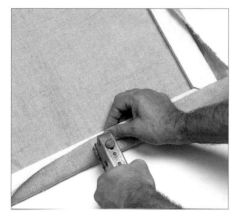

4 Fold the excess canvas over the stretcher bars, ensuring the canvas threads run parallel to the bars. Drive a staple into the centre of opposite sides. Repeat on the other sides.

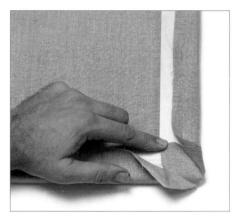

5 Insert one staple to each side of the centre staple on opposite sides, half way between the centre staple and the edge. Repeat on the other sides. Fold in the canvas corner and hold in position.

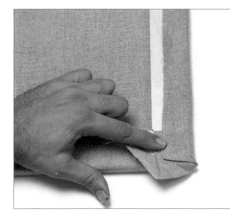

6 Fold over the flap of canvas on one side of the corner, pull it taut and hold it firmly in position with your fingertip.

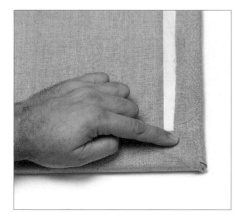

7 Fold over the remaining flap of canvas and secure with a staple to make a neat mitre, keeping your finger well away from the staple gun.

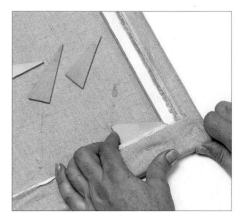

8 In each corner, push two wedges into the slots in the stretcher bars. If the canvas sags, the wedges can be pushed in further to keep the canvas taut.

Priming canvas

Canvas is usually sized and primed (or, increasingly, just primed) prior to being worked on. This serves two purposes. The process not only tensions the fabric over the stretcher bars but also (and more importantly in the case of supports used for oil) seals and protects the fabric from the corrosive agents present in the paint and solvents. Priming also provides a smooth, clean surface on which to work.

In traditional preparation, the canvas is given a coat of glue size. The most widely used size is made from animal skin and bones and is known as rabbit-skin glue. It is available as dried granules or small slabs. When mixed with hot water the dried glue melts; the resulting liquid is brushed over the canvas to seal it.

Increasingly, acrylic emulsions are used to size canvas. Unlike rabbit-skin glue, the emulsions do not have to be heated but are used diluted with water.

The traditional partner to glue size is an oil-based primer. Lead white, which is toxic, together with titanium white and flake white, are all used in oil-based primers. In order to penetrate the fibres of the canvas, it should be the consistency of single cream; dilute it with white spirit if necessary.

Traditional primer can take several days to dry, however; a modern alternative is an alkyd primer, which dries in a couple of hours.

Primers based on acrylic emulsion are easier to use. These are often known as acrylic gesso, although they are unlike traditional gesso. Acrylic primer should not be used over glue size, but it can be brushed directly on to the canvas. Acrylic primers can be used with both oil and acrylic paint, but oil primers should not be used with acrylic paints.

Primer can be applied with either a brush or a large palette knife. If a brush is used the weave of the canvas tends to be more apparent.

If you want to work on a toned ground, add a small amount of colour to the primer before you apply it. Add oil colour to oil primer and acrylic colour to acrylic primer.

Boards

Several types of wooden board make good supports for both oil and acrylic work. The boards can simply be primed with an acrylic gesso, or canvas can be glued to the surface; a technique known as marouflaging. There are three types of board in common use: plywood, hardboard (masonite) and medium-density fibreboard (MDF).

Plywood is made from several thin layers of wood or veneers glued together to form a rigid sheet. The surface veneers are usually made from hardwood and are smooth.

Hardboard is made from exploded wood fibre and is available both tempered and untempered. Tempering with oils or resins makes it harder and more water resistant. Use the softer-surfaced, untempered board, as the hard and somewhat oily surface of tempered board can resist paint. Some hardboards have a rough and a smooth side; you can paint on either side, depending on the effect you want.

MDF, made from compacted wood fibres, is perhaps the best board to use as it is stable and warp resistant. Both sides of MDF are hard and smooth.

All these boards can be found in a range of sizes. If used at a size where they begin to bend, mount rigid wooden battens on the reverse to reinforce them.

Priming board

Wood was traditionally sized with rabbit-skin glue and then primed with a thixotropic primer in the same way as canvas; nowadays, most artists use ready-made acrylic primer or acrylic gesso primer, which obviates the need for sizing. Acrylic primer also dries much more quickly.

Before you prime your boards, make sure they are smooth and free of dust. You should also wipe over them with methylated spirits to remove all traces of grease.

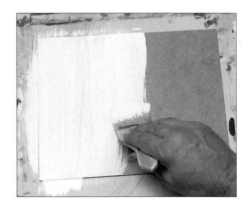

1 Using a wide, flat brush or a decorator's brush, apply primer over the board with smooth, vertical strokes. For a very large surface, apply the primer with a paint roller. Allow to dry.

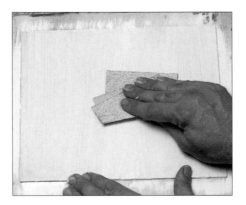

2 Rub the surface of the board with fine-grade sandpaper to smooth out any ridges in the paint. Blow or dust off any powder.

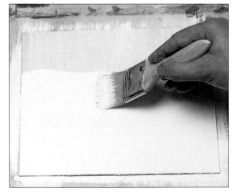

3 Apply another coat of primer, making smooth horizontal strokes. Allow to dry. Repeat as many times as you wish, sanding between coats.

Covering board with canvas

Canvas-covered board is a lightweight painting surface that is particularly useful when you are painting on location. Covering board with canvas gives you a support that combines the strength and low cost of board with the texture of canvas. You can use linen or cotton duck, which makes it a good way of using up remnants of canvas; calico, which is a cheap material, is also suitable. Acrylic primer is used to stick the canvas to the board. It looks white when it is first applied, but dries clear. When you have stuck the canvas on to the board, you should leave it to dry for an hour or two in a warm room. Prime the canvas with an acrylic primer before use.

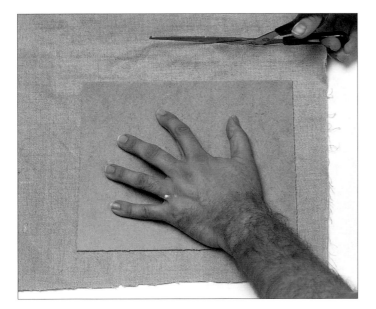

1 Arrange the canvas on a flat surface. Place the board on the canvas. Allowing a 5cm/2in overlap all around, cut out the canvas with a pair of sharp scissors.

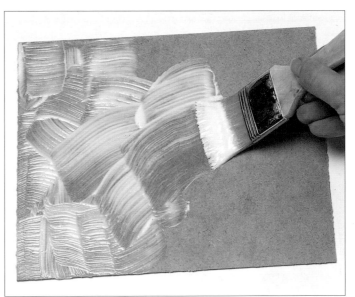

2 Remove the canvas from the work surface. Using a wide, flat brush or a household decorator's brush, liberally brush matt acrylic medium over the surface of the board.

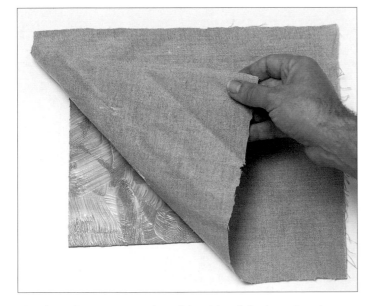

3 Place the canvas on the sticky side of the board and smooth it out with your fingertips, working from the centre outwards.

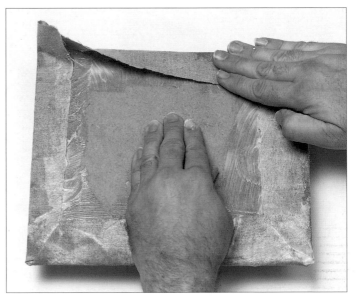

4 Brush acrylic medium over the canvas to make sure that it is firmly stuck down. Place the board canvas-side down on an upturned plate or bowl so that it does not stick to your work surface. Brush acrylic medium around the edges of the board. Fold over the excess canvas, mitring the corners, and brush more medium over the corners to stick them down firmly.

Canvas paper and board

Artists' canvas boards are made by laminating canvas – or paper textured to look like canvas – on to cardboard. They are made in several sizes and textures and are ideal for use when painting on location. However, take care not to get them wet, as the cardboard backing will disintegrate. They can also be easily damaged if you drop them on their corners. They are ready sized and can be used for both oils and acrylics.

Oil and acrylic papers are also available. Both have a texture similar to canvas and can be bought as loose sheets or as sheets bound together in blocks. Although they are perhaps not suitable for work that is intended to last, they are perfect for sketching and making colour notes.

Oil and acrylic papers ▶
Oil and acrylic papers have a texture similar to canvas.

Paper and illustration board

Although best suited to works using water-based materials, paper and illustration board, provided they are primed with acrylic primer, can also be used for painting in oils.

Watercolour papers provide ideal surfaces for gouache work. The papers are found in various thicknesses and with three distinct surfaces – rough, hot pressed (which is smooth) and NOT or cold pressed, which has a slight texture. Watercolour boards tend to have either a rough or a hot-pressed surface. Illustration board tends to be very smooth and is intended for use with gouache and linework.

Illustration board ▶
Used with gouache, illustration board is very smooth and good for finely detailed work.

Varnishes

Traditionally, varnish was applied to oil paintings to protect them from atmospheric pollution and dirt. Varnish also had an aesthetic purpose: oil painting techniques often result in a paint surface that looks uneven, with dull and shiny areas depending on the amount or type of painting media used. A varnish unifies and enhances the colour, bringing the whole painted surface together beneath a uniform gloss or semi-matt sheen.

The painting must be completely dry before it is varnished, otherwise the drying paint will contract beneath the less flexible varnish and cause the varnish to crack. Oil paintings can take months or even years to dry, depending on the thickness of the paint. Acrylic paintings can be safely varnished with acrylic varnish after a few hours. Watercolours and gouache paintings are normally framed behind glass, so they are protected and there is no need to varnish them.

All varnishes should be flexible. They should remain clear and non-yellowing and be easily removable. Varnishes are made from both natural and synthetic materials. The two traditional natural varnishes are damar and mastic. However, mastic varnish has a reputation for going dark and yellowing with age. It also tends to become cloudy, if it is prepared in damp air, leaving behind a surface bloom.

Varnishes made from natural resins are being replaced by synthetic varnishes made from Ketone and acrylic resins. Synthetic-resin varnishes have several advantages, as they do not yellow with age or become brittle. They can be used on both oil and acrylic paintings. They are also very tough. However, you cannot mix synthetic resin varnishes with oil mediums or turpentine. Several manufacturers market a range of these resins. They are manufactured to dry to a gloss or a matt finish and can be mixed together to provide varnish with varying degrees of sheen.

There are also spray varnishes, both removable and non-removable, which dry to give gloss, satin or matt finishes. They can be used on both oil and acrylic paintings. They are quick drying, but need to be used with care in order to achieve uniform coverage.

Applying varnish

Make sure the painting is completely dry before you varnish it. Always use a clean varnish brush and work in a dust-free environment.

The technique ▼
Place your painting flat on a surface. Dip a large, flat brush in your chosen varnish and apply it in smooth, even strokes in one direction. Do not scrub the surface or you will create air bubbles. If you go over any area more than once the finish will be uneven.

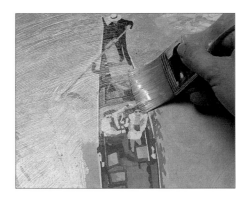

Different types of varnish

Varnishes are pale or colourless and it is difficult to tell the difference between the types by their appearance. Here are some of the most widely used.

Acrylic matt varnish
Synthetic varnishes can be used on oil and acrylic paintings. The one shown here dries to a matt finish.

Wax varnish
Wax varnish is used on oil paintings. It is made from beeswax mixed with a solvent. The wax is brushed over the work and allowed to stand for a short time. The excess is then removed with a rag and the surface buffed. The more the surface is buffed, the higher the resulting sheen.

Acrylic gloss varnish
This synthetic varnish dries to a gloss finish.

Retouching varnish
Retouching varnish is used on oil paintings and can be used at any time while the work is in progress. It is used to revive sunken areas where the paint looks dull. Both damar and mastic thinned with solvent can be used as retouching varnish.

Damar varnish
Damar varnish is used on oil paintings. It is made from the resin of the damar tree, which is found throughout Indonesia and Malaysia. The resin is mixed with turpentine to create a slightly cloudy liquid. The cloudiness is caused by natural waxes in the resin, and clears as the varnish dries. Damar does yellow with age, but it is easy to remove it and replace it with a fresh coat. The varnish dries very quickly.

Auxiliary equipment

Art stores are like candy stores, with shelves full of handsome-looking, colourful materials and equipment. Despite what the manufacturers' catalogues would have you believe, by no means all are essential – but there are several articles, such as the ones shown on these two pages, that are virtually indispensable and will make it easier for you to work.

Easels

Buying a good easel will make working on even a modest-sized support easier. It will also give you a psychological boost, inspiring you to greater things. There are several questions that you need to ask yourself when buying an easel. What size of work do you intend to produce? Are you going to use the easel on location or in the studio? If it is going to be used in your home or studio, is the room large enough?

The medium in which you like to work is also an important consideration. Oils are invariably painted with the support vertical, as are acrylics if used at the consistency of oil paint. However, if you are using fluid washes, then you will be working with the support horizontal, or nearly so, in order to prevent the paint from running. The same is invariably the case with gouache.

With any upright easel, stability is a primary consideration. Always test the stability of your chosen easel by placing on it the largest support that you intend to use.

Portable easels need to be lightweight, so that they can be easily transported, easy to erect and stable. They are usually made of wood, although a limited range is available in metal. Portable easels usually have three telescopically adjustable legs, so that you can set up the easel on uneven ground. The support is held between adjustable clamps and can be angled at any position from the horizontal to the vertical. Large portable easels can double as studio easels but they are generally not as stable.

A variation on this type of easel is the portable box easel, which incorporates a box that will hold all the equipment needed for a day's painting. Everything folds and packs away

Table easels ▲
The simplest table easels can be adjusted to hold a support horizontally or at varying angles up to about 45 degrees. They are perfect for working on gouache and acrylic paintings using thin, fluid paint.

Portable box easel ▶
Everything you need for a day's painting on location can be stored in the box beneath the easel.

neatly, while a carrying handle makes transportation easy. Some box easels even come with carrying straps, so that you can transport the easel on your back, like a rucksack – perfect for location work.

There is a comprehensive range of studio easels, with a model available to suit all styles and sizes of work. They are expensive, but a good studio easel will last a lifetime. Made of wood, studio easels are based around two distinct shapes – the A shape and the H shape. Both hold the support vertically.

H-shaped easels can handle larger canvases, with larger models being raised and lowered by means of a ratchet system. Some lighter-weight easels fold and convert into an easel that can hold a drawing board horizontally.

A-shaped easels are invariably smaller than H-shaped easels. They also fold flat easily, which makes them more suitable for use when space is at a premium. The height is adjusted by means of a series of catches that lock the support into position.

A less expensive alternative is the radial easel. These easels can hold a reasonably sized support. They have three short legs that give reasonable stability and can be adjusted in height.

◄ **Studio easel**
This is just one of many kinds of studio easel available. Buy one that is sturdy enough to hold a large canvas.

Drawing boards

Unless you are working on a rigid board or stretched canvas, you will need a drawing board on to which you can secure or stretch your paper or watercolour board. Art stores stock boards made from thick, smooth plywood in a range of sizes. It is sometimes possible to find boards made from jointed timber with screwed cross-pieces in second-hand stores, and these are worth buying as they will last a lifetime.

There are also boards intended for location work, which have a long strap running diagonally across the board and can be placed over the shoulder and neck, allowing you to hold the board in position while you are standing, without using your hands.

Mahl stick

Another useful piece of equipment when oil painting at an easel is a mahl stick, which consists of a light rod of wood (bamboo) with a soft leather ball secured on one end. This simple piece of equipment can be held in one hand and rested on the edge of the work. You can then rest your painting hand on the rod, which is positioned over the area being worked on. This steadies the hand, making it easier to do fine detailed work, and also keeps your painting hand clear of any wet paint so that you do not run the risk of smudging the paint.

If you do not want to go to the expense of buying a ready-made mahl stick, it is very easy to improvise and construct one yourself. Simply buy a length of dowelling or similar lightweight wood, wrap old rags around one end, and tape them in position with masking tape.

Mahl stick ▼
The mahl stick shown here comes in two parts, which can be screwed together to make one long stick so that it can be used when working on large canvases.

Applying paint

Brushes are the obvious means of applying paint to the support, and a wide range is available. The marks they make depend on both the shape of the brush (round or flat) and the material from which it is made. Hogshair bristle, which is often used for oil and acrylics brushes, is stiff and relatively unbending, and creates definite-shaped marks, while the sable or synthetic/sable mixes used for gouache and watercolour brushes are more pliable and create a softer mark. Of course, you can also use watercolour and gouache brushes for acrylic paints if you are using the paint thinly.

There are also many other things that you can use to make marks. Some are designed specifically for painting, while others are everyday household items. Experiment to see what effects you can achieve. Dip fabrics, from coarse but evenly textured linen to pretty, delicate lace, into paint to transfer their patterns to the support; press twigs, pieces of cardboard, or even out-of-date credit cards into paint and scrape them over your painting surface to make straight lines; dip scrunched-up aluminium foil or plastic food wrap in paint and press it on to the support to make random textures; even apply paint with your fingers, just as you did when you were a child.

Unusual paint applicators

There is a huge range of paint applicators on the market – some of which are useful, while others are little more than manufacturers' gimmicks. Each type makes a different kind of mark.

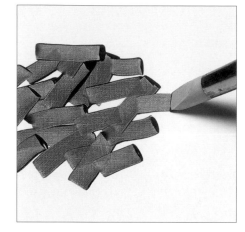

Paint shaper ▲
Available in a range of sizes and forms paint shapers consist of a shaped rubber tip fitted into a metal ferrule, which in turn is fitted into a wooden handle, just like a brush. The type of mark you can make depends on the size and shape of the tip. Paint shapers are best used with reasonably thick acrylic or oil paint; you can also use them with thin acrylic paint, gouache or watercolour.

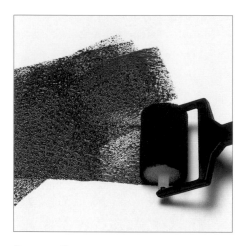

Foam roller ▲
Foam paint rollers, like those used in household decoration, are a great way of covering a large area quickly – when you want to prepare a toned ground, for example. They can also be used to achieve textural effects. They are available in various sizes and are inexpensive enough to be discarded when they are too dirty to use.

Foam brush ▲
This consists of a wedge of synthetic foam attached to a handle. It can be dragged across the support to make broad marks in which the texture of the foam is evident. You can also dip the tip in the paint to make straight lines.

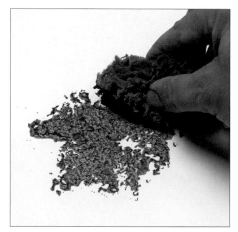

Sponge ▲
Sponges are a great way of creating texture for things like lichen on stone or random clouds and are particularly useful for landscape work. Synthetic sponges give a more even texture than the natural sponge shown here.

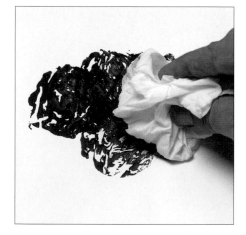

Rag or paper ▲
Rags and scrunched-up absorbent paper are used in the same way as sponges to create textured marks for particular subjects, although the textures that they create tend to be more irregular.

Brushes for oils and acrylics

Brushes for oils and acrylics tend to be made from bristle, which is relatively hard and unyielding. This means that the marks tend to have a distinctive shape. Synthetic nylon brushes are much softer.

Round brushes

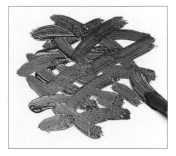

Short strokes ▲
With the brush handle more or less parallel to the support, you can quickly build up an area of paint by making short strokes.

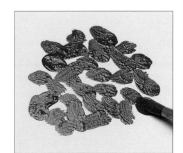

Rounded marks ▲
Holding the brush at 45 degrees to the support means that you are using the tip of the brush. This creates more rounded marks.

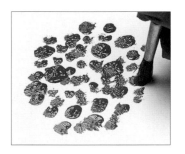

Dots ▲
Holding the brush almost perpendicular to the support and dabbing it on to the support creates small dots and stipples.

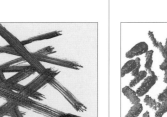

Long strokes ▲
Stroking the brush over the support as if you were drawing with a pencil allows you to make long, flowing marks.

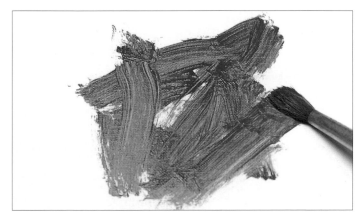

Rough, uneven texture ▲
Scrubbing on paint using the side of the brush creates a rough, uneven texture that is ideal when you want to cover a large area but do not want a flat wash of colour.

Flat brushes

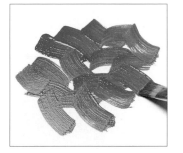

Long strokes ▲
Making long strokes with a flat brush held parallel to the support, the wedge-like shape of the brush head is evident.

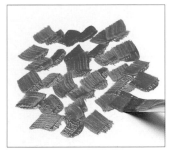

Short strokes ▲
Short, wedge-shaped strokes can be used to deliver thick paint to the support – a technique used to create heavy impasto.

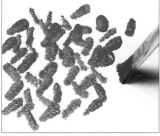

Dots ▲
Holding the brush almost perpendicular to the support and dabbing it on to the support creates short lines and wedge-shaped marks.

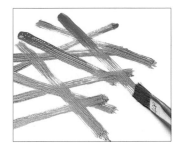

Thin strokes ▲
Use the edge of the brush to make thin marks, applying light pressure so as not to splay the bristles. The marks can be straight or curved.

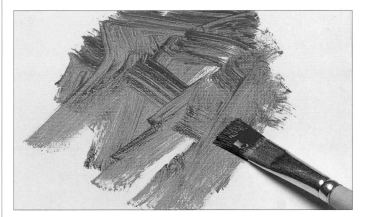

Rough, uneven texture ▲
Scrubbing on paint using the side of the brush creates a rough, uneven texture in the same way as with a round brush and is useful for scumbling one colour over another.

Brushes for gouache

The brushes used for gouache tend to be the same as those used for pure watercolour – soft sable and sable/synthetic mixes. For control and fine mark making, make sure that you buy brushes that hold their shape well. Although sable brushes are more expensive than synthetics, they will last longer if you look after them.

Round brushes

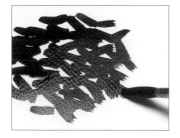

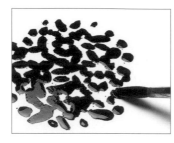

Short strokes ▲
Made using the point of the brush and, depending on the amount of pressure applied, short strokes are reasonably even in width.

Rounded marks ▲
Dabbing the end of the brush on to the support produces blob-like dots, the size of which depend on the consistency of the paint.

Flat brushes

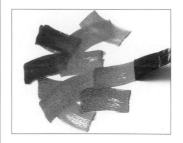

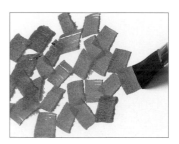

Long strokes ▲
Dragging the whole width of the brush over the support while applying even pressure results in a mark of an even width.

Short strokes ▲
Made using only the top half of the brush, short strokes create even and relatively broad rectangular-shaped marks.

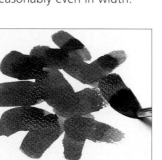

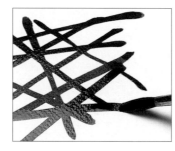

Applying pressure ▲
Holding the brush almost perpendicular to the support and applying pressure splays out the bristles, creating broad marks.

Long strokes ▲
As with oil and acrylic brushes, stroking the brush over the support and applying steady pressure makes flowing marks of even width.

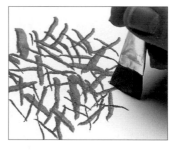

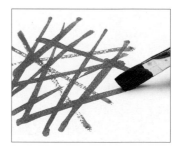

Fine marks ▲
Holding the brush upright and dabbing it lightly on to the support results in a thin, often slightly curved mark the width of the brush tip.

Long strokes using one edge of the brush ▲
For fine lines, use only one edge of the brush rather than the whole width and apply steady pressure.

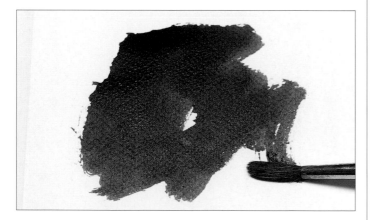

Rough, uneven texture ▲
Scrubbing on paint using the side of the brush creates a rough, uneven texture that allows some of the support or underlying paint layer to be seen.

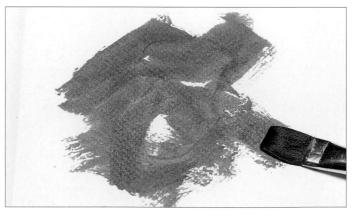

Uneven texture ▲
As with the other brushes, scrubbing on paint using the side of the brush rather than the tip creates a random, uneven texture in which individual brushmarks cannot be discerned.

Painting knives

Painting knives are available in several shapes and sizes, in both metal and plastic. They are ideal for thick, impasto-like applications. Painting knives are generally used for oils and acrylics, although it is also possible to use gouache straight from the tube; however, the texture will not be as pronounced as when using oils or acrylics.

Painting knives using oils and acrylics

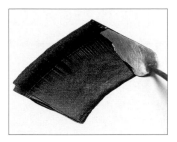

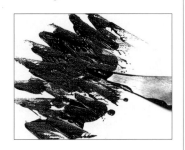

Broad marks ▲
Spreading paint on to the canvas with the flat of the knife, as one would when icing a cake, creates a flat, even application of paint.

Press on and lift off ▲
Pressing the knife on to the support and then lifting it off, without dragging it, makes marks that echo the shape of the knife.

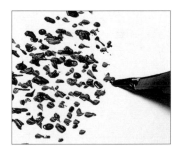

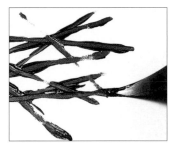

Dots ▲
Dotting the tip of the knife on to the support creates short, sharp marks that are useful for detail and adding highlights.

Uneven lines ▲
Because the paint is thick and does not spread evenly, dragging the tip of the knife across the support creates lines that vary in width.

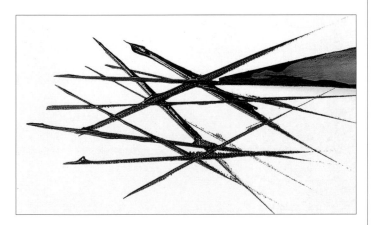

Thin strokes using the knife edge ▲
Turning the knife on its edge and pressing it on to the support, or dragging it across the surface, creates thinner lines that are even in width – a good technique for straight edges.

Painting knives for gouache

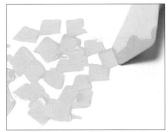

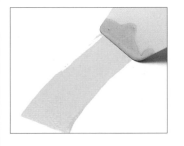

Broad marks ▲
For broad marks, smear the paint over the paper using the flat of the knife. The technique is exactly the same as for oils and acrylics.

Short marks ▲
Pressing one flat edge of the knife on to the paper and smearing the mark a little creates short marks the width of the knife.

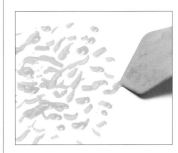

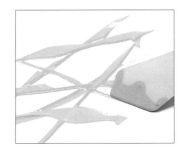

Dots ▲
Dotting the tip of the knife on to the paper creates fine points that could be used to depict pollen inside a flower, leaves on trees, or highlights.

Long, uneven marks ▲
Using the edge of the knife and angling it at about 45 degrees to the paper creates long, uneven marks that are good for loose, linear work.

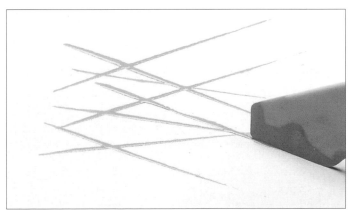

Press on and lift off ▲
Pressing one sharp edge of the knife at an angle of 90 degrees creates a crisp, clean line of even width on the paper. To make longer lines pull the knife across the support.

Tone

If you want to show that an object is three-dimensional, you need to master the art of depicting tone. Tone is simply the relative lightness or darkness of a colour. Another term that you may come across in art books is "value" – but the meaning is exactly the same.

The apparent lightness or darkness of a subject depends on several things. First, it depends on the quality, intensity and direction of the light source: if one side of an object is brightly lit (for example, a still life illuminated by sunlight streaming in through a window to the side of the set-up), it will be lighter in value than the side that is in shadow or shielded from the light. Second, the tone depends on the relative lightness or darkness of the colours present within that subject.

In order to create the illusion of three-dimensional form on a flat, two-dimensional surface, more than one tone needs to be in evidence. If you draw a circle and paint it a uniform mid-tone red, all you will see is a flat red disc. If, however, you paint one side of your circle red and then gradually darken that red colour as

you paint across the circle to the other side, the circle appears to become a sphere, one side apparently hit by the light and the other side in shadow.

In general, strong light makes colours appear brighter and more intense. It also increases the tonal gap, or the range of tones evident between the lightest tone and the darkest. This is known as contrast. An image with a strong tonal contrast will look more three-dimensional and appear to have greater depth than an image that lacks contrast. Used well, tone can also play an important part in conveying mood and atmosphere.

Colour also has an important part to play when you are assessing tonal values. When you are painting an image, a black object in bright light still needs to look black, just as a white object in shadow still needs to look white. A light-coloured object in bright light or deep shadow will look lighter than a dark colour in light or shade. In reality, however, very different colours can have the same tonal value, with even comparatively light colours looking surprisingly dark in the right lighting

conditions. Perhaps the best way to appreciate this is to look at a black-and-white photograph, where colours that are very different can look tonally the same or very similar.

Pure hues have distinct tonal values. Prussian blue is very dark in value, while lemon yellow is very light. This is best seen when positioning a hue against its matching tonal value on a value scale. However, similar hues can have very different tonal values, while different hues can be very similar in tone.

A pure hue straight from the tube is usually made darker by adding black or a mixture of other colours. A colour is lightened by adding white.

Colours and tonal equivalents ▼
Although there are hundreds of tonal values between black and white, the brain can only distinguish the differences between a few – as shown in the tonal scale, below. The second row shows the tonal equivalent – the relative lightness or darkness – of a number of different hues.

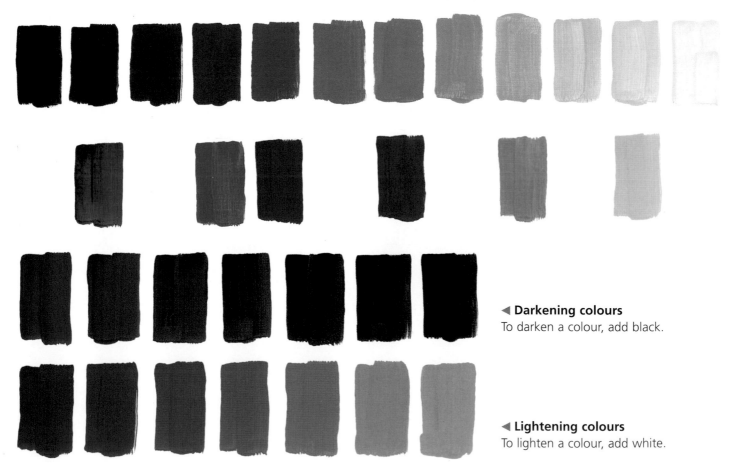

◄ **Darkening colours**
To darken a colour, add black.

◄ **Lightening colours**
To lighten a colour, add white.

Practice exercise: **Seeing in tones**

This exercise, painted in shades of grey, provides the opportunity to translate colours into tone. You may be surprised to discover that colours that you think of as being very different – the red of the pepper and chillies and the green of the broccoli, for example, or the red and dark blue of the cloth – are very similar in tone. Note, too, how many variations in tone there are within one colour – for example, in the white areas of the cloths and on the white plate. These differences are essential in conveying a feeling of light and shade.

In this exercise, the very brightest areas are left unpainted. Start by working out where these are, and then where the next lightest tone occurs. Working from light to dark in this way allows you to build up the tones very gradually. Remember that acrylic paint looks slightly darker when it is dry than it does when it is wet. Test all your mixtures first by applying them to a piece of scrap paper or board and waiting for them to dry.

It's often hard to be sure in the early stages that you've got things right, so be prepared to re-assess matters once you've put down several tones then make adjustments if necessary.

Materials
- *B pencil*
- *Canvas board*
- *Acrylic paints: Mars black, titanium white*
- *Brushes: small flat*

The set-up
This still life contains all three primary colours – red, yellow and blue – as well as black and white. The tablecloths and the lemons may turn out to be much darker than you might imagine, while even the darkest object (the aubergine [eggplant]) contains areas of bright highlight that help to define its form.

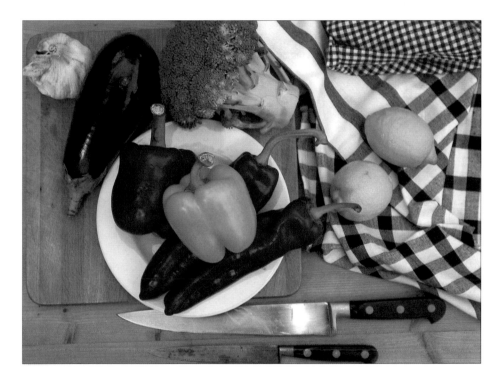

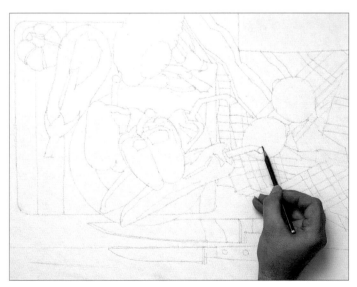

1 Using a B pencil, lightly sketch the subject. Put in as much detail as you need: although it's quite time-consuming to draw the checks of the cloths, for example, they will enable you to place the shifts in tone accurately. Similarly, the highlights on the vegetables will help you to define their form.

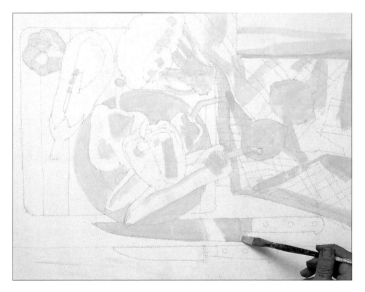

2 Mix the lightest tone from Mars black and titanium white. Using a small flat brush, paint the highlights on the aubergine, broccoli stalk, peppers and cloths. Use the same tone for the garlic, lemons and the blade of the topmost knife, except for the very brightest highlights.

▶

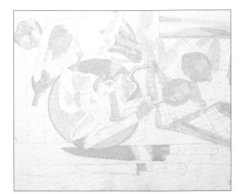

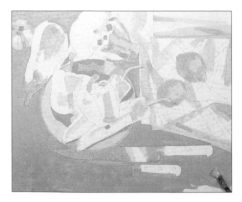

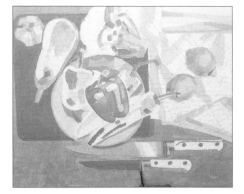

3 Look carefully to see where apparently uniform colours change tone. Add a little black to the mixture to darken it slightly and paint the cast shadows on the plate, the shaded edges of the lemons and the broccoli florets. Go over the first tone where necessary to darken it.

4 Now add more black to the paint mixture for your third tone. Darken the individual segments and the papery top of the garlic. Brush tone 3 over the wooden table and chopping board and around the main subject, taking care to cut around any light areas.

5 The chopping board is darker than the table on which it rests, so add still more black to the paint to make tone 4 and go over the chopping board again. Use the same tone to deepen the shadows on the peppers and chillies. Also use it to paint the rivets on the knife handles and the blade of the lower knife, which is somewhat tarnished and darker in tone.

Tip: When assessing tones, half-close your eyes: you will be able to see the differences more clearly.

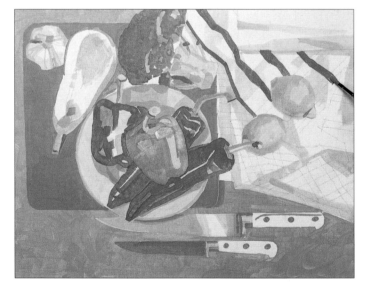

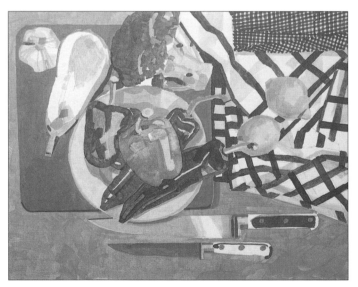

6 If you think the highlights that you put down in the early stages look too pale – as here on the yellow pepper, for example – darken them a little. Add more black to make tone 5. Using short brushstrokes, dab the paint over the broccoli florets, leaving some of the underlying tone showing through in places. Use the same tone on the large red pepper and chillies, leaving the highlights untouched, and on the blue-and-white cloth in the background.

7 Still using tone 5, continue working on the cloths. Note how the direction of the stripes changes with the folds in the cloth. Paint a thin shadow under the edge of the chopping board; this helps to separate it from the table and defines its form. Painting around the rivets, paint the dark wooden handle of the topmost knife.

Tip: You may find it helps to switch to a smaller brush, as you're working on very small, crisply defined areas at this stage in the painting.

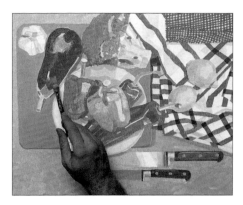

8 Add more black to make tone 6 and paint the darkest parts of the blue-and-white cloth – the squares where two blue bands overlap. Paint the aubergine, brushing around the light areas, and the handle of the lower knife.

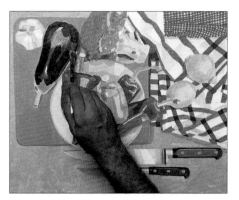

9 Using tone 6, darken the left-hand side of the red pepper. Add more black to make the darkest tone. Paint a thin strip along the top of the topmost knife. Use the same tone for the darkest parts of the aubergine and chilli peppers.

The finished painting
In this painting, seven tones plus the white of the support have been used to create a convincingly three-dimensional portrayal of a multi-coloured still life. It is interesting that colours that appear to be very different from one another (the red of the peppers and the green of the broccoli florets, for example) turn out to be very similar in tone. When you've done this exercise, you might like to try setting up another multi-coloured still life. Although it might seem difficult at first, you will quickly become adept at interpreting colours as tones; it is a vital part of making your paintings look rounded and three-dimensional.

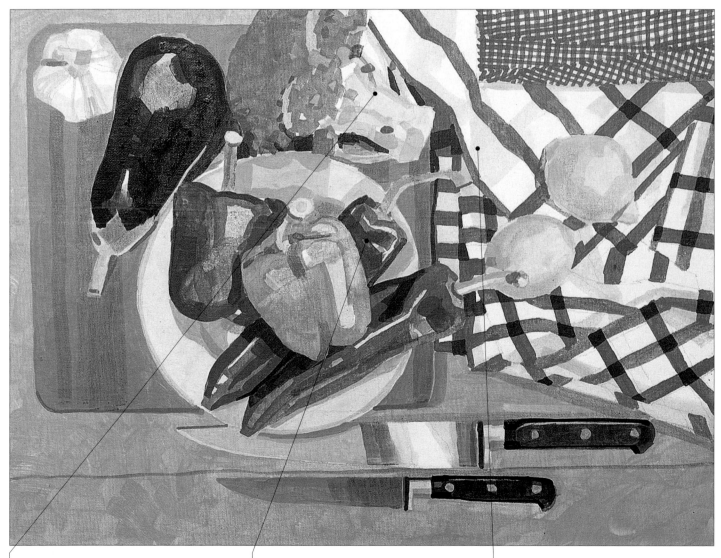

The pale green of the broccoli stalk is almost the same tone as the yellow pepper, although you might expect it to be considerably darker.

The darkest part of the chilli is almost as dark as the aubergine, although you might expect it to be lighter in tone.

Don't assume that things you know to be white will actually appear pure white: as you can see, some tone is evident in the white of the cloth.

Scaling up

People often paint from photographs. Some artists argue that this kills spontaneity, as there's a risk that you end up slavishly copying rather than interpreting what's in front of your eyes, but it's a perfectly valid way of painting. It isn't always practical to paint a scene from life, and photographs give you the opportunity to collect reference material when you're on your travels, or simply going about your daily business, and then work them up into a painting at your own convenience.

Some artists also make a small-scale sketch before they start on the painting itself. There are several reasons for doing this. First, it is a good way of deciding on the best composition: a quick sketch establishes the work's centre of interest and shows how the different elements of the scene relate to one another. Second, it enables you to work out the tonal values of the scene. This is just as important in colour work as it is in a monochrome drawing or pen-and-ink work, as an accurate assessment of tones is one of the things that will make your painting look three-dimensional.

But whether you're painting from a photo or from life, once you've got your reference material how do you transfer it on to a larger canvas or support?

It takes a certain amount of confidence to do this purely by eye, without any guidelines to help you – although, like anything else, you'll get better with practice. Luckily, there is a tried-and-tested means of scaling up. It involves superimposing a grid on your preliminary sketch or photo and marking a larger grid on your canvas. You can then copy the scene, one square at a time, and the lines of the grid will give you a good guide to where to position things. You can see, for example, that your subject's eye or the edge of a vase coincides with the edge of the second square down – so all you have to do is make sure that you draw it in the same position in your larger grid.

In a complicated scene such as a building or an elaborate still life, you might want to subdivide some of the squares. Any method that enables you to keep track of where you are in the sketch is fine.

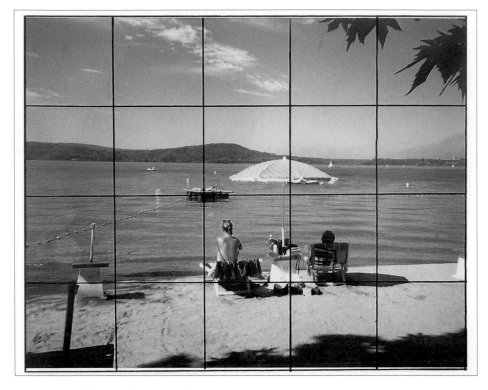

Acetate grid over photograph ▲
Draw a grid on acetate (available from craft and art supply stores) and place it over your photograph. Then draw a grid on your paper or canvas, keeping the same proportions. If, for example, the grid on your photo is five squares across and four squares down, the grid on your canvas should be the same – although the squares will be larger. You can then transfer the contents of each square in turn to make your underdrawing or sketch.

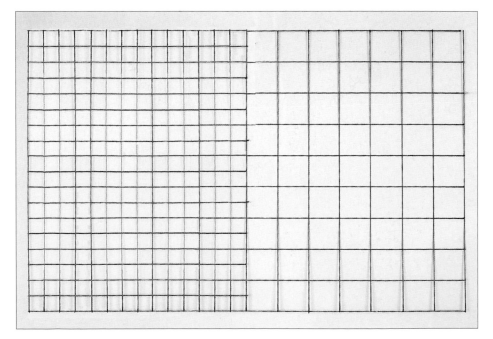

Different-sized squares within the same grid ▲
In areas where you need more guidelines, simply divide the squares of the grid into smaller squares.

Practice exercise: **Scaling up a small sketch**

The method for scaling up a small composition sketch is exactly the same as for scaling up a photograph. If, for example, the grid on your sketch is five squares across and four squares down, the grid on your canvas should contain the same number of squares – although they will be larger than the squares on the sketch. The grid system can also be used to make a drawing or sketch smaller, simply by reducing the size at which the grid is drawn on the support.

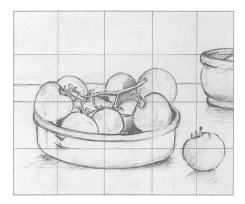

1 First make your initial sketch freehand and divide it up with a grid of evenly sized squares. The number of squares is up to you, but they should all be the same size.

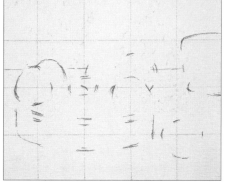

2 Then lightly mark a grid on the canvas on which you're going to make your painting, keeping the same proportions. Lightly mark the main intersections – the points where the edges of your subject touch on the lines of the grid.

3 Start joining up the intersections, working square by square and referring continually to your initial sketch to check that each shape is occupying the same area on your canvas as it did on the sketch. Already, your subject is beginning to take shape.

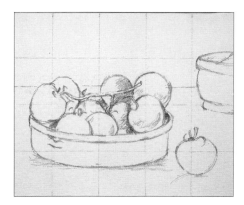

4 Continue transferring information until your underdrawing is complete. At this point, if you wish, you can also put in some shading to act as a tonal guide.

The finished underdrawing

When you have put down as much information as you need, you can begin the process of painting. The amount of detail that you put into your underdrawing depends at least in part on the complexity of your subject and is entirely up to you. Remember that an underdrawing is merely a guide to help you place elements correctly and work out the tones.

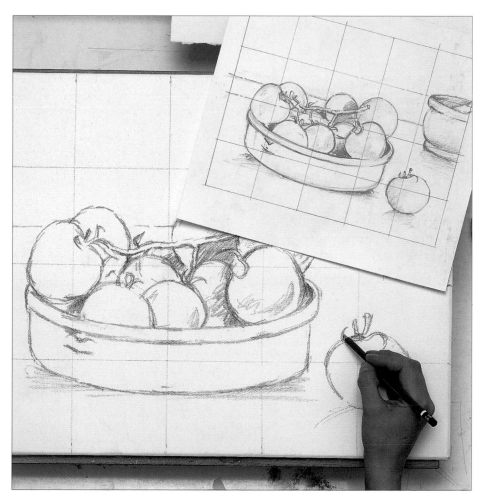

Underdrawing

An underdrawing is exactly what it says – a preliminary sketch on the canvas or paper, over which you paint your picture. Although some artists launch straight into a painting, most people – particularly if they are new to painting – like the reassurance that an underdrawing provides. It allows you to set down the lines of your subject, and erase and change them if necessary, before you commit yourself irrevocably to paint.

Your approach to the underdrawing will depend partly on the medium in which you're working. If you're painting in a transparent or relatively transparent medium such as watercolour or thin acrylic paint, you need to make sure that your underdrawing is light enough to be covered by the subsequent layers of paint. With thicker and opaque mediums, such as oils or impasto acrylics, the underdrawing can be heavier.

The style of your underdrawing also depends on the subject. If you're painting buildings, for example, it's important to get the angles of the roofs and windows right – so you might want to make a fairly detailed underdrawing that gives you plenty of guidelines to follow when you start to apply the paint. The same might apply to a complicated still life, in which lots of different elements overlap each other. For a loose, impressionistic landscape, on the other hand, a few sweeping lines might suffice.

But providing linear guidelines to follow is only one function of an underdrawing. It should also give you information about the tonal range of the scene, so that you know where the light and dark areas are. This can be in the form of loose scribbles and cross-hatching that roughly define the different areas.

For most purposes, an ordinary pencil is all you need, but it is not your only option. The underdrawings on these two pages are all made in different mediums, chosen for a specific reason.

Underdrawing in charcoal ▼

The lovely sweeping lines of the ground and foliage, counterbalanced by the strong upright lines of the tree trunks, are what attracted the artist to this subject. The intention is to produce an atmospheric landscape, in which an overall impression of the scene is more important than precisely rendered detail. Charcoal is perfect for this, as you can make broad sweeping strokes across the support using the side of the charcoal. It is also superb for blocking in areas of dark tone. To prevent the charcoal from mixing with the paint and muddying the colours, always brush off any excess, and spray fixative (available from all art supply stores) over the underdrawing.

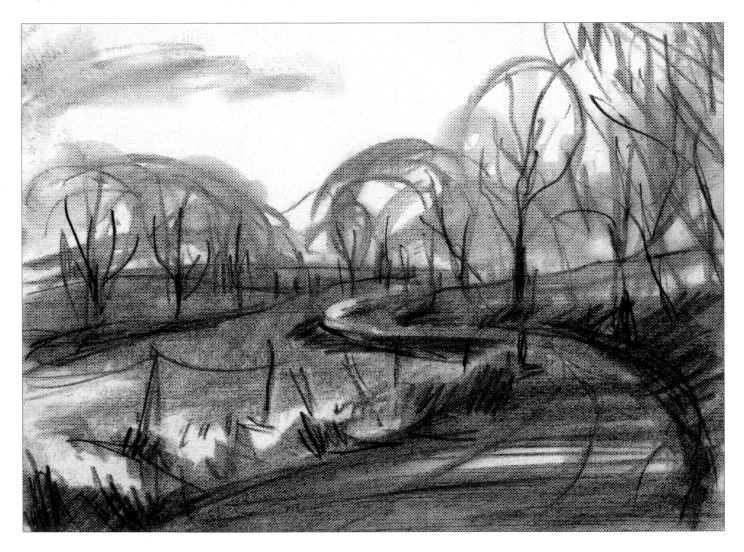

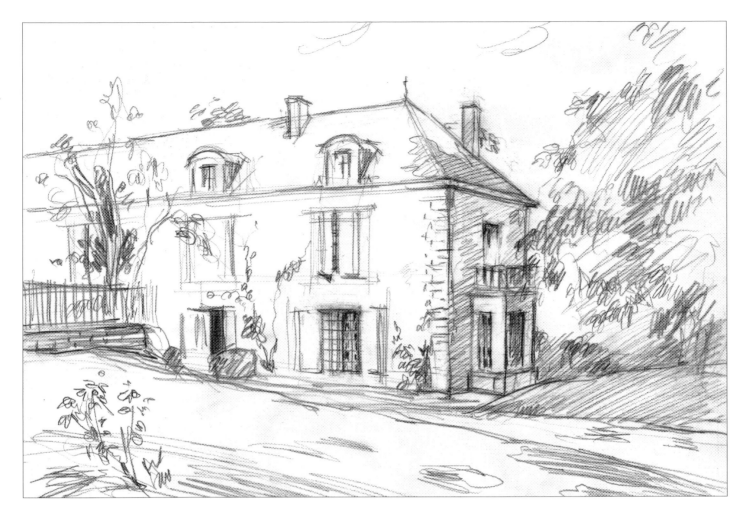

Underdrawing in pencil ▲

Architectural subjects generally require quite a detailed underdrawing: whenever you are painting buildings in two-point perspective, as here, it's vital that you get all the angles right and position all the different elements (windows, chimneys and so on) correctly in relation to one another. A complicated still life is another subject where the relations between one object and its neighbours are critical. A sharp pencil allows you to do this and cross-hatch small, more densely shaded areas such as the window recesses and foliage. It also produces a relatively light underdrawing that will easily be covered by subsequent layers of paint.

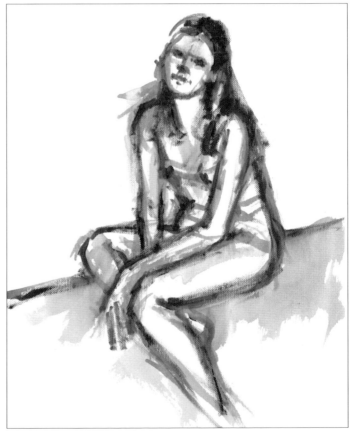

Underdrawing in acrylic paint ▶

The boundary between an underdrawing and an underpainting is sometimes blurred, but if we define an underdrawing as a linear approach, then this certainly qualifies. The brush has been used in the same way as a pencil or pen to indicate the tilt of the head and body and the position of the facial features. There is also some indication of tone within the subject. The choice of burnt sienna is an appropriate one, as it hints at the warm flesh tones of the subject.

Underpainting

The main difference between an underdrawing and an underpainting is that the former is primarily linear in approach while the latter provides more tonal information by roughly blocking in the main shapes and tones before applying colour. Whether you choose to make an underdrawing or an underpainting is entirely a matter of personal choice. Both, however, enable you to work out your composition and the tonal structure of the scene before you begin to apply colour and refine the detail of your subject.

Underpaintings are used in both oil and acrylic paintings. In both mediums, the colour is diluted to a thin consistency – oils with turpentine or other thinner, acrylics with water to which matt medium has been added – to prevent any shine on the underpainting. Because the paint is so thin, alterations can be made by wiping a turpentine- or water-soaked rag, depending on the medium, over the paint – something that is much more difficult to do in the later stages of a painting, when the paint has been applied more thickly.

Underpaintings for works in acrylic must always be made in acrylic paint. Under-paintings for works in oils can be made either in acrylics (provided the support has previously been primed with an acrylic primer) or oils. The benefit of using acrylics for the underpainting, of course, is that they are fast drying. Even fast-drying oil colours, such as flake white and diluted earth colours, need to be left to dry for a couple of days, while a thin acrylic underpainting will dry in a matter of minutes.

Colours for underpaintings

Many artists favour the traditional method of making a monochrome underpainting in neutral colours, generally greys or browns.

Others block in the light and dark tones in a rough approximation of the final colours. This allows you to check the overall colour balance of the work at a very early stage.

A third approach is to use a contrasting or complementary colour for the underpainting. The great Flemish artist Peter Paul Rubens (1577–1640), for example, often used terre verte (a muted green) as the underpainting colour in his nudes, as it complements the pink flesh tones and cools the shadows.

Practice exercise: **Monochrome underpainting**

The advantage of a monochrome underpainting is that it enables you to concentrate on tone rather than colour. It also provides a tonal base for any subsequent glazing technique. Work boldly without putting in textural detail.

Materials
- *Acrylic paper*
- *Acrylic paints: ivory black, titanium white*
- *Brushes: small flat*

The set-up
The tones in this still life need to be carefully assessed if the objects are to be made to look convincingly three-dimensional. Set up a table lamp to one side of the still life, so that the objects cast strong and clearly defined shadows, as this will make it easier for you to assess both the direction and the intensity of the light – and hence to work out the relative tones of the various objects.

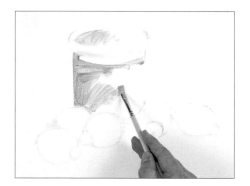

1 Mix a light grey and loosely draw in the outline of the lemons and the pot. Darken the tone slightly and block in the pot.

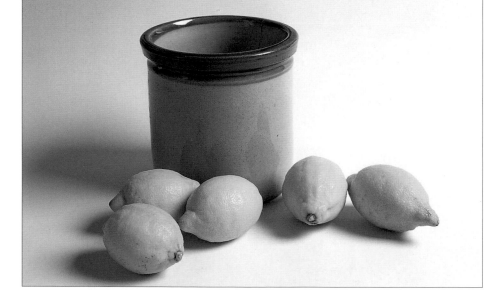

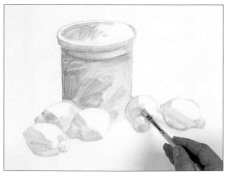

2 Apply the same tone to the inside of the pot, which is in shadow, and to the shaded sides of the lemons, again roughly blocking in the colour.

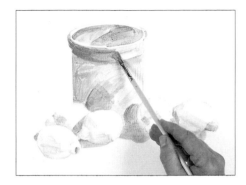 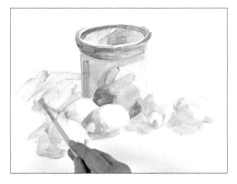 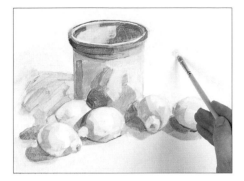

3 Add a little more black to the mixture to darken it further, and indicate the shadows cast by the lemons. Use the same mixture to paint in the outer rim of the shaded side of the pot.

4 Darken the inside lip of the pot and paint in the darker reflections and the shadows cast on its outer surface. Use the same mixture to apply a tone over the area of shadow on the left of the image.

5 Add white to the mixture to make a very light grey and paint the lightest area of the image – the brightly lit backdrop on the right of the still life. Complete the blocking in by using white on the highlights.

The completed underpainting
The underpainting has deliberately been kept loose and sketchy in style, but it has allowed the artist to work out his composition and it provides all the tonal information needed to make a more detailed and resolved painting. Once you have worked out the tonal structure of the still life, you can think about putting in the colour and textural detail.

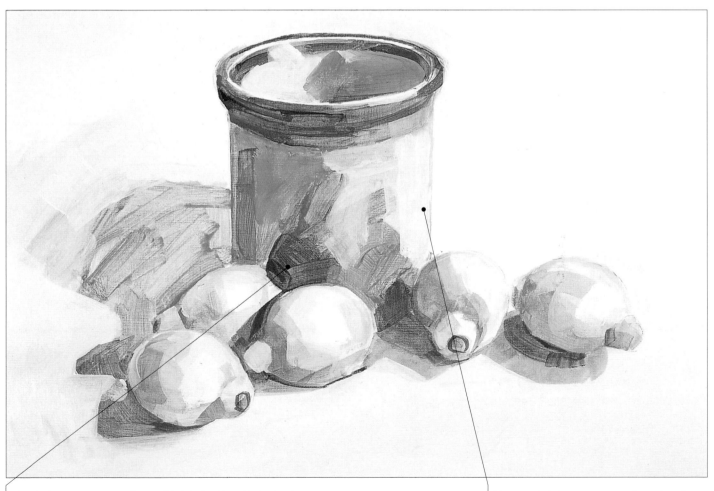

The darkest areas are only roughly blocked in: this is simply a preliminary to making the painting, so do not attempt to smooth out brushstrokes or put in any kind of detailing.

The very brightest areas can be painted as pure white.

Toned grounds

Some artists like to paint on a coloured, or toned, ground rather than on white canvas or paper. There are two main reasons for doing this. First, it can be difficult to judge colours against a white ground, particularly in the early stages of a painting when there are few, if any, other colours on the support to which you can relate them. In this situation, most colours tend to look darker than they really are – and so you may overcompensate by making your mixes lighter than they should be. If you start on a mid-toned, neutral-coloured ground, however, it is much easier to assess tones correctly.

Second, working on a toned ground establishes an overall colour "key" or mood for your painting. If you allow the colour of the ground to show through in places, it helps to unify the painting.

A toned ground may be either transparent or opaque. On a transparent ground, some of the colour of the support is reflected back up through the paint, giving a more luminous, vibrant feel to the painting. For this method, the paint should be heavily diluted (with water for acrylic or gouache paints, or with a thinner such as turpentine or household white spirit for oil paints), and spread over the support in a thin layer, using a brush or a lint-free rag. An opaque ground is used with opaque painting methods such as impasto, where the influence of the white ground is not so important. For an opaque ground, mix your chosen colour with either white paint or primer.

Acrylic paints dry quickly, whereas an oil ground may take a whole day or even longer to dry. To speed things up, many oil painters tone the ground with acrylic paint. (It is possible to paint oils on top of acrylics, but not the opposite way around, as this is likely to make the paint crack.)

What colour should you use to tone the ground? Some artists use a colour that is in keeping with the subject – a warm pink or orange for a nude study, or earth colours for a landscape. Others prefer a contrast, such as a hint of yellow beneath a brilliant blue sky or a reddish brown to warm up a landscape. Opt for a neutral tone that is mid-way between the lightest and darkest values in your painting.

How to tone a ground

Whether you apply paint with a rag or with a brush is largely a matter of personal preference. The important thing is to use a thin layer of paint. It doesn't matter if some brushes strokes are visible or if the paint is slightly streaked; in fact, this gives a more lively, spontaneous effect.

Applying paint with a rag

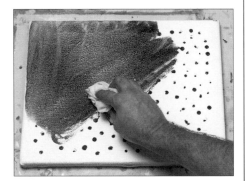

1 Dab your chosen colour (which can be oil or acrylic) over the canvas.

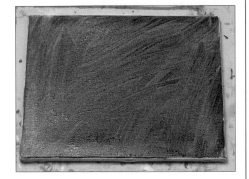

2 Dip a rag in the appropriate thinner (white spirit, turpentine or low-odour thinner for oil paint; water for acrylics), and rub the rag over the canvas to spread the paint over the surface. It is a good idea to wear rubber gloves. Leave to dry.

The prepared ground ▲

Applying paint with a brush

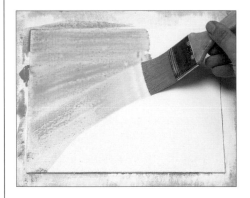

1 This method can be used with oils, acrylics or gouache. Mix a thin wash of your chosen colour and, using a large, flat brush, apply the paint to the surface, varying the direction of the brushstrokes.

The prepared ground ▲
Always allow the prepared, toned ground to dry completely before you begin your painting.

> **Tip**: When choosing a colour for your toned ground, whether you decide to go for a neutral grey or a toning or a contrasting colour, opt for a neutral tone that is midway between the lightest and darkest values in your painting. Soft colours – earth colours such as raw sienna or burnt umber, or soft blues, blue-greys and greens – tend to work well.

Practice exercise: **Teapot on a warm ground**

For your first attempts at using a toned ground, try painting a simple subject on different colours of ground to see what difference it makes. You will probably find that the differences are quite subtle; nonetheless, the colour of the ground will have an impact on the overall mood and colour temperature of the painting.

In this exercise, the artist decided to work on a warm ground that would complement the colour of the copper lustre teapot. The warm underpainting also serves to accentuate the coolness of the blues used to paint the background and table cloth. She then went on to paint the same subject on a white and a blue ground; the results can be seen overleaf.

Materials
- *Acrylic paper*
- *HB pencil*
- *Acrylic paints: burnt sienna, cerulean blue, titanium white, phthalocyanine green, ultramarine blue, cadmium red, cadmium yellow, alizarin crimson*
- *Brushes: medium flat, small round, fine round or rigger*

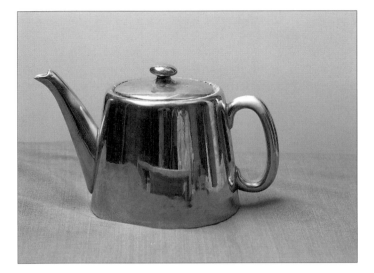

The set-up
Choose a simple subject on a plain background – but look for an interesting interplay of colours and tones.

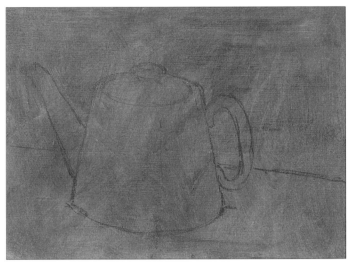

1 First, tone the support with burnt sienna acrylic paint. It doesn't matter if the coverage is slightly uneven. Leave to dry, then sketch your subject using an HB pencil.

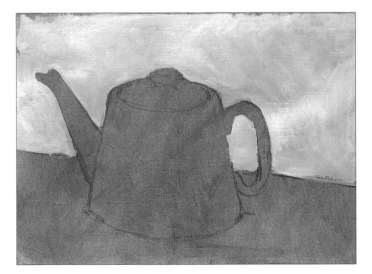

2 Mix a very pale blue from cerulean blue and titanium white. Using a medium flat brush, block in the background above the table. The pale blue serves as a complementary colour to the burnt sienna ground and the contrast between the two gives the painting more impact.

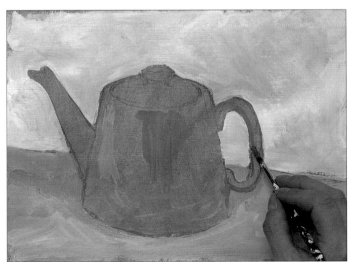

3 Mix a bluish green from phthalocyanine green, ultramarine blue and titanium white and paint the cloth on which the pot is resting, darkening the mixture by adding more green for the shadow cast by the teapot's spout. Use the same colour for the inner edge of the handle and a very dilute version of the mixture for the cooler areas within the teapot, where the colour of the cloth is reflected up into the metallic glaze.

▶

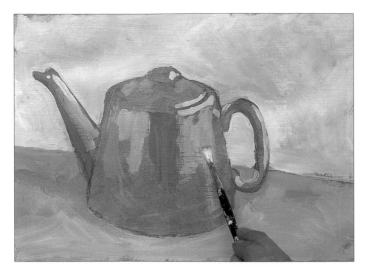

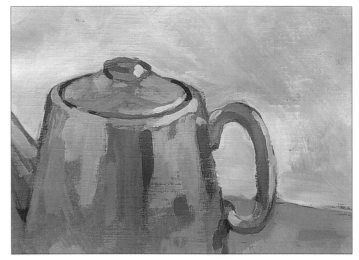

4 Mix a pale, yellowish gold from cadmium red, cadmium yellow and titanium white. Using a small round brush, put in the very brightest, irregularly shaped highlights, where light is hitting the glazed surface of the teapot. Note that the colour of the highlights is applied as a very thin layer of paint; consequently, it is slightly modified by the underlying burnt sienna of the ground.

5 Mix a dark purple from alizarin crimson and ultramarine blue. Using a fine round or rigger brush, "draw" a very fine line around the lid to imply the shaded recess in which the lid sits. Use the same colour to paint the thin line of shadow under the pot. Add more phthalocyanine green to the bluish green mixture from Step 3 and paint the reflections of the cloth at the base of the pot.

The finished painting

The burnt sienna ground gives an overall warmth and richness to the painting, as can be seen in the background, where hints of it remain visible through the thin blue-white paint.

It also serves as the deepest copper colour within the pot; the ground colour has not been painted over in these sections and this helps to unify the painting.

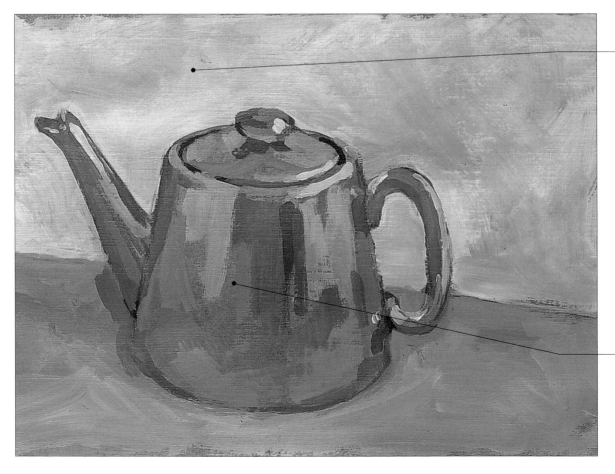

Hints of the toned ground remain visible through the thin blue-white mixture used to paint the background.

The burnt sienna ground is not completely covered over; here, it serves as the deepest copper colour within the pot.

White ground ▶

The artist also painted the same scene on a white ground. A white ground tends to reflect a certain amount of light, even through a relatively opaque colour, which has the effect of making the overall key lighter. There is less interplay of colours within the metallic glaze of the pot and the highlights have been left as white, rather than painted on later.

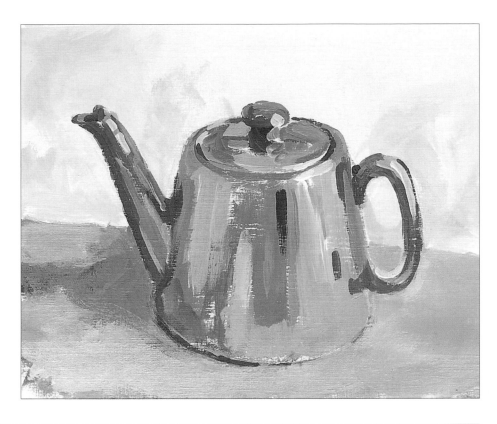

Blue ground ▼

The version painted on a blue ground is cooler in mood. However, the blue ground is a good complementary colour for the coppery pot. Even small areas of blue underpainting, if allowed to show through, will have an effect on any adjacent colours.

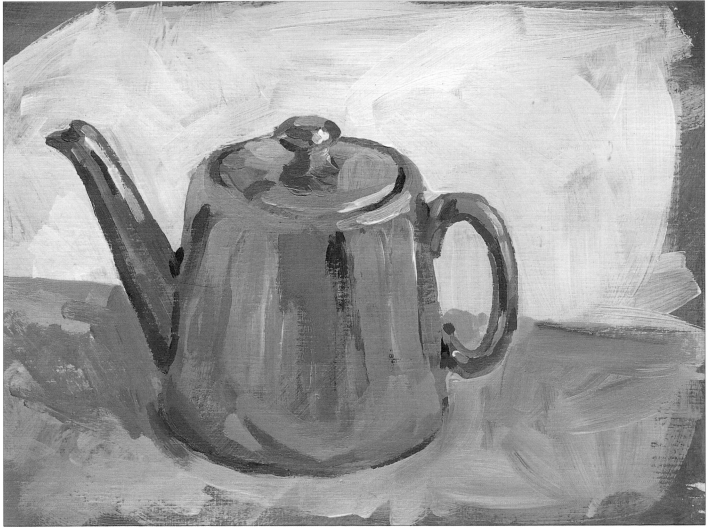

Washes

Laying a wash – a thin layer of transparent colour – is common practice in both gouache and acrylic painting, just as it is in watercolour painting. (The nearest equivalent in oil painting is glazing.) The idea is to apply fluid, thinned paint over areas that are too large to be covered by a single brushstroke. Washes are often used to form a base colour over which the image is then developed. As this tends to involve working over a large area, or even covering the whole of the support, always mix far more paint than you think you'll need: it's surprising how quickly you use it up, and if you run out, it can be very difficult to re-mix exactly the same shade. Before you apply the paint, prop your drawing board up on the easel at a slight angle, so that the paint can flow easily down the paper.

When using gouache paint or acrylic thinned with water and applied in the same way as watercolour, there are various types of wash. A flat wash is a smooth, even layer of colour with no discernible differences in tone or visible brushmarks. In a gradated wash, the colour shades from dark to light (or vice versa). A variegated wash, as the name suggests, consists of more than one colour. All washes are applied in a similar way, with the paint either merging wet into wet into another colour or spreading naturally over a damp support.

The main difference between gouache (or watercolour) and acrylic washes stems from the way in which the paints are manufactured. In gouache and watercolour paints the pigments are bound with gum, which holds them together even when they are diluted with water to the point where the paint appears to be virtually colourless. In acrylic paints the pigments are bound with an acrylic resin, which gives the paint body and substance; but if the paint is diluted too much, it begins to break down and any wash will look thin and lifeless. Because the paint has body, acrylic washes are easier to control than watercolour and gouache. When using acrylic paint as a thin wash on canvas or board, add either a flow-improving medium or a retarding medium so that the thin paint brushes out evenly.

Laying a wash

This sequence demonstrates the technique of laying a flat wash and is the same for acrylics, gouache and watercolour. When you are working in acrylics, however, it is a good idea to add a little flow-improving medium, as this increases the flow of the paint; very thin paint tends to puddle rather than brush out evenly across a surface. For a gradated wash, add more water to the paint as you work down the paper. For a variegated wash, change to a different colour part way through.

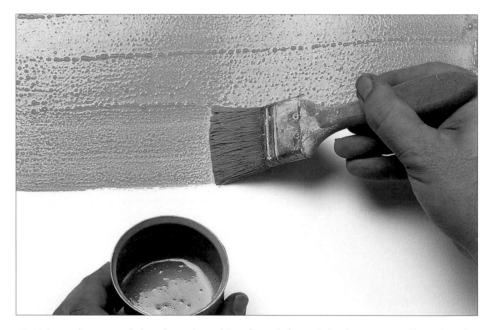

1 Using a large wash brush and working from left to right, lay a smooth stroke of colour across the paper. Quickly re-load your brush with more paint. Pick up the pool of paint at the base of the first stroke with your brush and continue across the paper, again working from left to right.

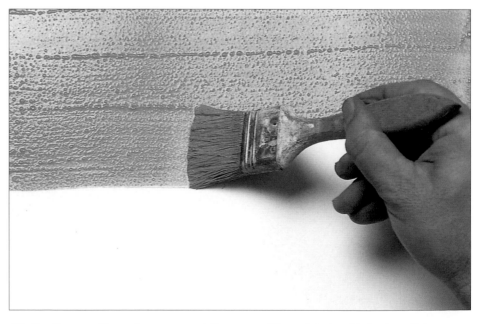

2 Continue until you have covered the paper. The paint should dry to a flat, even tone with no variation or visible brushmarks.

Practice exercise: **Italian landscape**

In any landscape, open spaces are essential: the viewer's eye needs somewhere to rest after taking in the detail of trees, hills and other features. In this exercise, such spaces are provided by the series of flat washes laid over the paper, which also help to lead our eye through the scene.

Note how the tone deepens and becomes warmer with each successive wash: this is a classic device in landscape painting and a very simple way of creating a feeling of recession, as colours generally look paler and slightly cooler the further away things are.

Materials
- *Watercolour board*
- *B pencil*
- *Acrylic paints: cadmium red, cerulean blue, ultramarine blue, olive green, cadmium yellow*
- *Flow-improving medium*
- *Brushes: large round, medium round, small round*

The scene
Here we are looking into the sun and so the scene appears somewhat hazy. This makes it easier to paint: relatively little detail is discernible, so you can get away with painting generalized shapes and concentrate on assessing the tones correctly.

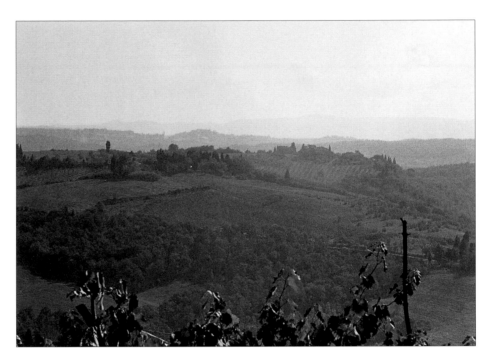

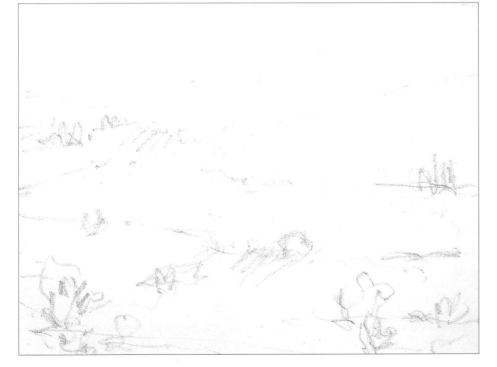

1 Using a B pencil, sketch the scene so that you have some guides for placing the main features. You don't need to include a lot of detail, but put in the outlines of the hills and the main trees and clumps of vegetation.

Tip: Successively darker washes will create a sense of recession in the landscape, so you don't need to include a lot of tonal information in the drawing.

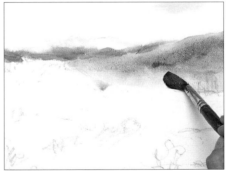

2 Using a large round brush, wash very pale, dilute cadmium red over the sky. The colour is so pale that is it barely perceptible, but it adds warmth to the image. Wash very pale cerulean blue mixed with a few drops of flow-improving medium loosely over the sky. Add more paint to the mixture to darken it and paint the most distant range of hills. Darken it still further by adding ultramarine blue and a tiny amount of cadmium red and brush in the next line of hills. Mix a dark green from cerulean blue and olive green and paint the next range. With just four simple washes, the landscape is already beginning to take on a sense of depth.

▶

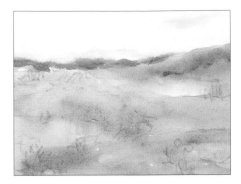

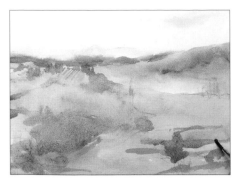

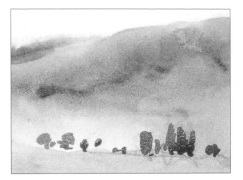

3 Wash olive green over the foreground, darkening the colour by adding cadmium red as you move down the paper. The warmer colour brings this area of the painting forwards and suggests the earth showing through the vegetation.

4 While the foreground is still slightly damp, mix dark and mid-toned greens from varying proportions of olive green and cerulean blue, and using a small round brush, put in the main areas of vegetation. Use vertical brushstrokes for the cypress trees along the horizon and dab the paint on using a circular motion of the brush for the main wooded area on the left.

5 Mix a mid-green from olive green and ultramarine blue and, using a small brush, block in the shapes of the cypress trees in the middle distance, just below the nearest range of hills. Because the underlying paper has dried out quite considerably by this stage, the paint you add now does not spread over the surface and the trees retain their neat, crisp shapes.

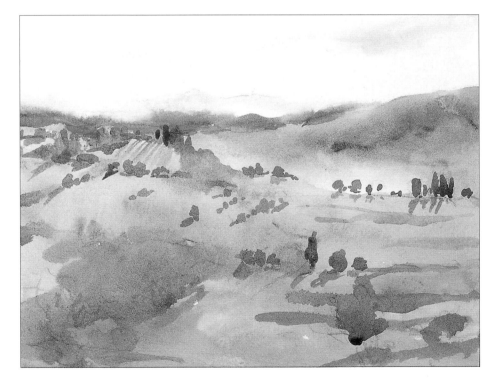

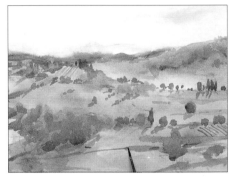

7 Mix a warm brown from olive green and cadmium red and, using a medium round brush, dot this mixture into the foliage areas. Use the same mixture to paint furrows and shadows on the land.

6 Continue putting in the mid-green detail in the middle distance, using the same colours as before and alternating between the different greens on your palette as appropriate. Paint the shadows cast by the trees in a neutral grey created by mixing cadmium red and ultramarine blue. With just a few washes and simple strokes, the scene is already turning into a delightful little landscape.

Tip: The trees are so far away that little detail is evident. A general impression of their shapes and tones, created by applying small blobs of paint and using short brushstrokes, is sufficient. When painting any type of vegetation, your brushstrokes should follow the direction in which the plant grows — so short vertical strokes are perfect for the cypress trees.

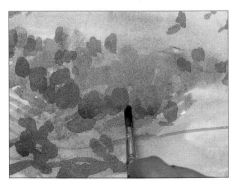

8 Mix a very dark green from ultramarine blue and olive green and dab it into the wooded area on the left. Again, generalized shapes are sufficient.

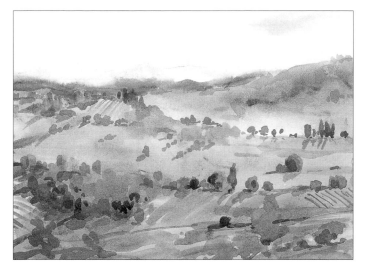

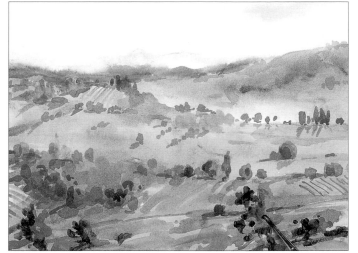

9 Wash the brown mixture from Step 7 over the foreground, adding some cadmium yellow to the mixture when you come to paint the immediate foreground. The warmth of the yellow has the effect of bringing this area forwards in the painting and makes it seem closer to the viewer.

10 Mix a dark brownish green from olive green and cadmium red. Using a small round brush and loose strokes, put in the trees in the foreground. You can use thicker, more textured, paint here: along with the darker colour, this is another means of making the area appear closer to the viewer.

The finished painting
Washes form the basis of this charming and atmospheric Italian landscape, and the detail of the trees and other vegetation is developed over the top once the washes are dry.

The tones of the washes have been carefully chosen to create a feeling of recession, while the earth colours in the foreground give a sense of warmth.

Areas of flat colour provide a resting space for the eye of the viewer.

Note how the washes become darker and warmer in tone as we move towards the foreground.

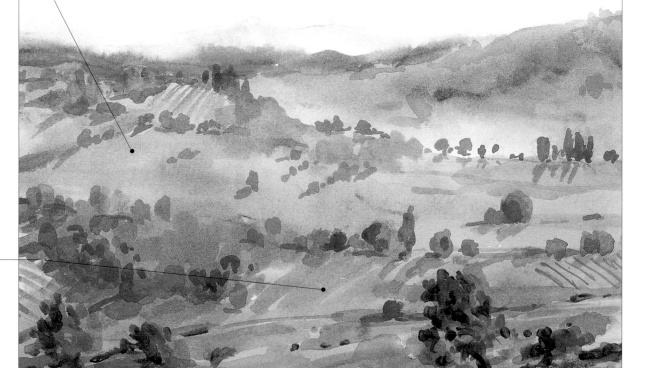

Wet into wet and blending

Allowing one wet paint colour to merge into another on the support is a very exciting way of painting and it can create some extremely atmospheric effects. The thinner the paint, be it oil, acrylic or gouache, the more the different colours will bleed into one another.

With gouache and acrylic paints mixed with lots of water, the technique is akin to that used in watercolour painting and the result depends on how wet the first colour is. If the first colour is still very wet, any subsequent colour will spread and blur, and the result will be soft and somewhat hazy – perfect for subjects such as skies or reflections in water. If the first colour or the support has dried a little, however, the paint will not spread so far – and the brush marks will have a harder edge.

Working wet into wet in this way will always be slightly unpredictable – but that is one of the charms of the technique and, with practice, you will get better at judging how far the paint is likely to spread.

Oil paints, even when mixed with relatively large amounts of thinner, tend to have a certain amount of body and they do not spread on the support in the same way. However, because oil paints take such a long time to dry, you can blend wet colours together on the canvas with the brush to create both optical and physical colour mixes.

In landscapes, this is a useful technique for certain atmospheric effects, such as clouds and fog. It is also invaluable when you are painting subjects with subtle transitions from one tone to another – skin tones, for example, or soft fabrics in a still life. The amount of blending that you do is up to you. It is possible to blend colours so smoothly that the brushstrokes and the transition from one tone to another are virtually imperceptible; alternatively, you can loosely brush one wet colour over another, so that the two retain their own identity but appear to be mixed when the painting is viewed from a distance. Such optical mixes often create a more lively effect than physical mixes.

Very thin oil paints mixed with thinner but no added oil are often used to block in a painting. As the thinner evaporates, the paint dries sufficiently to allow further work, using progressively thicker paint, after a relatively short period of time.

On a wet base colour ▼

If the first colour is still very wet, any subsequent colour will spread, blurring at the edges. The extent of the spread depends on how wet the underlying colour is; this is something that you will learn to judge with practice.

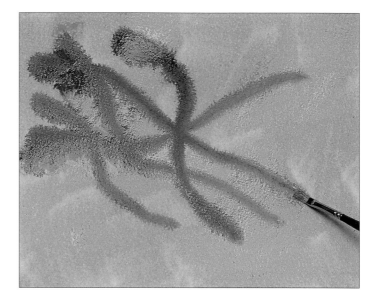

Blending paint with a fan brush

Thick oil and acrylic paints can be blended on the support, rather than in the palette, to create another colour. This technique is very effective where subtle gradations of colour are required.

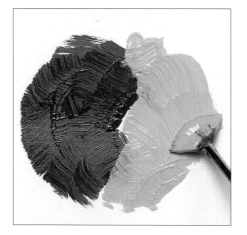

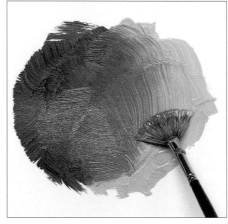

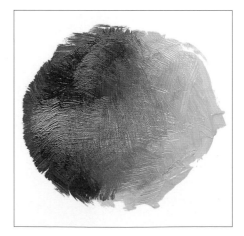

1 Put the two colours down separately on the support. Here, we used cadmium red and cadmium yellow.

2 Using a fan brush, gently stroke one colour into the other so that the two blend together.

3 The two colours merge physically on the support to create a third colour – here, orange.

Blending wet acrylic paint with water

When acrylic paint touches an area that is already wet, it will spread and blur within the wet area. If you do not want this to happen, make sure you allow colours to dry throughly before applying an adjacent one!

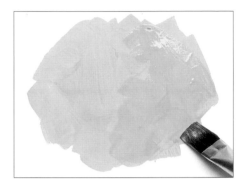

1 Put the first colour down on the support and leave it to dry. Brush clean water over part of the first colour.

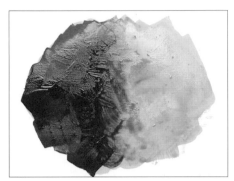

2 Apply the second colour, painting up to the edge of the area that you wetted with clean water.

3 The second colour spreads into the wet area and mixes optically to create orange.

Practice exercise: **Autumn leaves**

In this exercise, red and green paints are allowed to merge into each other, blending together on the support to create subtle, soft-edged shifts from one colour to the next. Painting autumn leaves is a great way of practising the wet-into-wet technique, as you don't need to be terribly precise about where one colour ends and the next one begins.

Materials
- *Watercolour board*
- *2B pencil*
- *Acrylic paints: alizarin crimson, cadmium yellow, phthalocyanine green, titanium white*
- *Brushes: large round, fine round*

The scene
These vine leaves are just beginning to turn from a glossy green to a rich red.

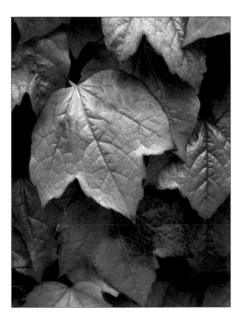

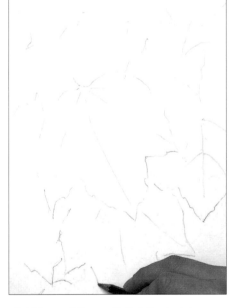

1 Using a 2B pencil, lightly sketch the outline of the leaves and the main veins.

> **Tip**: This is a relatively simple scene in which the tones on the leaves will be built up wet into wet, so all you need to do at this stage is delineate the shapes within which you'll be working.

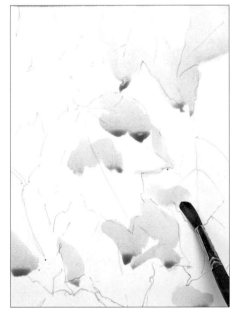

2 Mix a warm, dilute red from alizarin crimson and a little cadmium yellow. Using a large, round brush, loosely brush the mixture over the red parts of the leaves. You don't need to be very precise about where you place the red, but try not to allow paint to spill outside the leaves.

▶

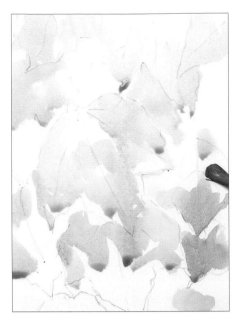

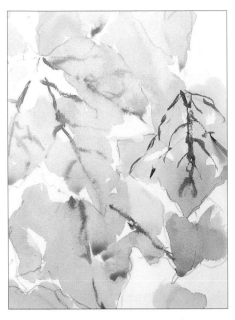

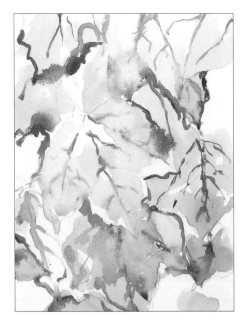

3 Mix a bright green from cadmium yellow and phthalocyanine green. While the red paint is wet, brush the mixture over the brightest green leaves, allowing it to merge into the red. Add more phthalocyanine green to darken the mixture, and paint the leaves on the bottom right of the image.

4 Mix a very dark green from phthalocyanine green and alizarin crimson. Using a fine round brush, put in the most prominent veins. Hold the brush by the end of the handle, almost vertically to the support, and lightly touch it on to the support to get some variation in the line.

5 Mix a dark red from alizarin crimson and a little phthalocyanine green and outline the edges of some of the redder leaves.

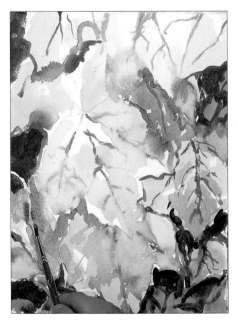

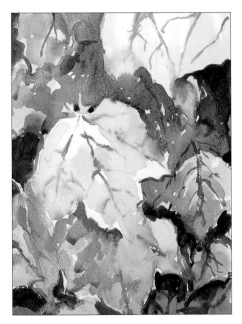

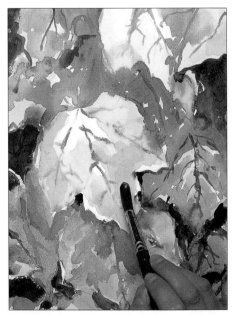

6 Using the dark green from Step 4, block in the spaces between the leaves. While the paint is still wet, mix some alizarin crimson into the dark green and drop it into the spaces, wet into wet. This looks much more interesting than a flat wash of a single colour as dark shadow areas are rarely, if ever, uniform in colour.

7 Continue working on the dark, shadowy spaces between the leaves. Defining these spaces will make the shapes of the leaves stand out more clearly from the background.

8 Now build up colour on the leaves. Darken the red leaves by brushing on a very dilute mix of alizarin crimson, dropping in some green in places so that the two colours merge wet into wet. Add more cadmium yellow to the bright green mixture from Step 3 and brush it on to the central leaf, which is catching the light.

The finished painting

By working wet into wet, the artist has achieved some lovely, subtle colour shifts in the leaves, with pink merging into red and red into varying shades of green. The joy of painting in this way is that you can allow the paint to flow of its own accord and do a lot of the work for you. The detail of the leaf veins was added when the first washes had almost dried, so these lines are crisper without overpowering the initial washes. By holding the brush near the end of the handle, however, the artist has been able to make lovely flowing lines like those used in Chinese brush painting or calligraphy. The result is an atmospheric, spontaneous-looking study.

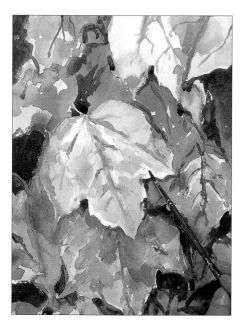

9 Combine your basic red and green mixtures to make a very dark, almost black colour. Using a fine round brush held almost vertically, put in the very dark veins on the shaded red parts of the leaves. Mix a soft pink from titanium white and alizarin crimson and paint the pink leaf tips.

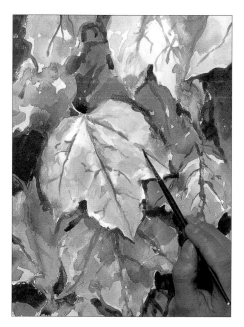

10 Continue to build up the tones on the central leaf, which is in the most prominent position, adding more of the yellowish-green mixture from Step 8. Finally, use the dark green mixture from Step 4 to put in the veining on the central leaf, holding the brush loosely by the end of the handle to make flowing calligraphic marks.

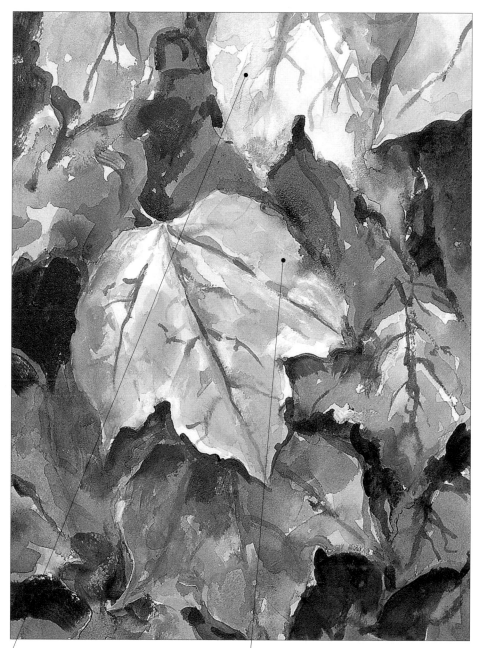

When one colour is applied on top of a colour that is almost dry, the second colour has a clearly discernible edge.

When two colours are allowed to merge wet into wet, the transition between the two is virtually imperceptible.

Painting alla prima in oils

The term *alla prima* comes from the Italian for "at the first" and is used to describe a work (traditionally an oil painting) that is completed in a single session. No underpainting is made, and often there is no preliminary drawing. Reasonably thick, creamy paint is applied using direct and expressive brushstrokes.

Even though they are made using a relatively thick layer of paint, alla prima paintings are invariably technically accurate, as the paint dries at a similar rate over the whole image. There is no problem of an underpainting of a different consistency dry-ing at a different rate and possibly causing the paint to crack at some point in the future.

The alla prima technique is well suited to portrait work and to landscape work done on location, as well as to preliminary studies. Size is an issue, as the work must be no larger than can be comfortably completed in a single session. To help facilitate the uniform drying of the paint, the same painting medium (preferably one that does not accelerate drying time) should be used throughout.

Practice exercise: **anemones painted alla prima**

Fresh spring flowers require a fresh, spontaneous approach, and painting them alla prima is a great way of capturing the delicate texture of the petals. Although the arrangement of leaves and stems looks complex, look for generalized shapes rather than trying to capture every single element. Look at the spaces between leaves, as defining these "negative shapes" will make the shapes of the leaves stand out more clearly.

The set-up
Although this vase of flowers looks so informal that you might imagine the flowers have simply been placed there, with no thought as to their arrangement, the artist has carefully positioned them so that some flower heads are fully open while others are seen from the side. This gives the artist the opportunity to explore the structure of the blooms and makes for a more interesting picture. The colour distribution, too, is important: the reds and purples balance each other well.

Materials
- *Canvas board*
- *B pencil*
- *Oil paints: phthalocyanine green, yellow ochre, burnt umber, cadmium yellow, titanium white, quinacridone red, ivory black, phthalocyanine blue, purple lake*
- *White spirit (paint thinner) or low-odour thinner*
- *Brushes: small flat*

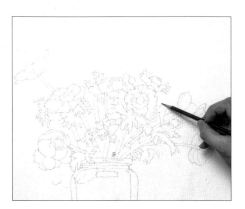

1 Using a B pencil, make a careful drawing of the flowers on the canvas. Establishing the shapes of the individual elements at this stage will make it easier later on: without an underdrawing, the mass of different greens in the bottom half of the image is potentially very confusing.

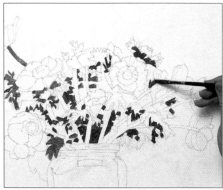

2 Mix a dark green from phthalocyanine green, yellow ochre and burnt umber, thinning the mixture with just enough solvent for the paint to come off the brush easily: too much solvent will make the paint too fluid and hard to control. Using a small flat brush, begin painting the darkest leaves and the spaces between the stems.

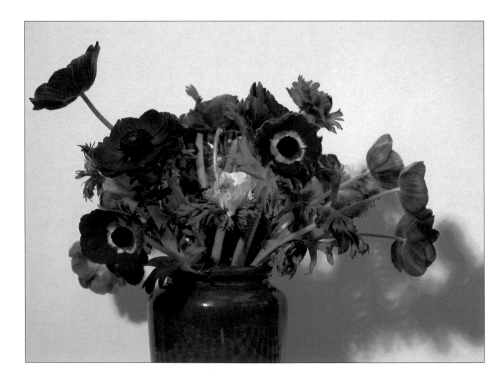

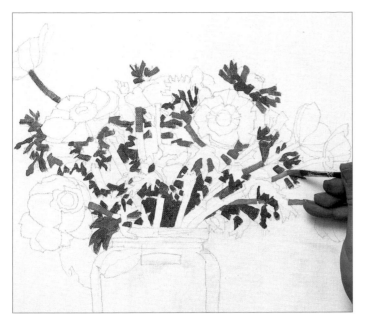

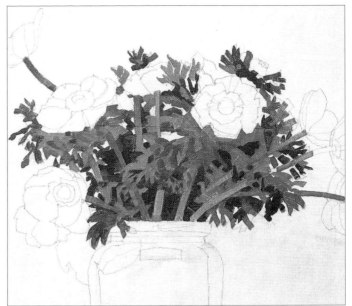

3 Continue adding the green leaves, using short single brush strokes to build up the forms. Lighten the mixture by adding cadmium yellow, a tiny amount of yellow ochre, and titanium white. Alternate between the two greens as you work, so that you begin to establish a sense of light and shade, and make a conscious effort to vary the angle at which you hold the brush, as this will result in marks of different thicknesses.

4 Still using various green mixtures, gradually build up the mosaic of colour and form. Note that some of the greens are very light (achieved by adding more white to the mixture), while some are very dark (achieved by adding a little quinacridone red): work slowly and methodically, so that you do not lose track of where you are in the painting, and refer continually to your still-life set-up. Use the underdrawing only as a guide.

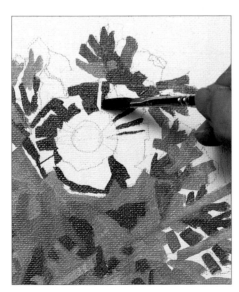

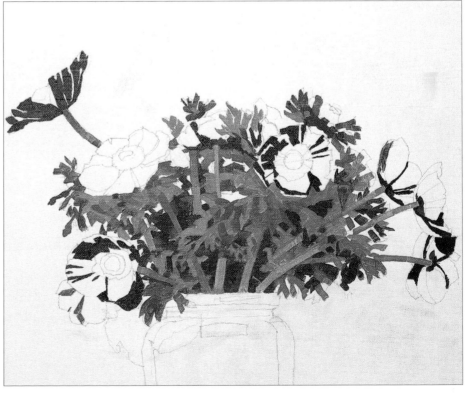

5 Mix a dark red from quinacridone red, a little ivory black, cadmium yellow and yellow ochre, and start putting in the darkest reds of the anemone flowers. There are several tones of red within the same flower, so you will need to look closely to establish where the darkest reds occur. Use the same mixture for the delicate veining on the petals, using the edge of the brush to create very fine lines.

6 While the dark red mixture is on the palette, use it to paint all the dark reds that you can see on the other flower heads. This is not only an economic use of paint, but it also forces you to work across the whole painting, rather than concentrating on one area and running the risk of overworking it.

▶

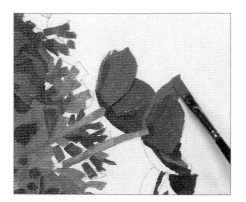

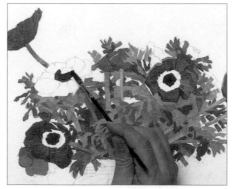

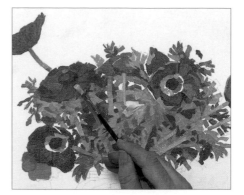

7 Lighten the red mixture by adding titanium white and a little cadmium yellow, and begin putting in the mid tones on the anemone flowers, working around the deep reds that you have already established in the previous two steps. Use just the tip or the thin edge of the brush and apply only light pressure, as this allows you to place your strokes very precisely and paint small, delicate areas with ease.

8 Mix a bluish-black colour from phthalocyanine blue and burnt umber and, with a few short and carefully controlled strokes, paint the dark mass that lies at the centre of each flower.

9 Mix a yellowish green from white, a little of the original green mixture and yellow ochre and touch this colour around the dark flower centres. Mix a dark purple from purple lake and a little phthalocyanine blue and paint the darkest parts of the purple flowers, delineating the individual petals. Mix a lighter purple from quinacridone red, phthalocyanine blue and titanium white and paint the lighter purple areas.

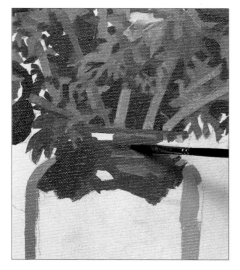

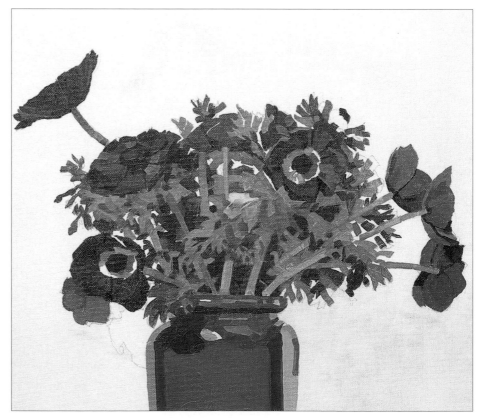

10 Add white to the light purple mixture from the previous step and paint over the lightest areas around the centre of the purple flower. Use some of the light green mixture that you used to paint the stalks to put in the light colour on the ceramic vase, leaving the brightest highlights untouched.

11 Add purple lake and a little burnt umber to the original dark green mixture that you used in Step 2 and paint the darker reflected colours that can be seen on both sides of the vase, taking care to paint around the highlights that you painted in Step 10. The vase is now beginning to look much more rounded and three-dimensional: the use of different tones of green helps to give it form, while the highlight shows us which direction the light is coming from and helps to enliven the composition.

Tip: Look carefully at the shapes of the shadows cast on the wall: although the flowers are soft, rounded shapes, some of the shadows are quite angular. Using a flat brush allows you to make precise marks: use a corner of the wedge shape to fill in detail, the end of the wedge for thin straight lines, and the full width to cover larger areas.

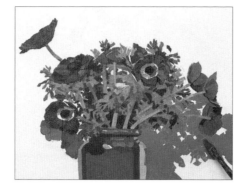

12 Now paint the shadow that the flowers cast on the wall behind. Mix a purplish grey from the purple flower colour, the red mixture used in Step 7, and phthalocyanine blue. Loosely brush in the shadow, remembering to leave gaps to indicate where the light shines through the flowers on to the wall.

The finished painting

Add lots of titanium white and a little yellow ochre to the shadow colour and put in the background. Working alla prima allows you to blend the colours on the support and capture the delicacy of the papery petals to perfection. The finished painting is a lively and realistic-looking interpretation of a loose arrangement of spring flowers.

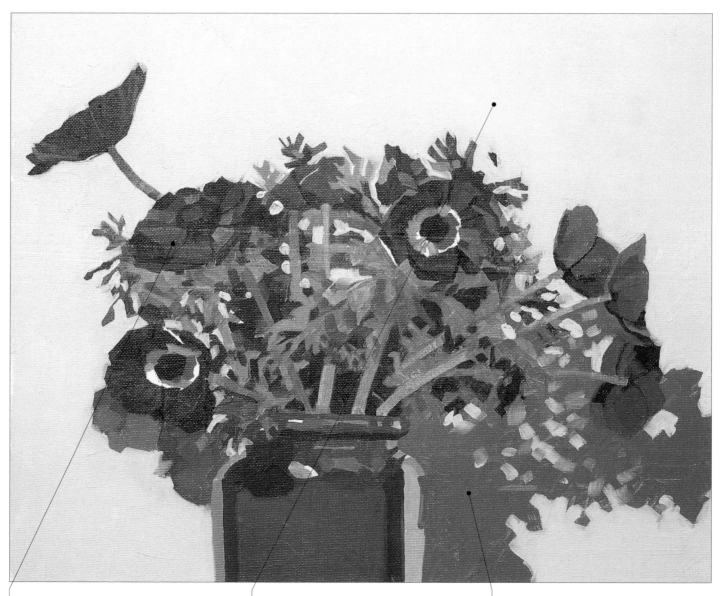

Thin layers of paint, blended wet into wet on the support, create the delicate veining and subtle coloration of the anemone petals.

The background is painted in a single, thin layer of a pale purplish grey, using short brushstrokes of lighter paint to soften the shadow edges.

The cast shadow has the effect of throwing the vase of flowers forward.

Glazing

A glaze is a transparent layer of paint that is applied over a layer of paint. As with traditional watercolour, light passes through the transparent glaze and is reflected back by the support or any underpainting. Glazing is a form of optical mixing as each glaze colour is separate from the next, with the mixing taking place within the eye. Each glaze needs to be dry before the next layer is applied, otherwise the colours will simply mix together as they would on the palette. Glazing techniques can be used with both oils and acrylics.

Glazed colours reflect light more readily than opaque colours, which tend to absorb light. This gives glazed works a richness and luminosity that can be lacking in paintings done using conventional mixing techniques.

Traditionally, the work began with an involved tonal underpainting in monochrome over which the colours were carefully glazed. Depending on the subject, the underpainting can be made using a warm brown, black, or even green. However, glazing techniques can also be used in conjunction with more opaque painting techniques. Glazes made over opaque layers of paint can liven up dull areas of colour, or make warm areas of colour appear cooler or cool areas warmer. This is particularly useful when painting portraits. A single colour glaze is often used over the entire picture area once it is finished and dry, which has the effect of bringing an overall harmony to the colours.

Lightness or darkness of the glazed colour ▼
Traditionally, glazed colours were applied over a tonal underpainting. It is the tones in the monochrome underpainting that determine the lightness or darkness of the colours glazed on top.

Physical colour mixing ▼
Physically mixing cadmium yellow (below left) and dioxazine purple (below right) creates a dull brown (bottom left). When the same two colours are glazed one over the other, the integrity of both remains intact and the result is a brighter mix in which the two colours combine optically (bottom right).

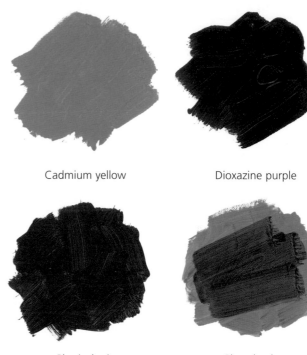

Cadmium yellow   Dioxazine purple

Physical mix   Glazed colour

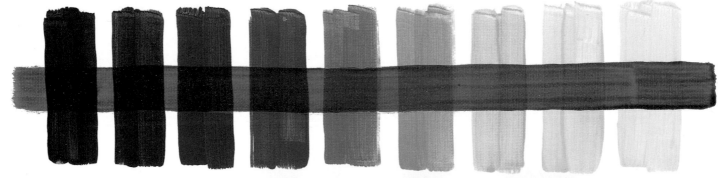

Mediums for glazes ▶
When using oil paint, which is less opaque than acrylic, use a glazing medium. With acrylic paints use a gloss painting medium; this not only thins the paint but also increases its transparency. Acrylic paints are ideal for glazing, as they dry very quickly. Certain colours, which are by their nature more transparent, are more suitable for glazing techniques than others, but even opaque colour can be used.

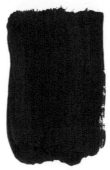

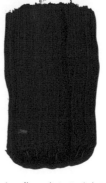

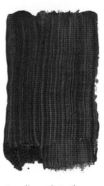

Oil paint straight from the tube

Oil paint plus glazing medium

Acrylic paint straight from the tube

Acrylic paint plus gloss medium

Practice exercise: **Glass jar and chiffon**

Glazing is the ideal technique for painting transparent and semi-transparent subjects such as this tiny glass jar and chiffon scarf, as it allows colour to be built up gradually until the right density is achieved. The final effect of both transparent glass and transparent fabric is skilfully achieved Careful observation is the key, as there are many subtle shifts of tone within the scene, even though the number of colours in this particular exercise is relatively small.

Remember that you need to allow each glaze to dry completely before you apply the next one, otherwise the colours will combine in a muddy mess.

Materials
- *Oil paper*
- *B pencil*
- *Oil paints: phthalocyanine green, raw sienna, alizarin crimson, ultramarine blue; zinc white*
- *Thinner*
- *Drying linseed oil*
- *Brushes: medium flat, small round*

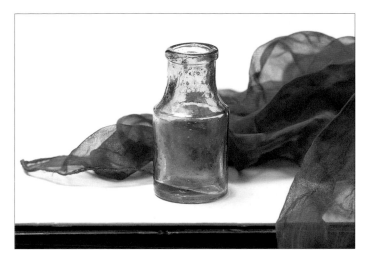

The set-up
Although the chiffon scarf is casually draped, it naturally falls into folds, some of which are several layers thick, and you have to assess the depth of colour very carefully. The scarf can also be seen through the glass jar, although its colour here is modified by the green of the glass.

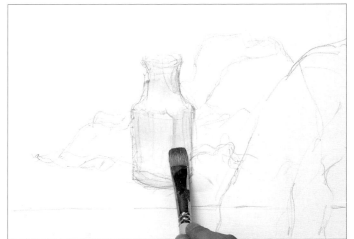

1 Using a B pencil, make a light underdrawing, putting in the lines of the main folds in the chiffon scarf as a guide. Mix a bluish green from phthalocyanine green and a tiny amount of raw sienna. Using a medium flat brush block in the jar, leaving some areas untouched for the highlights in the glass. Indicate the cast shadow to the right of the jar.

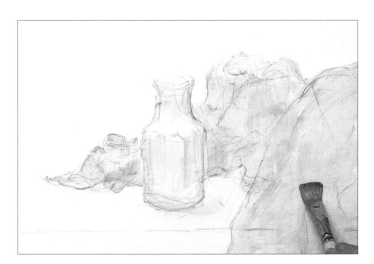

2 Mix a pale pinkish red from alizarin crimson with a little raw sienna. Paint the scarf. Your brushstrokes should run in the same direction as the folds in the fabric; you will find that the flat brush makes it easier to paint the edges of the folds.

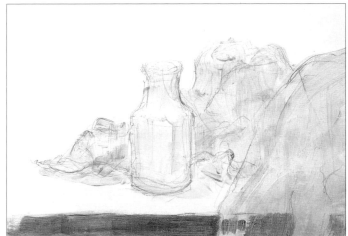

3 Mix a neutral grey from alizarin crimson and a little phthalocyanine green, and paint the shadow under the scarf. Mix an orangey brown from raw sienna and alizarin crimson and paint the shelf edge. Add a little phthalocyanine green and glaze it over the shelf to get some variation in colour. Use this mixture for areas where the wood can be seen through the chiffon.

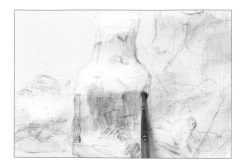

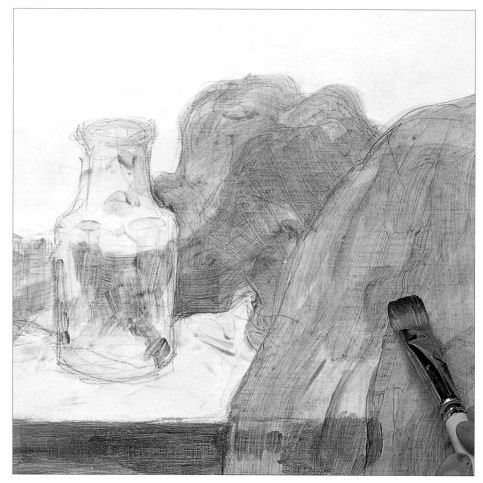

4 Mix a cooler version of the scarf colour used in Step 2 by adding a tiny amount of phthalocyanine green and paint the scarf that can be seen through the jar. At this stage, simply block in the area of colour without making any attempt to work out the tones.

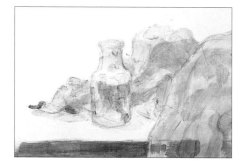

5 Glaze this cooler colour over the most deeply shaded parts of the scarf. Already the scarf is beginning to take on some depth.

6 Mix a very pale, dilute raw sienna and brush it lightly over the white background to warm up this area and make the contrast between it and the still life less stark. Using the medium flat brush, glaze alizarin crimson over the deepest-coloured parts of the scarf, where several layers of fabric overlap each other.

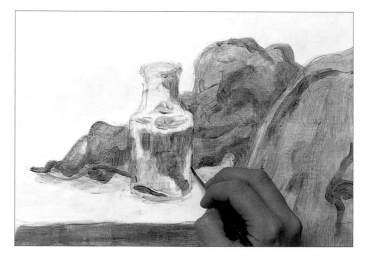

7 Glaze the cool pink colour from Step 5 over the deepest folds in the fabric. Mix a dark blue-green from phthalocyanine green and ultramarine blue and, using a small round brush, darken the colour of the jar where necessary. Glaze this blue-green colour over some of the dark reds in the jar. Note how the two glazes modify each other: the red is cooled by the green.

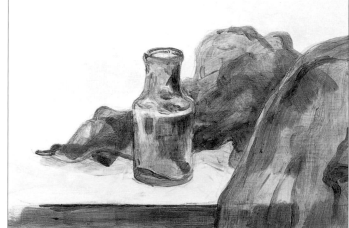

8 Continue building up the dark green colour of the jar, remembering to work around the highlights. Glaze more of the pink mixture over the most deeply coloured parts of the scarf, where several layers of fabric fall in soft folds on top of one another. Use a cooler (bluer) mix inside the jar, as the colour of the scarf in this area is affected by the green of the glass.

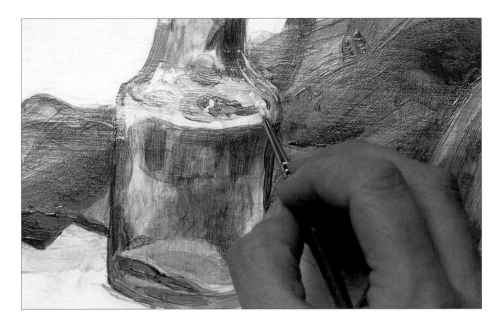

9 Glaze more dark green over the jar to make a stronger contrast, so that the jar comes forwards in the scene. Reinforce the highlights in the jar with zinc white (or zinc white mixed with a tiny amount of blue-green, as appropriate).

> **Tip**: Even in clear glass, highlights are rarely, if ever, pure white. Instead they are tinged with a hint of the colour of any nearby objects that are reflected in the glass. Here, the highlights are created by using a paler version of the green used for the glass jar.

The finished painting
Thin layers of paint have been skilfully applied to build up the colours and tones. Where several layers of sheer fabric overlap one another, glazes are the perfect means of building up the colour to the right density. Each glaze modifes the preceding colour, creating optical mixes that are more lively than could be achieved by mixing colours in the palette.

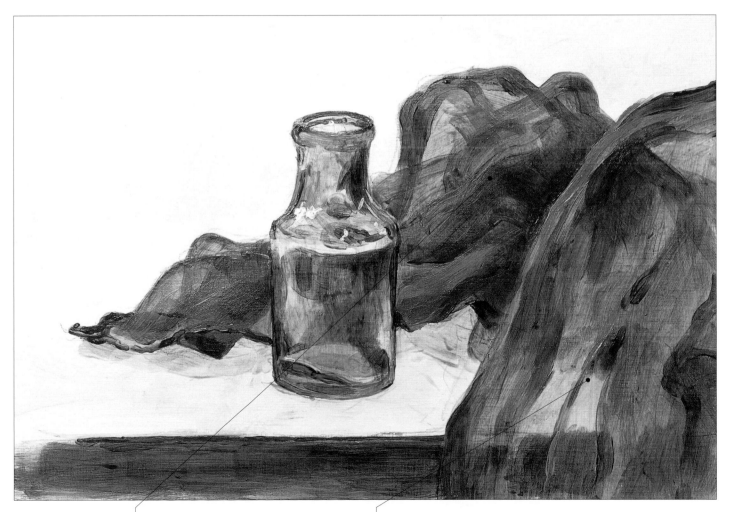

Several glazes of different colours are used for the deepest-coloured areas.

One layer of thin paint is enough to portray the delicate wispy nature of the fabric.

Scumbling

Scumbling is the technique that involves applying dry, semi-opaque paint loosely and roughly over a dry underlayer, leaving some of the underlayer visible to create optical colour mixes on the support. The technique also produces interesting surface textures in which the marks of the brush or other paint applicator may still be seen. The technique can be used with oils, acrylics, gouache, watercolour and pastels. The texture of the support plays an important part in scumbling techniques, which tend to be more successful on rough surfaces than on smooth. Having said that, however, subtle scumbling is useful for adding variation and relief to large areas of flat, uninteresting colour on smooth supports.

Scumbling is a great way of modifying colour while keeping the painted surface looking lively. For example, if an area looks too hot, you could scumble a cool colour over the top – and vice versa. Or you might choose to use the technique to paint an area of deep shadow, which is rarely if ever a uniform, flat colour; the colours thus applied will create an optical mix that looks much more lively and interesting than a physical mix of the same hues. There are lots of subjects for which scumbling is appropriate. Masses of foliage seen from a distance, clouds racing across a stormy sky, torrents of water, worn stone or distressed wood: all consist of intermingling colours and can benefit from the fresh, spontaneous look that scumbling can achieve.

Whatever medium you are using, when applying a scumble you should always work loosely and freely. If you're using a brush, scrub the paint on to the support with the brushstrokes going in different directions or even in a circular motion. A bristle or synthetic brush is best, as the fibres are hard and separate from one another; with a soft-haired watercolour brush, the fibres would stick together and detract from the irregular effect of the technique. It is best to save old, worn brushes for this technique as the scrubbing action will quickly damage the bristles of good brushes. You can also scumble paint on using a rag or sponge, or even your fingers.

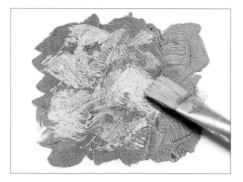

Broad scumble ▲
Here, a stiff mix of paint is scumbled over the dry, slightly impasto paint applied previously. The paint catches on some of the brushstrokes, but in other areas the underlying layer still shows through.

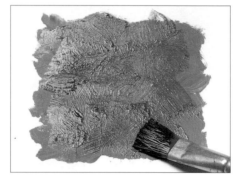

Transparent scumble using acrylics ▲
For a more transparent scumble and delicate optical colour mixes, add acrylic medium to the paint. This increases the transparency of the paint.

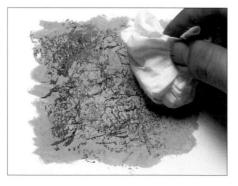

Light scumbling with a rag ▲
To allow more of the first layer to show through, dip a rag or absorbent kitchen paper into your chosen colour and lightly touch it on to the support, so that the paint adheres only to the peaks of the brushstrokes of the first layer.

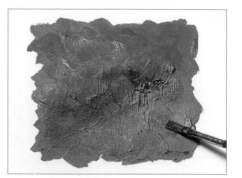

Scumbling to add interest ▲
An area of dry, flat colour can be made more interesting by scumbling a slightly different colour over it.

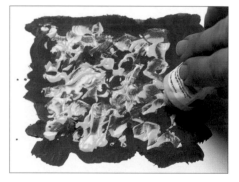

Heavily textured scumbling ▲
For a more textured look, dot the paint on to the support straight from the tube. You can use this technique with both oils and acrylics.

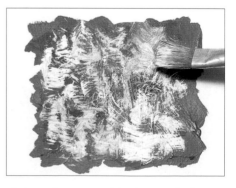

Light colour scumbled over dark ▲
Use a stiff, dryish mix of paint and remove some of it from the brush prior to making the mark, in the same way as you would with drybrush techniques. This allows more of the first layer to show through.

Practice exercise: **Distressed wood and metal**

Scumbling is the perfect technique for painting weathered wood and metal, as it allows underlying colours to show through and creates interesting textures. Keep your paints fairly thick and dry, and apply the paint unevenly, so that the colour is not uniform.

Build up the scumbles gradually. If you apply too much heavy paint all at once, the subtlety of the effect will be lost. A few drops of acrylic medium improves the paint flow. In this exercise, which is painted on cardboard, the medium also acts as a size; even though the cardboard has been primed, it is still porous, and the medium prevents the paint from sinking into the surface.

Materials
* Cardboard primed with acrylic gesso
* HB pencil
* Acrylic paints: alizarin crimson, phthalocyanine green, raw sienna, titanium white
* Matt acrylic medium
* Brushes: large round, small round, small flat

The scene
The artist came across this magnificent but rather scary-looking door knocker on a trip to Venice; small details such as this are often as evocative as views of an entire building.

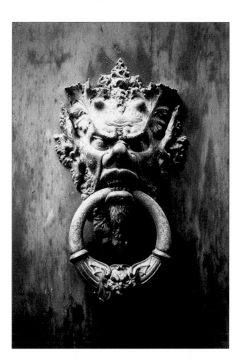

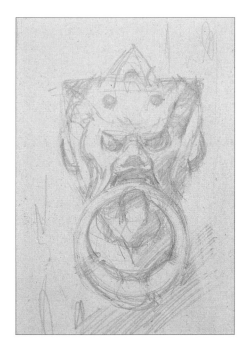

1 Using an HB pencil, sketch the scene. Although the subject is small in scale, the changes in tone from one plane to another need to be carefully rendered, so make sure you put in all the detail you need. Your pencil marks will be fully covered by the paint.

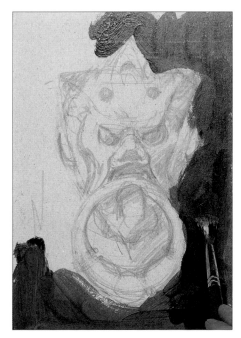

2 Mix a dark, almost black, green from alizarin crimson and phthalocyanine green and add a few drops of matt acrylic medium. Using a large round brush, start painting the background.

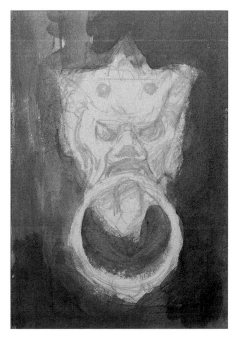

3 Lighten the mixture for the top left of the painting, which is catching more of the light. Add some raw sienna to the mixture and brush it wet into wet into the background to get some variation in colour.

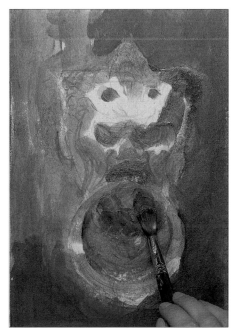

4 Mix a warm brown from raw sienna and alizarin crimson and dab it loosely over the darkest parts of the metal door knocker. This will serve as a warm base for subsequent applications of paint.

▶

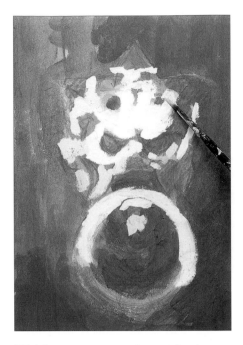

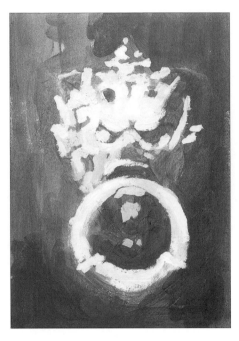

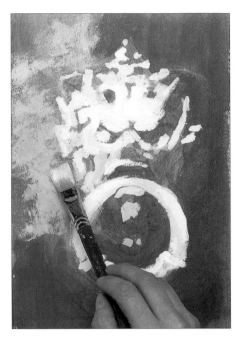

5 Mix an opaque, pale metal colour from titanium white, raw sienna and a little phthalocyanine green. Using a small round brush, brush it over the lightest areas, adding more green to the mixture for those areas that are slightly cooler in tone.

6 Continue to paint the door knocker, alternating between the warm and cool mixtures used in the previous step as necessary in order to build up the form. Leave to dry.

7 Mix an opaque white from titanium white and the cool green mixture. Using a medium flat brush, loosely scumble it over the wood of the door, allowing some of the underlying colour to remain visible, creating the effect of worn, distressed paintwork.

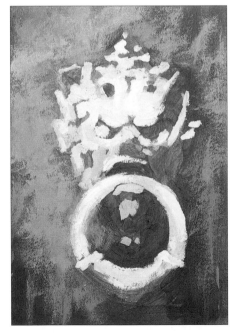

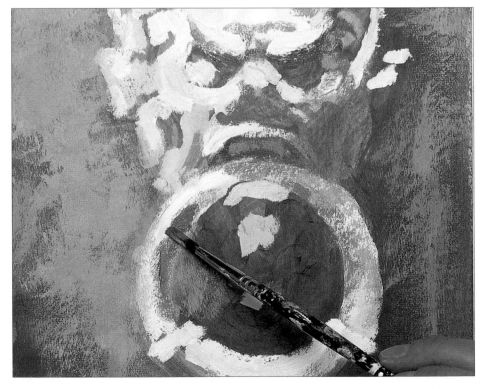

8 Continue to scumble paint over the door, varying your mixtures by adding more green for some parts and more raw sienna for others. Remember that the light in the scene is coming from the top left, which means that the bottom right is darker and more deeply shaded.

9 The scumbling on the door establishes the mid tones of the painting, which makes it easier to assess how dark the very shaded parts need to be. Mix a dark, brownish green from raw sienna, alizarin crimson and phthalocyanine green. Using a small brush, put in the dark recesses on the face, adding more raw sienna on the right-hand side. Scumble the same colour over the round knocker.

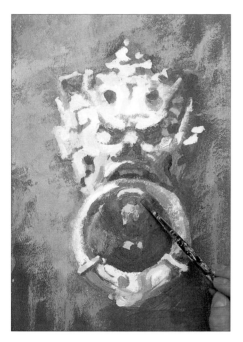

10 Build up the form by continuing to add shaded recesses on the face.

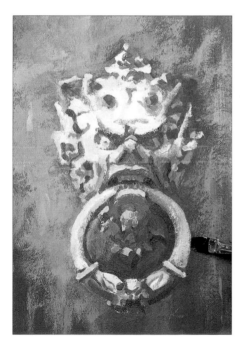

11 Refine the details, using opaque mixtures of all the colours on your palette. Use a small flat brush to sharpen the outline of the door knocker with dark greens and blue-green mixes.

Tip: The shape of the flat brush makes it easier to give objects a crisp, sharp outline.

The finished painting
This painting shows just how effective scumbling can be when painting worn and weathered surfaces. Although only a limited number of colours were used, the various layers of paint imply not only the way the wooden door has been bleached by years of exposure to the sun and rain, but also create rough textures. The use of warm and cool tones of the same colours creates a convincing sense of light and shade, even though the light source itself (the sun) is not visible. This helps to build up the form of the door knocker and make it look three dimensional.

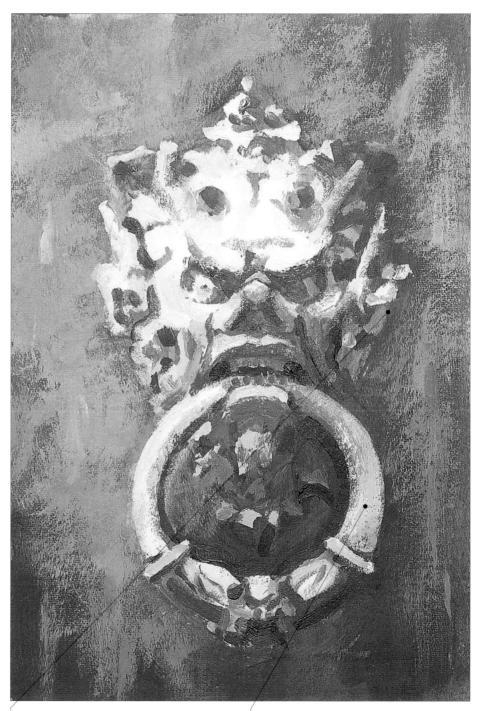

Rough scumbling adds texture to the image.

Here, the scumbling hints at the rustiness of the metal.

Impasto

Impasto techniques involve applying and building the paint into a thick layer and are not unlike icing a cake. The word impasto is Italian for "dough" and describes the consistency of the paint used. In reality, the paint is usually more like butter; it is easy to spread and manipulate, but retains the mark of any brush or implement used to apply it. The consistency of paint straight from the tube is usually about right.

Given the amount of paint that can be used in even a modest-sized work, it can be economical to mix the paint with a medium specifically designed for impasto work. In the case of oil paint, these mediums contain drying agents that speed up the paint's drying time and cause the paint to dry at a uniform rate regardless of thickness. The medium also adds bulk to the paint without affecting its colour, so you use less paint – an important consideration given the cost of many oil paints. Acrylic paints can be bulked out using heavy gel medium and texture pastes.

By its nature, working with impasto techniques precludes the inclusion of fine detail. The work should be well planned, but painted as freely and intuitively as possible to keep it fresh. One solution is to use impasto work over an underpainting. If you are using oil paint (following the important oil-painting rule, painting "fat over lean"), use thin paint to which you have added plenty of thinner. Alternatively make the underpainting in thin acrylic paint and do the impasto work in oils.

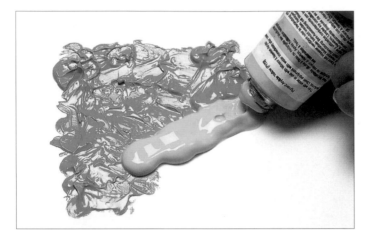

Using paint straight from the tube ▲
With both oils and acrylics, you can squeeze paint straight from the tube on to the support. More often than not, artists will apply paint to the support in this way and then work into it using a painting knife or other implement.

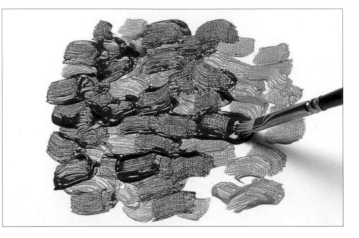

Using a brush ▲
You can also squeeze the paint on to your palette and apply it with a brush. Paint from the tube is invariably of the right consistency for impasto work. Provided you do not overbrush, the brushmarks will stand proud and evident.

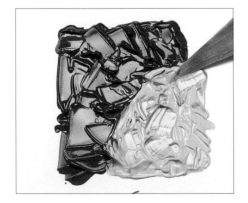

Using a painting knife ▲
You can drag and press a painting knife into thick paint and also blend colours together on the support. The marks you make will depend on the size and shape of the knife. The knife can also be used to scrape into wet paint to create textures and to remove paint that has been incorrectly positioned.

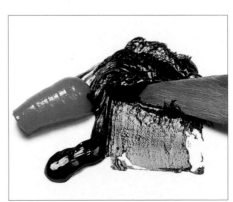

Adding impasto medium to paint ▲
There are a number of so-called impasto mediums, for both oils and acrylics, that can be mixed into the paint on the palette. The one shown here is a quick-drying impasto medium designed specifically for use with oils. If you are using acrylic paints, use a heavy gel medium.

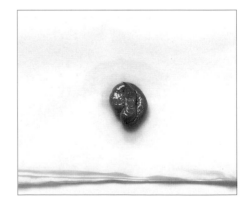

Blotting up excess oil ▲
If your paint is too oily when you squeeze it out of the tube, it will tend to spread and flow too easily. To overcome this, simply squeeze it on to absorbent paper (a paper towel or blotting paper); the paper will absorb the oil, leaving behind a blob of thick paint.

Practice exercise: **Pumpkins painted impasto using acrylics**

Pumpkins are highly textured vegetables: there are clear indentations on the outer surfaces delineating the different segments, while a tangled mass of fibres and hard seeds on the inside provides you with the perfect opportunity to practise impasto work. The coloration, too, gives you the chance to apply the paint thickly, dabbing on different colours to achieve the necessary variations in tone. Adding acrylic gel medium to the paint thickens it and makes it ideal for impasto work, as it holds the marks of the knife or brush. It also makes the paint go further.

Materials
- Primed canvas
- 2B pencil
- Acrylic paints: burnt umber, cadmium red, cadmium yellow deep, phthalocyanine blue, alizarin crimson, cadmium yellow medium, yellow ochre, titanium white, sap green, cadmium orange
- Acrylic gel medium
- Brushes: small flat, medium flat
- Medium trowel-shaped painting knife

The set-up
Arrange the pumpkins on a table or shelf, aiming for good contrasts of size: it looks more interesting if at least one vegetable is laid on its side, so that you can see the cut-off stalk. Look at the angle of the stalks, too: here, the artist has positioned the largest and the cut pumpkins with their stalks pointing towards each other, which helps to direct the viewer's eye through the picture. Cut at least one of the pumpkins open to reveal the seeds and fibres inside.

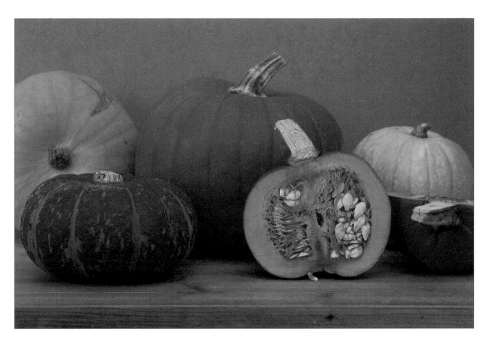

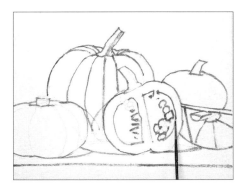

1 Using a 2B pencil, lightly sketch your composition. You do not need to put in all the detail, but indicate the striations on the largest pumpkin (these curved lines will make it easier for you to get the overall shapes right). Add the angles of the stalks, and the main internal divisions in the cut pumpkin so that you have some guidelines for when you begin to paint. When you are happy with the sketch, go over the lines in burnt umber acrylic paint, using a small flat brush. If you wish, you could underpaint the picture at this point, using watered-down acrylic paint.

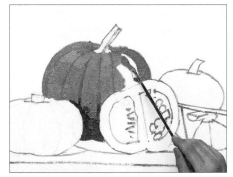

2 Mix a warm dark orange from cadmium red, cadmium yellow deep, and a little burnt umber, adding acrylic gel medium to the mix to thicken it. Using the edge of the brush, paint the segments on the surface of the largest pumpkin. Mix a dark brown by adding phthalocyanine blue and alizarin crimson to the orange mixture and paint the deep shadow at the base of the pumpkin. Add cadmium yellow medium to the orange mixture to lighten it, and block in the sections, carefully painting around the stalk of the cut pumpkin.

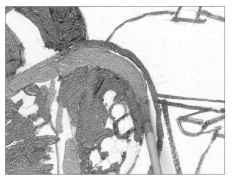

3 Using the same dark orange mixture, outline the cut pumpkin and block in the dark area around the seeds in the middle, delineating the largest of the individual seeds in the same colour. Add yellow ochre and titanium white to the mixture and paint the fibrous area with loose, horizontal brushstrokes, varying the proportions of the mixture to create tonal variety. Add more cadmium yellow and white to the mixture and paint the pumpkin flesh around the outside of the seeded area, using a full range of brushstrokes to work around the shapes.

▶

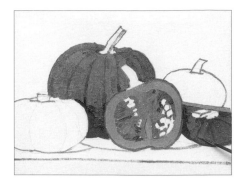

4 Using the same mixture as in Step 2, paint the shadow between the cut pumpkin and the pumpkin on the far right. Paint the individual segments of the pumpkin on the right, then paint the cut surface in a mixture of cadmium yellow medium and titanium white. Add cadmium red to the basic warm orange mixture and block in the segments of the pumpkin.

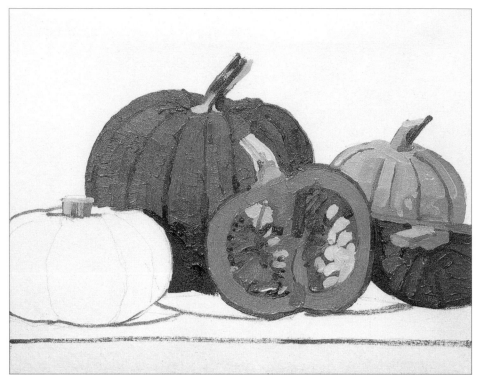

Tip: Use a hairdryer to speed up the drying time of thick acrylic paint. Once you are sure that the first layer is completely dry, you can apply further layers to build up the impasto effect without disturbing the underlying paint.

5 Mix a pale, greyish-green from titanium white, phthalocyanine blue, yellow ochre and the basic orange mix and outline the segments of the small green pumpkin on the right. Add more white to the mixture and block in the segments. Mix a pale beige for the seeds of the cut pumpkin from titanium white, yellow ochre and the pale green mixture. Use the pale beige for the top of the stalk and the pale grey-green mixture for the base of the stalk. Mix a darker green, using the grey-green mix plus orange, and paint the stalks of the two pumpkins on the far right, using the dark green for the shaded sides to create a sense of light and shade.

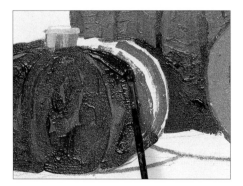

6 Mix a mid-tone green from sap green, yellow ochre, a little phthalocyanine blue and titanium white, and outline the segments of the green pumpkin on the bottom left of the picture. Dab the same mixture over other parts of the pumpkin too. Mix a darker green from sap green, phthalocyanine blue and alizarin crimson and paint around the first green. Brush the paint on thickly, using the side of the brush, to build up interesting textures.

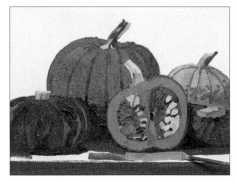

7 Use the same greens to reinforce the dark lines and shadow areas on the green pumpkin on the right, which are too light in relation to the rest of the image. This also helps to create a visual link across the painting. Mix a dull brown from the dark green mixture, cadmium red, yellow ochre and white and paint the table edge, using horizontal brushstrokes to echo the direction of the wood grain. Add yellow ochre and cadmium orange to lighten the mixture, and paint the table top.

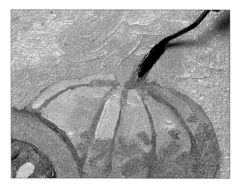

8 Add yellow ochre and titanium white to the pale brown mixture. Using a medium flat brush, paint the background, constantly varying the direction of the brushstrokes and allowing the brushstrokes to remain visible in order to enhance the impasto effect. Using the edge of a trowel-shaped painting knife, press some of the dark brown mixture on to the stalks to create a fibrous, woody texture.

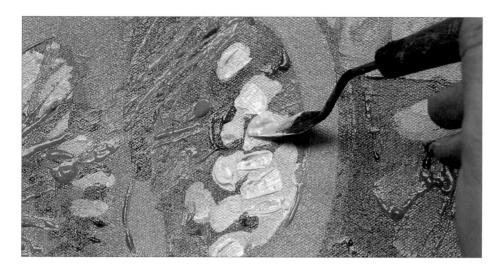

9 Dip the tip of the painting knife into the basic orange mixture and drag it over the fibrous area in the middle of the cut pumpkin to make a series of uneven lines. Add titanium white to the background colour and, using the painting knife, shape the seeds in the cut pumpkin.

The finished painting

Using the paint thickly has allowed the artist to create a range of interesting textures that are perfectly suited to the subject – fine lines for the fibres inside the cut pumpkin, achieved through both brushwork and the use of a painting knife; splotches of thick colour on the bumpy exterior surface of the vegetables.

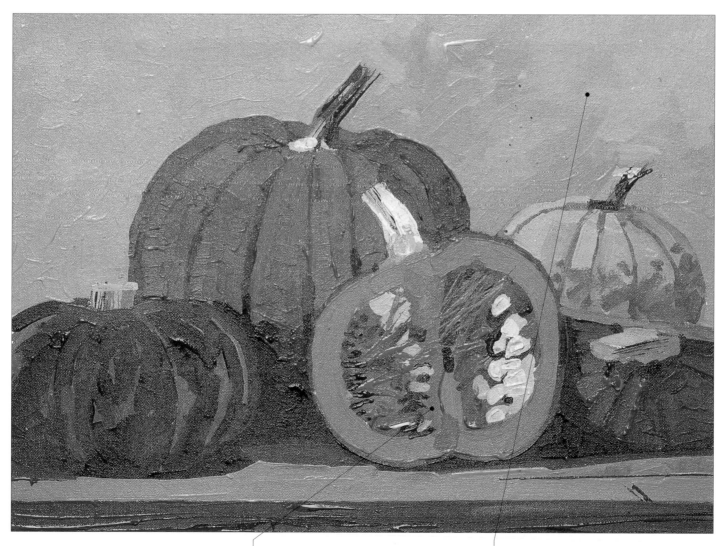

The fibres and seeds are created by dragging and dabbing the edge and the end of the painting knife on to the support.

Allowing the brushstrokes to remain visible creates texture and offers visual relief in an otherwise flat area.

Practice exercise: **Impasto landscape in oils**

With its scrubby vegetation and pebbly path, this Mediterranean cliffside scene provides many opportunities for working impasto. In a landscape such as this, however, it is generally helpful to include some quieter, flatter areas, such as the sea and sky, for the viewer's eye to rest on. This exercise is painted entirely with a painting knife.

Materials
- *Canvas-covered board primed with acrylic gesso*
- *HB pencil*
- *Oil paints: phthalocyanine blue, titanium white, ultramarine blue, alizarin crimson, cadmium lemon, sap green, burnt sienna, raw sienna*
- *Rag*
- *Small painting knife*

The scene

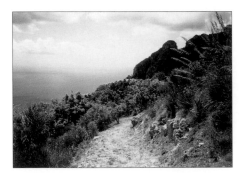

This is a classically composed scene, with the main cliff falling at the intersection of the thirds and the path leading our eye through the picture. The contrasting textures – the relative smoothness of the sea and sky versus the pebbly path and dense vegetation – make a picture that is full of interest.

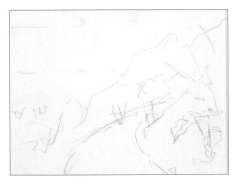

1 Using an HB pencil, lightly sketch the scene so that you have a rough guide to where to place the different elements.

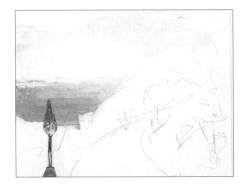

2 Mix a pale blue from phthalocyanine blue and titanium white. Using a rag, smear it across the sky. Add more phthalocyanine blue and, using a small painting knife, put in the sky, smoothing the paint out so that the coverage is fairly even.

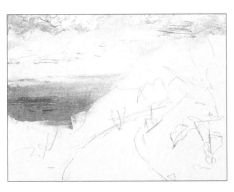

3 There are some deep shadows on the sea; paint these in using ultramarine blue. Still using the painting knife, apply strokes of thick titanium white for the clouds. The rough impasto work helps to give a sense of volume to the clouds.

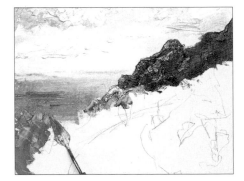

4 Mix a dark purplish blue from alizarin crimson and ultramarine blue and smear it over the rocky, exposed area of cliff on the right, adding some sap green to the mixture as you work down towards the path. To capture the jagged feel of the rocks, pull the paint up with the tip of the knife to form small peaks. Mix a bright green from cadmium lemon, sap green and a little burnt sienna and begin putting in the lightest parts of the foreground vegetation on the left, dabbing in a more yellow version of the mixture in parts.

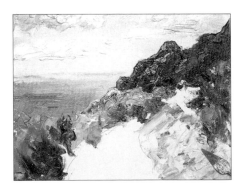

5 Mix a pale brown from raw sienna and white and paint the rough-textured ground to the right of the path.

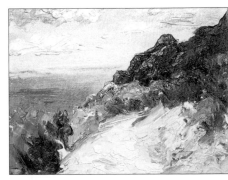

6 Add more raw sienna to the mixture and include some darker browns in the vegetation.

> **Tip**: When painting the vegetation, angle the painting knife so that it follows the direction in which the plants naturally grow.

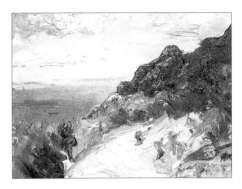

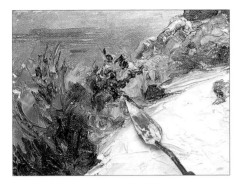

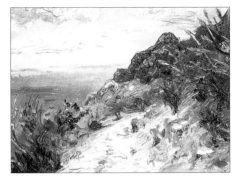

7 Mix a pale purple from ultramarine blue, titanium white and a little alizarin crimson and use this mixture to put in the shaded sides of the foreground rocks that lie to the right of the path. Paint the bright highlights where the sun hits the tops of the rocks in titanium white.

8 Mix a very dark green from ultramarine blue and sap green and put in the very darkest areas of the plants that are growing on the cliff side, dabbing the paint on with the tip of the painting knife. Add some alizarin crimson to the mixture and put in some slightly curved strokes, using the side of the knife, for the taller stems and branches.

9 Continue to build up textures in the vegetation and rocks, using the same colours as before. Vary the way that you apply the paint, sometimes using long thin strokes of the side of the knife and sometimes dabbing the paint on with the tip of the knife. Paint the tall, thin grass strokes on the right-hand side of the painting using a mixture of raw sienna and white.

The finished painting

Impasto work adds great vitality to this image: you can almost reach out and feel the texture of the rocks and plants. The artist has also made full use of the range of marks that can be made with a knife, from smoothing out the sky and sea areas with the flat of the knife to dabbing on small blobs of paint with the tip, and even dragging the side of the knife over the canvas to create long, flowing marks for the thinnest stems and branches.

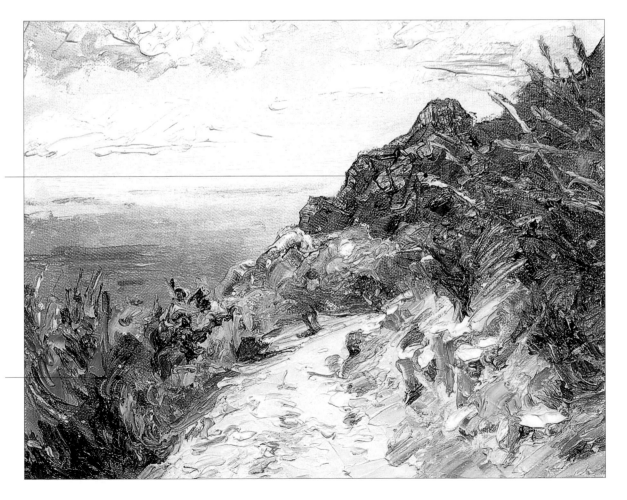

Thick oil and acrylic paint can be pulled up with the tip of the knife to form small peaks, as here.

Note how the knife marks echo the direction in which the plants grow.

Removing paint

There are three main reasons for removing paint from your canvas or support: to get back to the original support, either so that you can reveal the underlying colour or so that you can paint over the area again and correct a mistake; to remove excess paint from an area that is too heavily impastoed or has become clogged with paint; and to work into paint to create textured marks.

Removing paint to get back to the original support

If the underlying colour is very strong, it's best to try and remove it so that it doesn't affect any subsequent glazes. The method that you select depends on the medium you are using and on whether the paint is wet or dry.

To remove wet acrylic paint ▼
Dip a rag in water and wipe it through the paint.

To remove dried gouache paint ▼
You can remove gouache paint that has dried by brushing clean water over the paint to soften it. You can then lift off the colour with your brush or a rag and paint over the affected area again. Note that this technique cannot be used with acrylic paint as once it has dried, the paint is no longer water soluble.

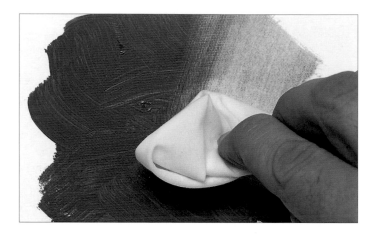

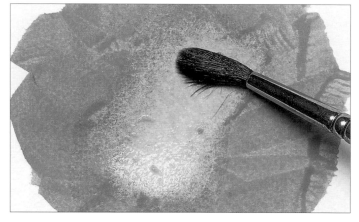

Removing excess paint

When you're doing very heavy impasto work in oils or acrylics, the canvas can become clogged with paint. If the effect is as you desire, then allow the paint to dry before applying more paint. If the effect is not what you intended, scrape off the paint and start again. Thick oil paint remains wet for weeks, so it can be scraped off the support at leisure. Thick acrylic dries in hours, so it needs to be scraped off immediately. To remove excess paint, use one of the following methods.

Scraping off paint with a knife ▼
Hold the edge of the knife perpendicular to the support, press down firmly, and drag the knife through the wet paint to remove any surplus. This leaves a flat area of colour, in which no brush marks can be seen.

Tonking
An alternative method is a technique known as tonking – named after the British artist Henry Tonks (1862–1937).

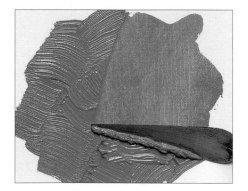

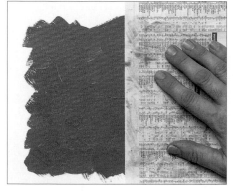

1 Place a sheet of newspaper over the affected area and smooth it down with your hands.

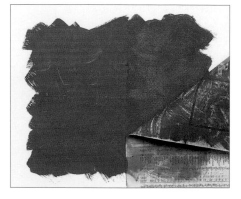

2 Peel away the paper, removing any excess paint in the process. The result is more textured than using a knife.

Working into paint to create texture

Thick paint has a pleasing texture that comes from the marks left by the bristles of the brush. This, combined with the texture of the support, is often all that is needed. However, greater verisimilitude can often be achieved when replicating the textures present on whatever is being painted by working into the paint.

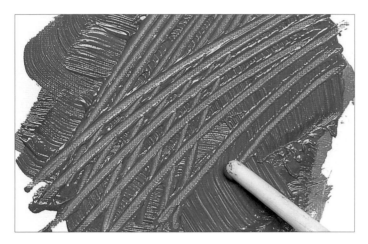

Sgrafitto – wet paint ▲
You can make textured marks in paint by scraping into the paint with the end of a brush. Alternatively, use a twig, the tip of a craft knife or the edge of a piece of cardboard.

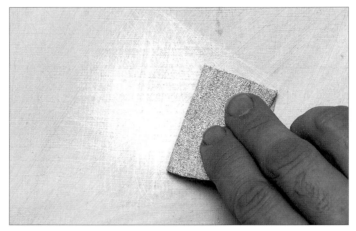

Sandpaper – dried acrylic or gouache paint ▲
To create texture on dried acrylic and gouache paint, lightly rub sandpaper or another abrasive material over the area. Do not rub so hard that you damage the support.

Practice exercise: **Watermelons**

Two methods of lifting off paint are used in this exercise – tonking and scraping off paint with a knife. Tonking creates some texture, whereas scraping off paint leaves a much flatter, smoother surface.

Acrylic paints are used here, although the subject and techniques that the artist employed would work equally well in oils. As acrylics dry quickly, it is a good idea to add a little retarding medium to your mixes as this gives you longer to work into the paint. Even so, it is best to work on relatively small areas – one melon at a time – finishing one off before the next.

Materials
* Board primed with acrylic gesso
* B pencil
* Acrylic paints: cadmium yellow, titanium white, phthalocyanine green, olive green, alizarin crimson, cadmium red
* Retarding medium
* Small painting knife
* Newspaper
* Brushes: flat wash, medium flat, small flat

The scene
The artist came across these watermelons on a market stall. Red and green are complementary colours and almost always work well together. The jagged lines of the cut melons counterbalance the rounded forms of the whole fruits.

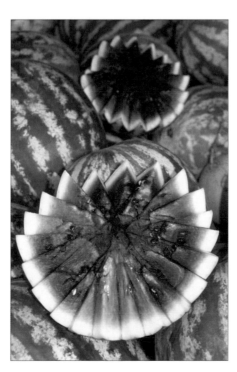

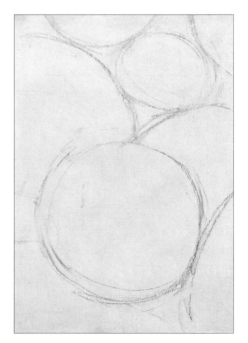

1 Mix a pale yellow from cadmium yellow and titanium white and, using a flat wash brush, cover the board. Leave to dry. Using a B pencil, draw the outlines of the fruits. At this stage, you don't need to put in the jagged outlines of the cut melons: an indication of the overall shape, which you can use as a guideline, is sufficient.

▶

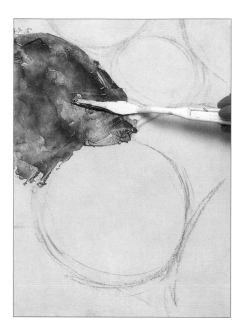

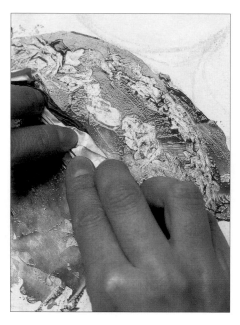

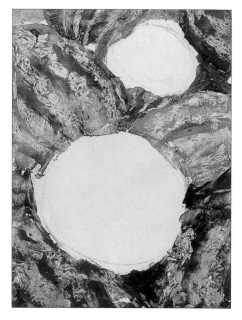

2 Mix a dark green from phthalo-cyanine green and olive green, adding a little retarding medium to the mixture to give yourself longer to work. Using a small painting knife, cover the first uncut watermelon with the mixture. The coverage does not have to be completely even, but try not to go outside the pencil lines.

3 Tear off a piece of newspaper and scrunch it up into a long, thin strip. Press it firmly into the paint and lift it off to reveal the toned ground underneath. Note the lovely random textures and markings that this creates: it would be much more difficult to achieve this effect by painting on the lighter colour with a brush.

4 Repeat Steps 2 and 3 until you have painted all the uncut watermelons, varying the dark greens by adding more cadmium yellow for some fruits and more olive green for others. Using a medium flat brush, fill in the spaces between the melons with a very dark green. The image immediately takes on more of a sense of depth.

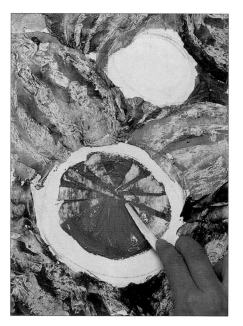

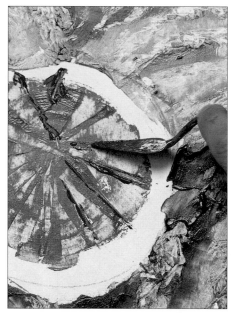

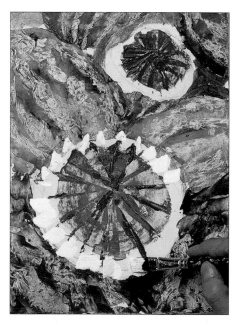

5 Mix a pinkish red from alizarin crimson, cadmium red and titanium white. Paint the red flesh of the cut melons, leaving a broad band of yellow around the edge. Place the knife tip in the centre of the melon, with the knife on its side, and scrape it clockwise, lifting off wedge-shaped areas of paint.

6 Darken the pink mixture from the previous step by adding more alizarin crimson. Dip the side of the knife into the paint and press it on to the melons to create the jagged cuts in the surface. This helps to create shading and makes the surface of the melons look three-dimensional.

7 Mix an opaque yellow from cadmium yellow and titanium white. Using a medium flat brush, paint the zigzag-shaped cut edges of the melons.

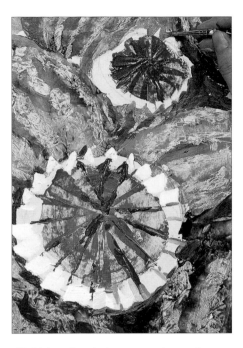

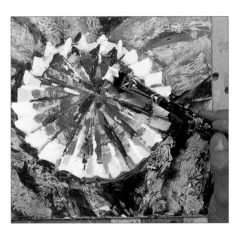

9 Mix pale pink from alizarin crimson and titanium white and touch in the pale pinks in the melon flesh, taking the colour to the melon rim in places. Mix a pale off-white from titanium white and a little cadmium yellow and put in some thin highlight lines on the melon flesh.

The finished painting
This is a lively and energetic painting that uses the technique of lifting off paint to great effect to create interesting textures.

8 Using the dark green mixture from Step 2 and a small flat brush, cut in around the edges of the melons to sharpen the shapes.

Tip: The dark green makes the watermelons stand out more.

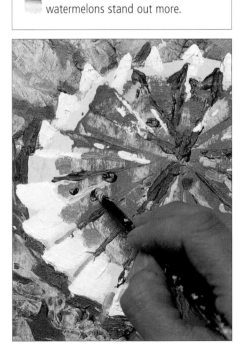

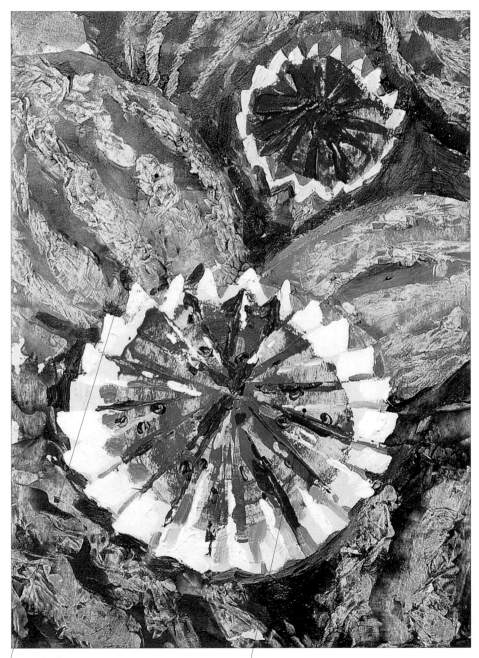

10 Mix together the dark green from Step 2 and the dark red from Step 6 to create a colour that is almost black. Paint the pips, using a small brush, and then scrape off the highlights on the pips using the end of your brush handle.

Colour has been lifted off to reveal the toned ground beneath, creating the pale stripes on the outside of the watermelons.

Scraping paint off with the side of a painting knife creates flatter, less textured areas of colour.

Drybrush

The technique of drybrush work means precisely what it says: the brush is loaded with the minimum amount of paint and then skimmed gently over a dry surface so that it catches on the "peaks" or raised tooth of the paper or canvas, leaving part of the support showing.

It is important to splay out the bristles of the brush (or to use a fan brush) so that the individual bristle marks are evident on the support. Make sure your paint mix is not too wet: keep a rag or a piece of absorbent kitchen paper handy to blot off any excess paint, so that your brush is only very lightly loaded.

Drybrush work is a great way of conveying the texture of things like wood or weathered stone, which have a linear quality within them.

Using a fan brush ▶
A fan brush is ideal for drybrush work as the bristles are naturally splayed out.

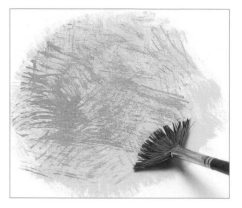

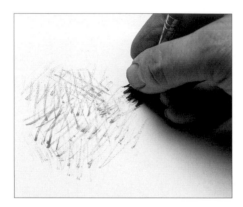

Splaying out bristles ▲
If you do not have a fan brush, you can splay out the bristles of an ordinary brush between your finger and thumb in order to create the same kind of drybrush marks.

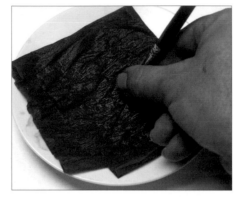

Loading the brush with paint ▲
If you simply dip your brush into your palette, there is a risk that you will overload it. To avoid this, splay out the bristles and gently pull them over a paper towel soaked in paint.

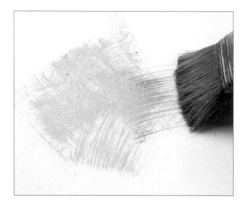

Drybrush work over a large area ▲
To cover a large area, dip the tip of a large bristle or household decorating brush in paint and gently drag it over the support, holding the brush at 90 degrees to the support.

Practice exercise: **Seashells**

The delicate, linear markings and ridges on seashells such as these make them the perfect candidates for the drybrush technique. Because the shells are very light in tone, the artist decided to start from a mid-toned ground. She used button polish, which serves both to tone and to prime the ground, although you could equally well use acrylic gesso mixed with burnt umber paint.

Materials
- *Cardboard primed with button polish*
- *HB pencil*
- *Acrylic paints: titanium white, ultramarine blue, raw sienna, cadmium red, cadmium yellow*
- *Brushes: small flat, fine round*
- *Absorbent kitchen paper*

The set-up
This simple still life consists of two large shells on a white background, simply lit from one side. One of the shells is placed upside down, enabling us to look inside it. Always look at your still-life subjects from different angles to find out what makes the most interesting composition.

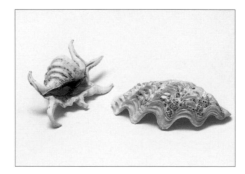

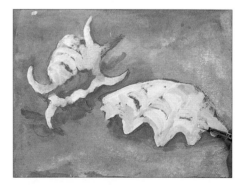

1 Sketch the shells with an HB pencil. Paint the background in a dilute wash of white and ultramarine. Paint the shadows in a purplish grey mixed from ultramarine and raw sienna. Mix a warm-toned mix of white and raw sienna and a cool-toned mix of white and ultramarine. Alternating between them, begin painting the shells.

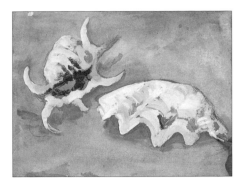

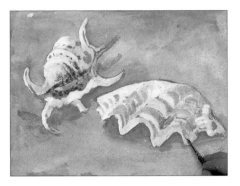

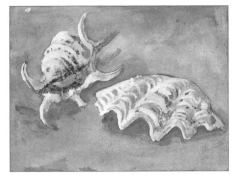

2 Mix a purplish colour from cadmium red and ultramarine blue. Load the paintbrush, dab off any excess paint on a piece of kitchen paper, and paint the dark colour on the inside of the left-hand shell. Add white to the mixture to make it more opaque and put in the dark markings on the other shell. Using a fine round brush and the warm-toned mixture from Step 1, drybrush the grooves on the shell.

3 Mix a dark purple from cadmium red and ultramarine blue and drybrush on the markings on the interior of the left-hand shell. Add a tiny amount of raw sienna to the cool-toned mixture from Step 1 and put in the slightly shaded areas of the right-hand shell, making sure your brushstrokes follow the direction of the grooves on the shells to reinforce the three-dimensional impression.

4 Mix a very pale yellow from cadmium yellow and titanium white and paint the tops of the ridges on the right-hand shell. Continue putting in the dark patterning on the shells, using the drybrush technique all the time to create texture and imitate the rough, irregular markings on the shells.

The finished painting

These shells have a jagged and irregular surface. Drybrush work is the perfect way to paint the small, spiny ridges. As the brushes are skimmed only lightly over the surface of the support, the technique also allows underlying colours to show through, conveying the mottled, irregular coloration of the shells very effectively. The key with any isubject like this is not to overwork it and lose the spontaneity of the image.

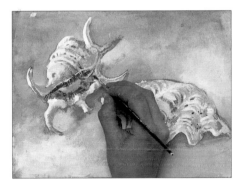

5 Mix a mid-toned grey from titanium white, cadmium yellow and raw sienna. Scumble the mixture over the background, carefully brushing around the shadows. Using the purple mixture from Step 3, reinforce the lines in the left-hand shell.

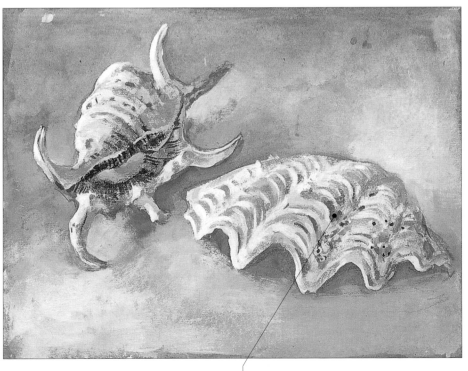

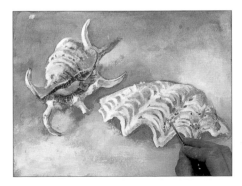

6 Reinforce the dark patterning on the shells where necessary, using the same colours as before.

Drybrush work captures these small ridges to perfection.

Gouache techniques

The techniques that are used when painting in gouache are very similar to those used when working in watercolour, and these two pages give a brief summary of the most common methods. Like watercolour, gouache is water soluble – but unlike watercolour (which is transparent), gouache is opaque. This means that, because of its opacity, light pale colours can be painted over dark colours, just as one would when using certain oil or acrylic techniques. However, gouache paint can also be heavily diluted with water and used in semi-transparent washes, as one would use watercolour paint. It is common practice to combine the two approaches in the same work.

Wet on dry

Paint applied to a dry surface creates marks that retain their edge and shape, and the paint tends to stay where it is put. However, the underlying support or paint layer must be completely dry before you apply a second layer, or else the effect will be lost. As gouache can easily be made re-soluble when it is re-wet, wet colour needs to be applied over a dry colour using quick, sure brushstrokes in order not to pick up any of the underlying colour.

Wet paint applied to dry paper ▼
Below, the first (red) wash was allowed to dry completely before strokes of yellow paint were applied on top. The yellow has not spread at all, but retained its original edges. As gouache is opaque, of course, it is possible to apply a light colour on top of a dark one without the underlying colour showing through – unlike watercolour.

Wet into wet

Paint applied to a surface that is already wet with paint or water will bleed and spread, creating a soft, seductive blend of colour. The technique takes practice to control, as the results can, to a certain extent, be unpredictable. The extent and speed of the paint spread depends on the wetness of the surface. On a damp surface, paint will spread slowly, within a contained area. On a visibly wet surface, paint will spread rapidly and not always in a predicted direction. However, you can control the direction in which the paint spreads by tilting the support.

Masking

Masking is done to prevent paint from getting on to unwanted areas or to create an edge that would be impossible using any other method. Masking fluid can be used with thin washes, although heavy, thick paint can prevent the dry fluid from being removed. Masking tape and film (frisket paper) can be used to create straight edges or cut to create curved edges. Torn paper can be used in the same way as tape, while torn fabric with frayed edges can create wonderful effects.

Different types of mask ▼
Masking fluid and thin strips of torn and untorn masking tape were applied to the unpainted paper before a wash of orange paint was brushed over the whole area. When the paint was dry the masks were removed, revealing the unpainted paper underneath.

Wet paint applied to damp paper ▼
Applied over a slightly damp first layer, the red paint has spread a little.

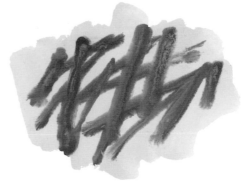

Resist techniques

Wax candle or wax crayon can be used to draw on to the dry support or dry paint work. When the area is painted over, the wax will repel the watery paint, which will only settle in areas where there is no wax. If the paint is too thick it will settle on the wax and the effect will be lost. The exact result depends on how much pressure you apply and on the type of surface on which you are working: the wax will leave more broken marks on a rough surface than on a smooth one. Resists are a useful technique for painting waves or turbulent water, trackways and ploughed fields.

Candle wax ▼
Here, a candle was rubbed over parts of the unpainted paper before a wash of green paint was applied. The wax repels the water in the paint, leaving a textured effect.

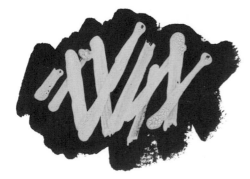

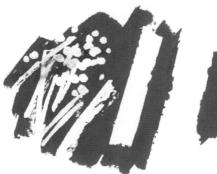

Spattering

Gouache paint can be spattered on to a dry or a wet surface: blobs of paint spattered on to a dry surface will retain their shape, while blobs spattered on to a wet surface will soften and spread. Very wet paint tends to make larger blobs, as more paint is picked up by the brush and leaves it easily when the brush is tapped. Thick paint clings to the brush and is reluctant to leave it when tapped, resulting in a fine spatter. The distance that you hold the brush from the support also has an effect on the spatter density and size. It is hard to control exactly where spatters will go, and you may need to mask certain areas of your painting to prevent blobs of paint accidentally falling on them. Spattering is a useful technique for painting pebbles or gravel paths.

Spatter texture ▼
Paint can be spattered by tapping your finger against the handle of a brush loaded with paint or by pulling back the bristles of the brush with your fingertips to release a fine spray. Many artists keep old toothbrushes to use for spattering.

Sgrafitto

The technique of scratching into paint is known as sgrafitto. It is used to create texture and highlights. You can scratch or scrape into dry paint to reveal previously applied paint or the surface of the support. Any sharp implement can be used, as can abrasives such as sandpaper. Once made, the scratch marks can be left as they are or worked over using more paint. Sgrafitto can also be used to remove areas of paint to correct mistakes, although the technique is less successful if so-called staining colours have been used, as they tend to soak into the support and stain the paper fibres to a greater depth than non-staining colours. Sgrafitto techniques are best used on heavy or thick supports as there is less risk of cutting through the paper.

Sandpaper and craft (utility) knife ▼
On the left, fine sandpaper was rubbed over a wash of dry paint – a useful technique for creating texture on rock faces or areas of grassland. On the right, paint was scratched off using the tip of a knife – good for highlights such as sun touching water.

Sponging

Both natural and man-made sponges can be dipped into paint and used to create textural effects and apply washes of colour. Natural sponges tend to have a more random texture than man-made sponges and leave a more pleasing mark. Various shapes and sizes are available, and sponges can be cut or pulled apart for work on small areas. Thin mixes of gouache tend to soak into the sponge, so you will need to mix up a large quantity of paint. Thick paint, however, tends to be picked up only on the sponge surface. Complex textural marks can be made by building up a sequence of sponge marks in layers, allowing each one to dry before you apply the next. You can also dip sponges in water and wipe them over the paper surface to remove paint.

Natural sponge ▼
Here you can see the effect of pressing a sponge loaded with paint several times over the same area: the paint is quite dense, but the pattern is sufficiently broken to create a textured effect that is useful for painting things like distant areas of foliage.

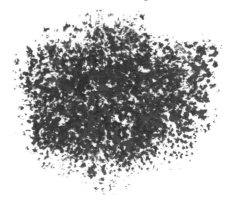

Drybrush

Any type of brush can be used to apply drybrush marks, but fan brushes intended for blending oil or acrylic paint are particularly effective. If you do not have a fan brush, you can create the same effect by loading a brush with paint and then splaying out the bristles with your fingers before applying the brush to the support. The technique can be slow, but if it is applied with care and patience it is possible to build a beautiful textured surface. Paint needs to be used sparingly or the effect will be lost. Drybrush is a useful technique for painting the flow and fall of fabric, birds' feathers and animal fur.

Drybrush marks with splayed-out brush ▶
This technique creates the effect of regularly spaced lines, with areas of the support showing through the paint.

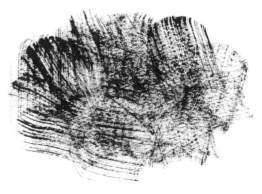

Practice exercise: **Combining gouache techniques**

This simple still life gives you the chance to practise different gouache techniques within the same painting: overlaying colours; wet into wet and wet on dry; various ways of creating textures, including spattering and sponging; and exploiting the natural chalky consistency and opacity of gouache paint.

The artist chose watercolour board as the support for this painting, as it has a smooth surface that is ideal for capturing fine detail.

Crabs and other shellfish, such as lobsters, langoustines and mussels, make fascinating subjects for still lifes as their shells contain many variations in colour, providing you with the ideal opportunity to practise assessing different tones.

In this project the darkest colours are put down first – unlike pure transparent watercolour, where you have to work from light to dark. Establishing the dark colours first gives you a strong guide to follow for placing the individual elements of the scene. It also keeps the colours looking fresh and lively: light gouache colours contain proportionally higher amounts of chalk, which means that any colours that are put down on top of them may pick up some of the chalk and lose their clarity. Dark gouache colours, on the other hand, contain very little chalk, so any light colours that are put down on top of them will not pick up the chalk. Nonetheless, the chalk content of the paint also makes it ideal for this particular subject as it allows you to recreate the slightly matt surface of the crab shell.

Materials
- *Watercolour board*
- *HB pencil*
- *Gouache paints: cadmium red deep, lamp black, raw sienna, phthalocyanine blue, cadmium red medium, cadmium yellow lemon, yellow ochre, cadmium yellow light, zinc white*
- *Brushes: fine round, medium round*
- *Cardboard*
- *Pencil: red*

The set-up
In terms of both its size and its colour the crab dominates the composition. The red-and-white tablecloth and napkin echo the coloration of both the crab shell and the plate on which it is set; they also offer a contrast of texture. The lemons, with their slightly pitted outer skin, provide an interesting contrast of texture and colour.

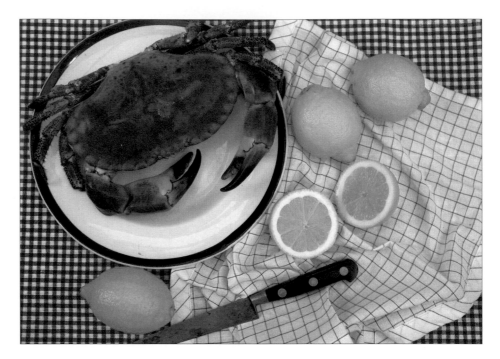

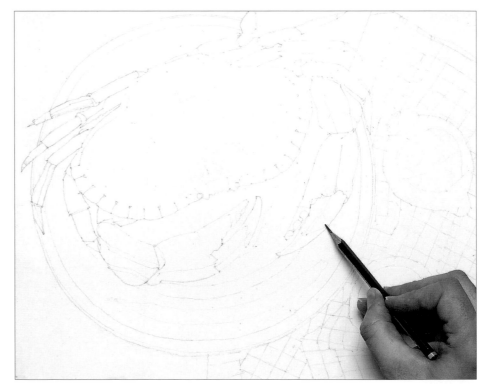

1 Using an HB pencil, make an underdrawing of your still-life set-up. It is easy to lose track of where you are in a painting like this, so make sure you put down all the information you are likely to need. The segments of the crab claws, the indentations on the shell, and the lines of the draped napkin are all useful guidelines.

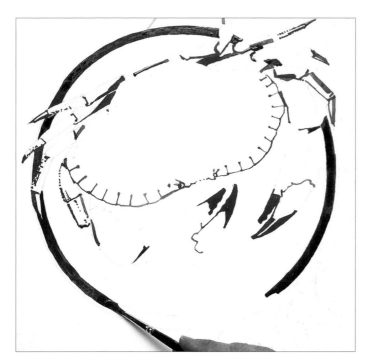

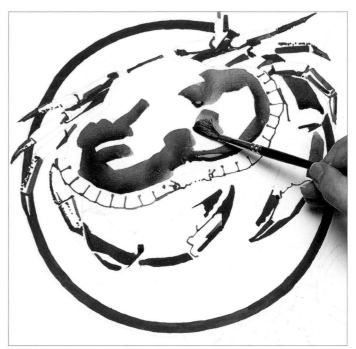

2 Mix a dark reddish brown from cadmium red deep, lamp black and raw sienna. Using a fine round brush, paint the darkest red of the crab shell and claws. Add a little more lamp black and some phthalocyanine blue to the mixture and paint the very dark tips of the claws. Mix lamp black and phthalocyanine blue together and paint the border of the plate. Leave to dry.

3 Mix a dark, brownish red from raw sienna and cadmium red medium. Using a fine round brush put in the next darkest parts of the crab claws, taking care to follow the hard-edged, angular shape of the segments. Switch to a medium round brush and begin to apply the same colour to the body of the crab, using the side of the brush to scrub on the colour.

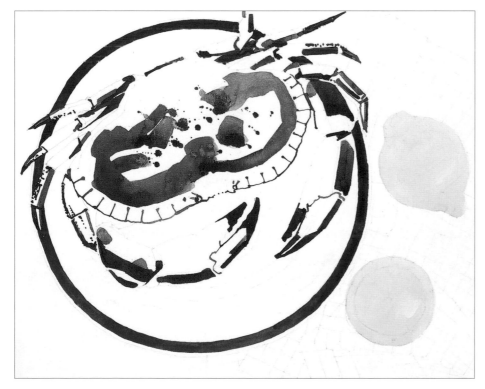

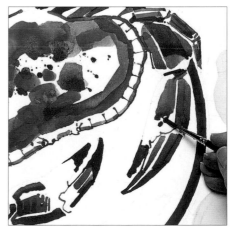

5 Add more cadmium red deep and a little yellow ochre to the brownish red mixture from step 3 and paint more of the crab shell and claws. This is a slightly lighter and redder tone than the ones used to date; with the transition from dark tones to mid-tones, the three-dimensional form of the crab is becoming more evident.

4 Spatter some of the brownish red mixture from Step 3 over the body of the crab and leave to dry. While you are waiting for the brown paint to dry, brush cadmium yellow lemon over the lemons in order to establish the base colour. Leave to dry.

▶

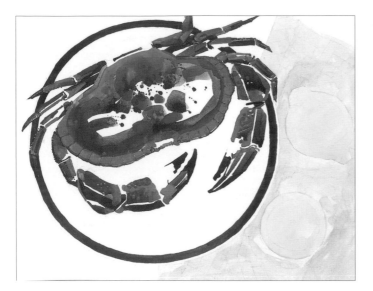

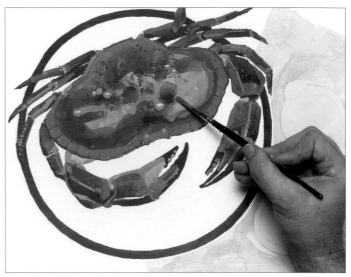

6 Add cadmium yellow light to the mixture to make it more orange and paint the lighter tones around the end of the shell and claws. Now start to put in some colour on the red-and-white napkin on the right. Although it looks predominantly white, the white is not as bright and pure as the brightest areas on the plate, so mix a pale, yellow-tinged grey from yellow ochre, zinc white and a little lamp black. Using a medium round brush, brush the mixture over the napkin to establish the underlying colour. Leave to dry.

7 Add some cadmium red deep to the orange mixture from the previous step and lightly dot it over the crab's shell. Leave to dry.

> **Tip**: Study the crab shell carefully before you apply the paint. The indented areas are slightly darker in tone, and this helps you to convey the gently undulating nature of the hard shell.

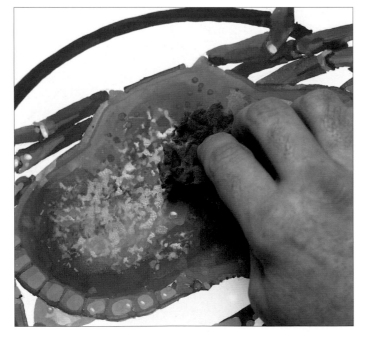

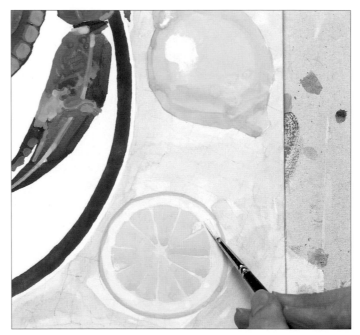

8 Mix a very pale yellow from yellow ochre and white and, using a fine brush, paint the bright highlights on the shell – around the scalloped edge, for example. Mix a pale and dilute reddish orange from cadmium red medium and cadmium yellow light. Dip a clean sponge into the mixture and dab it over the shell to build up tone and texture. Leave to dry. You may want to repeat the sponging to build up more texture, but do not make any decision on this until you've seen how the first application looks.

9 Mix a warm yellow from cadmium yellow lemon and a tiny amount of cadmium red medium and paint the lemon in mid-tones, leaving some of the underlying colour as the highlight, the outer rim of the cut lemon, and the segments of the cut lemon, with spaces between the segments. Paint the pith of the cut lemon in a mixture of cadmium yellow lemon and zinc white. Mix a greener yellow from cadmium yellow lemon with a little phthalocyanine blue and paint the shaded underside of the whole lemon.

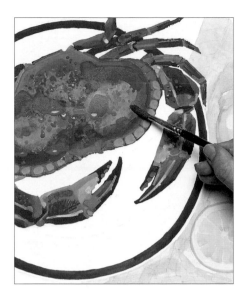

10 Continue building up texture on the shell, using the same mixtures as before. To create more tonal variation, dip a brush in clean water and scrub over any areas that you judge to be too dark, in order to soften the paint; you can then either lift off some of the paint, rinsing your brush periodically as you do so, or re-blend it.

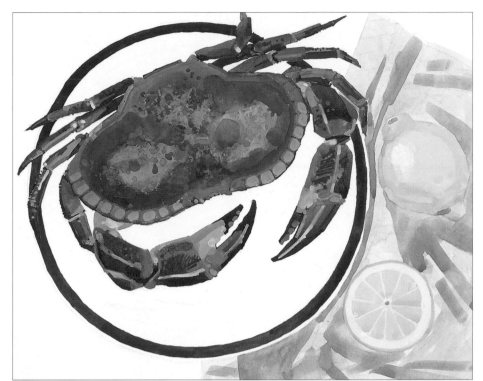

11 Using the same grey as before, block in the shadow areas on the napkin. Leave to dry. The cloth is now starting to look three-dimensional, as the folds in the cloth gradually take shape.

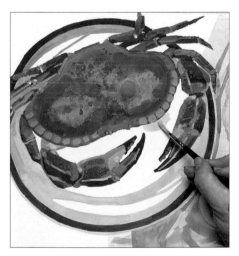

12 Mix a cool grey from phthalocyanine blue, lamp black and white and, using a medium round brush, paint the shadows cast on the white plate by the crab's body. Use the same colour to paint the shadow cast by the plate itself.

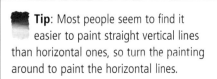

Tip: Most people seem to find it easier to paint straight vertical lines than horizontal ones, so turn the painting around to paint the horizontal lines.

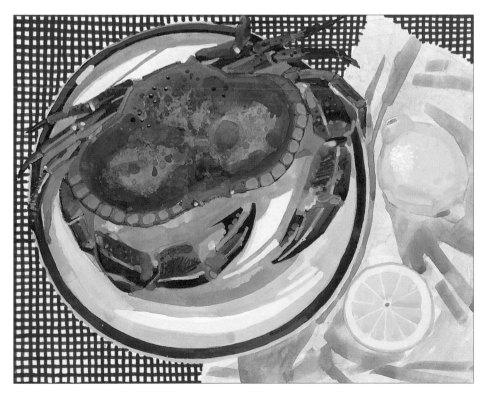

13 Add lots of zinc white to the shadow mixture to make a very pale grey and paint the remainder of the white plate, leaving a few of the very brightest highlight areas untouched. Using a fine brush, paint the vertical red lines of the red-and-white cloth on which the plate sits; you may find it easiest to rest your painting hand on your other hand or on a straightedge to steady it. Leave to dry, then paint the horizontal lines.

▶

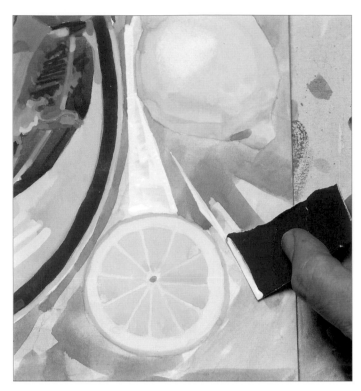

14 Dip the edge of a piece of cardboard in white paint and press it on to the support to create the highlights on the napkin, scraping and dragging it over the surface like a flat brush and "painting" around the shadows. This allows you to create sharp edges that would be harder to achieve with a brush.

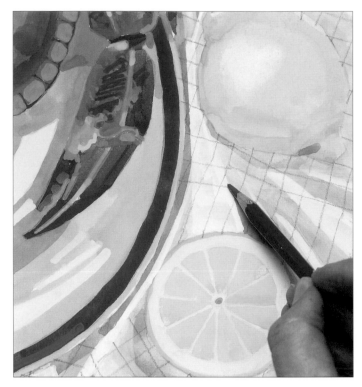

15 Draw thin red lines on the napkin with a red pencil, noting how the lines change direction with the folds in the cloth. The pencil marks are softer and thinner than you could achieve with a brush, which ensures that this area does not compete for attention with either the crab or the red-and-white cloth on the left of the image.

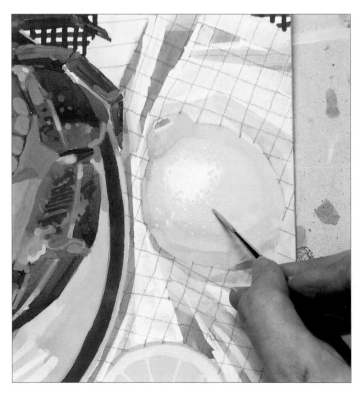

16 Using a fine round brush, stipple cadmium yellow light over the surface of the whole lemon to create the pitted texture of the skin.

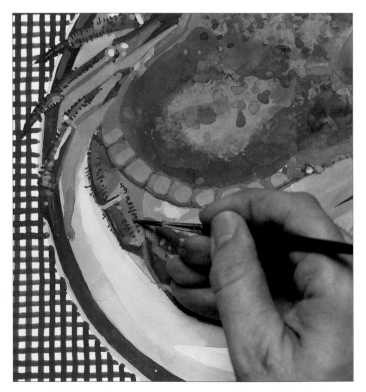

17 Mix a dark reddish brown from cadmium red, phthalocyanine blue and raw sienna and stipple it on to the crab claws for extra texture.

The finished painting

This is a richly textured still life that demonstrates the versatility of gouache. Although the composition is simple, it has been handled with skill. The colours are well balanced, with the red of the cloths echoing the tones in the crab shell and the white of the plate and cloths and the bright yellow of the lemons offsetting the deeper tones used elsewhere.

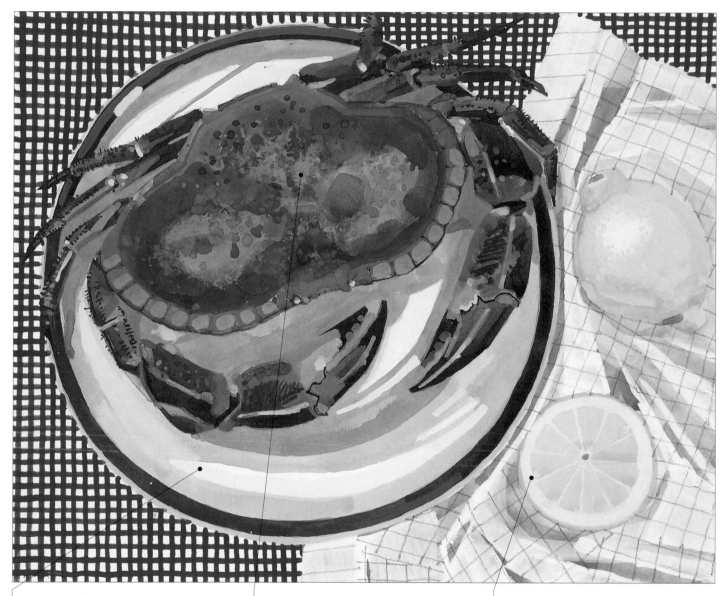

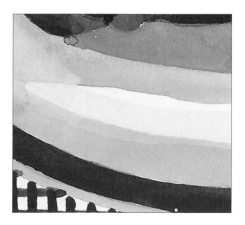

The brightest highlight areas on the plate are left unpainted.

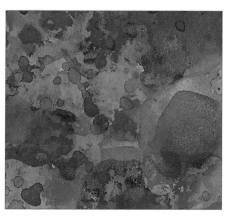

Spattering, sponging and wet-into-wet applications of paint combine to create a range of lively textures on the crab shell.

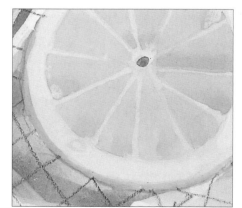

The chalky, opaque nature of gouache paint is ideally suited to painting the pith of the lemon.

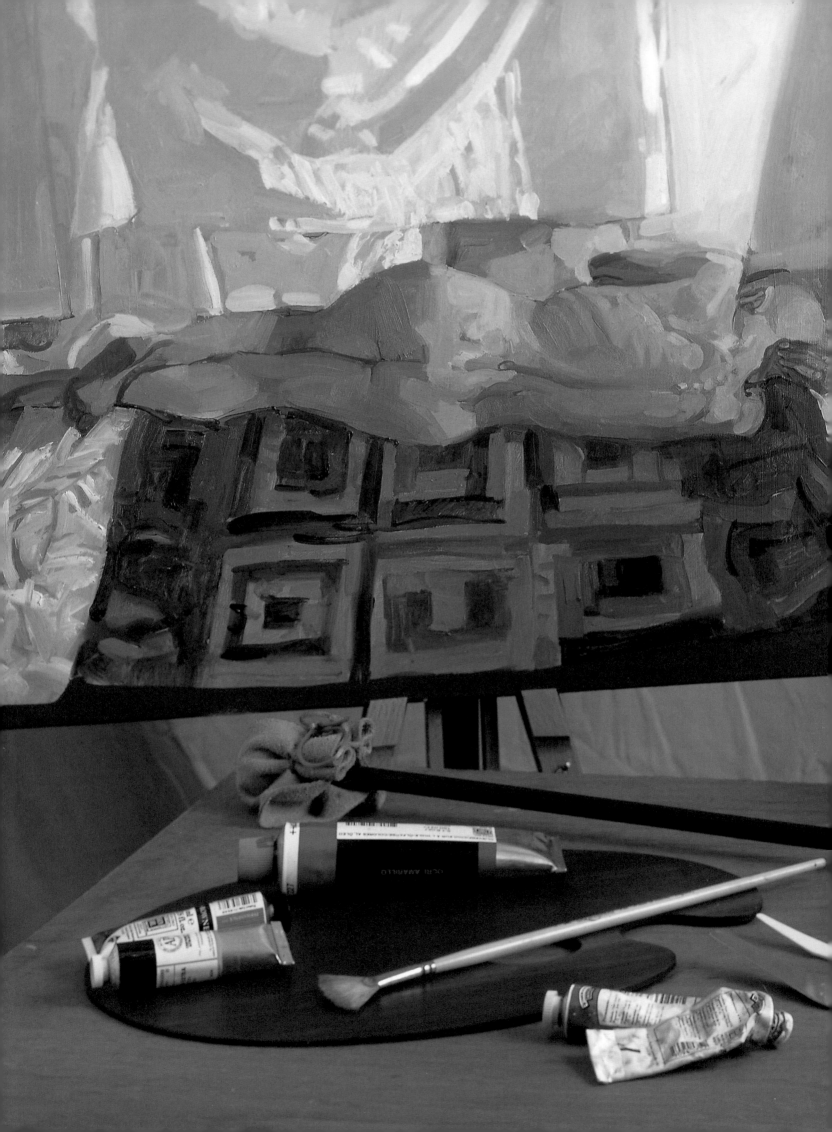

Painting projects

Painting flowers and leaves

From tiny meadow flowers growing in the wild to hot-house exotics such as orchids, flowers and leaves are an infinitely appealing subject to paint. The approaches to painting them are equally varied. If it's the subtle coloration of the blooms and foliage that appeals to you, or a particular species of flower, you might choose to concentrate on a single leaf or flower – or even to close in on one or two petals so that your work becomes semi-abstract. Bouquets of cut flowers allow you to explore a number of different blooms in the same arrangement. Alternatively, you might want to paint a floral landscape – a field full of poppies or lavender, perhaps.

Whatever approach you take and whatever medium you are working in, start with the overall shape. Make studies in your sketchbook, looking at how the petals and leaves overlap, where the flower head sits in relation to the stalk, the size and shape of the leaves and so

on. The better you understand the structure, the better your painting will be.

Colour is undoubtedly one of the main reasons for painting flowers; the rich golds and russets of autumn leaves are stunning. If you are painting in oils or acrylics, thin glazes are a good way of conveying the delicacy of petals and leaves; the colours mix optically on the support, creating subtle blends that would be difficult, to achieve in the palette. The equivalent technique in gouache is to work thinly in semi-transparent washes, allowing each wash to modify the wash beneath.

Working wet into wet in any medium will enable you to convey subtle shifts of tone. In gouache and thin acrylics, you can allow the colours to flow and merge on the support of their own accord; although the technique is somewhat unpredictable, with practice you will have more control. In thicker acrylics and in oils, working wet into wet allows the artist to blend the

paint on the support, feathering brush-strokes to create subtle transitions in tone.

Textures are important too. Exploit the full range of textural techniques at your disposal – drybrush work for linear details on petals or leaves, scumbling one colour over another, dabbing paint on thickly with a painting knife to convey a mass of small flowers.

If you're painting several flowers together, choose a viewpoint that allows you to see some of them from the side, rather than straight on. This makes it easier to see the structure of the bloom and make it look three-dimensional; it also makes for a more interesting painting.

Alchemilla and roses ▼
This lovely oil study effectively contrasts both colour and shape, the delicate and "frothy" stems of bright, yellowy green alchemilla providing a lovely foil to the more rounded forms of the roses.

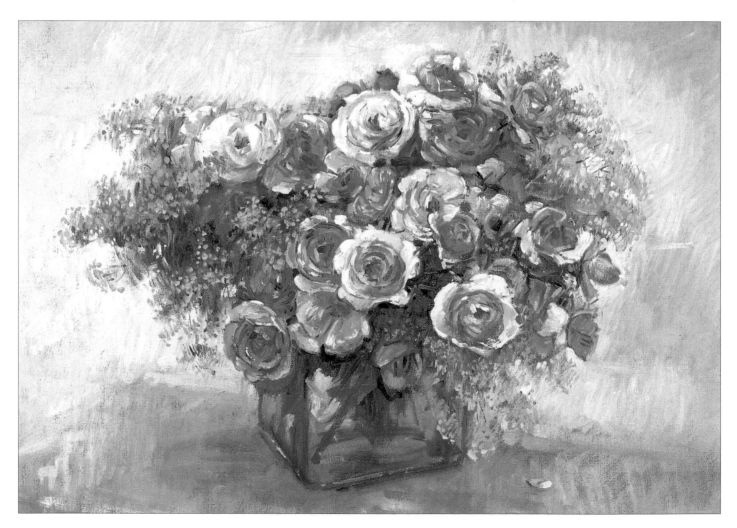

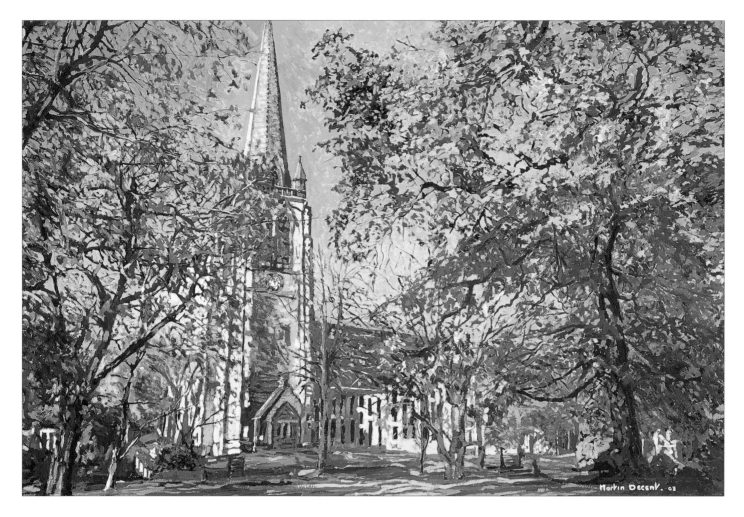

Autumn day ▲
Here, the foliage makes a natural-looking frame for the church, the warm-coloured leaves enhancing the pale colour of the stonework.

Lovage, clematis and shadows ▶
In this scene, it the shadows cast by the stems, rather than the flowers that caught the artist's eye. They bring the painting to life

> **Tip**: Match the technique to the flower: use delicate wash or glazing techniques for delicate flowers and more robust textural techniques for more substantial blooms.
> • Subtle coloration, where one colour blends imperceptibly into another, is best painted using wet-into-wet techniques.
> • Flowers and leaves have a strong underlying structure, which should always be shown. These structural differences are what separates one species from another.

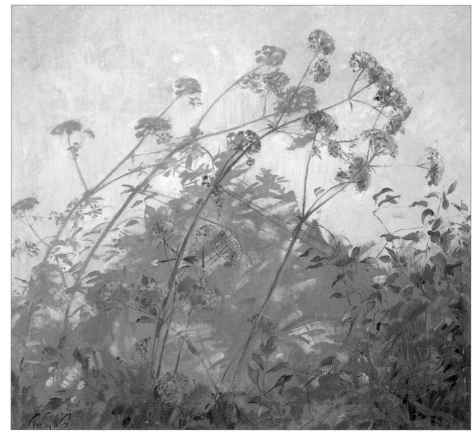

Irises

You don't have to venture outside to create convincing nature studies: in this project, a vase of irises is painted to look like flowers growing in the wild. They have been given a background of subtle washes and brushstrokes of yellowy green that give the impression of a luxuriant flower meadow. The artist has also selected a low viewpoint, so that we feel as if we are lying down in the grass and looking through the stems. You could try the same approach with other relatively tall wild flowers, such as poppies.

This project also gives you the chance to explore an interesting means of creating subtle paint textures by pressing plastic food wrap into wet paint: who would have thought that something so mundane could be put to such creative use? The paint seeps into the crinkles in the food wrap; when it is completely dry the food wrap is removed, leaving behind linear marks that perfectly convey the delicate veining and papery texture of the flower petals.

You need to work quickly, while the paint is still wet, so tear off appropriately sized pieces of food wrap in advance. Stretch them out between your fingers and place them on the wet paint following the direction in which you want the lines to run. Tap them down gently with your fingertips – but do not rub, or you will smudge the paint. Above all, wait until you are sure that the paint is completely dry before you attempt to remove the food wrap. The technique is a little unpredictable, but that is part of its charm and the results more than repay the effort.

Materials
- *140lb (300gsm) rough watercolour paper*
- *Pencils: 2B or water-soluble*
- *Acrylic paints: ultramarine blue, light blue violet, dioxazine violet, Hooker's green, medium yellow, Hooker's green deep, yellow ochre, titanium white*
- *Brushes: medium round; fine-tipped round or rigger*
- *Plastic food wrap*
- *Masking fluid*
- *Ruling drawing pen*

The set-up
Place your flowers in a vase and experiment until you find an arrangement you are happy with. You will probably need to remove or add stems to get the effect you want, but remember to look at the spaces between the stems, as well as at the flowers, as the placement of the stems is an important part of the composition. You may also need to adjust the height of the vase in order to get the right viewpoint: the flower heads should be slightly above your eye level.

Nowadays, you can buy good-quality very convincing-looking artificial flowers. Although they do not have the same texture and subtlety of colour as real flowers, they can show you the botanical structure very clearly. If you are interested in painting flowers, it is also worth building up your own personal collection of gardening books and cuttings from magazines and seed catalogues to use as reference material for your paintings.

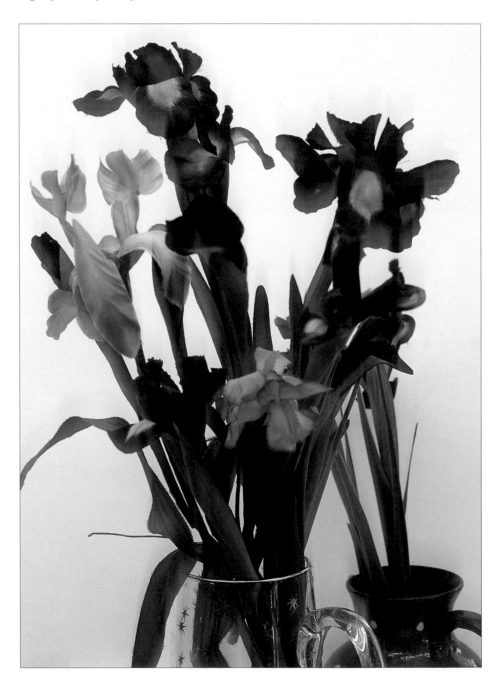

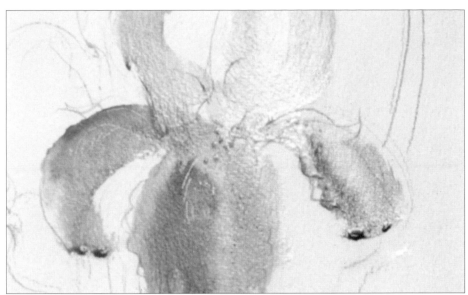

1 Lightly sketch the flowers in pencil. Here, the artist used a blue water-soluble pencil to delineate the flowers; the linear marks will disappear when paint is applied. However, an ordinary graphite pencil would work just as well.

2 Using a ruling drawing pen, stipple masking fluid into the flower centres and mask the edges of the leaves where they catch the light. Allow the masking fluid to dry completely. Working on one flower at a time, brush clean water over the petals. Drop a watery mixture of ultramarine blue and light blue violet into the damp area, adding a touch of dioxazine violet on the lower petals. The paint will spread within the damp area, and the colours will merge with no harsh edges.

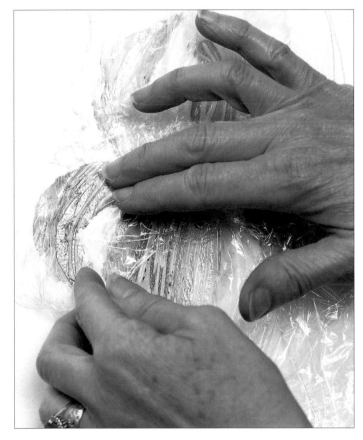

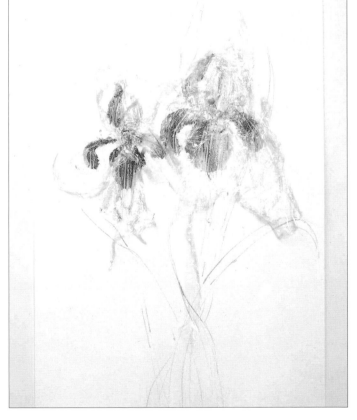

3 Working quickly while the paint is still wet, stretch a small piece of plastic food wrap out in your fingers and press it gently but firmly on to the first petal. Make sure that you lay the food wrap out following the direction of the striations in the petals.

4 Repeat the process until all the petals have been covered. Provided the wash is still wet, you can lift off the food wrap two or even three times to reposition it if necessary, but remember that you will lift off paint every time you do this: take care not to get paint on to areas outside the petals.

▶

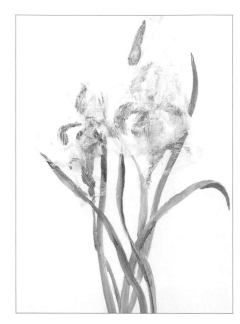

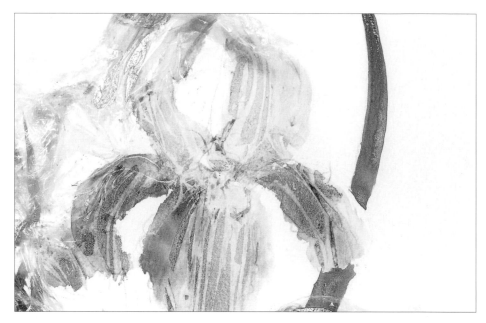

5 Begin painting the leaves in Hooker's green, adding medium yellow for the lighter-coloured leaves. While the paint is still wet, brush a little dioxazine violet along the shaded lower edge of some leaves; this helps to show how the leaves twist and turn, and it provides a visual link with the colour of the flowers. Paint the papery sheathes at the base of the petals in a mixture of yellow ochre and Hooker's green and cover with plastic food wrap, taking care not to dislodge any of the food wrap from the petals as you do so.

6 When you are sure that the petals are completely dry, carefully peel off the food wrap. Note how some of the paint has been blotted off, creating the delicate papery texture and veining that is so characteristic of iris petals.

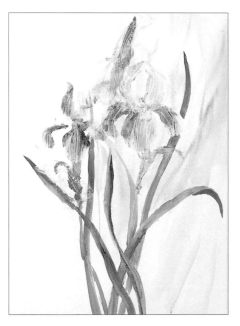

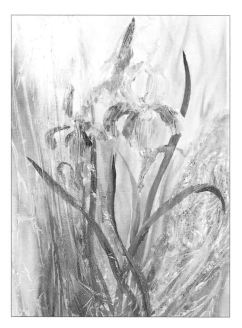

Tip: Colour is one of the ways in which you can imply distance in your paintings, as colours look paler the further away things are from the viewer. In this project, the use of different tones of green for the iris stalks and leaves makes it seem as if we are looking through a sea of waving stems and grasses, with only the flowers and leaves in the immediate foreground being in sharp focus and strong colour – a simple but effective technique.

7 Mix a pale, watery yellow-green from medium yellow, yellow ochre, Hooker's green and a little light blue violet. Wet the background with clean water. Don't worry if some water goes over the painted areas; the paint will not lift off provided it is completely dry. With flowing, calligraphic strokes that imitate the shape of the leaves, brush the yellow-green mixture over the right-hand side of the background. Paint a few more strokes in Hooker's green deep, which is darker, to imply that these leaves are closer to the viewer.

8 Add light blue violet to the previous yellow mixture and, as in the previous step, paint loose, leaf-like strokes to the left and right of the central flowers in order to create an atmospheric, but realistic-looking background. While the paint is still wet, apply plastic food wrap over these areas in exactly the same way as you did for the petals, stretching it taut from top to bottom so that it runs in the same direction as the leaves.

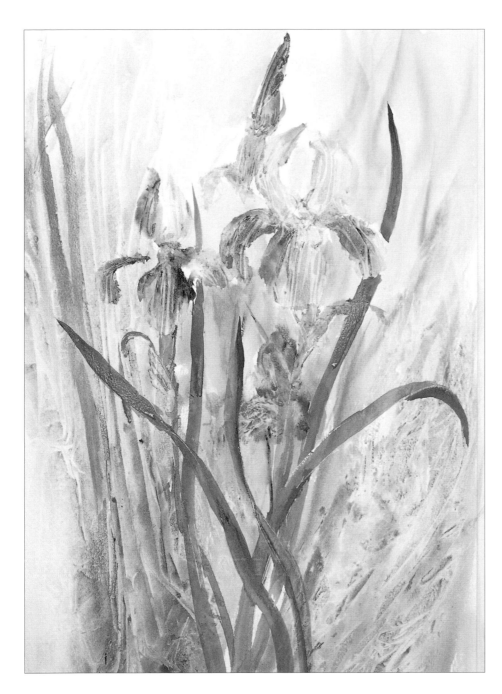

9 When the paint is completely dry, remove the plastic food wrap. In the space between the two main flowers, brush in the shape of another flower head, using a paler, bluer mixture of the previous flower colours. Because it is paler than the main flowers, it gives the impression of being further away. Leave to dry.

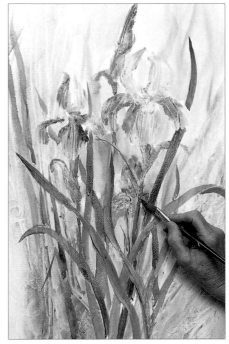

10 Using the same green mixtures as before, brush in more dark leaves in both the foreground and the background. Look carefully at the points where leaves overlap: it should be obvious which leaves are in front and which are behind.

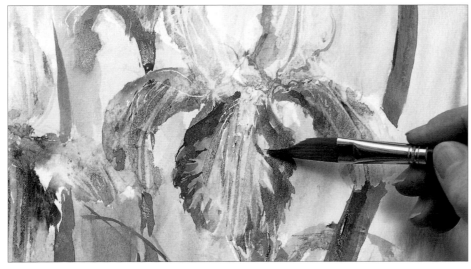

11 Using the tip of the brush, paint fine lines of dioxazine violet on to the petals of the top right-hand flowers to reinforce the striations in the petals that were left when you pulled off the plastic food wrap. Your brushstrokes should be delicate squiggles rather than flat applications of colour, as this helps to create texture. Leave to dry, then rub off the masking fluid from the centres of the flowers.

▶

Assessment time

Now it is time to assess exactly how much more work you need to do in order to complete the painting. At present, the flowers merge into the background because the colours are a little too pale: the tones need to be strengthened and darkened in order to make the flowers stand out more. In the final stages of a painting, it is often necessary to adjust the tones that you put down to begin with. The flowers are also somewhat soft and indistinct – the delicate textures created by pressing the food wrap into the wet paint need to be reinforced with some careful and subtle brushwork. It would be very easy to overdo things and lose the subtlety of the painting, so mix and assess any darker tones very carefully before you apply them to the support and use a fine-tipped brush so that you can control where you place your brushstrokes.

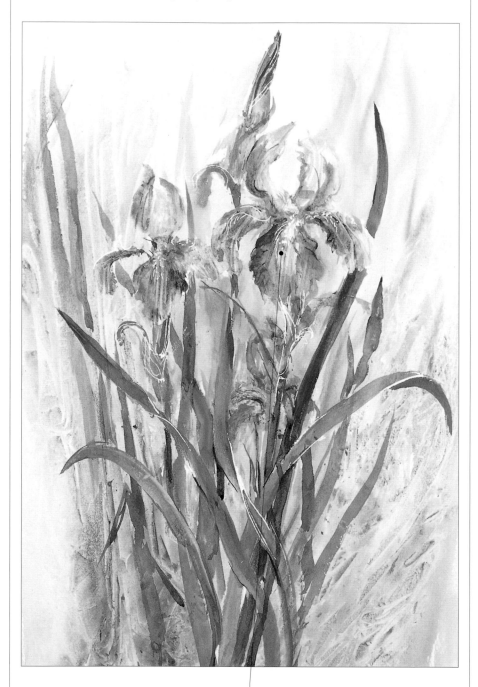

The flowers are too soft and indistinct.

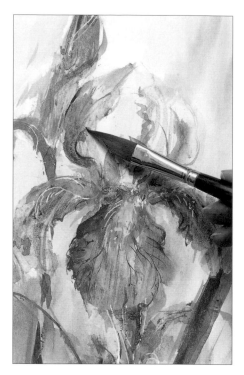

12 Brush medium yellow into the flower centres. Strengthen the petal colour using the same ultramarine blue and light blue violet mixtures as before. Note that the upper petals are bluer in tone than the lower ones.

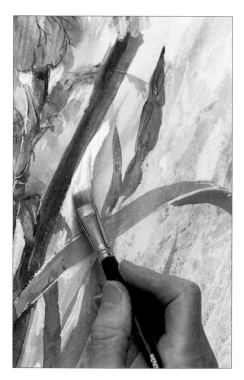

13 Mix a pale, opaque yellow from medium yellow and titanium white. Brush this into the spaces between the leaves where necessary to reinforce the shapes of the leaves.

The finished painting

This is a delicate study that captures the characteristics of the flower to perfection. The clever use of tone, with darker tones in the foreground and lighter ones further back, has created a convincing sense of depth. The papery texture of the petals is created through a combination of calligraphic brushstrokes and blotting off paint.

Soft yellows and greens provide a natural-looking background that allows us to concentrate on the flowers.

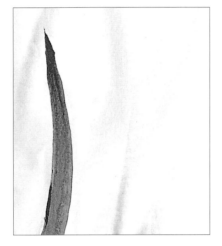

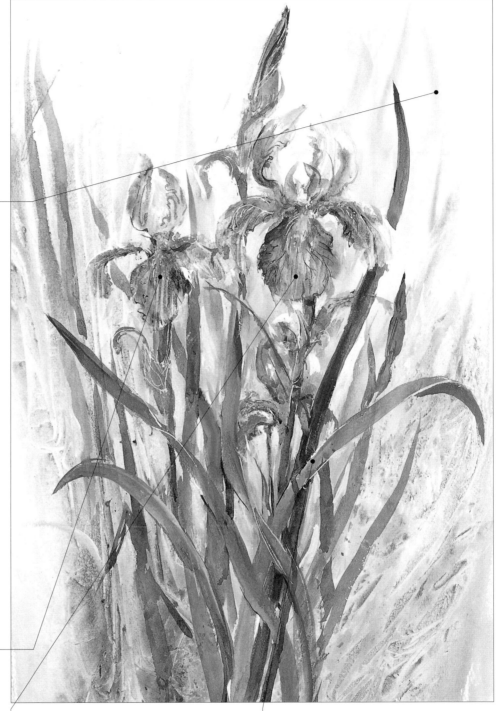

The vertical lines on the translucent petals are created by pressing plastic food wrap into wet paint and lifting it off when dry.

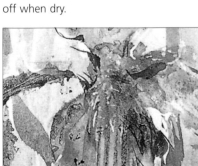

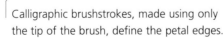
Calligraphic brushstrokes, made using only the tip of the brush, define the petal edges.

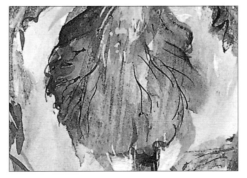

The leaves twist and turn over one another, enlivening the composition.

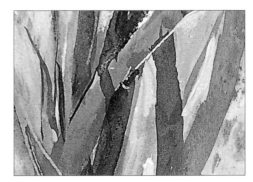

Floating leaf

A landscape doesn't have to be a grand, panoramic view that stretches far away to the distant horizon: little details, such as this brightly coloured leaf floating in a mountain stream, can be just as appealing and atmospheric.

Although this little stream and rocks might not, at first glance, appear to contain much colour, there are many subtle variations in tone, and it is essential that you take time to observe the scene closely and work out where these changes in tone occur.

This looks like a very simple scene, but in practice you would have to be very lucky to find a leaf floating exactly where you want it to be! However, one of the advantages of painting is that you can alter reality to make a better picture – so feel free to introduce a leaf where none exists in real life or to change the angle at which it lies across the stream to make a more interesting composition.

One of the advantages of using gouache for a scene such as this is that, because you can paint light colours over dark ones, you can put in the highlights on the sparkling water right at the end, when everything else is in place. If you were using pure, transparent watercolour, you would have to reserve the white of the paper for the highlights or scratch off paint using the tip of a craft (utility) knife, with the risk of damaging the surface of the support. With gouache, you can spatter on white paint for a random effect or dot it on with a fine paintbrush for a more controlled look. Use permanent white gouache for highlights: it has better covering power than zinc white, which is best reserved for mixing with other colours in order to lighten them.

Materials

- *Watercolour board*
- *HB pencil*
- *Masking film (frisket paper)*
- *Craft (utility) knife*
- *Gouache paints: cadmium yellow deep, sap green, ultramarine blue, flame red, indigo, Vandyke brown, permanent white*
- *Brushes: medium round, fine round, old toothbrush*

The leaf ▶
Here, the artist decided to make a floating leaf the main centre of interest. It makes a bold splash of colour against the darkness of the water.

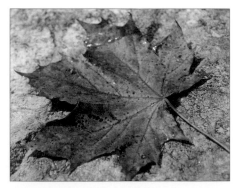

The stream ▼
When you are painting a moving subject, such as this flowing stream, a photograph can help you to capture the way the light plays on the scene.

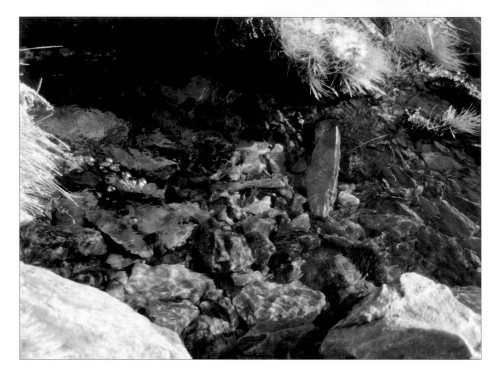

Tonal sketch ▼
Making a tonal sketch helps you to work out the main areas of light and shade before you begin painting, although it does not have to be as detailed as the one shown here.

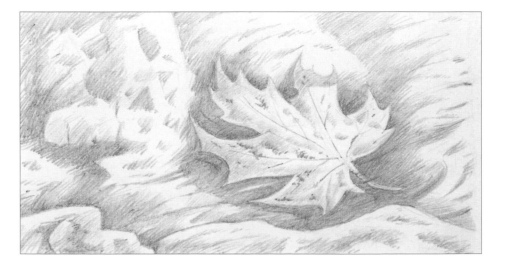

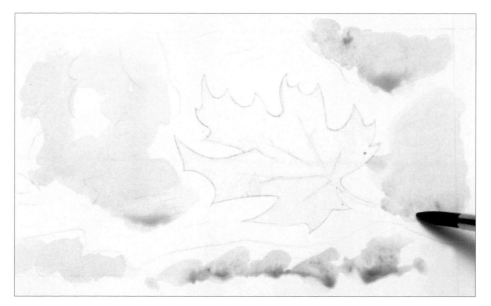

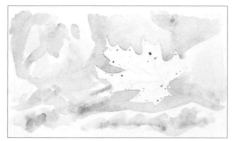

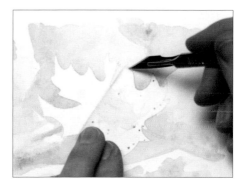

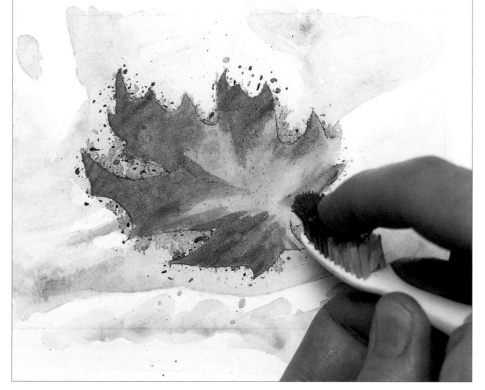

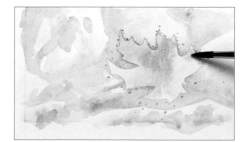

1 Lightly sketch the scene on watercolour board. Stick masking film (frisket paper) over the image and, using a craft (utility) knife, cut around the floating leaf. Peel the masking film off the rest of the image, leaving the leaf covered. Using a medium round brush and a dilute mix of cadmium yellow deep, paint the underwater rocks. Mix a dilute bluish green from sap green and ultramarine blue and dab it over the water area.

2 Continue dotting ultramarine blue over the water, brushing the colour over the rocks and leaving the highlight areas untouched. Leave to dry.

Tip: If you are worried about cutting into the board when you cut out the leaf for the mask, trace the entire underdrawing on to tracing paper and stick masking film over the trace. Put the trace on a cutting mat, cut out the mask, and position the masking film on the relevant part of the image.

3 Using the tip of the craft knife to lift up the edge of the masking film, peel the film off the leaf.

4 Mask off everything except the leaf. Brush very dilute cadmium yellow deep over the leaf. Add more pigment to the mixture and drop it into the centre of the leaf, allowing it to spread of its own accord. Brush flame red, wet into wet, around the edges.

5 Brush flame red over the tips of the leaf, leaving the central portion of the leaf light yellow. Dip an old toothbrush into the flame red paint, hold it over the leaf, and gently pull back the bristles to spatter droplets of paint on to the leaf.

Tip: Practise on a scrap piece of board first until you are confident that you can make spatters the right size. Do not pull too hard: the spatters should be small.

▶

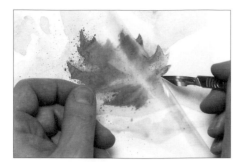

6 Gently peel off the masking film to reveal the whole painting.

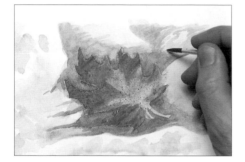

7 Mix a dark blue from indigo and Vandyke brown and, using a fine round brush, paint around the leaf and surrounding rocks. Brush small strokes of cadmium yellow deep over the rocks to deepen the tone.

Assessment time
The colours and shapes of the leaf and rocks have been established, as have the areas of water. This is a good start, but the image still looks rather flat and one-dimensional at this stage. There is little sense of depth, and it is a little hard to tell which rocks are above the water level and which ones are covered by the flowing stream. The painting is also rather static: there is also no real feeling of movement in the water.

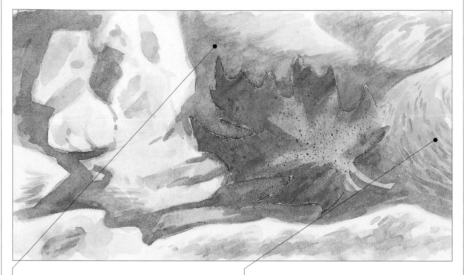

More sense of movement is needed in the water. This can be achieved with fine brush strokes

These rocks lack form. Greater definition of the rock and the water next to it will help.

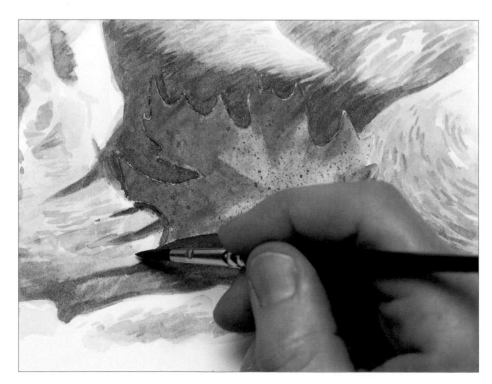

8 Using a fine round brush, go over the water again with ultramarine blue paint, sharpening the outline of the leaf. With short brush strokes, brush a mixture of cadmium yellow deep and flame red over those areas of the rocks on the left that stick up above the water.

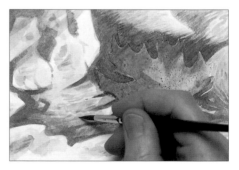

9 Using indigo, paint shadows on the rocks.

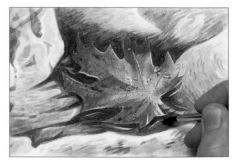

10 Brush small, curved strokes of permanent white into the water around the leaf to indicate ripples.

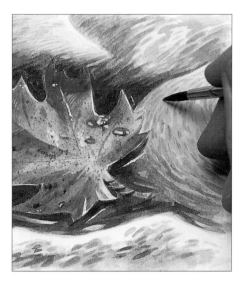

11 Mix together sap green and ultramarine blue and build up the texture in the strip of greenish water at the base of the image. Continue building up the tones and textures over the whole image. It is better to work across the whole painting than to concentrate on just one area, otherwise you risk overworking one part at the expense of the rest.

The finished painting

This is a simple little scene that many landscape artists might pass by in favour of a grander view. It is a study in contrasts – the softness of the water versus the solidity of the rocks, the vibrant colour of the leaf versus the muted tones of the water. The brushwork is controlled, with the brush strokes in the water following the direction of the water flow to create lifelike ripples. Note how the main centre of interest – the leaf – is positioned slightly off centre and at an angle to add interest to the composition.

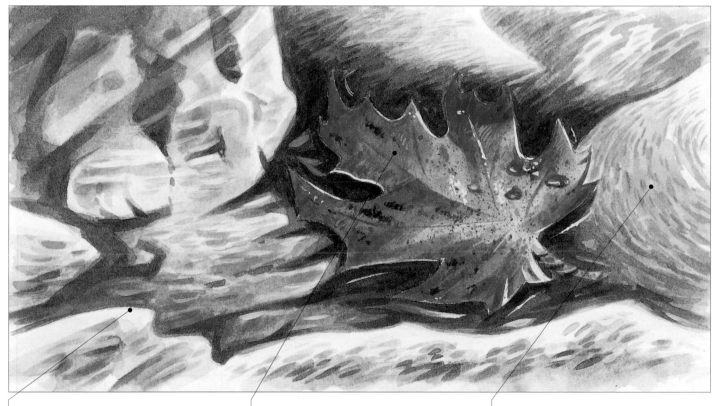

Water flows over the rocks in this area, and so the detail and texture are deliberately subdued.

Wet-into-wet spatters and wet-on-dry applications combine to create a lively texture on the leaf.

This rock stands clear of the water; more detail and texture are evident here than in the submerged rocks.

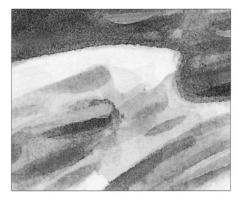

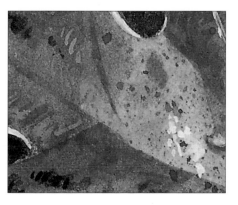

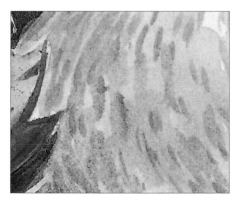

Tulips in glass vase

In this simple still life, a bunch of pink and green parrot tulips has been placed in a turquoise glass vase that complements their shape beautifully. When you paint a subject like this, with overlapping shapes and twisting stems, remember to look at the spaces between as well as at the flowers and stems themselves. Note, too, how the water in the vase distorts the shapes of the stems and how the semi-opaque glass affects the colours of anything seen through it.

In order for the form of the flowers to stand out, opt for a neutral, plain-coloured background. Here, the vase was placed on a window ledge in front of a sheer muslin curtain, which diffuses and softens the light it lets through, creating a subtle contre-jour effect. But even though the background is a plain colour, you will see that there are lots of tonal contrasts within it. Even the gentlest of folds in the

fabric will create shadows that you must render tonally. Try half-closing your eyes when you look at the scene, as this will subdue the detail and make it much easier for you to assess where the tonal changes occur.

One difficulty with painting cut flowers is that they either wilt and perish or turn upwards towards the light. You may find that your still life is not still at all: over a period of just a few hours, the flowers may droop and change position. If you're painting in oils, and creating a painting over a number of painting sessions several days apart, this can be a real problem. Work quickly in the early stages to make sure you capture the position, shape and colours while the flowers are at their best – or take photos for reference.

Another problem with this set-up is that natural light can change considerably over several sessions. As you can see from the

photographs below, in the first session the light was very overcast and uniform. During the final painting session a few days later, strong sunlight cast oblique shadows on the scene, and the artist incorporated them into the final painting to add drama and interest. This project, above all else, is an exercise in painting the effects of light.

Materials

- *Stretched and primed canvas*
- *Oil paints: olive green, raw sienna, viridian, yellow ochre, Indian yellow, lemon yellow, titanium white, madder lake, Caesar purple, cadmium red, cobalt blue, cerulean blue, phthalocyanine turquoise*
- *Turpentine*
- *Brushes: selection of small and medium filberts and sables*
- *Rag or absorbent kitchen paper*

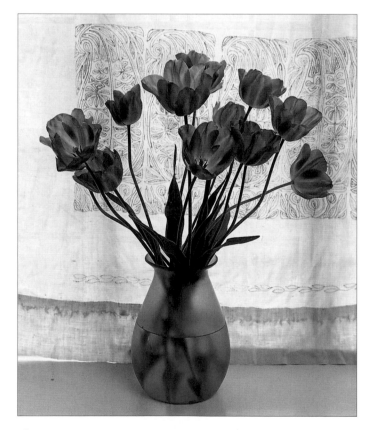

The set-up
A vase of spring tulips, loosely arranged, was placed on a window ledge. The light coming from outside, which was soft and uniform, was diffused still further by the semi-transparent muslin curtain. As a result, there are few shadows in the scene and the colours are muted.

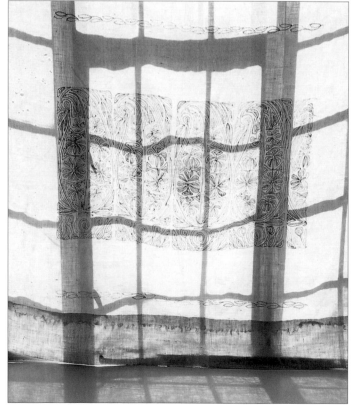

Change in lighting
At the beginning of the final painting session, the sunlight outside was much stronger than it had been originally. The glazing bars of the window cast interesting oblique shadows on the muslin curtain, which the artist decided to exploit in the final painting.

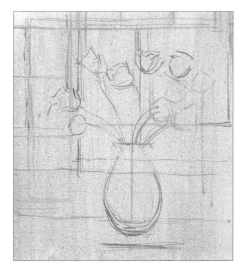

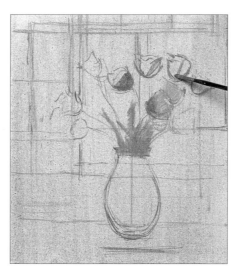

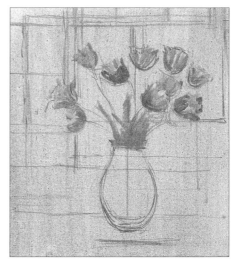

1 Mix a dull brown from olive green and raw sienna. Using a small brush, draw the overall lines and shapes of the flowers and vase. Put in the glazing bars, which can be seen through the curtain, and the window ledge.

Tip: Put down guidelines, such as a vertical line through the centre of the vase. Turn your painting upside down to check the shapes. This makes it easier to see objects as geometric forms.

2 Mix greens for the leaves and stalks (viridian, yellow ochre and Indian yellow for the warmer dark and mid-toned areas, and viridian, lemon yellow, and titanium white for the more acidic areas). Mix pinks for the flowers (madder lake and white, with a touch of blue for the cooler shades, and Caesar purple and white). Vary the proportions of the colours to give a good range of tones. Using a mid-toned and a slightly bluer green, put in the stalks and leaves protruding from the vase. Start to block in the flowers.

3 Continue to block in the flowers, adjusting the proportions of the colours in your mixes to get the right tone. Because of their position in relation to the light, some flowers are much warmer in tone than others: add a little cadmium red for these mixes. In others, where petals overlap, a deeper shade of purple can be seen. Work methodically and spend as much, if not more, time looking at your subject as you do looking at the canvas: you need to assess tones and colours continually as you work.

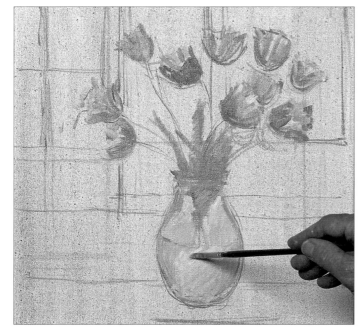

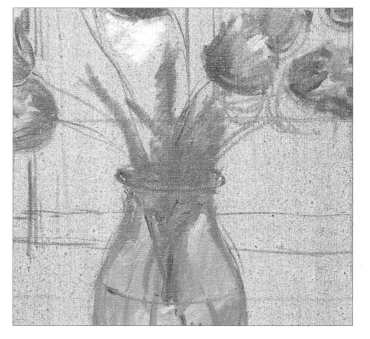

4 Using various dark greens, paint the stalks. Mix a bright blue from cobalt blue and titanium white and put in the darkest areas at the top of the vase, and the water line halfway up. Mix cerulean blue and white for the light blues in the top half of the vase, and a greener blue for the water.

5 Paint the stems that are underwater, using a darker green. The shapes are slightly distorted by being seen through water; the colours are also softened by the opaque glass of the vase. You can create these effects by blending the green into the underlying wet paint.

▶

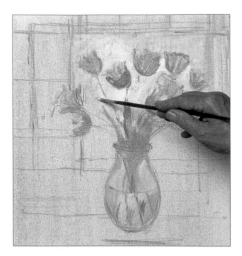

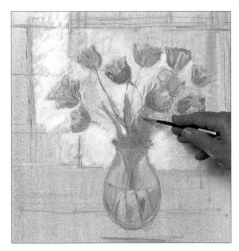

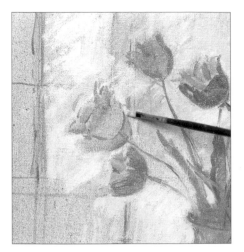

6 Mix a pale, creamy brown colour by adding Indian yellow and white to the bright green that you used you used on the flower heads. Begin blocking in the dark panel in the centre of the muslin curtain behind the flowers, taking care not to obliterate the lines of the glazing bars completely.

7 Outside the central panel, the curtain is lighter in tone. Mix blue and white and scumble the colour on loosely, allowing some of the toned ground to show through to create the texture of the woven fabric. Paint more of the stems, noting how they twist and turn over one another.

8 At this point, the artist decided to alter some of the flowers on the left, as he felt that the painting was weighted too heavily towards the right-hand side. Because oil paint stays wet for so long, you can simply wipe it off with a rag soaked in turpentine and re-paint if necessary.

Assessment time
The basic elements and tones of the composition have been established, but more form is required. Both the vase and the flowers look rather flat at this stage and tend to merge into the background.

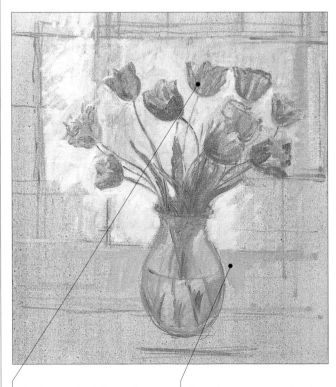

The flowers look flat and one-dimensional.

There is no sense of depth to the window ledge.

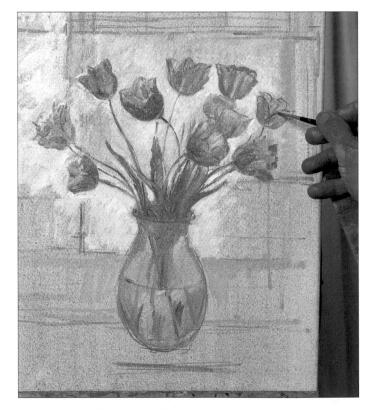

9 Using the tip of a small sable brush, sharpen the edges of the flowers to give them a crisp outline, and put in some linear detail on the petals, using a deep purplish pink and a bright, acidic green as appropriate. You can see that the flowers almost immediately begin to take on more of a sense of form and to stand out more clearly from the neutral-coloured background; they are no longer merely flat blocks of colour.

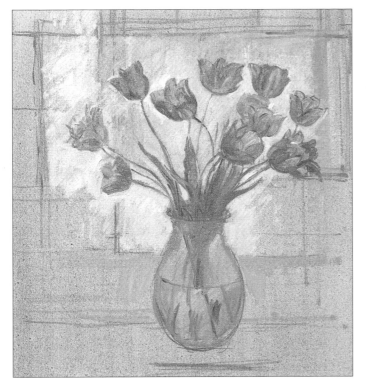

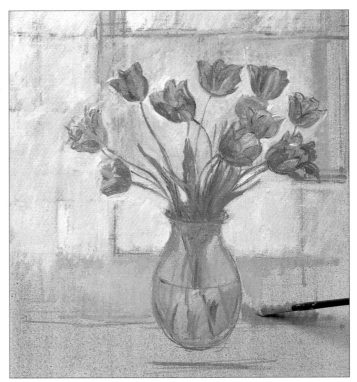

10 Continue to refine the details, working on the tonal changes within the petals to create some sense of depth and form. As before, half-close your eyes as you look at the scene, to see where the changes in tone occur.

11 Paint the deep hem of the curtain in the same mixture that you used for the central panel. The darker colour means that the flowers have something to register against. Don't obscure the glazing bars; they will be reinforced later.

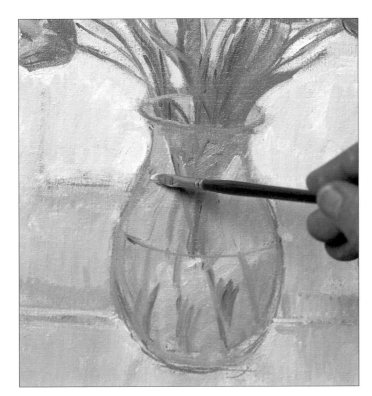

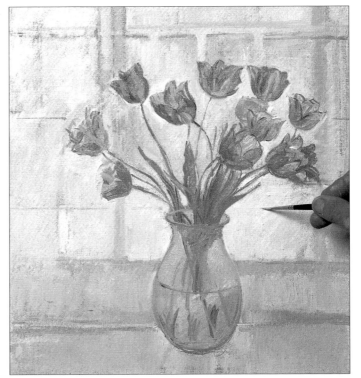

12 The vase is reflected in the window ledge. Put in this reflection, using slightly curved brushstrokes that echo the form of the vase, and leaving some gaps to create the effect of shimmering light. Work more pale blue into the vase interior, carefully painting around the flower stems.

13 Using the same neutral background colours as before, work around the vase, sharpening the edges and softening any areas that are overly blue. Using a pale, neutral blue-grey, strengthen the glazing bars that can be seen through the fabric.

▶

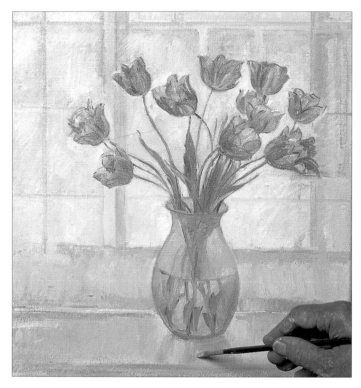

14 Strengthen the greens of the stems in the water. Look at the negative spaces between the stems as well as at the stems themselves. Reinforce the shadow cast by the vase on the window ledge.

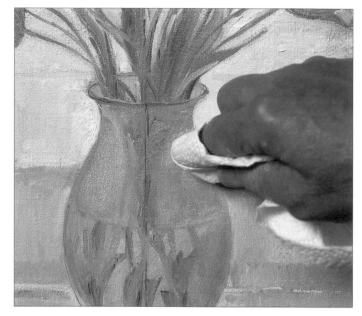

15 At this point, the artist realized that the shape of the glass vase was not quite right. He also felt that the blue he had used for the vase was not vibrant enough. Because the paint was still wet, he was able to scrape it off with a knife and repaint, using a mixture of phthalocyanine turquoise and white. He then wiped off some of the turquoise paint with a piece of absorbent paper to soften the colour and create the effect of light being diffused through the glass.

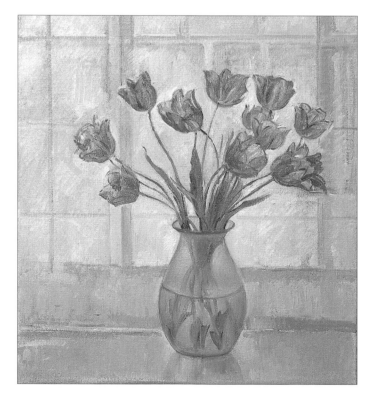

16 Gently stroke a paler version of the phthalocyanine turquoise and titanium white mixture used in Step 15 over the top half of the vase, blending the colours wet into wet, to heighten the effect of soft, diffused light coming through the glass.

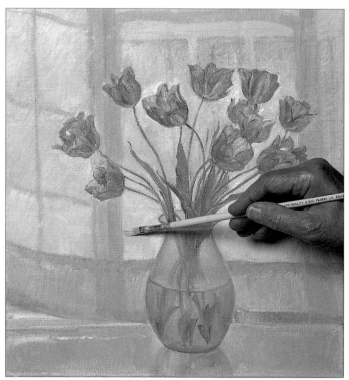

17 In the final stages, the lighting changed. Mix a range of greys from cobalt blue, white and a little Caesar purple and put in the shadows cast by the glazing bars. Warm up the neutral background mixture by adding Indian yellow, and scumble it over the background.

The finished painting

This is a charming study in the effect of diffused and reflected light. The texture of the translucent petals and the opacity of the blue vase have been beautifully captured in soft blends of colour. Loose scumbles of various warm- and cool-toned neutral mixes convey both the texture of the muslin curtain and the effect of light shining through it.

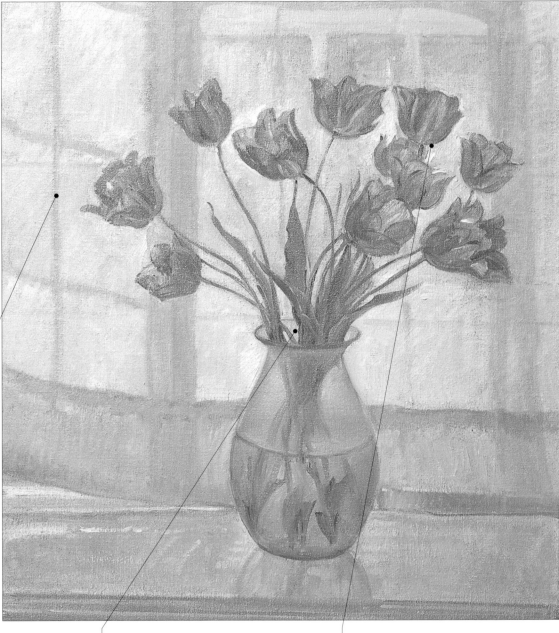

The glazing bars can still be seen through the curtain, although their shadows are more prominent.

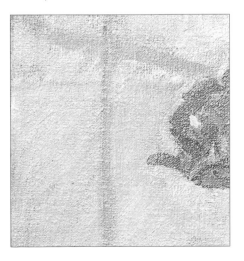

The glass distorts the shapes and softens the colour of any objects that can be seen through it.

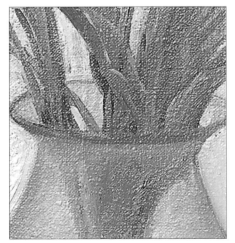

Linear details applied using the tip of a fine brush help to bring the flowers forwards in the scene.

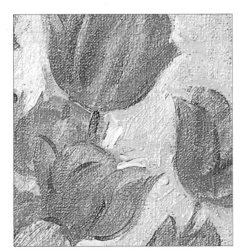

Woodland path

This project is about interpreting what you see and conveying the mood of the scene, rather than making a photorealistic rendition. That does not mean that observation is not important, however. When you are painting a scene like this, look at the overall growth patterns. Are the tree trunks tall and straight or do they lean at an angle? Do the branches droop and spread on either side of the trunk, like weeping willows, or is the foliage weighted towards one side, like maples and Scots pines? Is the shape of the tree basically conical (like many conifers) or rounded (like oaks)?

Look at where the shadows fall, too – and remember that the shape made by the shadows should match the shape of the objects that cast the shadows. Above all, make sure that the shadows are dense enough, as the contrast between the dark and the brightly lit areas is what gives the work a three-dimensional quality.

This scene also gives you the useful opportunity to explore many different textures – the tangled undergrowth and criss-crossing branches, the rough texture of the path and the peeling bark on the trees. Again, try to capture the mood rather than placing every detail precisely. Spatters of paint convey the rough texture of the ground, while the colour of the tree trunks and the patterning of the bark call for more carefully placed brush strokes.

Here the artist also added a few small pieces of collage in the final stages. This is optional, and you may think that the image does not need it; however, provided you do not overdo things it is well worth experimenting with simple techniques like this, as they can bring an added dimension to your work.

Materials
- *Watercolour paper primed with acrylic gesso*
- *4B pencil*
- *Masking fluid*
- *Medium-nibbed steel dip pen*
- *Gouache paints: phthalocyanine green, brilliant yellow, raw umber, raw sienna, zinc white, scarlet lake, jet black, phthalocyanine blue*
- *Brushes: large wash, small round, old toothbrush*
- *Newspaper*
- *Gum arabic*

The scene
Although there is no real focus of interest in this scene, the textures and the contrasting shapes (the sweeping curve of the path against the strong vertical lines of the tree trunks) make it very rewarding to paint. The shadows over the foreground also add interest.

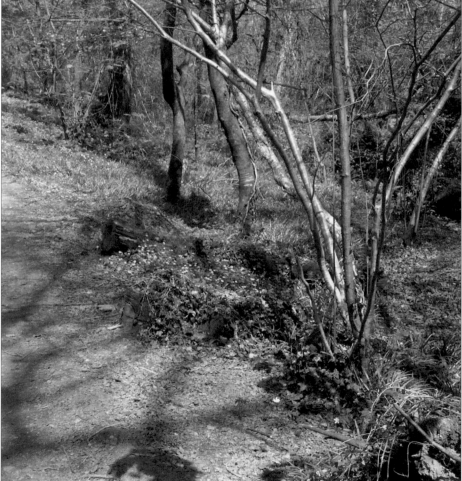

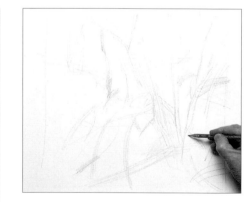

1 Using a 4B pencil, sketch the scene, putting in as much detail as you feel you need. Your underdrawing will help you to keep track of where things are once you start applying the paint.

> **Tip:** You do not need to get all the branches in exactly the right place in your underdrawing, but you should try to be faithful to the general patterns of growth and the rhythms of the scene. Although this is a fairly loose, impressionistic painting, it must look convincing – but it is also important to try to capture a sense of spring-like growth and energy in the scene.

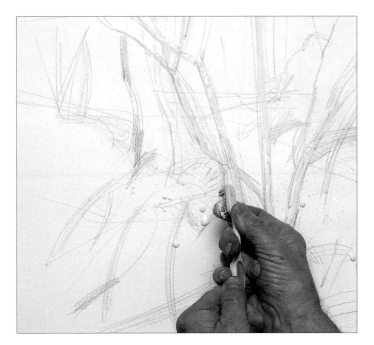

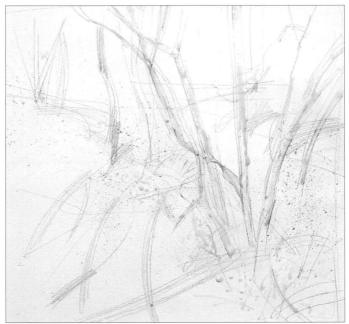

2 Using a medium-nibbed steel dip pen and masking fluid mask the lightest trunks and branches. Also mask any branches that are lighter than their immediate surroundings, even if they are brown in colour rather than a light, silvery grey. Using an old toothbrush, spatter some masking fluid over the undergrowth. Leave to dry: this won't take long, but it is essential that the masking fluid is completely dry before you apply the first washes of colour.

3 Before you begin the painting stages, take some time to make absolutely sure that you have masked all of the light-coloured areas of branches and foliage that need to be protected. Even though gouache is opaque and it is perfectly possible to paint light colours over dark ones, such corrective measures should only be used as a last resort – otherwise you run the risk of losing some of the freshness and spontaneity of the painting.

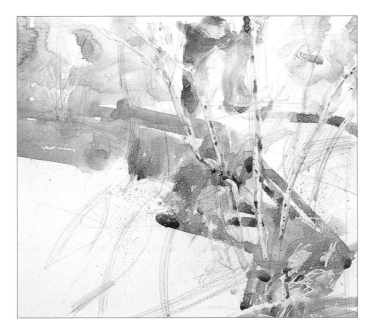

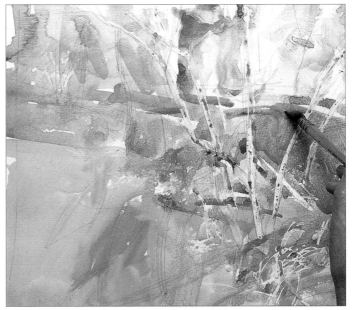

4 Mix a dilute, bright green from phthalocyanine green and brilliant yellow. Using a large wash brush, put in broad horizontal strokes for the band of undergrowth that runs across the centre of the scene. Mix a duller green from phthalocyanine green and raw umber and repeat the process in the foreground. For the tree trunks in the background, put in vertical strokes of raw sienna and raw umber, occasionally adding some green to them.

5 Mix a dilute yellowish brown from zinc white and raw umber and brush the mixture lightly over the earth in the foreground, allowing some of the support to show through to create some texture in this area. The earth on the far right, behind the band of undergrowth, is warmer in tone, so paint this in raw sienna. While the paint is still wet, touch a little scarlet lake into it so that it spreads of its own accord.

▶

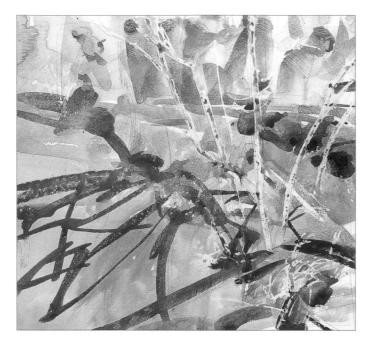

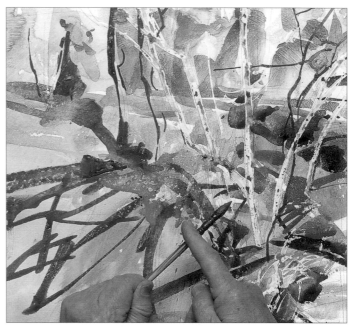

6 Mix a very dark greenish black from jet black, phthalocyanine blue and phthalocyanine green and paint the little stream in the background. Add raw umber to the mixture and paint the cast shadows on the ground.

7 Add more phthalocyanine green to the mixture and paint the shapes of the trunks in the background. Using the bright green mixture from Step 4, spatter colour over the foreground for the low-growing plants alongside the path.

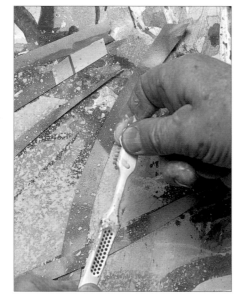

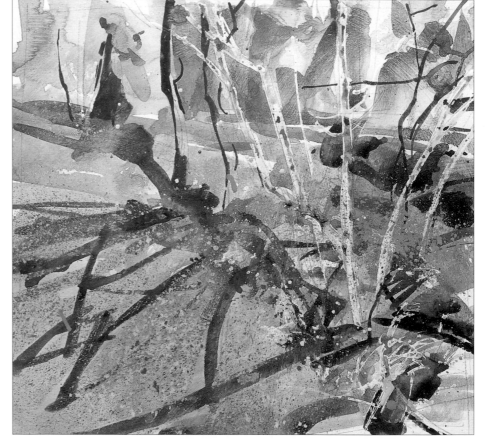

8 Roughly cut masks from newspaper the same shape as the largest cast shadows on the ground and lay them in position. (There is no need to stick them down.) Mix brilliant yellow with white, load an old toothbrush with the mixture, and spatter it over the foreground, pulling the bristles back with your fingertips.

9 Repeat the spattering process with a mixture of white and raw umber to create the rough, pebbly texture of the path in the foreground. When the paint is dry, remove the newspaper masks: the scene is now beginning to take on more depth and texture.

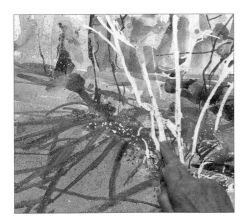

10 There are some warm, pinkish tones on the path, so mix scarlet lake and white and lightly spatter a little of the mixture over the foreground. Leave to dry completely, then rub off all the masking fluid.

Tip: When you have removed a little of the masking fluid, squash it together into a ball and rub it over the surface of the painting like an eraser. Any remaining fluid will stick to it – and it is a lot easier on your fingertips.

Assessment time

Now that you have removed the masking fluid, it is easier to see what must be done to complete the painting. Although the general shapes are all there, at this stage the painting lacks depth: you need to increase the density of the shadows.

The exposed areas are too stark and bright and contain no detail.

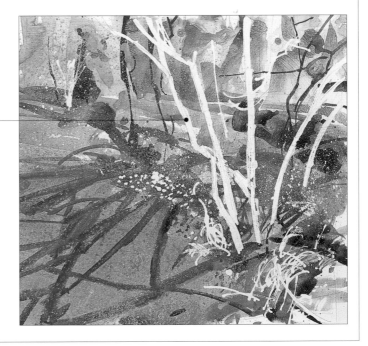

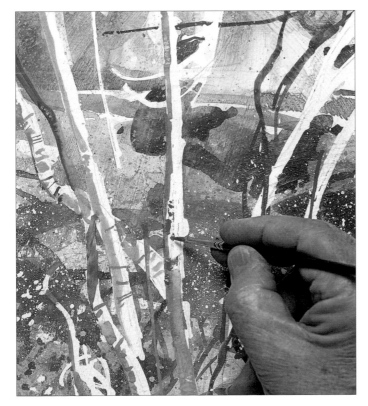

11 Mix a pale brown from raw sienna and white. Using a small round brush, paint the shaded sides of the exposed tree trunks. Add raw umber to the mixture and paint the shadows cast on the tree trunks by other branches.

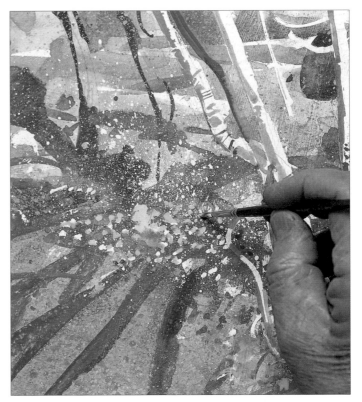

12 Mix brilliant yellow with a little phthalocyanine green and, using a small round brush, dot in the yellow flowers in the undergrowth, making the distant dots slightly smaller than those in the foreground.

▶

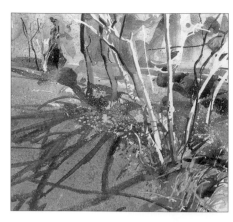

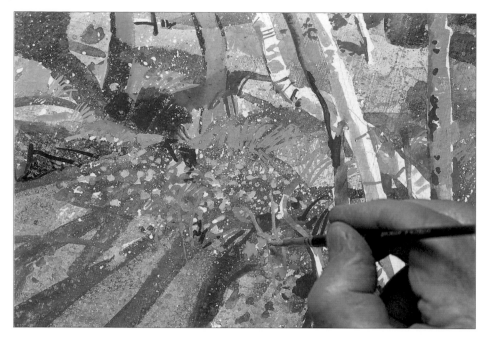

13 Using various versions of the dull green mixture from Step 4, paint the exposed grasses on the bottom right of the painting, keeping your brushstrokes loose and flowing.

> **Tip**: Vary the greens, as this will look more natural. Some grasses are more mature than others, and some are more shaded, hence the variations in tone.

14 The yellow flowers in the centre look a little too vibrant, so tone them down by dotting some of the dull green mixture from the previous step into this area. Put in some solid areas of green, too, obliterating the exposed whites and re-establishing any shadow areas that have been lost on the grasses. Using mid-toned browns, reinforce the lines of trunks in the background.

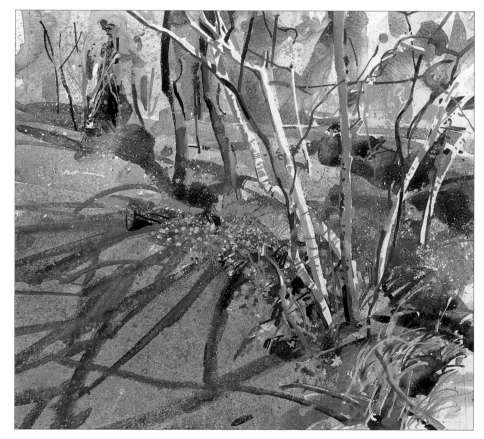

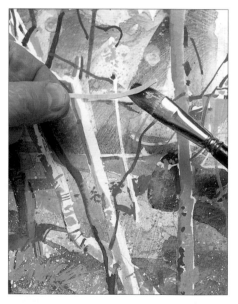

15 You might consider the painting finished at this point, but here the artist decided to enhance the three-dimensional quality of the upper part of the image by incorporating a little collage. If you do this, take care not to overdo it, or the result could end up looking messy and overworked.

16 Paint strokes of branch-coloured paint on a piece of scrap paper and leave to dry. Cut out curving, branch-shaped pieces and brush a little gum arabic on to the reverse side. Position the pieces on the painting and brush gum arabic over the top to fix them in place. Leave to dry. (The advantage of using gum arabic is that, unlike ordinary glue, it can be painted over if necessary.) The collage element adds depth and texture to the image.

The finished painting

This is a lively and atmospheric painting of a woodland path in dappled sunlight. The strong vertical lines of the tree trunks and the diagonal lines of their shadows give the picture a feeling of energy that is echoed by the textural details and bold applications of colour. The palette of colours chosen by the artist is muted but natural looking. Although the scene looks deceptively simple, there is much to hold the viewer's attention.

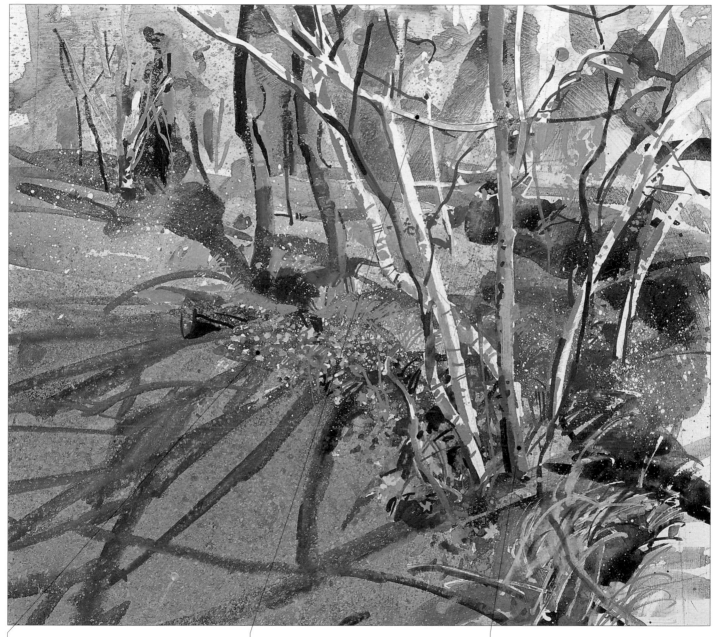

Spatters and dots of colour convey the texture of the path and the tiny flowers.

The use of collage on some of the branches is subtle but effective.

Carefully placed brushstrokes are used for the grasses and tree bark.

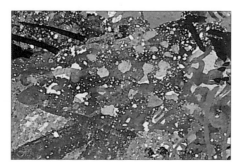

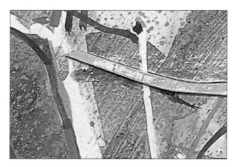

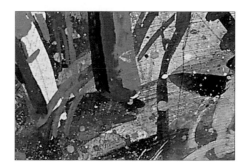

Painting animals and birds

One of the most obvious difficulties of painting animals and birds is that, unlike people, they cannot generally be persuaded to sit still. However, with relaxed subjects such as a sleeping cat or dog or a rabbit held in its owner's arms, you stand at least some chance of being able to put down the basic lines of the 'pose' before the animal moves. Sketching a family pet that you already know well is a good introduction to animal painting.

When you feel ready to paint moving animals and birds, spend time simply watching them, without even attempting to put brush to canvas. You'll soon see patterns emerging – the way a cat licks itself clean, or a dog sniffs at the ground, or a caged bird hops from one perch to another, for example. Try to fix these movements in your mind so that you can

incorporate them into your paintings. Reference photos may help, provided you don't rely on them too much – but there is no substitute for sketching from life, even though your first attempts will probably not be very successful.

A little knowledge of basic anatomy is a great help, just as it is when you're painting people. Knowing the names of all the joints and muscles won't get you very far, but having some idea of how the joints are articulated or the sequence in which an animal's legs move will. Until the early days of photography, for example, jumping horses tended to be depicted with their front legs stretched out in front and the back legs stretched out behind; think of the paintings of George Stubbs (1724–1806). Now we know that they launch themselves off their back legs with

their front legs brought close to the body and tucked in tightly.

When it comes to painting feathers and fur, aim to convey a general impression rather than capture every single hair, otherwise your painting will look fussy and overworked. Painting wet into wet is a good way to achieve this as you can work a second fur colour into or over a first to create subtle blends on the support. Drybrush is also a good technique for rendering fur and feathers, especially when used with a fan blender.

Swans ▼
The ripples in the water and the sparkling sunlight give this painting a lovely sense of movement. Note how many different tones have been used to paint the birds' white feathers.

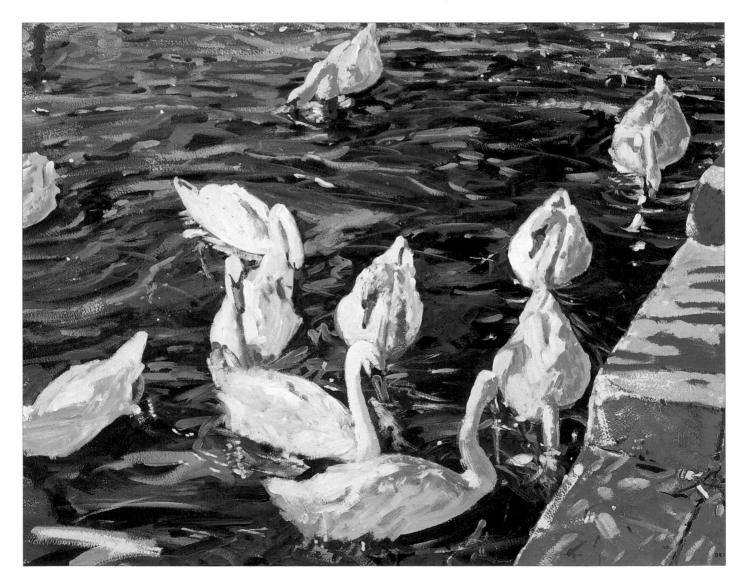

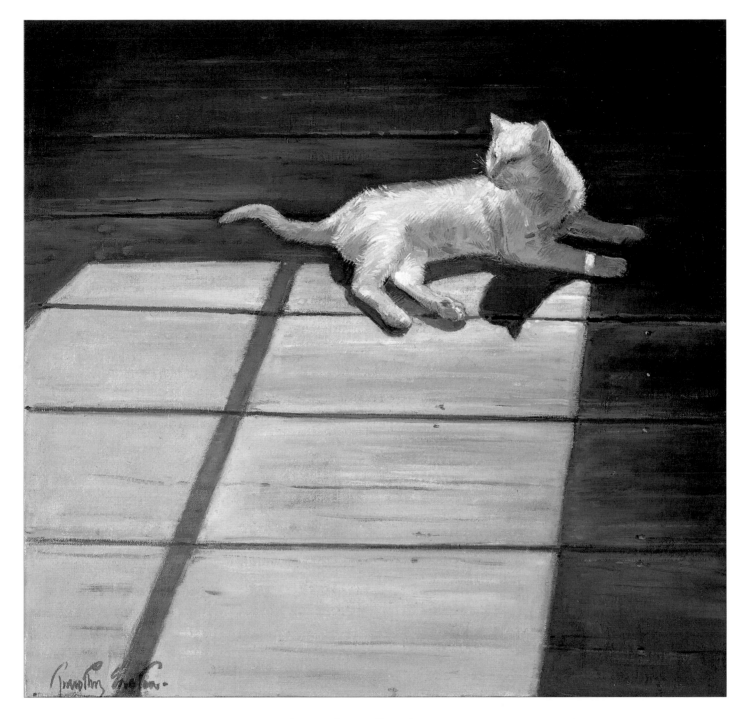

Studio window reflected ▲

Anyone who owns a cat will recognize this as a typical cat "pose" – legs sprawled out, head erect and ears pricked for the slightest sound. Quick sketches of such poses made while the animal is at rest are a good way of capturing its character and personality.

Turning fish ▶

The artist has skilfully conveyed the movement of the fish with his treatment of the light shining on the water and the ripples on the surface.

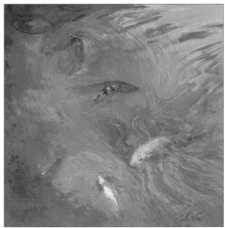

Sleeping cat

It is lovely to be able to put your painting skills to good use to paint a portrait of a cherished family pet. Because you know your animal so well, you will easily be able to find a pose that sums up its character and personality, and a painting like this would make a wonderful gift for another family member. Here, the artist combined a quick snapshot of the sleeping animal with a background of brightly coloured leaves from his garden.

There are several ways to approach painting fur. In a water-based medium such as acrylic, you might choose to apply loose, impressionistic washes of colour wet into wet, so that the the paint blends on the support to create subtle transitions from one tone to another, perhaps lifting off colour with clean water to create lighter-toned areas. In this project, we build up the colour in thin glazes, gradually darkening the shaded areas until the right density is achieved, with each layer of paint being allowed to dry before the next one is applied. Use short brushstrokes that follow the direction in which the fur grows, and an almost dry and very fine brush. This creates the impression of individual strands of hair and is a particularly effective way of conveying the texture of the fur.

The project also gives you the chance to practise masking. Because you need to mask out large areas in the early stages of the painting, use masking film (frisket paper) rather than tape or fluid. Masking film is used by draughtsmen and is available from most good art supply stores. To ensure that the film adheres firmly to the support and that no paint can seep under the edges, choose a smooth surface, such as illustration board.

Materials
- *Illustration board*
- *Masking film (frisket paper)*
- *Craft (utility) knife*
- *Gouache paints: cadmium yellow deep, flame red, burnt sienna, Vandyke brown, indigo, permanent white*
- *Brushes: medium round, fine round*

The cat
The artist used this photograph as reference material for the cat's "pose" and the colour and texture of its fur. However, the striped wallpaper does not make a very attractive background.

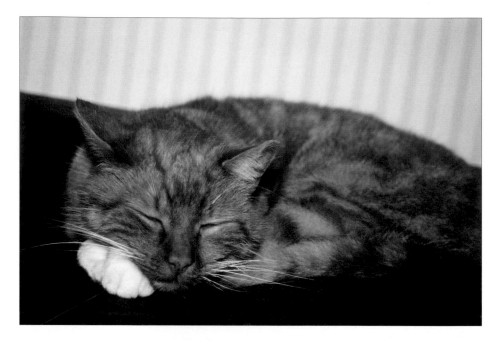

The background
These leaves provided a colourful and natural-looking background against which to position the cat.

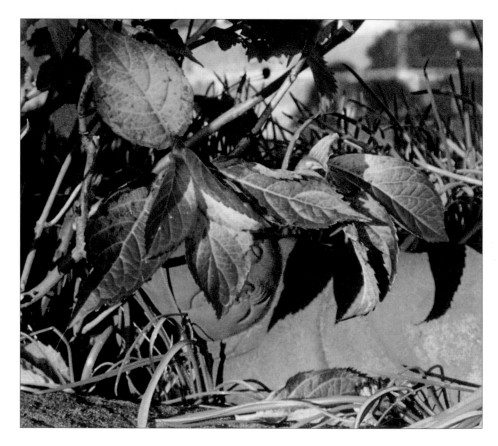

Compositional sketch

When you are combining two or more references in a painting, you must give some thought to the relative scale of the different elements. Make a quick sketch, in colour or in black and white, before you begin painting.

Tonal sketch

This cat is predominantly ginger in colour, but there are many different tones within the fur. Making a tonal sketch in pencil or charcoal enables you to work out not only the different tones but also the composition of your painting.

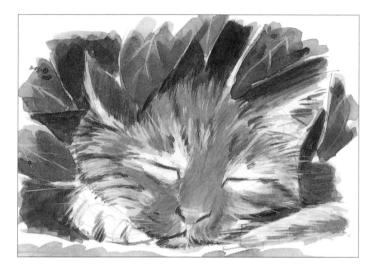

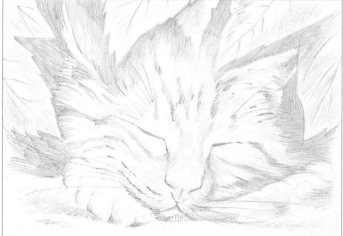

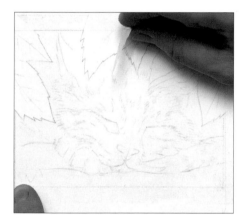

1 Referring to your initial sketch, lightly draw the cat using an HB pencil, indicating the main clumps of fur. Draw the veins on the leaves. Place masking film (frisket paper) over the sketch and, using a craft (utility) knife, cut around the outline of the cat. Peel away the masking film that covers the leaves.

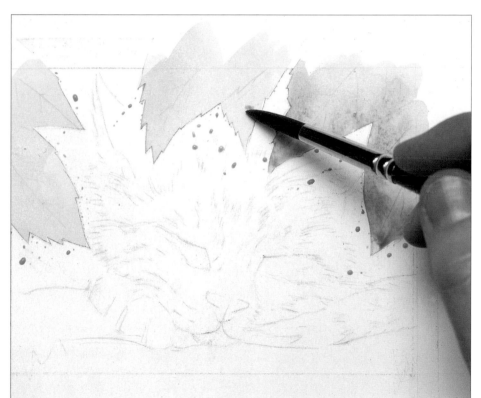

Tip: The last thing you want is for paint to seep under the masking film on to the area of the painting that you are trying to protect. Working in one direction only, wipe a clean tissue or soft rag over the film to smooth out any wrinkles and ensure that the film is stuck down firmly. It is best to work towards the cut edges of the film.

2 Using a medium round brush, brush cadmium yellow deep gouache paint over all the leaves to establish the underlying colour. While the paint is still wet, rinse your brush in clean water and drop flame red over the tips of the leaves. The two colours will combine wet into wet to make a warm orange, creating soft-edged transitions of colour. It is important that you leave the paint to dry completely before you move on to the next stage; like watercolour, gouache paint dries very quickly, so this should only take a minute or two, but if you want to speed up the drying time, you can use a hairdryer on a warm setting. Hold the dryer well away from your painting so that you do not accidentally blow the red paint away from the tips and into the centre of the leaves.

▶

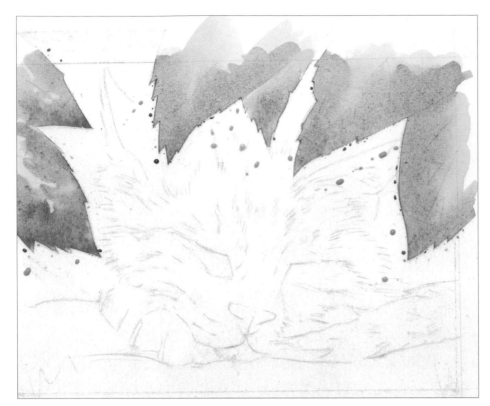

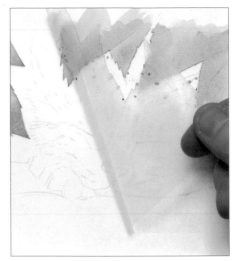

4 When you are sure that the paint is completely dry, carefully peel the masking film back from the cat. You can see how the leaves have crisp edges: it is easy to achieve this using a mask.

3 As you can see, the yellow and red merge together on the support in a way that looks completely natural. It does not matter if the colour is darker in some parts of the leaves than in others.

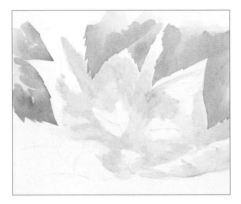

5 Mix a warm, yellowish brown from cadmium yellow deep and burnt sienna. Using the medium round brush, brush this mixture over the cat, leaving the white fur untouched. Your brushstrokes should follow the direction in which the fur grows. Leave to dry.

Tip: If you are worried about accidentally splashing colour on to the leaves when you paint the cat, cover them with the masking film that you removed in Step 1.

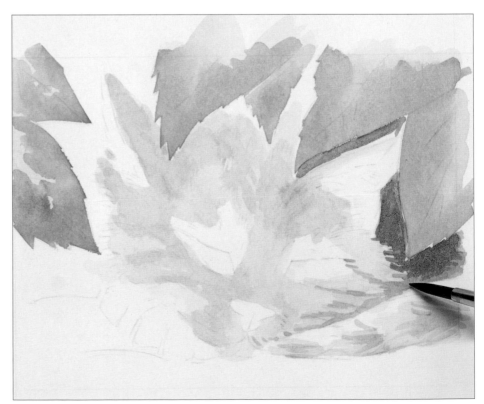

6 Mix a rich, chestnut brown from burnt sienna and Vandyke brown. Using a fine round brush, put in the dark fur on the cat's face, again using short brushstrokes that follow the direction in which the fur grows. Mix a darker brown from Vandyke brown and indigo and paint the dark fur around the edges of the ears.

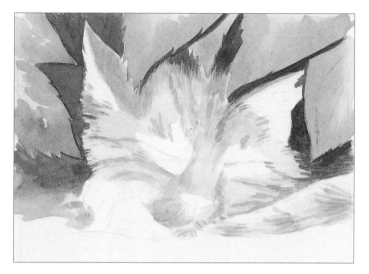

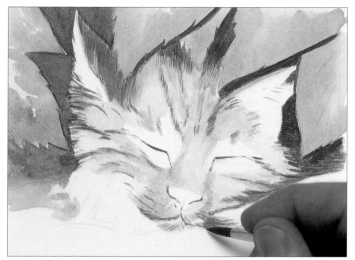

7 Use the same colour to paint the dark spaces between the leaves, so that the individual leaves stand out clearly.

8 Using Vandyke brown and the tip of the brush, start putting in the dark brown markings on the cat's face.

Assessement time

Brush a dilute version of the cadmium yellow deep and burnt sienna mixture used in Step 5 over the non-white areas of the cat's face to warm up the tones overall.

The painting is starting to take shape but more detail is needed to bring out the roundness of the face and the texture of the fur.

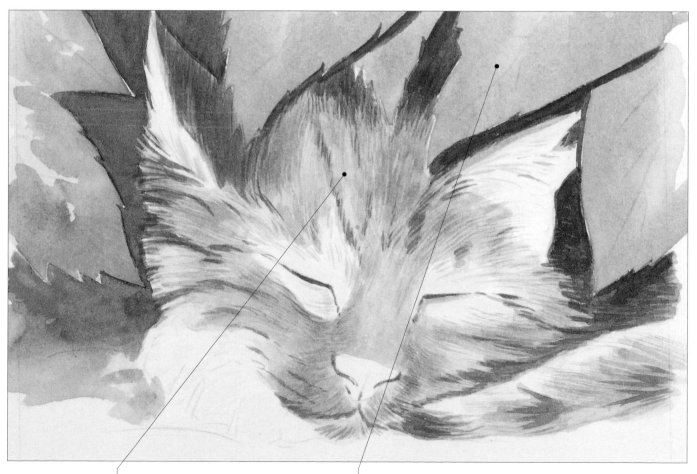

The fur contains little texture.

The cat merges with the background; the leaves do not yet look like leaves.

▶

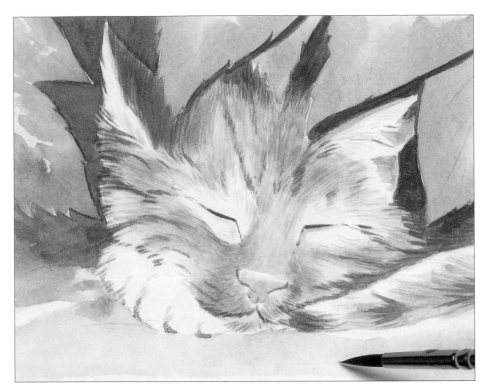

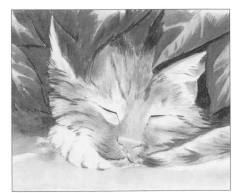

10 Mix flame red with a little cadmium yellow deep. Using a medium round brush, brush this colour over the leaves, allowing some of the original pale yellow colour to show through as the veins in the leaves.

9 Mix a very pale pink from flame red and permanent white and brush it on to the tips of the ears, which are slightly pink, and the tip of the nose. Using the Vandyke brown and indigo mixture from Step 6, put in the dark spaces between the claws. Add more water to the mixture. Brush clean water over the foreground and dot the indigo and Vandyke brown mixture into it.

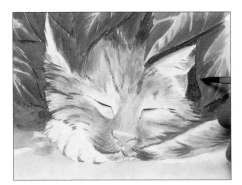

11 Using the same mixture, build up the intensity of the red, taking care not to go over the veins.

Tip: Remember that gouache looks slightly darker when it is dry than it does when it is wet, so wait until the paint is dry and assess its colour before you add another layer. It is better to build up the density of colour gradually: if you make the leaves too dark, they will overpower the cat, which is the main focus of the painting.

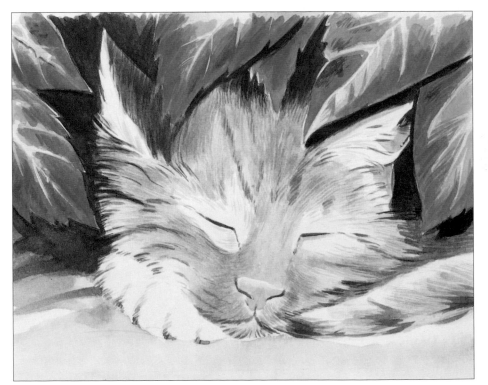

12 Using the indigo and Vandyke brown mixture, deepen the colour of the leaves. Note that the edges of the leaves are slightly serrated; use a fine brush to paint the serrations. Use the same colour to darken the very dark fur markings and the outlines of the mouth and nose.

The finished painting

This is a slightly whimsical but very appealing painting of a cherished family pet in a characteristic "pose". The leafy background provides a colourful foil for the animal and focuses attention on its face, while delicate brushwork captures the texture of the fur.

Here, the artist has used white gouache and a very fine brush to put in the whiskers and more fur texture in the final stages. It is up to you how much detail you put in: you might choose to build up the tones and textures more than has been done here.

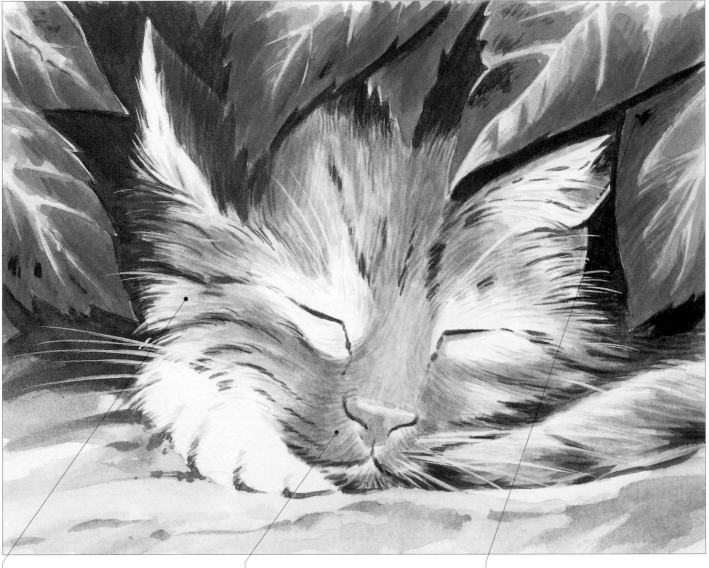

The texture of the fur has been built up gradually, using fine brushstrokes that follow the direction in which the fur grows.

Small details – the pink of the nose and the outline of the mouth – convey the character of the sleeping cat.

The richly coloured, textured autumn leaves provide a simple but dramatic backdrop to the portrait.

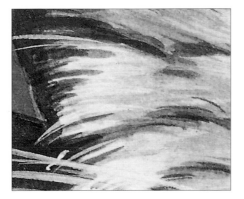
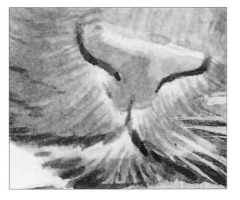
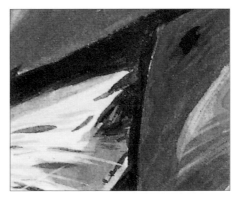

Farmyard chickens

Whether you are painting wild or domesticated animals, it is interesting to paint them in their environment – in this case, a corner of a farmyard, where the chickens are allowed to range freely, pecking at grain.

Before you begin painting, spend time observing how the chickens move. Although you might at first imagine their movements to be completely random, you will soon see a regular pattern emerging – a staccato rhythm of strutting and pecking, stabbing at the ground to pick up grains of wheat before throwing the head back to swallow. Try to fix this rhythm in your mind, as it will help you to anticipate what the bird is likely to do next. Look, too, at the way the movement of the head and legs affects the rest of the bird's body: when the head is tilted down, the rest of the body tilts up – and vice versa. Regardless of whether you are painting from life or from a photograph, accurately capturing the angle of the body in relation to the head will give added veracity to your work.

This project also gives you the opportunity to practise a number of different ways of capturing texture in acrylics. By applying very thin layers of paint in glazes, you can build up the slightly uneven coloration of the rusting cartwheel in the background, while the woodgrain on the wheelbarrow is painted using just the tip of the brush. Spatters of paint on the gravelled area in the foreground and thick dabs of paint applied to the chickens with a painting knife also add textural variety to the painting.

Materials
- *300gsm (140lb) NOT watercolour paper*
- *HB pencil*
- *Masking fluid*
- *Ruling drawing pen*
- *Acrylic paints: yellow ochre, raw sienna, burnt sienna, cadmium orange, cadmium yellow, Hooker's green, burnt umber, light blue violet, violet, cadmium red*
- *Brushes: medium chisel or round*
- *Small painting knife*

The scene
Although this is an attractive scene, with lots of detail, the colours are a little subdued. The artist decided to boost the colours a little and make more of the sense of light and shade in her painting, in order to make a more interesting and better balanced picture.

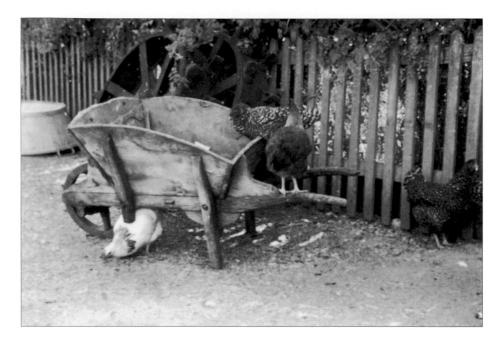

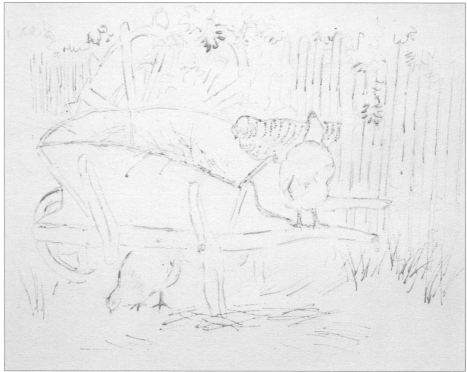

1 Using an HB pencil, make a light underdrawing of the scene to use as a guide. Dip a ruling drawing pen in masking fluid and outline the chickens. Mask out the lightest areas – the white dots on the chickens' feathers, the bright wisps of straw on the ground, and the brightest bits of foliage. Leave the masking fluid to dry completely.

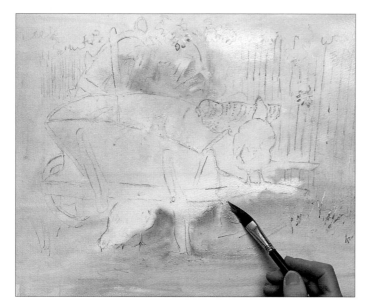

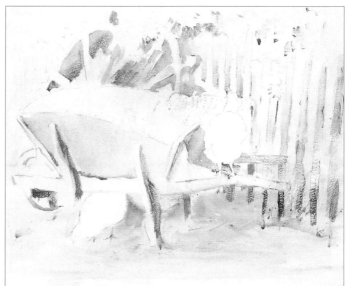

2 Mix up a dilute wash of yellow ochre and another one of raw sienna. Using a medium round brush, wash yellow ochre over the side of the wheelbarrow and the background foliage. Loosely brush raw sienna over the foreground, which is darker than the rest of the image. These two loose washes of warm colour establish the overall colour temperature of the scene.

3 Brush raw sienna over the fence posts. Add burnt sienna to the mixture and paint the triangular-shaped wedges inside the background cartwheel. Use the same mixture for the shaded portion of the wheelbarrow wheel and for the wooden supporting struts and handle of the barrow. In effect, what you are doing in these early stages is making a tonal underpainting of the scene.

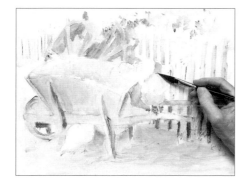

4 Brush a dilute mixture of cadmium orange over the straw lying in the wheelbarrow and on the ground, using short brushstrokes. Brush the same colour over the spokes of the cartwheel and the body of the brown hen perched on the wheelbarrow handle. Add more pigment to the mixture and paint the brown hen's head.

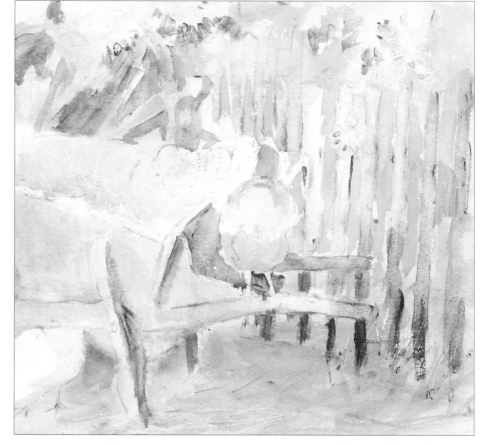

Tip: Always vary the length and direction of your brushstrokes to suit the subject. Here, broad sweeps are used to block in large areas such as the wheelbarrow, while short, individual strokes are used for the wisps of straw.

5 Mix a yellowy green from cadmium yellow and a little Hooker's green and wash this mixture over the bushes behind the fence. Add a little burnt umber to the mixture in places to get some variety of tone. Leave to dry.

▶

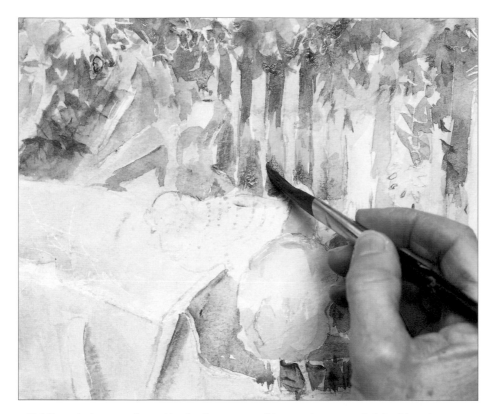

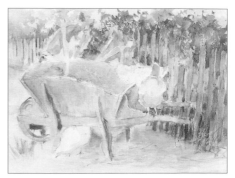

6 Mix a dark green from Hooker's green and burnt sienna and dab this mixture over the bushes, twisting and turning the brush to create leaf-shaped marks and allowing some of the underlying yellowy green from the previous step to show through. Note that some of the foliage pokes through the gaps and obscures part of the wooden fence posts.

7 Mix a purplish grey from light blue violet and burnt sienna and paint the shaded wheelbarrow interior and the shaded parts of the fence posts.

Tip: Neutral greys can be created by mixing together two complementary colours. This scene is relatively warm in temperature, and therefore two warm colours (light blue violet, which is a warm, red-biased colour, and burnt sienna, a warm reddish brown) were combined to produce the shadow colour. For a cool shadow colour (a snow scene, for example), mix cool, blue-biased complementaries.

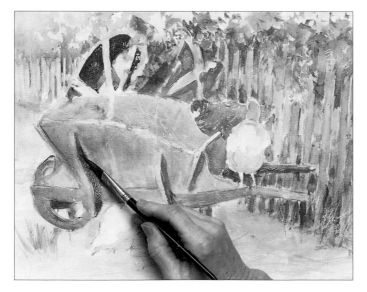

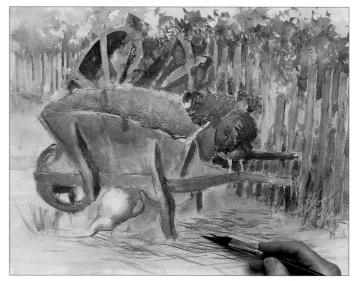

8 Mix a warm grey from violet and a little Hooker's green and paint the grey chicken on the wheelbarrow, leaving the beak untouched. Add burnt sienna to the mixture and paint the dark shadow areas inside the cartwheel and on the struts of the wheelbarrow.

9 Paint the dark feathers of the white chicken in light blue violet and brush the same colour loosely over the grey chicken on the wheelbarrow to create some variety of tone in its feathers. Mix a warm brown from burnt sienna and cadmium orange and paint the rim of the cartwheel. Brush burnt sienna over the body of the brown chicken on the wheelbarrow, allowing some of the underlying colour to show through. Splay out the bristles of the brush and brush thin lines of burnt sienna over the foreground.

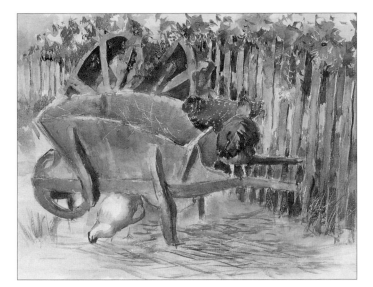

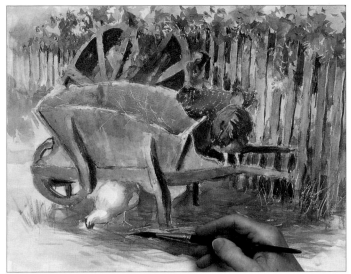

10 Paint the chicken combs in cadmium red. Mix a very dark green from violet and Hooker's green and dot this colour into the foliage, wherever there are really dark leaves or shaded areas. The different tones of green help to create a feeling of dappled light in the foliage.

11 Mix a purple shadow colour from violet and light blue violet, adding lots of water so that the mixture is very dilute, and brush this colour over the shadowed area underneath the wheelbarrow. When this is dry, brush thin, straw-like strokes of yellow ochre over the foreground.

Assessment time
Rub off the masking fluid. At this stage, the painting still looks rather flat and lifeless; the wheelbarrow and chickens do not stand out sufficiently from the background. You need to add more texture to both the foliage and the foreground areas and increase the contrast between the light and dark areas.

Stronger tonal contrast is needed in the foliage to help create a sense of light and shade.

More texture is needed – particularly on foreground elements such as the wheelbarrow.

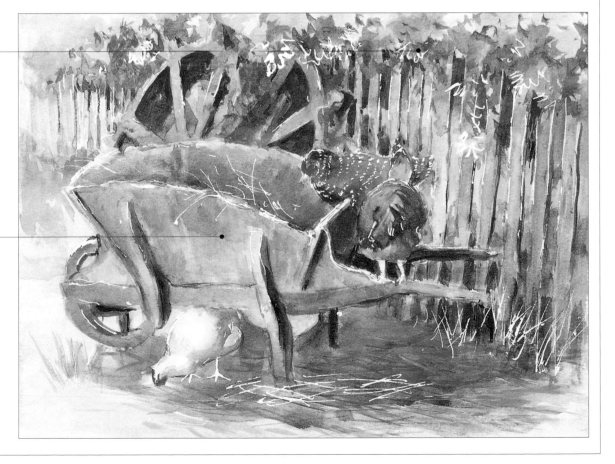

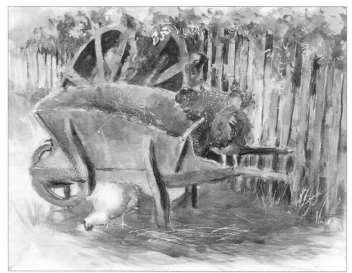

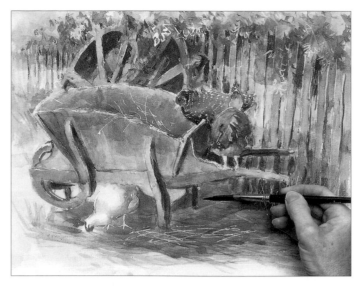

12 Mix a very dilute yellowy green from cadmium yellow, Hooker's green and a little yellow ochre and brush the mixture over the greenery at the top of the image to warm it a little. Brush pale yellow ochre over the exposed straw in the wheelbarrow and in the foreground. Brush very pale light blue violet over the gray chicken to tint the exposed dots.

13 Brush the purple shadow colour from Step 11 over the foreground to deepen the shadows and improve the contrast between the light and dark areas.

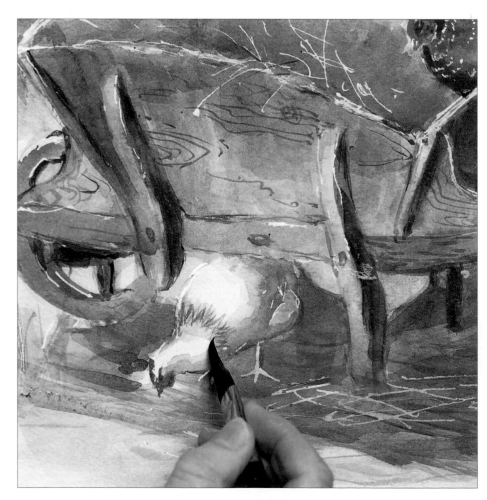

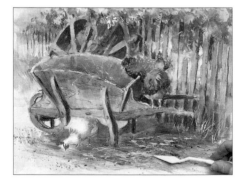

15 Spatter dark brown mixture over the foreground. Use the same colour to paint dark feathers on the brown chicken. Mix cadmium yellow with yellow ochre and apply light, textured strokes to the foreground.

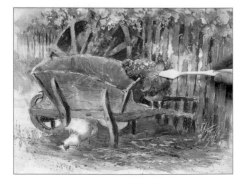

14 Mix a dark brown from burnt sienna and violet and, using the tip of the brush, "draw" in the wood grain on the wheelbarrow. Use the same colour to paint the "ruff" of dark feathers on the white chicken in the foreground.

16 Dot thick white paint over the grey chicken's body and yellow ochre over the brown chicken's body.

The finished painting

This is a charming farmyard scene that exploits the versatility of acrylics to the full. The paint on the rusty metal cartwheel and wooden wheelbarrow is applied in a similar way to watercolour – in thin layers, so that the colour and subtle variations in tone are built up gradually. Elsewhere – on the bodies of the chickens and the straw-strewn ground, for example – relatively thick impasto applications create interesting textures that bring the scene to life.

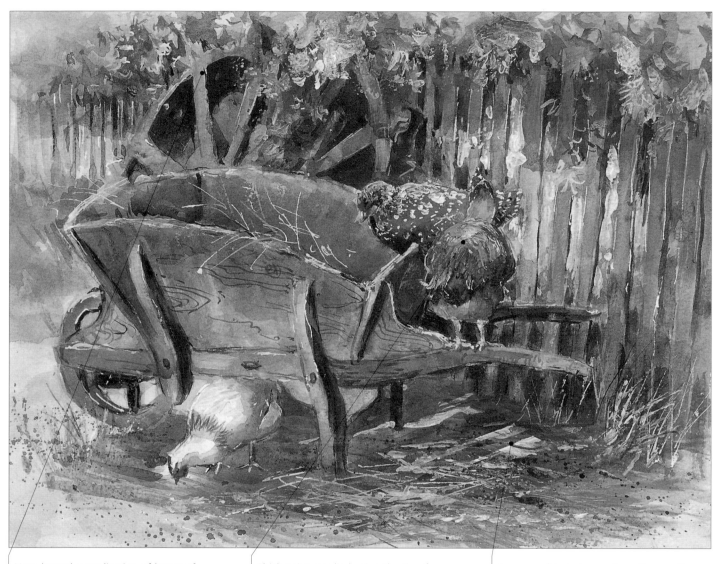

Note how the application of layers of colour, wet on dry, creates the texture of rusty metal.

Thick paint, applied using the tip of a painting knife, shows the texture of the ruffled feathers.

A range of techniques, from fine spatters to thick impasto work, is used to paint the pebble-strewn ground and loose straw.

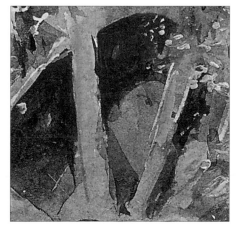
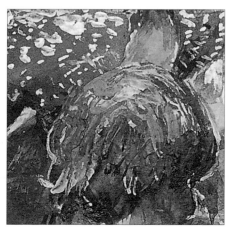
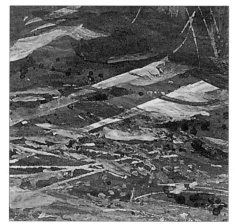

Tropical butterfly

Both butterflies and moths belong to the scientific order Lepidoptera, which means "scale-wing" in Latin, and most butterfly wings are covered with tiny, individually coloured scales arranged in partially overlapping rows, like tiles on a roof. Butterfly houses give you the chance to see all kinds of exotic, brilliantly coloured and patterned species that you might never be able to encounter in the wild. This peacock pansy butterfly (*Nymphalidae precis almana*) is indigenous to Nepal and neighbouring regions and is characterized by the eyespots on the wings, which act as a deterrent to potential predators.

The artist selected a smooth-surfaced board for this study in oils, for two good reasons: first, he wanted this to be a reasonably detailed painting and a smooth surface allows you to put in small details without the paint spreading and sinking into the support; second, he did not want the texture of the support to show through in the final painting.

To speed up the drying time and enable you to complete the painting in one session, use a medium to which a drying agent has been added, such as drying linseed oil.

As each scale on the wing is differently coloured, you will find infinitely subtle gradations of tone. One way of conveying both the texture of the wings and the subtlety of the colour shifts is to stipple the paint on, using the tip of the brush, to create optical colour mixes in the same way that the Pointillist painters such as Georges Seurat (1859–91) did. However, although some inks and liquid watercolours can come close, it is difficult to match the intensity of iridescent colours with even the brightest of pigments.

Materials
- *Smooth-surfaced board*
- *HB pencil*
- *Oil paints: chrome yellow, cadmium orange, geranium lake, brilliant pink, titanium white, ultramarine blue, turquoise blue deep*
- *Turpentine (white spirit)*
- *Drying linseed oil*
- *Brushes: selection of fine rounds, filbert*

The butterfly

With its dramatic eyespots and brilliant colouring, this peacock pansy butterfly makes an appealing subject for a painting. However, the artist decided not to include all the flowers, as he felt they detracted from the butterfly. It is perfectly permissible to leave out certain elements of a scene in order to make your painting more dramatic.

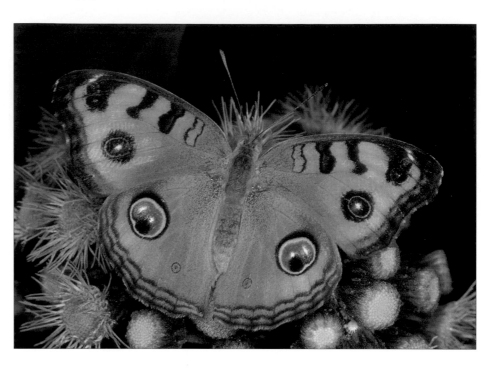

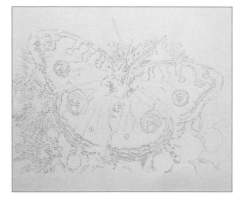

1 Lightly sketch the butterfly in HB pencil. It is entirely up to you how much detail you put into your underdrawing, but including the veins and the fringe-like pattern around the outer edge of the wings will make it easier for you to keep track of where you are in the painting.

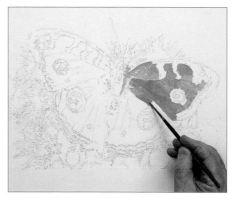

2 Using a fine round brush and alternating between chrome yellow and cadmium orange, start putting in the basic colour of the wings. Thin the paint with turpentine (white spirit) and mix it with drying linseed oil so that it is the consistency of single (light) cream.

Tip: Use a different brush for each colour, so that you do not have to keep stopping to clean brushes.

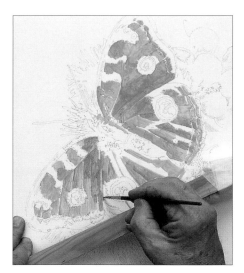

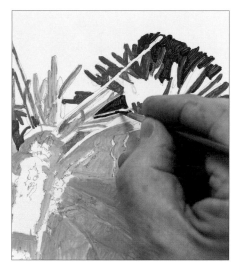

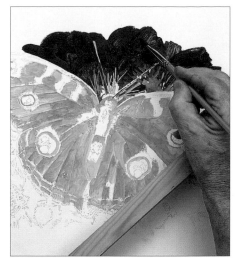

3 Continue until all the yellow is complete, looking closely at your subject to see the different tones. You may need to turn the support around and use a mahl stick to keep your hand clear of wet paint. If you do not have a mahl stick, you can improvize one by taping rags around one end of a thin piece of wood or dowelling, as the artist did here.

4 Mix a range of bright pinks from geranium lake, brilliant pink and titanium white and start painting the flowers on which the butterfly is resting. Mix a dark, purplish blue from ultramarine blue and geranium lake and start putting in the background, taking care not to get any colour on the butterfly. Again, use a mahl stick, if necessary, to keep your hand clear of any wet paint.

5 Continue painting the background, carefully cutting in around the flower tendrils.

> **Tip**: When you are clear of the butterfly and flowers, switch to a larger brush to enable yourself to cover the background more quickly.

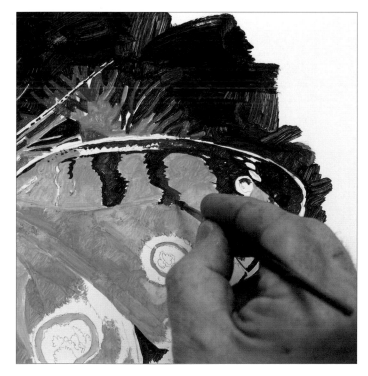

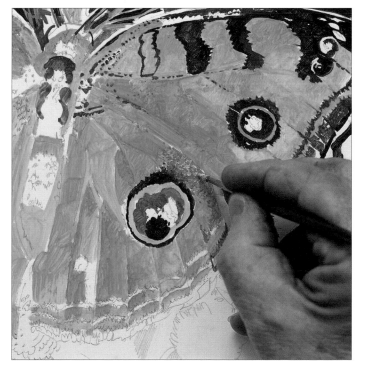

6 Using the same colours that you used for the flowers and background, start putting in some of the dark detail on the butterfly, using short brush strokes to convey the texture of the scales on the wings.

7 Paint the "eyes", using cadmium orange and the purple/pink mixture from the previous step and stipple the colour on with the tip of the brush to create an optical colour mix. Note that there are bluish-purple patches next to the two largest eyes: add more white and ultramarine blue to the mixture for these areas. Paint the "fringe" around the outer edge of the wings in oranges and pinks, as appropriate.

▶

Assessment time

The main elements of the painting are in place. All that remains is to add more fine detailing to the butterfly and complete the surrounding flowers and background, working carefully and methodically. Although the artist had originally intended to include the flowers to the right of the butterfly, at this point he decided that they would detract too much from the painting of the insect.

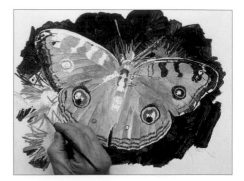

8 Using a fine brush and the same pinks and purples as before, paint the flowers on the left-hand side, gradually working down the painting. Paint as much of one colour as you can while you have it on your brush. When you have finished the flowers, paint the dark background.

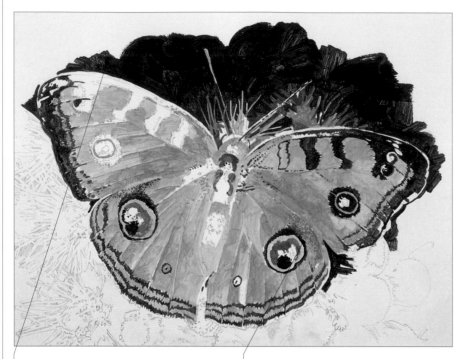

The dark background acts as a foil to the butterfly. Keeping its edges irregular adds to the informality of the study.

The detail is beginning to take shape; features like this are best put in during the final stages, when the underlying colours and shapes have been established.

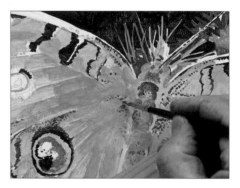

9 Paint the body of the butterfly, blending the colours on the support so that the brushstrokes are not visible.

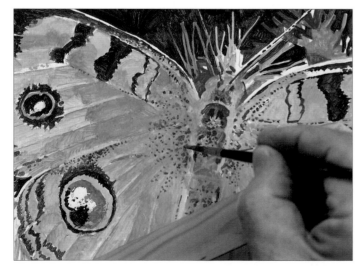

10 Continue painting the dots of colour on each side of the body. Although the dots are clustered more densely near the body, the same colours also run along some of the veins. Finish painting the "eyes" on the left-hand side of the butterfly, using the same colours as before.

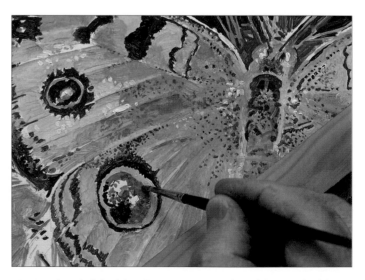

11 Mix a bright blue from turquoise deep blue and white and dot it into the whites of the "eyes". The patterning is now beginning to stand out strongly. Reinforce the orange areas around the two largest eyes with cadmium orange, deepening the colour with geranium lake where necessary.

The finished painting

Although this was never intended as a photorealistic painting, pointillist-style dots of colour help to capture the iridescent quality of the wings – something that cannot be achieved easily in paint. Much of the painting consists of a single layer of paint, which is appropriate for the thin, delicate structure of the insect. Note the clever use of different lengths of brush stroke to create texture: longer, blended strokes are used for the furry body, while short strokes and tiny stipples convey the individual scales on the wings. The artist has also used some artistic license in reducing the number of flowers so that the butterfly is more clearly defined against the dramatic, dark background.

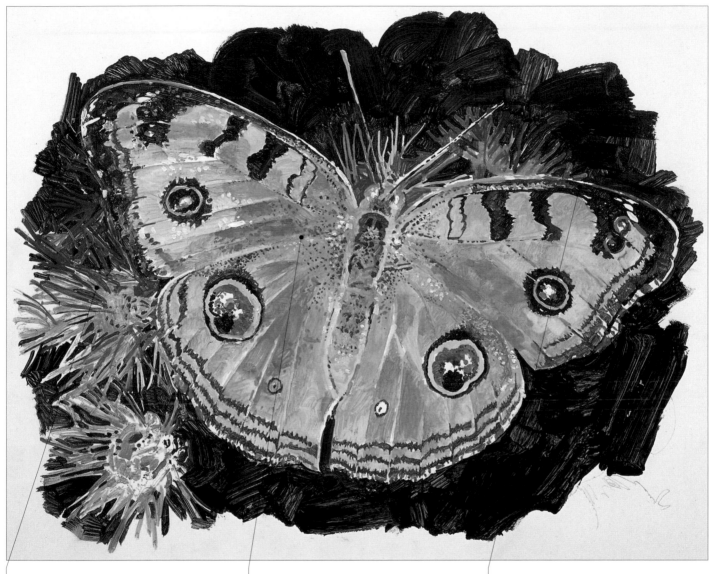

The flowers are loosely painted but echo some of the colours in the butterfly.

Different lengths of brush stroke create different textures.

The butterfly stands out clearly against the dark background.

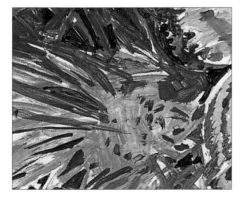

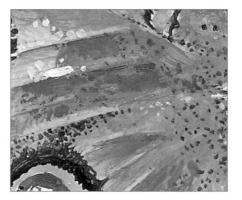

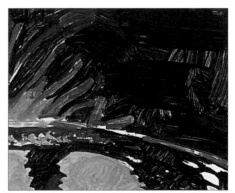

Painting landscapes

Landscapes are probably the most popular of all subjects to paint. Each season has its own mood and colours, each scene its own unique features.

The most important thing to decide on when painting a landscape is what constitutes your focal point. A grand panoramic view is all very well, but there must be something that holds the viewer's interest. Do not include too much, however, or your painting will look jumbled. Feel free to simplify and leave out any elements that do not contribute to the overall effect.

Once you have selected your focal point, decide where to place it within the picture area. Placing a subject in the centre of the picture is generally best avoided, as it tends to result in a static image – although there may be times when you deliberately do this to create a calm mood. One placement that almost always works well is "on the thirds" – roughly one-third of the way into the painting from both the horizontal and the vertical edge.

Use lines or curves, either real or implied, to help lead the viewer's eye to the focal point. You might, for example, choose a viewpoint that allows a river to snake its way through the scene in an S-shape, or have a secondary point of interest on an implied diagonal line.

Another important consideration is how much sky to include. Beginners often place the horizon line right across the middle of the image, which cuts the picture in half and looks rather boring. If you have an interesting sky, emphasize it by placing the horizon low down; conversely, a sliver of sky (or even no sky at all) places the emphasis on the land.

To convey a sense of scale and distance in landscapes, keep in mind that objects that are further away look smaller than those that are close by. Colour is another way of implying distance, as colours tend to look paler the further away they are. Texture, too, plays a part: more textural detail should be evident in the foreground than in the background.

Crooked tree against the dazzle ▼
The strong diagonal line that runs upwards through the painting from the bottom left gives a sense of energy to this very simple seaside scene.

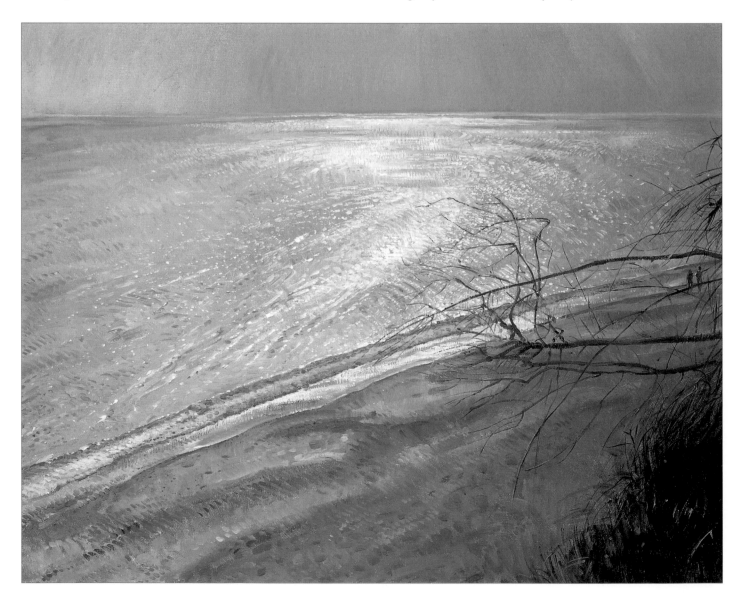

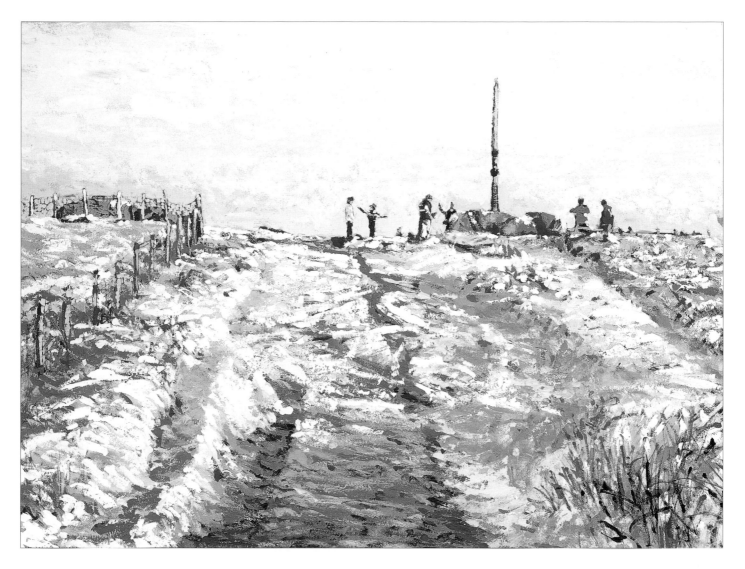

The view from here ▲
The lines of the fence and furrows
in the snow curve inwards, leading our
eye to the focal point of the image,
which is placed on the third.

River Laune, Ring of Kerry ▶
The main interest is in the rolling hills
and sinuous curve of the river. Note
how the sky is reduced to a relatively
small sliver near the top of the frame.

Tip: Use a full range of techniques
to suggest different surface textures.
• When working in impasto, incorporate
plenty of direction strokes to help
the eyes read the shape of the thing
being painted.
• Use a degree of artistic licence to
improve a scene by leaving things out or
even by adding elements that are not
there in reality.

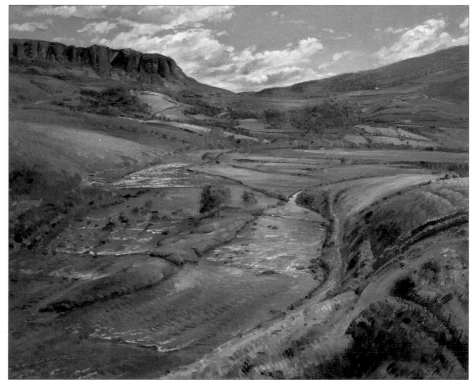

Stormy sky

Although the small strip of land and the high-rise buildings at the base of this picture provide an essential calm, static point on which the viewer's eye can rest, the main interest undoubtedly lies in the dramatic and bleak, stormy sky, with its dark, billowing clouds and the warm glow of the setting sun shining through them.

When you are painting clouds, remember that you need to make them look like solid, three-dimensional objects, not mere wisps drifting across the sky. You should also follow the rules of perspective and make clouds that are far away smaller than those that are directly overhead.

For this project use acrylic paint thinly, flooding the paper with generous washes of dilute colour. The aim is to create an impressionistic scene, with no hard edges to the clouds and very little detail in the buildings. Let the paint do as much of the work for you as possible, such as puddling at the base of damp areas to form darker tones at the base of the clouds. Soften paint edges by dabbing off any excess with a paper towel.

Materials
- *Watercolour board*
- *Acrylic paints: cerulean blue, alizarin crimson, burnt sienna, ultramarine blue, lemon yellow, titanium white*
- *Brushes: large round, medium flat*
- *Household plant sprayer*
- *Flow improver*
- *Absorbent paper towel*

The scene
The warm glow of an evening sunset contrasts dramatically with the glowering purple of the storm clouds in this scene. Note the complementary colours – purple and yellow – which almost always work well together. Although the silhouetted buildings along the skyline occupy only a small part of the picture area, they are critical in giving a sense of scale to the image.

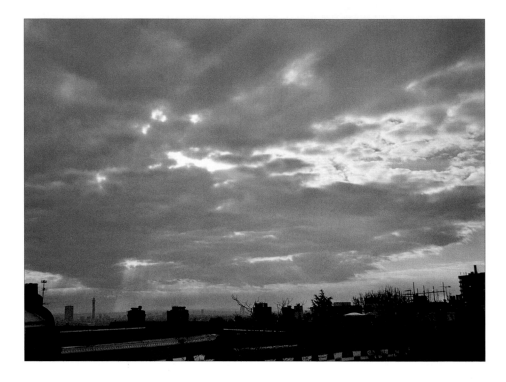

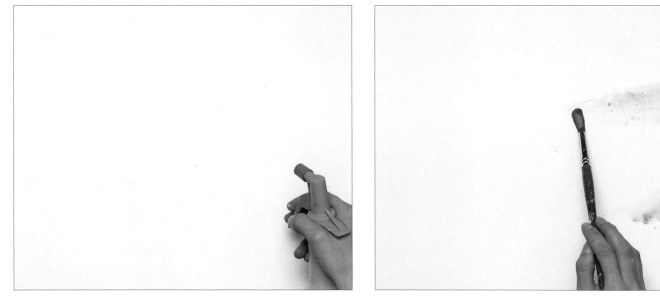

1 Using a household plant sprayer, spray clean water on to the board over the areas that you want to remain predominantly blue. (You could brush on water – but the spray gives a more random, less controlled coverage.)

2 Mix a few drops of flow improver into cerulean blue paint. Using a large round brush, drop the paint into the areas that you dampened in Step 1; it will spread and blur to give a soft spread of colour.

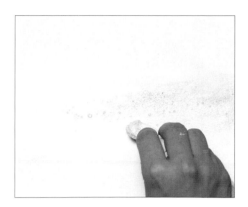

3 Scrunch up a piece of clean paper towel in your hand and dab it on to the blue paint to soften the edges.

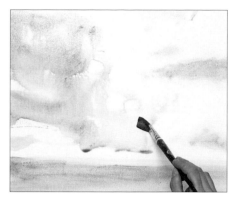

4 Mix a warm purplish blue from cerulean blue and alizarin crimson. and brush it over the land area at the base of the image with the large round brush. Mix a neutral purplish grey from burnt sienna and ultramarine blue. Spray clean water over the left-hand side of the painting and quickly drop in the neutral colour, allowing the paint to pool at the base of the damp area, as storm clouds are darker at their base.

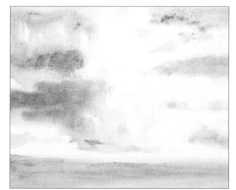

5 Soften the edges of the clouds by dabbing them with a paper towel, as in Step 3. While the paint is still damp, dot in more of the dark mixture in the top right of the painting.

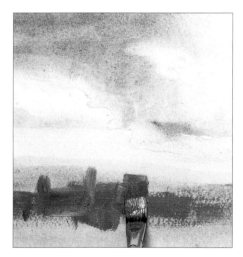

6 Using a watery version of the neutral purplish grey mixture from Step 4, brush in a dark line above the purplish base, adding more burnt sienna nearer the horizon to warm up the tones. Allow the paint to dry. Mix a warm purple from burnt sienna and ultramarine blue and, using a medium flat brush, make broad, rectangular-shaped strokes for the high-rise buildings along the horizon line, varying the tones so that the nearer buildings are slightly darker than those that are further away. Use strokes of different thicknesses to create a natural-looking variation in the shapes and sizes of the buildings.

Assessment time
You have now established the basic framework of the image and the main areas of colour – the blue of the open patches of sky, the dark storm clouds that dominate the scene, and the thin sliver of land with its high-rise buildings at the base. However, for the painting to look convincing, the clouds should be made more three-dimensional.

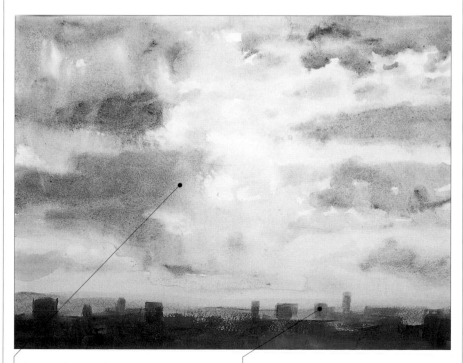

The clouds are soft-edged but do not appear to have volume.

Varying the tones of the buildings helps to create a sense of recession.

▶

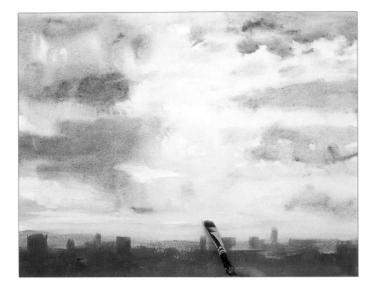

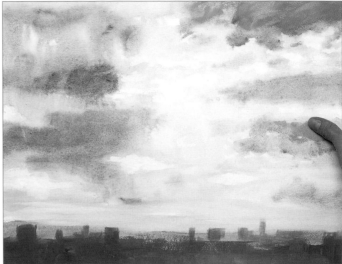

7 Mix a pale but warm, yellowy orange from lemon yellow, titanium white and a little burnt sienna. Brush this mixture into the breaks between the clouds, making horizontal brushstrokes that echo the direction in which the clouds are being blown in order to create a sense of movement in the sky. This adds warmth to the horizon and makes the dark storm clouds stand out all the more dramatically.

8 Continue adding this warm yellowy orange, adding more burnt sienna to the mixture as you get nearer the horizon; the sun is sinking, so the colours are warmer nearer the horizon. Mix an opaque blue from cerulean blue and titanium white, and brush this mixture over the top of the sky, smudging the paint with your thumb to soften the edges and get rid of any obvious brushstrokes.

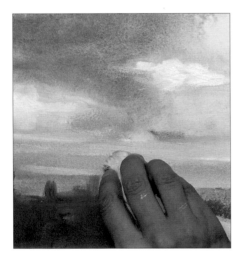

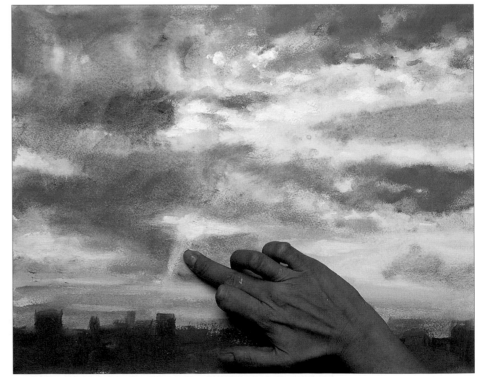

9 Dip a small piece of paper towel into the warm purple mixture that you used in Step 6 and squeeze out any excess moisture. Lightly stroke the paper towel over the yellow area just above the horizon to create streaks of storm cloud.

Tip: You could apply the paint with a rag or a sponge instead of a piece of paper towel. All these tools create a more random, spontaneous-looking effect than a brush and are very appropriate for a natural scene such as this.

10 Dab light opaque blue into the very dark area at the top of the picture, using your fingertips. Mix a purple from cerulean blue and burnt sienna and swirl it around the light area in the centre of the paper to darken it and give the clouds more of a feeling of depth. Mix a pale, warm yellow from burnt sienna, lemon yellow and titanium white and stroke on shafts of light coming down from the clouds with your fingertips. Using a flat brush, block in the shapes of the nearest buildings on the skyline; using warmer, darker tones in this area will make these buildings look closer to the viewer.

The finished painting

This is a convincing representation of a stormy sky at dusk. The colours are allowed to spread on damp paper and pool naturally, creating soft-edged shapes that are darker at their base and thus appear to have volume. Although the colour palette is limited and based mainly around the complementary colours of purple and yellow, the clever use of different tones of purple in the buildings at the base of the image creates a sense of recession.

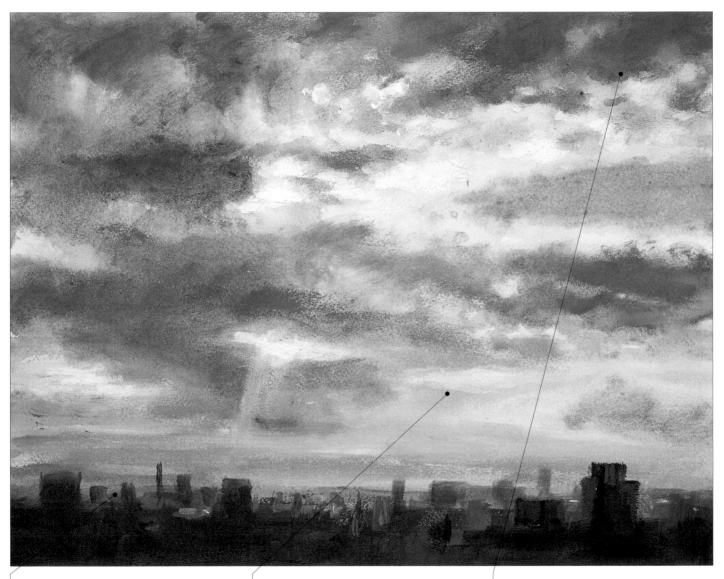

The silhouettes of the buildings along the skyline are painted as simple rectangles of colour, exploiting the natural shape of the flat brush.

Purple and yellow are complementary colours and almost always work well together. Here, they create a warm-toned yet dramatic-looking composition.

There are no harsh-edged colours in the sky – dabbing the wet paint with a paper towel helps to remove any potentially distracting brushmarks.

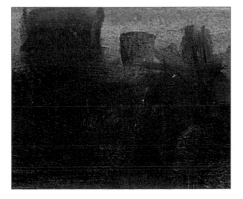

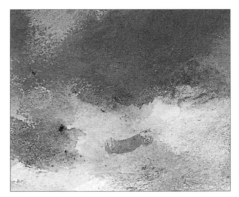

Rocky landscape

This is a dramatic and impressive vista of rocky outcrops surrounded by open moorland, which falls away rapidly to the sunlit landscape below.

The scene covers a wide area and there are lots of things to hold your attention – but don't allow yourself to get too caught up in the detail. Think instead about the general characteristics – hard rocks next to soft, springy vegetation, deeply shaded areas such as the side of the rock that is facing us versus brightly lit sections such as the fields.

There are also lots of different colours, from the muted grey of the rocks and the purple heather to the bright blue of the sky. You may find that it helps to half-close your eyes when you look at the scene, as this will help you to see it in terms of blocks of colour rather than as a landscape that consists of many different individual elements.

There are several things to bear in mind when trying to convey a sense of scale and distance. First, the further away things are, the smaller they look. Note the crag in the middle distance, for example: it's actually about the same height as the foreground crag, but because it's quite a long way away, we perceive it as being smaller.

Colour plays a part in this, too: generally, things that are further away appear paler in tone, so remember to make your colours paler as you move towards the horizon.

Finally, foreground elements should contain more detail and texture than those in the background.

Gouache is an interesting choice of medium for a scene like this. The slightly chalky nature of the paint makes the shaded rocks look almost hazy, as if our vision is affected by the bright sunlight that is streaming in from the right. At the same time, the opacity and covering power of gouache enable you to paint very precise, crisp highlights without any of the underlying colour showing through.

Finally, toning the ground a bright yellow, as the artist has done here, means that you begin your painting from a warm mid-tone, which sets the overall colour temperature of the sunlit scene and contributes to the mood of the painting.

Materials
- *Illustration board*
- *B pencil*
- *Gouache paints: cadmium yellow deep, cadmium orange, cadmium red, phthalocyanine blue, spectrum violet, cerulean blue, permanent white, Naples yellow*
- *Brushes: large wash, small round, large round bristle*
- *Rag or absorbent kitchen paper*

The scene
There are many interesting textures to paint in a scene such as this, from the springy heather that covers much of the ground, to the hard gritstone rocks. The lighting is important, too: note how the contrast between light and shaded areas helps to convey the direction of the light and makes what might otherwise seem like flat areas of vegetation appear three-dimensional.

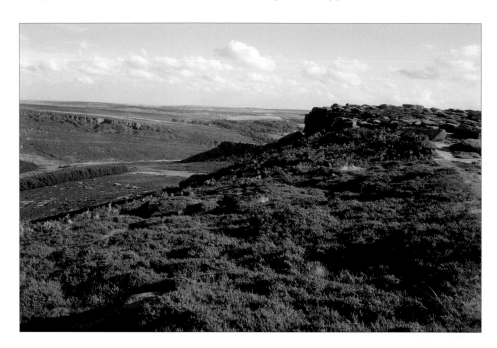

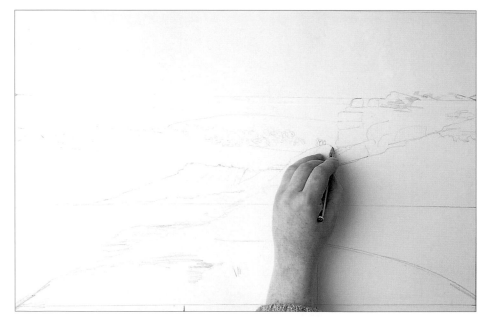

1 Using a B pencil, make a light underdrawing of the main elements of the scene, indicating the outline of the rocky outcrops. Make a series of flowing pencil strokes across the foreground to indicate shading within the moorland vegetation.

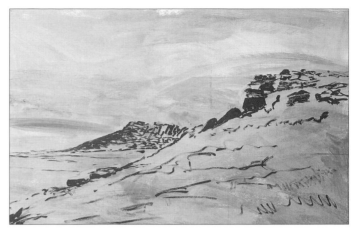

2 Mix a generous wash of cadmium yellow deep gouache paint and another one of cadmium orange. Using a large wash brush, loosely wash cadmium yellow deep over the whole of the paper. While the first wash is still slightly damp, brush cadmium orange over the bottom right of the painting – the rocky outcrop in the foreground. Leave to dry. The colour is uneven but it provides a lovely warm, toned ground on which you can develop your painting.

3 Mix a dark purple from cadmium red, phthalocyanine blue and spectrum violet. Using a small round brush loaded with very little paint, brush the mixture over the pencil marks made in Step 1. Holding the brush almost vertically, make short, spiky strokes for clumps of grass in the foreground and longer, calligraphic strokes on the rocky outcrop in the background. Block in the rocky outcrop in the foreground.

Tip: The use of a dark, solid colour (as an underpainted colour) on the large rocky outcrop in the foreground makes it appear closer to the viewer.

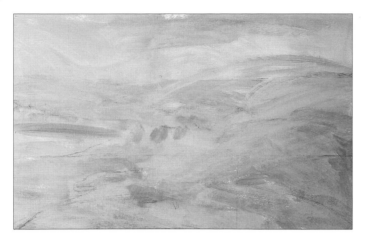

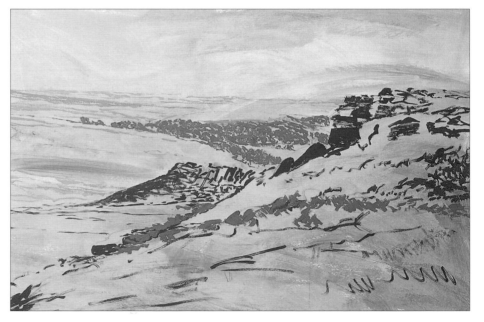

4 Mix a mid-toned greyish blue from cerulean blue, permanent white and cadmium orange. Using a small round brush again, brush in the horizon line and broken horizontal strokes to the left of the second outcrop of rock. You are starting to establish the undulating bands of vegetation that run across the scene. The use of a cool colour here helps to convey a sense of distance.

5 Now mix a dark green from phthalocyanine blue, cadmium yellow deep and a little of the purple mixture from Step 3. Using a small round brush, dab this mixture on loosely to create a triangular wedge of green for the wooded area in the middle distance, allowing the underlying colour to show through. Dab the same colour across the foreground hill.

Tip: Whenever you are painting vegetation, make your brushstrokes follow the natural direction of growth: use short, vertical brushstrokes for the trees in this scene.

▶

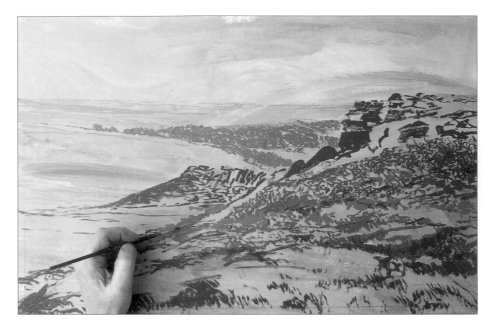

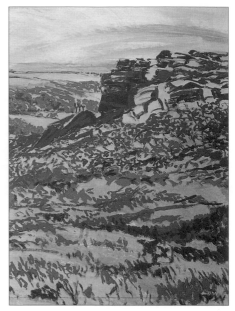

6 Continue dabbing on green and the purple mixture from Step 3, as in the previous step, in order to build up texture in the vegetation.

> **Tip**: Don't attempt to place each stroke precisely. Your aim should be to build up a general impression of loose, scrub-like plants rather than a botanically accurate rendition.

7 Using the purple mixture again, but varying the proportions of the colours in the mixture, block in the rocky outcrops, using vertical brushstrokes of varying lengths and widths and allowing some of the underlying rock colour to show through for the lighter-coloured rocks.

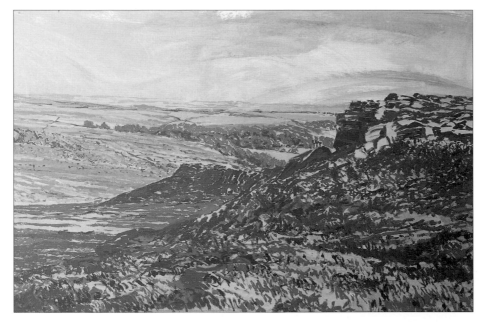

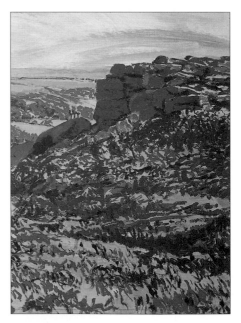

8 Continue darkening the colour of the foreground vegetation, using the same mixtures as before. Add permanent white to the purple mixture to lighten it and make it more opaque, and brush small horizontal strokes over the low-lying area beyond the second outcrop. This establishes the colour of the main vegetation in this area – the flowering heather. The area is so far away that the general colour is sufficient: there is no need to put in lots of textural detail.

9 Add more permanent white and a little phthalocyanine blue to the opaque purple mixture from step 8 and dab it over the shaded areas of the foreground rocky outcrop, allowing some of the underlying colour to show through. This helps to create the texture of the rocks, which have cracks and crevices running through them.

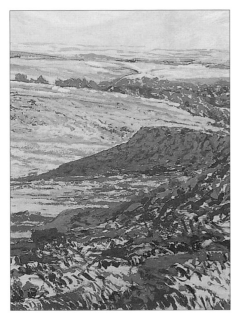

10 Mix a bright green from cadmium yellow deep and phthalocyanine blue. Brush small horizontal strokes of the mixture over the low-lying, sunlit fields in the background.

Assessment time
The contrast between the shaded and sunlit parts of the image is now becoming more apparent and the scene is taking on a convincing sense of depth and perspective. Note, in particular, how toning the ground yellow has imparted a warm glow to the sunlit areas.

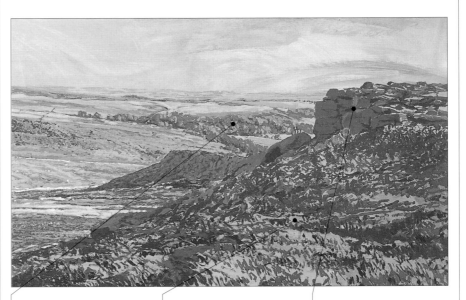

This bright green nestles between the two rocky outcrops and draws our eye to them.

The yellow in this area looks unnatural but gives a warm glow to this sunlit area.

The rocks are beginning to take form, but will require more texture if they are to look convincing.

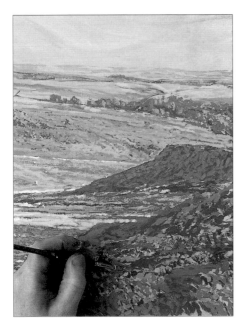

11 Mix a brownish pink from cadmium red, permanent white, Naples yellow and spectrum violet and dot and dab it over the foreground vegetation. As before, your aim is to create a general impression of the small, scrubby plants.

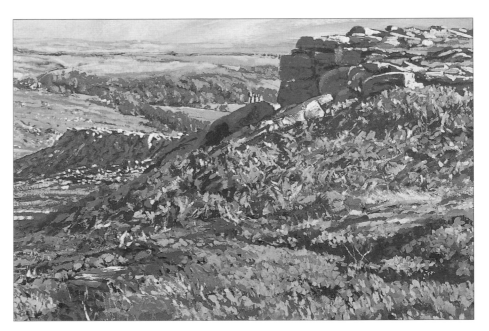

12 Using a small round brush, apply short strokes of permanent white and a little cadmium yellow deep to highlight areas of the rocks. This emphasizes the structure of the rocks, which have very distinct facets.

Tip: Permanent white gouache has good covering power, which makes it ideal for painting opaque highlights.

▶

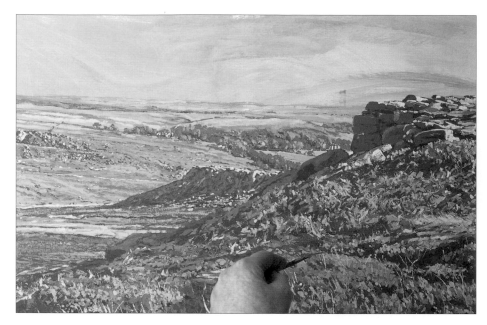

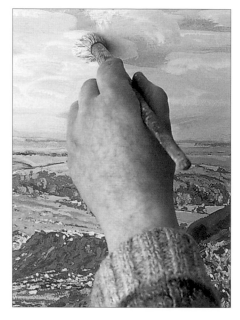

13 Continue to build up texture in the vegetation. Using a small, almost dry round brush loaded with permanent white paint, make a series of light vertical brushstrokes over the foreground to imply gently the taller grasses among the heather. Foreground texture is one of a number of ways in which the artist can imply that such areas are physically closer to the viewer.

14 Using a large round bristle brush, scumble dilute permanent white over the sky. Although gouache is opaque, the fact you are using a dilute mixture means that the white is slightly modified by the underlying yellow, which will give the impression of warm afternoon sunlight in the sky.

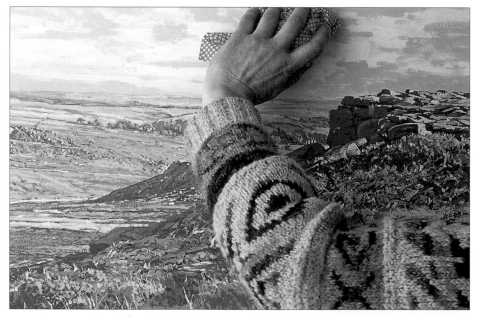

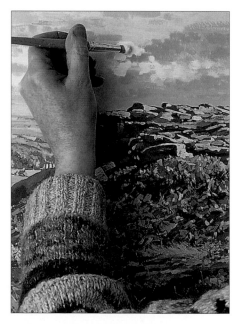

15 Mix a bright blue from cerulean blue and permanent white and brush it loosely over the sky, leaving some white shapes for clouds. Skies are never uniform in colour because of the effects of light, so darken the mixture by adding a tiny amount of cadmium red and put in a few strokes of this colour here and there to create some tonal variation. While the paint is still wet, gently dab a clean cloth or a piece of absorbent kitchen paper over the sky to soften the brushstrokes and blend the colours together on the support, so that the transition from one tone to the next is virtually imperceptible.

16 Reinforce the clouds with permanent white where necessary to make them stand out a little more dramatically, remembering to make them smaller as they recede towards the horizon.

The finished painting

Repeat the previous two steps if necessary to build up more colour in the sky. This is a strong and dramatic landscape that exploits the characteristics of gouache to the full. Wet-into-wet applications of paint in the sky create soft-edged cloud formations, giving a sense of movement that is counter-balanced by the solidity of the rocky landscape below. Texture in the vegetation is achieved through drybrush work and short brushstrokes. The natural opacity and chalky nature of gouache paint can be seen in the way the artist has painted the rocks, which look convincingly three-dimensional.

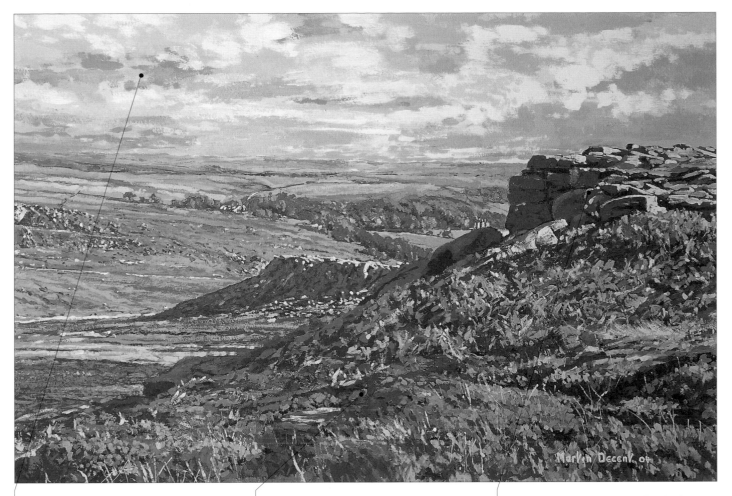

Note how darker tones are used for the undersides of the clouds, which are in shade. Clouds, just like any other feature of the landscape, are three-dimensional and it is important to give them volume.

Texture is a feature of this painting. The artist has used drybrush work and small dabs and dots of paint to create a convincing impression of the scrubby moorland vegetation.

Bright highlights are achieved with short strokes of opaque permanent white, while the shaded sides of the rocks are painted in an appropriately dull, chalky mixture of purplish grey.

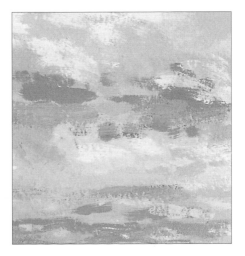

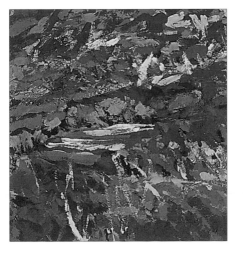

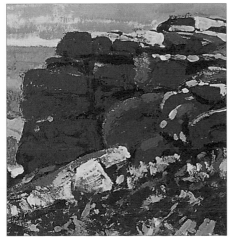

Sunlit beach

This simple-looking scene of an almost deserted beach on a bright summer's day gives you the chance to paint two of nature's most fascinating subjects – moving water and sparkling sunlight.

Painting the sea is an interesting challenge: how can you capture the constant ebb and flow of the water? As always, the more time you spend observing the scene the better. Although the movement of the waves may seem random, if you stand still and watch for a while you will soon see a pattern. Look at the shapes that the waves make as they roll in towards the shore and try to fix them in your mind.

One of the risks of painting in bright sunshine is that your eyes can be dazzled by the intensity of the light, with the result that you tend to make the scene too high-key. Instead of capturing the brightness of the scene, as you expected, you will find that your painting simply looks bleached out. Look for tonal contrasts within the scene and balance bright areas with dark, cooler shadows. The dark passages will have the effect of making the light areas look even brighter.

When painting highlights, don't try to put in every single one or your work will look overly fussy. Half-close your eyes: this reduces the glare, enabling you to break down the pattern of light more easily and put in just the key highlight areas.

Finally there is the question of how to paint the sky. If you're painting *en plein air* and the clouds appear to be fleeting, you may want to put them down quickly to capture the effects, whereas with a relatively static scene, you might concentrate on the land first. But remember that clouds have volume: look for the lights and darks within them to make them look three-dimensional.

Materials
- *Stretched and primed canvas*
- *Oil paints: olive green, cobalt blue, titanium white, alizarin crimson, cerulean blue, burnt umber, Indian yellow, cadmium red, black, lemon yellow*
- *Turpentine*
- *Brushes: small filbert brush, selection of small hogshair and sables*

The scene
The tide has receded, leaving shallow inlets illuminated by bright sunlight and large areas of exposed sand – an interesting contrast of colours and textures.

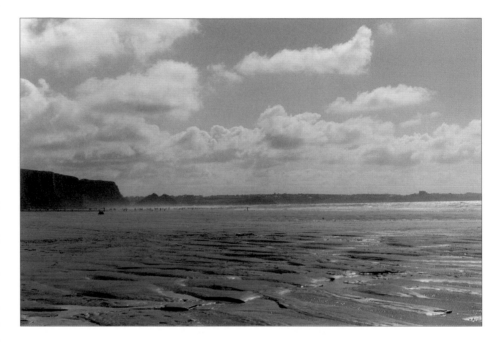

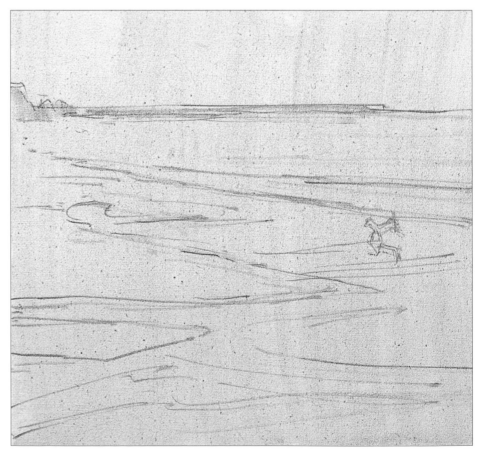

1 Using a thin mix of olive green, 'draw' the cliffs on the horizon, the lines of the waves and the little channels. At the outset the artist decided to add a small dog to the scene to focus the viewer's attention. Add its outline and shadow now.

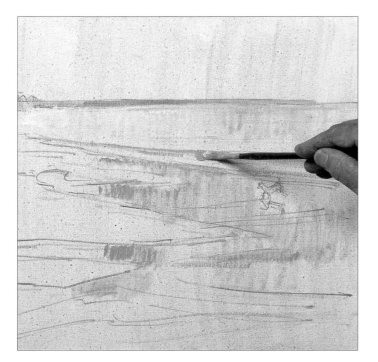

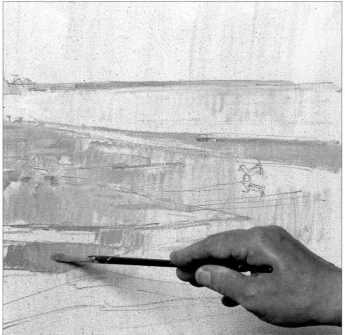

2 Mix a bright, light blue from cobalt blue and titanium white. Using a small filbert brush, loosely scumble the mixture over the shallow areas of water in the foreground of the scene. Add a little alizarin crimson to the mixture to make it slightly more purple in tone, and brush in the line of cliffs along the horizon in the background. Mix a paler blue from cerulean blue and titanium white and use this mixture for the most distant area of sea.

3 Add a tiny amount of burnt umber to the purplish blue mixture from Step 2 and blend this colour, wet into wet, into the darkest parts of the sea – the undersides of the waves that roll in towards the shore. Mix a rich, dark sand colour from burnt umber and Indian yellow and scumble this mixture over the sand, blending in a few strokes of cadmium red here and there, and adding purple for the very darkest lines along the edges of the water channels.

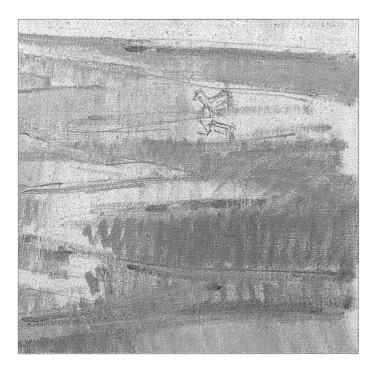

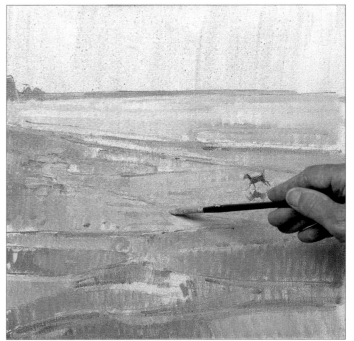

4 Add a little burnt umber to the bright blue mixture from Step 2, and scumble it over the deepest areas of the foreground water. Using short, vertical brushstrokes, loosely scumble various sand colours over the shallowest parts of the water, where the underlying sand is clearly visible.

5 Continue putting in the sand areas in the middle distance. Note that some areas are pinker and warmer than others; adjust the mixtures on your palette as appropriate. Block in the dog and its reflection in a dark mixture of olive green, black and a little burnt umber.

▶

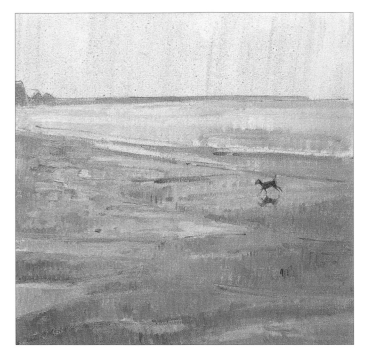

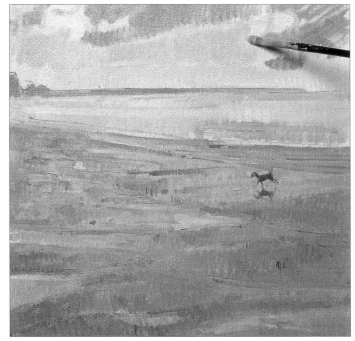

6 Continue to build up the tones in the water, using the same purplish blues as before to emphasize the darker areas. Overlay pale blue paint over the water-covered sand in the foreground, blending the vertical brushstrokes that you put down in the earlier stages to create the impression of sand seen hazily through shallow water.

7 Now start to work on the sky. Put in the clouds first, using light- and mid-toned greys mixed from burnt umber, cobalt blue and titanium white in varying proportions. Warm or cool the mixtures as necessary by adding a touch of pink or blue. Put in the bright blue of the sky using a mixture of cobalt blue and titanium white.

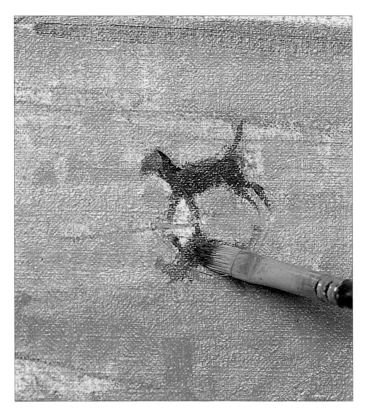

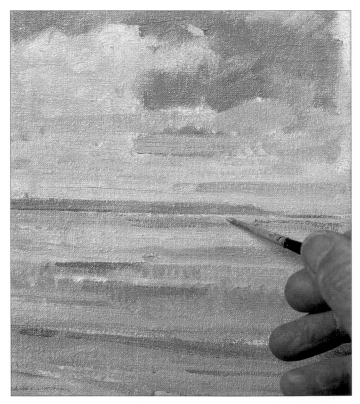

8 Use a darker version of the olive green, black and burnt umber mixture that you used in Step 5 to reinforce the shape of the dog and its reflection in the wet sand.

9 Now start to put in some of the reflected highlights on the crests of the waves, dotting in little specks of white tinged with yellow to give the impression of sunlight glancing off the surface of the water.

Assessment time
Now that the main elements and colours are in place, take time to assess the tonal balance of the painting as a whole. Although the orange of the sand and the blue of the sea are complementary colours and give the scene a lot of energy, they are both predominantly mid-tones. You need to reinforce the sense of sunlight within the scene – and, paradoxically, the way to do this is to make the dark areas darker, so that they form an effective contrast to the brightly lit parts.

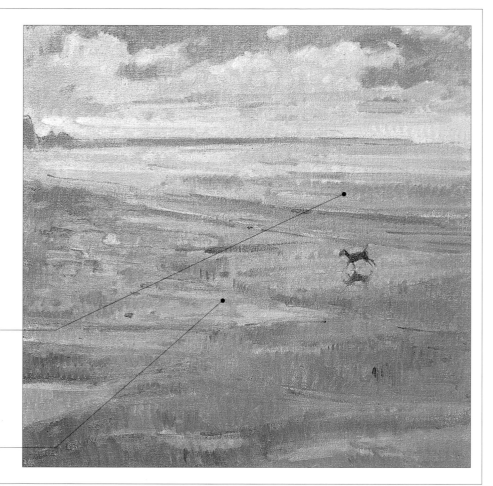

You need to create a sense of sunlight sparkling on the water.

The sand is little more than a block of colour at this stage; it needs more texture.

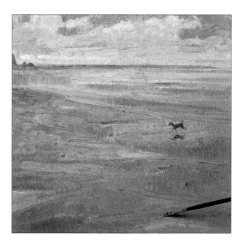

10 Darken the water channels in the foreground, using the same purples and blues as before.

Tip: Don't add any solvent to the paint for this process: using the paint straight from the tube means that it is relatively dry, so the colours do not turn muddy even though you are overlaying paint on a layer that it still wet.

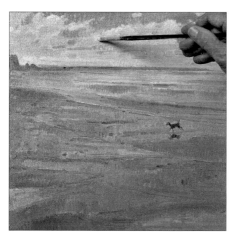

11 Touch some very pale yellow (made by mixing lemon yellow, a little Indian yellow and titanium white) into the top of the clouds to create the effect of warm sunlight.

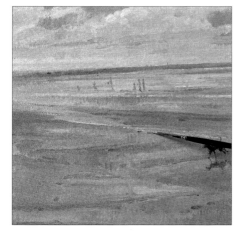

12 Look at the colours within the sea: it is by no means a uniform blue. Add a little purple to your blue mixes to put in the darkest parts of the small waves as they break on the shore. Loosely block in the figures, using a purplish blue-black. As they are silhouetted, with the sun behind them, little detail is discernible. Add a hint of yellow to titanium white and put in fine lines to create highlights on the foam-tipped wave crests.

▶

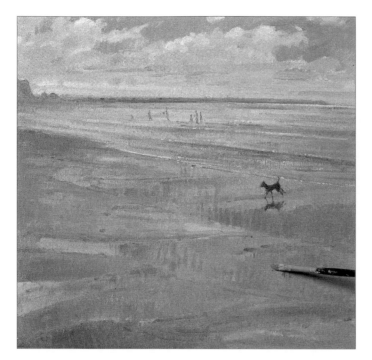

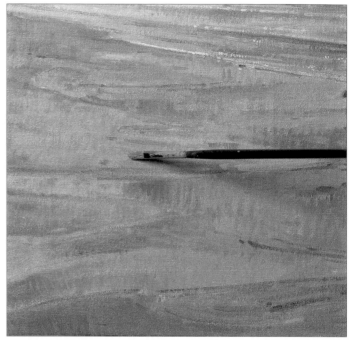

13 Continue putting lights and darks into the sea area, using small strokes and dotting in the highlights. In the deeper channels in the foreground water, use loose vertical strokes of a mid-toned blue to create the sense of light shimmering in the water. The brushstrokes will soon be blended out, but their direction is important as it helps to give the effect of sunlight glancing off the water.

14 Continue working on the foreground area, using the sand colour and blue mixes tinged with purple as appropriate. Gently and gradually blend the wet paint on the canvas and smooth out the brushstrokes.

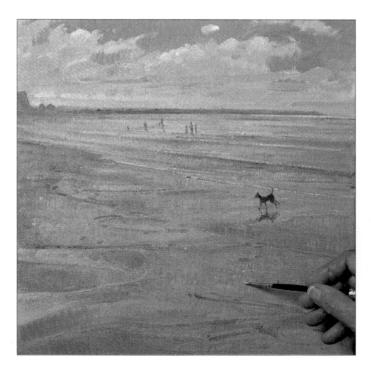

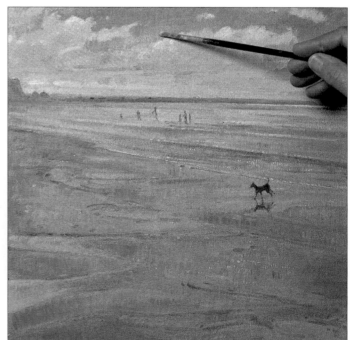

15 Create more variety and texture in the exposed sand area by dotting in other colours – a light yellow mixed from lemon yellow and white, and burnt umber lines and dots. Dot the pale yellow mixture that you used in Step 12 over the foreground to create the effect of sunlight sparkling on the water.

16 Mix a bright blue from cobalt blue and titanium white and scumble it over the top of the sky to darken it and allow the clouds to stand out more dramatically. The use of a dark colour at the top of the picture holds the viewer's eye within the frame, while the loose brushstrokes help to give an impression of movement in the sky.

The finished painting

This is an attractive painting of an almost deserted beach in summer. Lively brushstrokes convey the dark clouds scudding across the sky, and loose scumbles of colour over the water also help to convey a sense of movement. The viewpoint has been carefully chosen so that the wedge-shaped areas of sand in the foreground balance the composition and lead our eye through the painting. Although the dog and the silhouetted figures in the middle distance occupy only a small part of the scene, their position (roughly on the thirds) means that our eye is drawn to them.

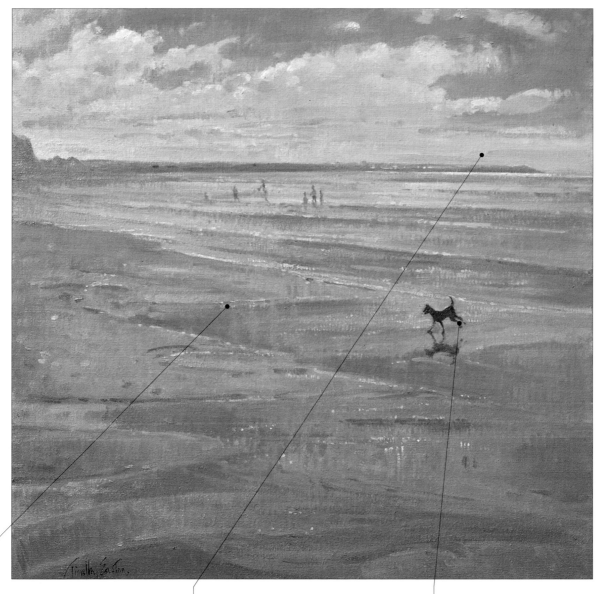

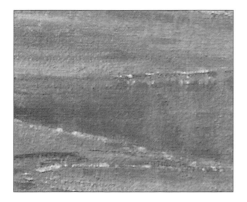

The use of complementary colours (blue and orange) imparts a sense of energy.

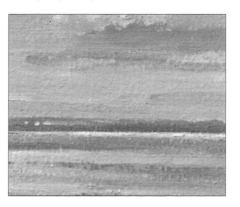

Specks of yellow create the effect of warm sunlight glancing off the water.

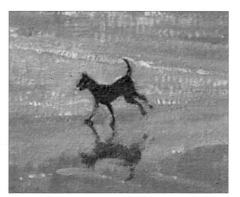

The dog occupies only a small area, but its position means that our eye is drawn to it.

Rolling hills

Sometimes when you are painting a landscape, a single element – a lone tree, a waterfall, a farm building, for example – attracts your attention; at other times, it's the sheer scale and drama of a broad panorama that draws you. In the latter case, however, it can be hard to evoke the same feeling of awe in the viewer that you felt on beholding the scene – and more often than not, the reason for this is that you have failed to provide a focal point in your image.

In the landscape shown here, gently rolling hills sweep far away into the distance in an idyllic rural setting that gives no hint of the hustle and bustle of the modern world. But even in the most rural of settings, evidence of former industries can often be seen. Although the quarries in which they were cut have long since ceased to operate, these abandoned millstones provide the artist with a focal point for his painting. Without them, the scene would look like an empty stage set, with nothing to hold the viewer's interest.

This project uses acrylic paint in a similar way to traditional watercolour, with the colours being built up gradually in thin glazes, so that each layer is modified by the underlying colours. It also incorporates a wide range of textural techniques, from drybrush work to less conventional methods such as pressing bubble wrap into the paint and dabbing on paint with your fingertips. There is no "right" or "wrong" way to apply paint to the support: use whatever tools you have to hand to create the effect you want.

Materials
- Card primed with acrylic primer
- B pencil
- Acrylic paints: cadmium yellow, cadmium red, phthalocyanine blue, burnt umber, magenta, titanium white, cobalt blue, cerulean blue
- Brushes: medium round, small round
- Rag
- Bubble wrap

1 Using a B pencil, make a light underdrawing of the scene, taking care to get the ellipses and angles of the millstones right.

The scene
The millstones are the focal point of the painting. Note how they form a rough triangle, positioned just off centre at the base of the image, leading the viewer's eye up the line of the hill and back down again to the foreground. When you paint a scene like this, make sure you spend time selecting the best viewpoint.

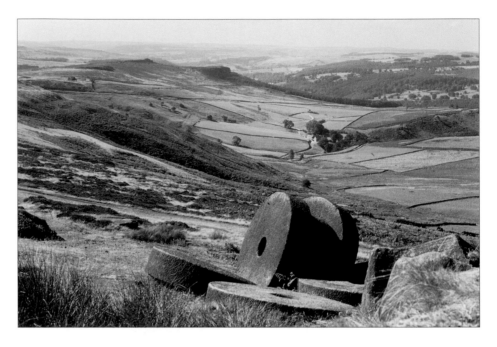

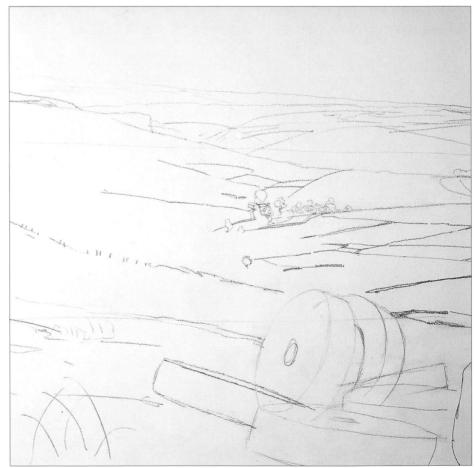

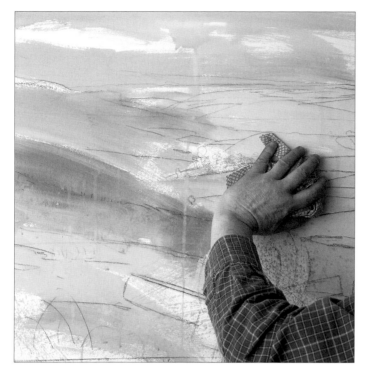

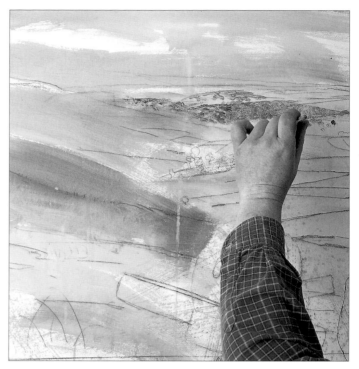

2 Using a rag, spread cadmium yellow acrylic paint straight from the tube over the support, leaving a few gaps in the sky area for clouds. Drop a little cadmium red over the centre left of the image and blend it into the yellow paint with the rag so that the two colours merge on the support, creating an orange, wedge-like shape. Leave to dry.

3 Mix a dark green from cadmium yellow and phthalo-cyanine blue. Using a medium round brush, scumble the mixture over the wooded hillside in the middle distance to give a generalized impression of trees. While the first green is still damp, add a little more blue to the mixture and dot this in for the darkest areas of green.

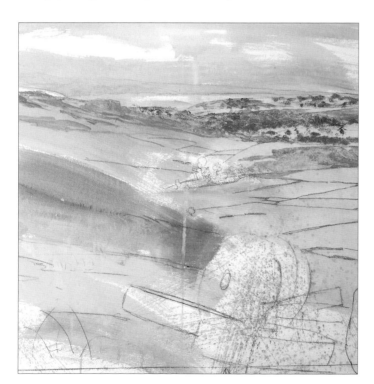

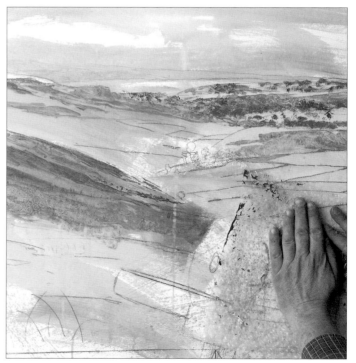

4 Mix a dull but warm orange from cadmium yellow, cadmium red and a little burnt umber and brush it over the distant escarpment on the left of the image and over the fields in front of the wood. The warm colour helps to bring this area forwards in the image.

5 Using a medium round brush, apply a thin glaze of magenta in a broad stroke over the slope of the hill on the left. Add a little phthalocyanine blue to the mixture and paint the crest of the escarpment behind it. While the paint is still wet, gently press bubble wrap into it to create some texture.

▶

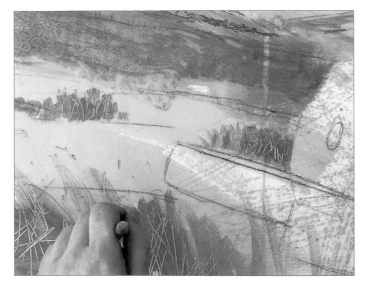

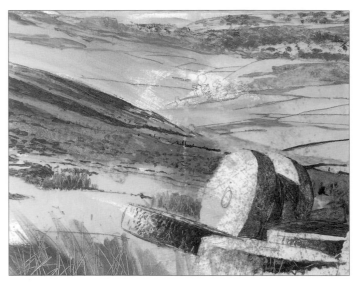

6 Add a little burnt umber to the dark orange mixture from Step 4 and brush it loosely over the bottom left corner of the painting. While the paint is still wet, lift off some of the colour by "drawing" the shapes of grass stems with the tip of a paintbrush.

7 Darken the hillside, using the same colours as in Step 5. Press bubble wrap into burnt umber paint and then press the bubble wrap across the bands of orange and magenta on the left to create loose, textured dots that echo the growth pattern of the vegetation. Paint the fence posts using a dark, reddish brown mixed from phthalocyanine blue and burnt umber. Mix a dark purple from cadmium red and phthalocyanine blue and brush it over the shaded sides of the mill-stones. For the darkest stones, use phthalocyanine blue.

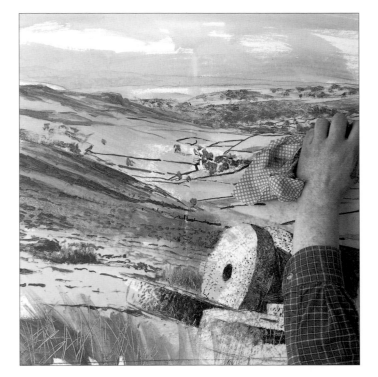

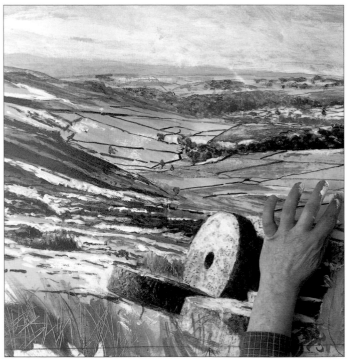

8 Dot in the shapes of the isolated trees in the middle distance, using the same dark orange that you used to paint the fields. Following your initial pencil marks, mark out the field boundaries in burnt umber. Roughly block in the buildings in the middle distance in magenta. Brush a broad sweep of magenta over the hill to the right of the buildings and wipe a rag over it to blur the colour.

9 Brush titanium white over the sky area, allowing a hint of the underlying yellow to show through to maintain the overall warm colour temperature of the scene. Re-establish the highlight areas on the ground by smearing on titanium white paint with your fingertips, which gives a more spontaneous-looking and random effect than applying the paint with a brush.

Assessment time

It is becoming clear which parts of the scene are in shadow and which are brightly lit, and the underlying yellows and oranges give a warm glow to the whole scene. Now you need to concentrate on putting in the greens and browns of the landscape and on building up the textures.

Note how the colours become paler in tone the further away they are.

The yellow used as a base colour on these sunlit fields will modify any glazes that are applied on top.

More texture is needed in the grasses in the immediate foreground.

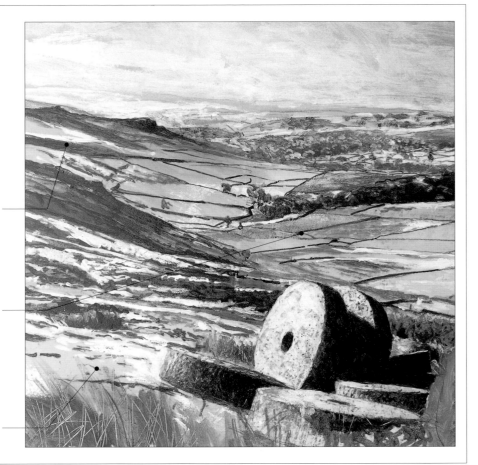

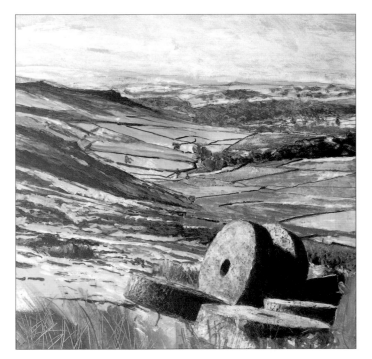

10 Reduce the starkness of the white areas by brushing over them with a thin glaze of the appropriate colour – cobalt blue over the wooded area, burnt umber over the shaded parts of the hillsides, and various yellow-orange mixtures over the sunlit fields. Note how the scene becomes more unified as a result.

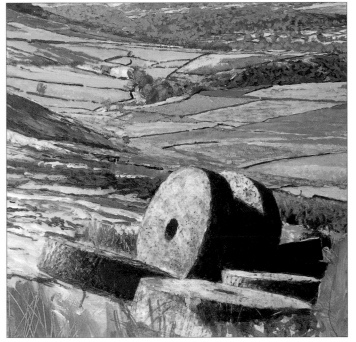

11 Mix a bright green from cadmium yellow and cerulean blue and, using a medium round brush, paint over the mostly brightly lit fields in the middle distance. Note that some of the fields contain crops, so leave the underlying orangey brown colour in these areas and take care not to go over the field boundaries.

▶

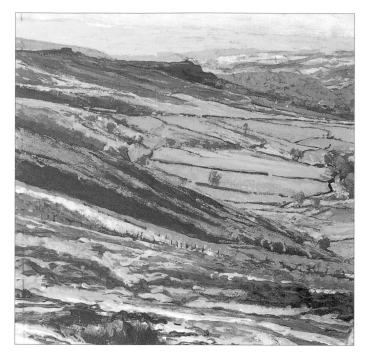

12 Add a little more titanium white to the mixture to lighten it and paint the most distant fields. Mix a neutral brown from cadmium yellow, cadmium red and phthalocyanine blue and use it to tone down the reddish areas on the hill to the left, which look too harsh.

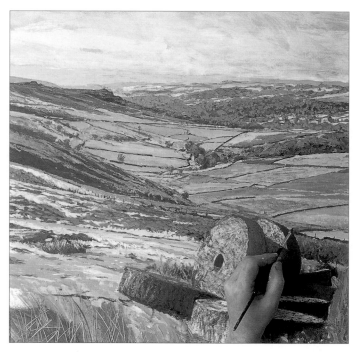

13 Mix a slightly darker green from cadmium yellow and phthalocyanine blue and paint the green grass in the immediate foreground. The use of a darker tone pulls this area forwards and makes it seem closer to the viewer. The shaded sides of the millstones look too red in tone and jump forwards too much. Mix a neutral brownish grey from cadmium yellow, cadmium red, cobalt blue and titanium white and paint over these areas, reinforcing the cast shadows with a slightly darker version of the same mixture.

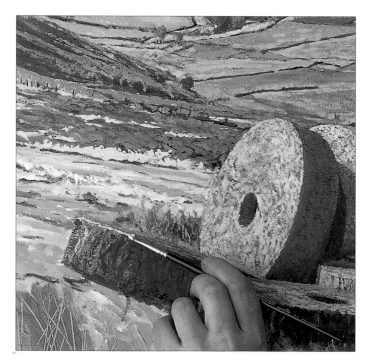

14 Using a very small round brush, paint a thin line of titanium white around the top edge of the millstone that is lying on its side, so that it appears to be rim-lit by the sun.

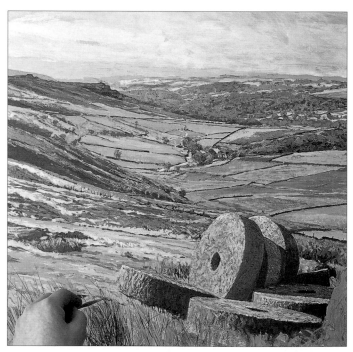

15 Using a small round brush, drybrush thin strokes of burnt umber over the foreground to the left of the millstones to add texture and create grass stems blowing in the breeze.

The finished painting

Finally, put in the sky using a bright blue mixed from cerulean blue and titanium white. This tranquil landscape simply glows with sunlight and warmth. The scene covers a wide area but the millstones in the foreground, which are positioned slightly off centre, provide a strong triangular shape at the base of

the image and a much-needed focal point. Although they occupy only a small part of the frame, the buildings in the middle distance provide a secondary point of interest, to which our eye is drawn by the gently sloping diagonal lines of the hills and fields.

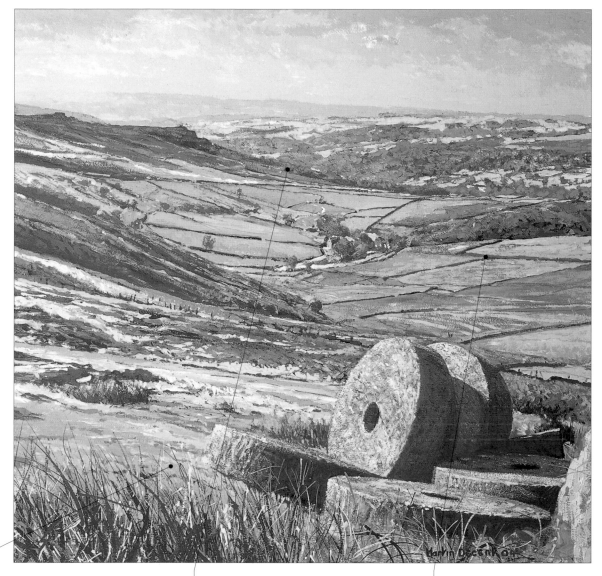

Strong textures in the foreground help to pull this area forwards and imply that it is closer to the viewer.

The sloping line of the hills leads our eye down towards the buildings, which form a secondary point of interest.

The greens and browns of the fields are modified by the underlying yellow, adding warmth to these rather subdued colours.

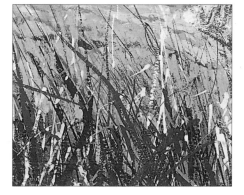

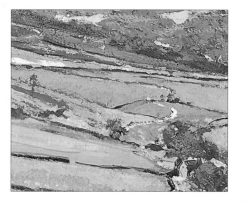

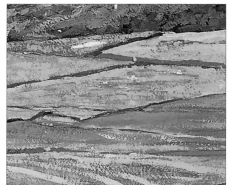

Painting still lifes

One of the advantages of painting still lifes is that all the elements are under your control: you don't have to worry about the weather or the light, your subject won't get up and walk away, and potential subjects are all around you in the form of everyday household objects. Nonetheless, planning your composition and making preliminary sketches to check you've got the balance right are absolutely vital.

In traditional still lifes there is normally some kind of thematic link between the various objects, although this is by no means essential. But do look for interesting contrasts of shape and texture. If, for example, you are painting fruit in a bowl, all of which are rounded in shape, introduce a tall, vertical element in the form of a vase in the background. Juxtapose the rough-hewn texture of a rustic wooden table with the smooth, shiny surface of glazed pottery, or the soft texture of velvet with the faceted edges of crystal. Such contrasts will add interest to your painting. Odd numbers of objects (three, five or seven) tend to look better than arrangements of even numbers.

Whatever subject you choose, the most common mistake is not to spend enough time arranging the set-up. When you've selected your subjects, move them around until you're happy with the grouping. Even very slight adjustments can have a big impact on the overall composition. Look at how the shapes overlap and at the overall balance of colours. Triangular compositions work well, as they encourage the viewer's eye to move around the picture. Placing all the elements in a straight line is rarely, if ever, successful.

Look at the spaces between the objects, too; they play an important part in the composition. If the objects are too far apart, they will look as if they don't belong together; if they are too close, the composition may look cluttered.

Another common mistake is including too many things: sometimes, as the saying goes, 'less is more'. If your set-up isn't working, try simplifying the composition by taking items away.

Keep the background simple, too. A plain-coloured wall or piece of fabric in an appropriate colour will allow your chosen objects to stand out – but don't leave too much space around the objects or the background will become too dominant.

Finally, remember to experiment with different viewpoints. It's interesting to note how different objects can look when viewed from above or below, rather than at normal eye level, making your paintings look much more dynamic.

Sweet Williams and cherries ▼
The colour of the flowers is echoed in the cherries that are randomly scattered over the table. The plain wood allows the flowers and fruit to stand out, while the diagonal planks lead our eye through the scene.

Tips: Spend time moving objects around and looking at your set-up from different viewpoints before you begin making your preliminary sketches.
• Take time to sketch a number of thumbnails in order to establish the composition.
• Arrange your still lifes on a board of wood so that, once you have set it up, the entire still life can be turned in order to alter the light.
• Try creating still-life set-ups using unusual or strange-looking objects, in order to create tableaux that are exciting and fresh.

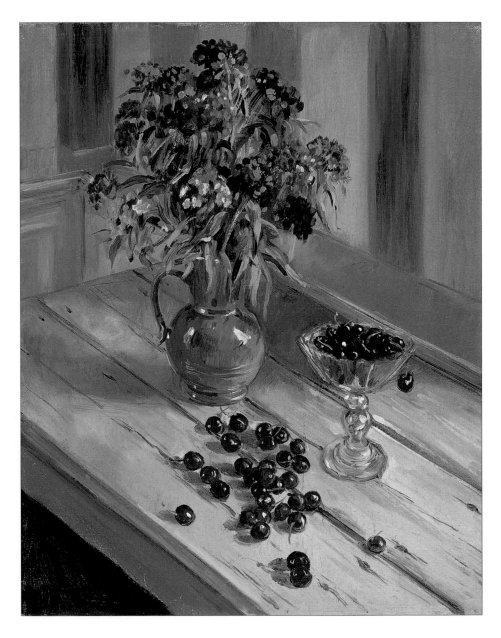

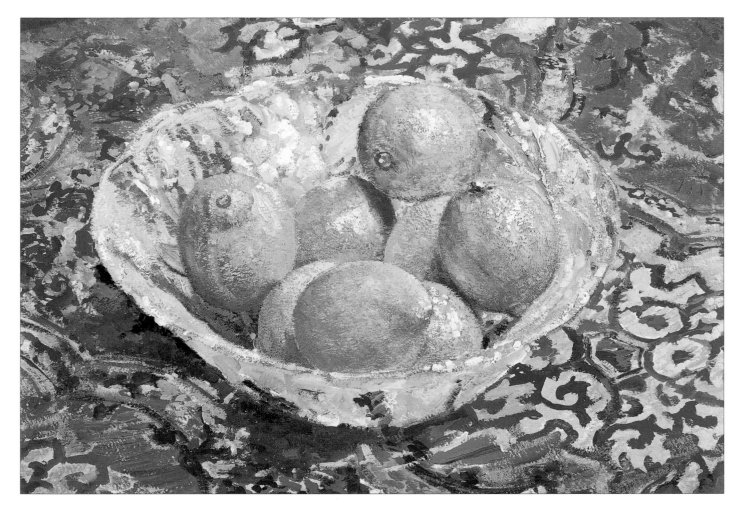

Lemons ▼

The simplest arrangements often work best. Here, lemons in an opaque glass bowl form the centrepiece of the image, their colours and shapes offset by the patterned tablecloth. Note that the bowl is not positioned in the centre of the image; there is slightly more space on the right-hand side, which prevents the image from looking bland and static.

The apple basket ▶

In this still life, in contrast to the painting shown above, the wicker basket in which the fruit are placed is highly textured and intricate. A brightly coloured background would distract, but the terracotta flagstones provide the perfect foil for both basket and fruit. The unusual viewpoint (from almost direcly overhead) enhances the feeling that the scene has been captured *en passant*.

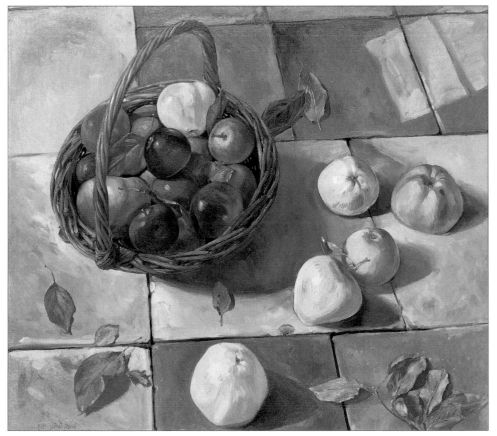

Still life with gourds

A still life does not have to be an elaborate scene in the style of the Dutch Old Masters such as Rembrandt: you can set up a scene on a corner of your table with just a few carefully chosen fruits.

Interestingly, one of the gourds in this painting is artificial – but it is virtually impossible to tell which one. Realistic-looking artificial fruits and flowers are readily obtainable from florists and craft stores and it is worth putting together a small collection of things that you can incorporate into your paintings. An added bonus is that they will not wilt or rot while you are in the process of painting them! Seashells, pieces of driftwood, pebbles and pine cones also make interesting subjects that you can pick up for free while out walking, as well as being attractive items to display around the home.

Odd numbers of objects – three, five, or seven – always seem to look more balanced in a composition than even numbers. Spend time over your arrangement: even a slight adjustment to the position of the your chosen subjects can make a substantial difference to the painting. Placing one object behind the others will give your painting more of a sense of depth: putting everything in a straight line almost always looks boring and static.

If you do not feel up to tackling a complicated background but still want to have something behind your main subject, a small piece of fabric is a good choice. Buy remnants from fabric stores in a variety of colours and patterns; they are inexpensive and don't take up much storage space.

Materials
- *2B pencil*
- *300gsm (140lb) rough watercolour paper*
- *Acrylic paints: yellow ochre, cadmium orange, Hooker's green, ultramarine blue, cadmium red, cadmium yellow, Hooker's green deep hue, titanium white, burnt sienna*
- *Brushes: wash brush, medium round brush that holds a good point*
- *Ruling drawing pen*
- *Masking fluid*
- *Paper towel*
- *Plastic painting knife*

The set-up
Before you start painting, spend time arranging the subjects you have selected for your still life and experiment with different arrangements and viewpoints until you find one that you are happy with: many amateur artists make the mistake of rushing this stage. Here, the gourds have been arranged to create interesting contrasts of scale, colour and texture. Not surprisingly, groups of three objects seem to work well in compositions that are roughly triangular in shape – and if you draw imaginary lines from the tip of the largest gourd down to the base of each of the two foreground gourds, you will see that this is what the artist has done here. The triangular shape of the composition is echoed in the way that she has chosen to drape the background fabric.

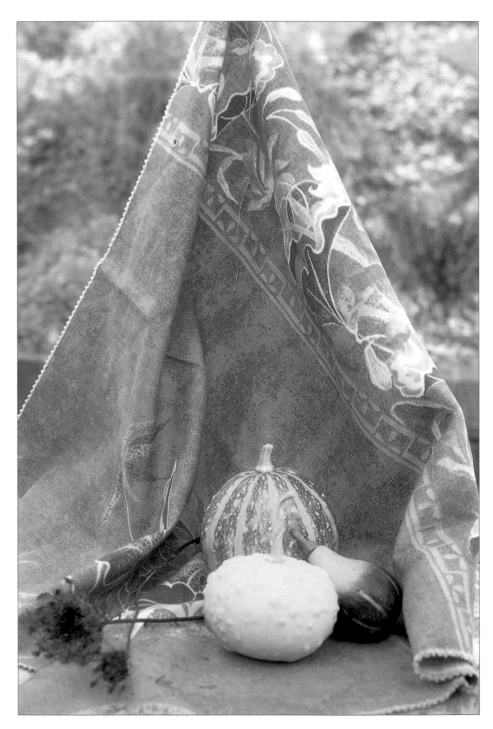

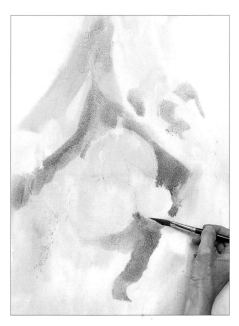

1 Using a 2B pencil, lightly sketch the still-life set-up. Put in some of the striations on the surface of the gourds, as the direction of the lines helps to show the curve of the fruits. Using a ruling drawing pen, apply masking fluid over the light-coloured patterns on the background fabric. Look at where the lines of the pattern break, as this indicates the drape of the fabric. Apply a little masking fluid over the dried cow parsley heads in the foreground, and allow it to dry completely.

2 Using a medium wash brush, wet the paper completely with clean water. Mix a pale wash of yellow ochre and brush it over the whole paper, scrubbing on cadmium orange, wet into wet, for the folds of the fabric and the gourds.

3 Mix a dark green from Hooker's green, yellow ochre and a little ultramarine blue. While the first wash is still slightly damp, start putting in the green of the background fabric around the gourds, using broad, confident brushstrokes.

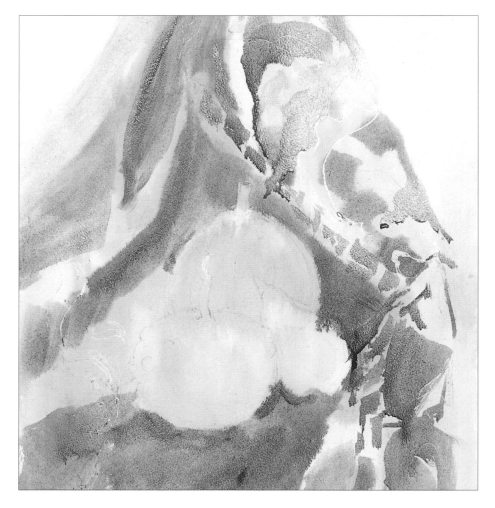

4 Continue painting the green of the background fabric, leaving the underlying yellowy orange wash showing through for the lighter parts of the fabric.

▶

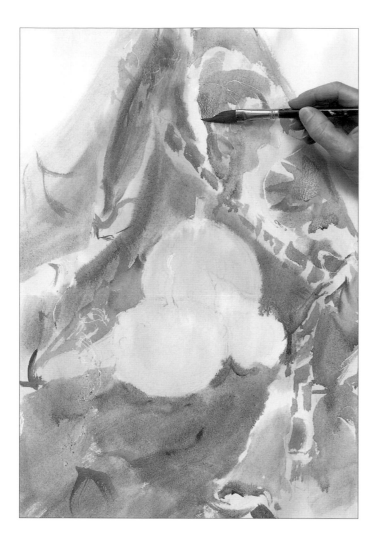

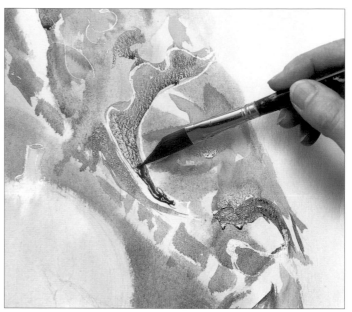

5 Mix a bright orangey red from cadmium red and a little cadmium orange. Using a medium round brush, start painting the red pattern on the fabric and some of the shadows in the background.

6 Mix a dark blue from ultramarine blue with a little Hooker's green and paint the blue pattern on the background fabric. Work quickly, with flowing brush strokes: getting the exact pattern is not important, but the curving lines enliven the painting and contrast with the solidity of the gourds in the foreground. Leave to dry.

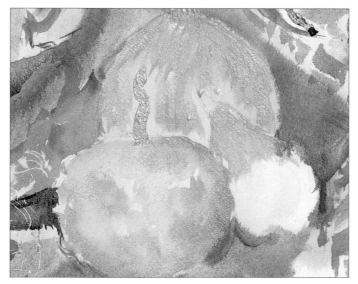

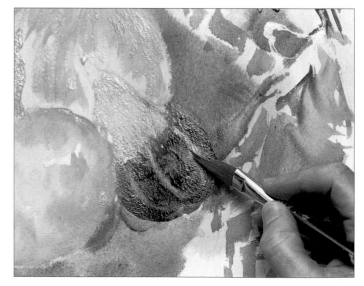

7 Now that the background is well established, you can turn your attention to the main subject – the gourds. Mix a warm orange from cadmium orange and a little cadmium yellow and brush it over the largest gourd, making sure your brushstrokes follow the striated lines on the fruit's surface. Use the same colour on the top half of the smallest gourd, and stipple yellow ochre on to the rounded gourd, which has a bumpy surface texture.

8 Mix a thick, bluey-green from Hooker's green deep and ultramarine blue and paint the base of the small gourd, working from the base upwards. As you get near the top half, brush on cadmium yellow, dragging the brush to soften the line between the two halves. Rinse the brush thoroughly. While the paint is still wet, drag the tip of the brush over the green half to lift off lines of paint and reveal the underlying yellow wash applied in Step 2.

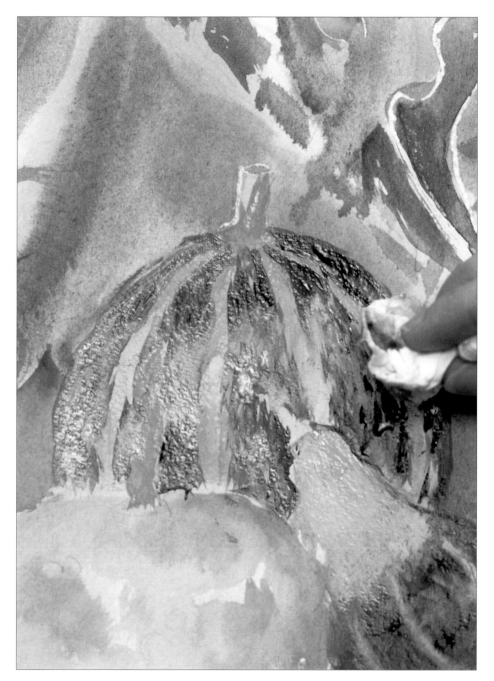

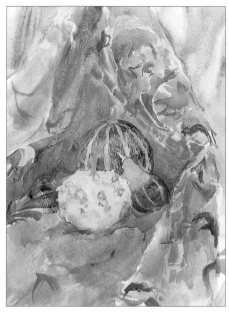

10 Mix a thick, warm yellow from cadmium yellow, titanium white and a little cadmium orange and paint the light areas on the rounded gourd in the foreground. Using the tip of the brush, dot on burnt sienna in places to indicate the bumpy surface texture. Mix ultramarine blue with titanium white and paint some of the pale, muted blues in the background fabric; loosely brush burnt sienna on to the right-hand side of the painting, outside the draped background fabric. Leave to dry.

9 Using the side of the brush, dab Hooker's green and Hooker's green deep over the largest gourd. It is not a uniform, flat colour, and alternating between the two greens helps to show up the texture. Leave broad lines of the underlying orange showing through. Outline the edge of the small foreground gourd in Hooker's green deep, so that it stands out more clearly. Dab off paint in places with a piece of paper towel to create more texture and visual interest.

Tip: Turn the paper towel around in your hand each time you press it on to the paper so that you are using a clean area and don't accidentally dab paint back on to the support.

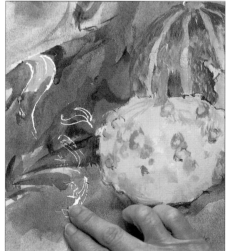

11 Using your fingertips, gently rub off the masking fluid from the cow parsley and the background fabric. Run your fingers over the surface of the painting to make sure you have removed all of the masking fluid.

▶

Assessment time
Take some time to stand back and think about what still must be done. The shapes, colours and patterns are all established, but the foreground gourd, in particular, still looks a little flat and needs to stand out more from the background.

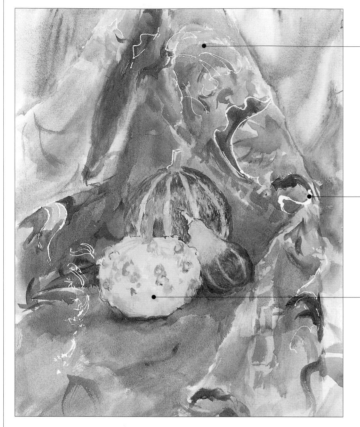

The background fabric should look more three-dimensional.

The areas protected by the masking fluid are distractingly bright.

The texture of this gourd is not as pronounced as it should be.

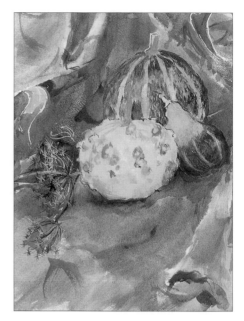

12 Mix a dark brown from burnt sienna and a tiny amount of Hooker's green deep and brush the mixture over the heads of cow parsley in the foreground. Mix cadmium orange with titanium white and, using the tip of the brush, "draw" the little florets of the dried cow parsley heads as criss-crossing, star-shaped lines. The shapes do not have to be exact; just aim to give an impression of the texture. The colour provides a visual link with the colours of the gourds and the warm orangey red of the background fabric.

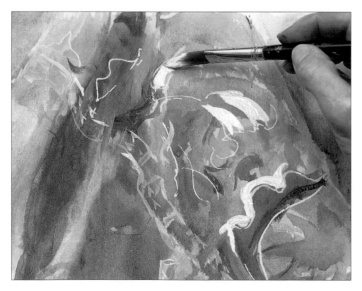

13 Mix a pale yellow from cadmium yellow and a little titanium white and brush over the exposed masking fluid lines on the background fabric. Mix a very pale blue from ultramarine blue and titanium white and paint flowing lines on the background fabric, noting how the fabric drapes.

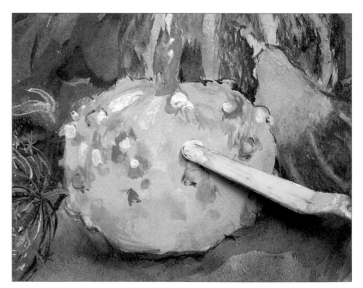

14 Using a plastic painting knife, dot blobs of the pale yellow mixture used in Step 13 over the surface of the bumpy gourd in the foreground, where the raised surfaces catch the light. This enhances the texture of the gourd and helps to make it look more three-dimensional.

The finished painting

Gourds and other autumn fruit and vegetables make attractive subjects for still lifes. Instead of painting the subject in photorealistic detail, the artist has interpreted the scene loosely, creating an animated painting that is full of swirls of colour and interesting textures. Too precise a rendering of the background fabric, in particular, could have resulted in an overly tight piece of work that lacked any sense of life.

Note the contrast between wet-on-dry paint applications on the fabric and the wet-into-wet blurs of the background.

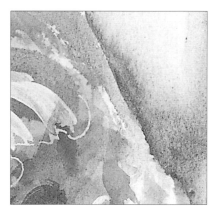

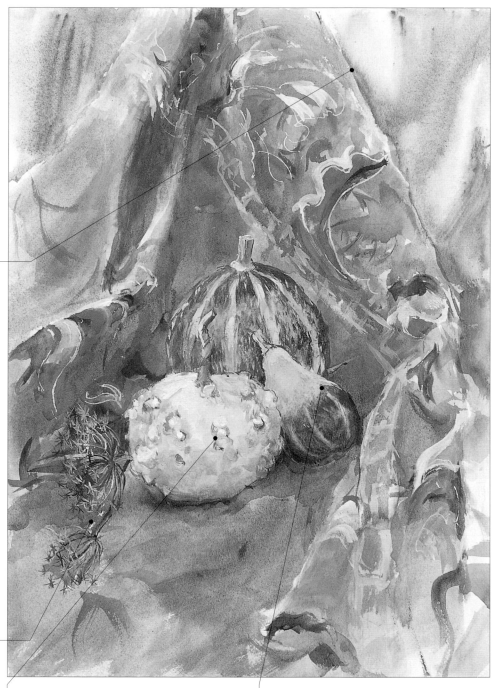

Specks of warm, bright yellow on the cow parsley help to bring it forwards in the painting.

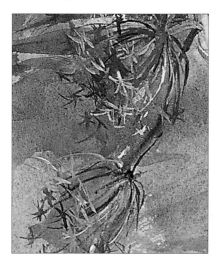

Dots of thick burnt sienna and pale yellow applied with a painting knife create the textured surface of the gourd.

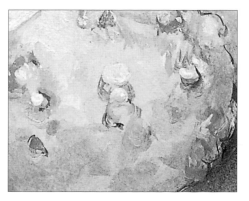

The yellow lines are created by lifting off wet paint with a damp brush or paper towel to reveal the underlying colour.

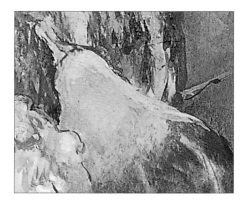

Still life with pebbles

This project is all about taking something very mundane and making a painting from it. Although we may tend to think of still lifes as being carefully controlled compositions, in which every element is deliberately placed, potential subjects are all around us. It's simply a matter of keeping your eyes open. In this project, a random arrangement of pebbles and lengths of twine in a small fishing harbour, which the artist came across quite by chance, has been transformed into a colourful painting that is full of texture and interest.

Of course, "found" still lifes still require a certain amount of input on the part of the artist. You have to decide how much of the scene to include, and where to place the edges of the painting. You may even have to move things around a little

to get the effect you want, although beware of doing too much as this can destroy the spontaneous, natural look.

In this project, the pebbles are more or less life-size. Painting a smaller subject than normal is a useful exercise, as you will have to look at things in a different way. If you often paint landscapes, for example, your initial instinct might be to scan the scene rapidly to gain an impression of the key elements; you will probably then spend time working out how best to make these elements stand out. When you concentrate on a small area, as here, every element counts: you need to slow down and look at how the different parts relate to one another in terms of their size, shape and colour, and adjust your position until you are sure you have got the

best viewpoint. At this scale, moving just one step to the left or right, backwards or forwards, can make a real difference.

Materials
- Illustration board
- B pencil
- Gouache paints: cadmium yellow deep, cadmium orange, burnt umber, phthalocyanine blue, ultramarine blue, zinc white, ivory black, cerulean blue, mid green, flame red, lemon yellow
- Brushes: large wash, old toothbrush, small round, fine round
- Rag or absorbent kitchen paper
- Small painting knife
- Acrylic gold size
- Gold leaf

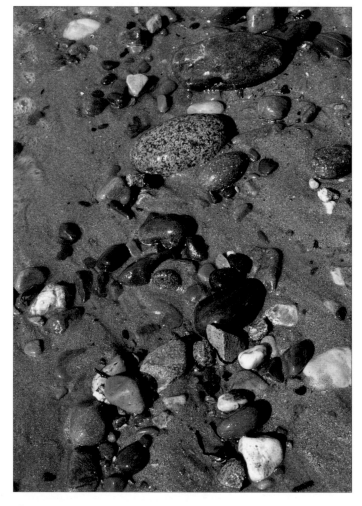

The scene
Pebbles in a harbour, glistening with water left by the retreating tide, present an interesting challenge. When painting a subject like this, look for contrasts of size and colour.

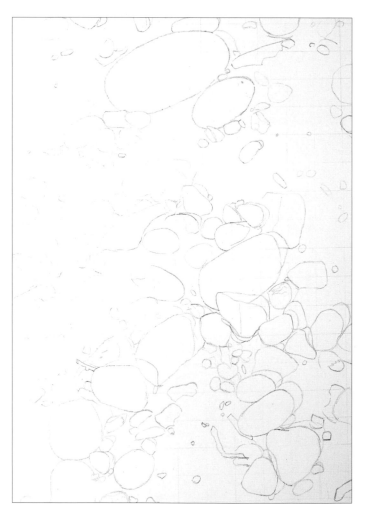

1 Using a B pencil, mark a grid of squares on your paper. Many of the pebbles are similar in size and shape, so the grid will help you to keep track of which pebble you are painting. Again using the B pencil, make a light underdrawing.

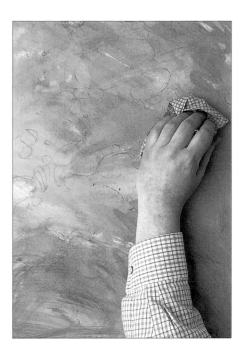

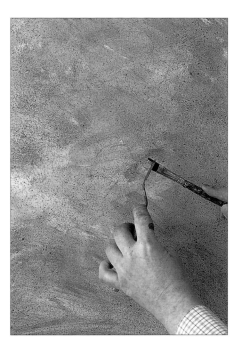

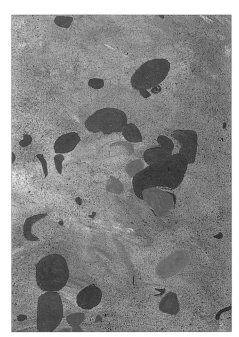

2 Mix separate washes of cadmium yellow deep and cadmium orange. Wash cadmium yellow deep over the whole paper. While it is still wet, brush in cadmium orange, leaving some areas as pure yellow. Press a clean rag or absorbent kitchen paper over the top right of the paper, to lift off some of the orange. Leave to dry.

3 Load an old toothbrush with burnt umber and any other colours that you can detect in the sand, and drag a painting knife through the bristles to spatter paint over the paper, creating a background of large-grained sand. (If you don't have a painting knife, an ordinary kitchen knife will work just as well.) Leave to dry.

4 Mix various blues and greys from phthalocyanine blue, ultramarine blue, zinc white and ivory black. Using a small round brush, begin putting in the pebbles. Note that you are simply placing the pebbles at this stage; although they look like flat circles and ovals, you will begin to build up the form later.

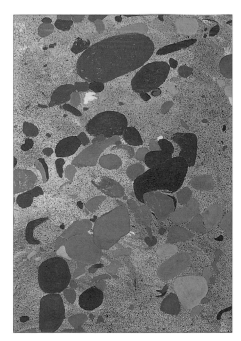

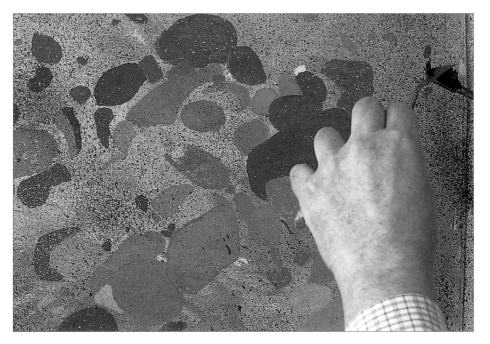

5 Continue putting in the pebbles, varying the colours. Some have a purple undertone; others have a greenish tinge, created from a base colour of mid green plus zinc white or ivory black, as appropriate. Leave to dry.

6 Load the toothbrush with cadmium yellow deep. Drag a painting knife through the bristles, as in Step 3, to spatter both the pebbles and the sand with yellow paint. Repeat the process with flame red and lemon yellow.

Tip: To get the size of the spatters right, try practising on a piece of card, holding the toothbrush at different distances from the painting.

▶

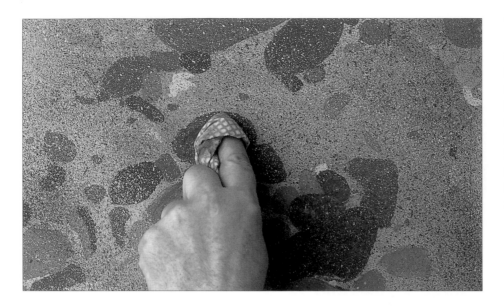

7 While the yellow spattering is still wet, drag a rag or a piece of absorbent kitchen paper over the spatters on some of the larger and darker pebbles to create streaked marks. On other pebbles, simply dab off any excess paint with a damp cloth to reveal the underlying colours, so that the spatters look like mica or other mineral crystals lodged within the stone, rather than lichen growing on top.

Assessment time

The initial blocking in of colours is complete, and the sand (which contains spatters of several different colours) looks convincingly textured, but at this stage the majority of the pebbles simply look like circles or ovals of dark colour positioned within the sand, rather than three-dimensional objects. The lighting is fairly flat and uniform, so there are no clearly defined shadows to help you, but if you look closely you will see differences in both tone and colour temperature, with the sides of the pebbles that are turned away from the light being cooler (bluer) in colour. As you complete the painting, you should concentrate on reinforcing these tonal contrasts and on giving the pebbles more texture.

Smudging wet paint over dry has created streaks of paint that provide a good basis on which to build up more texture.

The shape of the pebbles is clear, but so far they all look flat and one-dimensional.

The texture of the sand has been built up well by blending colours wet into wet and by spattering.

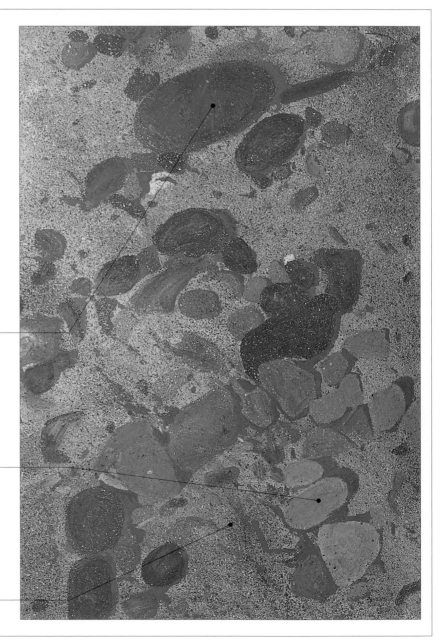

8 Mix a bright but chalky blue from cerulean blue and a little zinc white. Using a small round brush, brush this mixture over the brightest parts of any blue-grey pebbles. Mix a pale yellow from cadmium yellow deep, lemon yellow and zinc white, and a pale pink from flame red and white, and dab these mixtures over the large, pale pebble near the top of the painting, using short horizontal brushstrokes. Mix a dilute, neutral shadow colour from phthalocyanine blue and a little burnt umber. Paint the small shadows to the right of the largest pebbles; they immediately look much more three-dimensional.

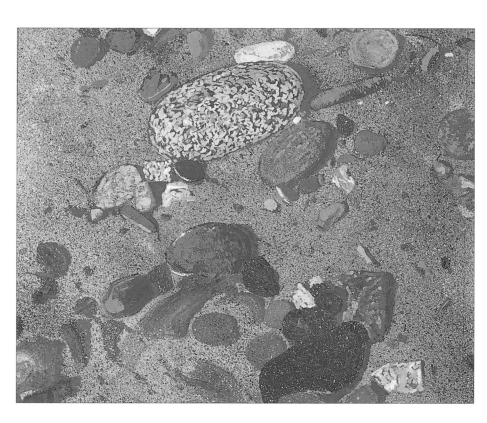

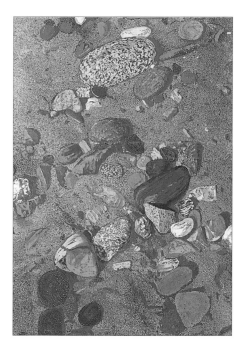

9 Continue to build up the texture and tonal contrasts within the pebbles, using all the colours on your palette – pale yellows and pinks, blue-greys, and almost pure white for the very lightest pebbles.

10 Vary your brushstrokes, stippling the paint in some places and using short strokes in others, but always allowing some of the underlying colours to show through.

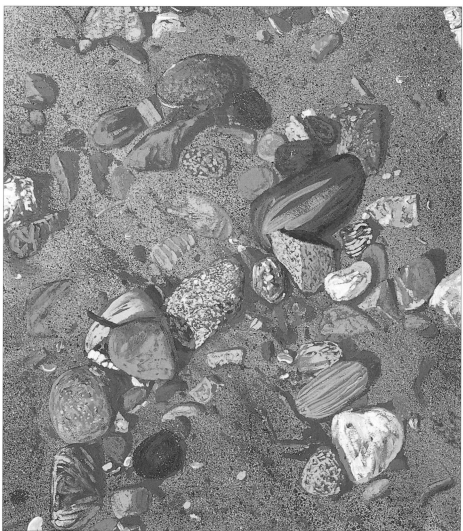

▶

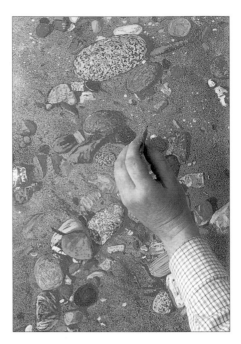

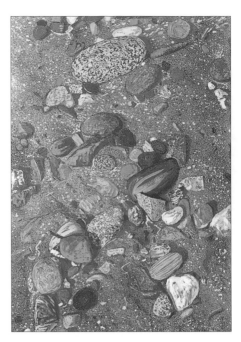

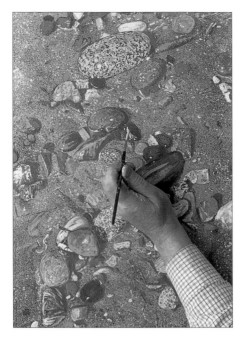

11 Using a very fine brush, stipple all the colours on your palette on to the sand to create the appearance of large grains of sand or very tiny pebbles. Stand back from your work at regular intervals in order to see how the whole painting is progressing.

12 Many different colours have now been spattered and stippled on to the sand, creating a suitably granular-looking background for the pebbles. Take time to assess whether or not the texture of the sand is complete before you move on to the next stage.

13 If some of the stones look too dark in relation to the rest of the image, stipple or dab on some of your very pale yellow mixture. Use artistic licence where necessary in your choice of colours and keep looking at the balance of the painting as a whole.

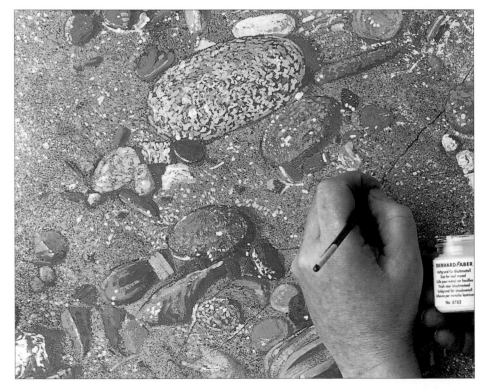

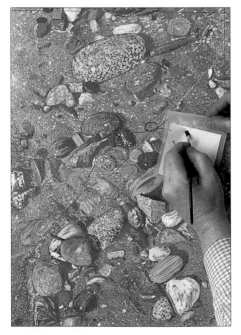

14 Now for the final touch – the twine that twists and turns its way through the pebbles, creating a dynamic diagonal line that draws our eye through the composition. Using a fine round brush, "draw" the line of the twine in acrylic gold size. Leave the size until it is tacky to the touch, following the manufacturer's instructions.

15 Lift a small piece of gold leaf by the backing paper and position it on the sized surface. Brush over the backing paper with a soft brush. Press a piece of kitchen paper over the gold leaf to ensure that it adheres firmly. Brush off any excess gold leaf with a clean, dry brush.

The finished painting

This is a deceptively simple-looking still life, but the gradual build-up of tones and textures makes it very convincing. A number of textural techniques have been used, and the artist has exploited the chalky consistency of gouache paint to give the pebbles solidity. The use of gold leaf for the twine is an imaginative touch that adds yet another texture to the image.

The trick with a painting like this is not to overwork it. Try to build up the image as a whole, rather than trying to finish one small area before you move on to the next. Taking time out at regular intervals, so that you can stand back and assess whether or not you've built up the textures to the degree that you want, is also important.

Just a hint of a shadow under the right-hand edge of the largest pebbles is enough to make them look three-dimensional.

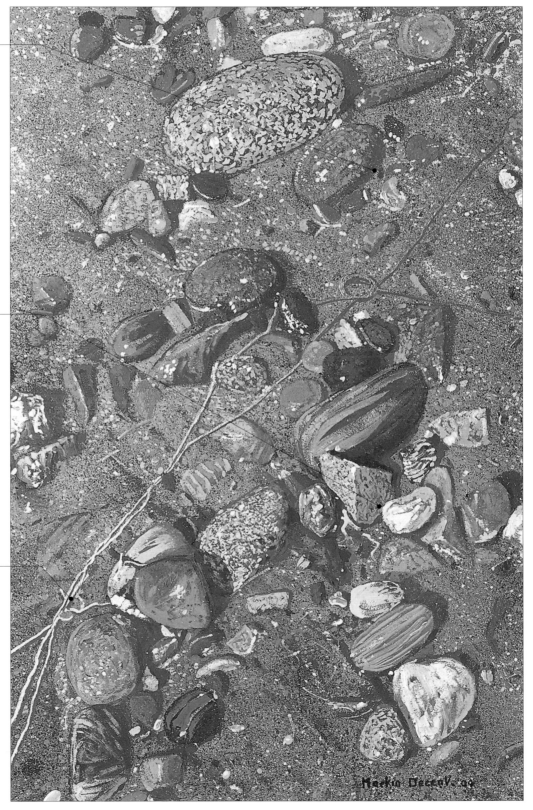

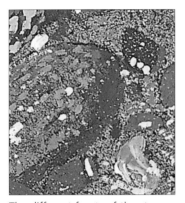

The different facets of the stones have been carefully observed.

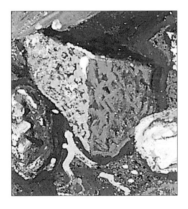

The twine, created by applying gold leaf, snakes its way through the image in a diagonal line.

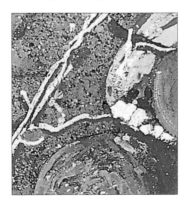

Lemons in glass dish

Less is very often more when painting still lifes; in other words, a small number of objects, carefully arranged, is often more effective than an elaborate set-up of many different elements. What could be simpler than a few lemons in a glass dish?

However, you still need to take time and care over your arrangement. Place the lemons so that they create an attractive overall shape, and look at the balance of the composition and at the spaces between the objects. Does the arrangement look too heavily weighted towards one side? Do the lemons make an interesting shape that draws our eye around the picture? Positioning the lemons at different angles and cutting one of them in half, so that we can see its internal structure, adds interest to the scene.

Because clear glass takes on the colours of the objects around it, you need to establish the background colour and the colour of any objects seen through the glass before you can turn your attention to the glass itself.

The highlights on both the dish and the lemons require careful study, but you should resist the temptation to put in every single one: too many highlights can easily detract from your main subject. Half-close your eyes, as this makes it easier to assess which highlights are the most prominent and therefore the most important.

Shadows are an essential part of the composition, too, with both the lemon on the table top and the glazing bars of the window casting interesting shadows that tell us about the direction and intensity of the light. Beginners sometimes make the mistake of adding black to the local colour of an object to make its shadow colour, but shadows often contain a hint of the complementary colour, as well as colours reflected from nearby objects. Here, for example, the lemon's shadow contains some violet – the complementary of yellow. Even within the shadows there are warm and cool colours and light and dark areas: never paint a shadow as a uniform, flat colour.

Materials
- *Stretched and primed canvas*
- *Oil paints: olive green, lemon yellow, cadmium red, cobalt blue, raw umber, alizarin crimson, titanium white*
- *Turpentine (white spirit)*
- *Brushes: selection of small and medium hogshair*

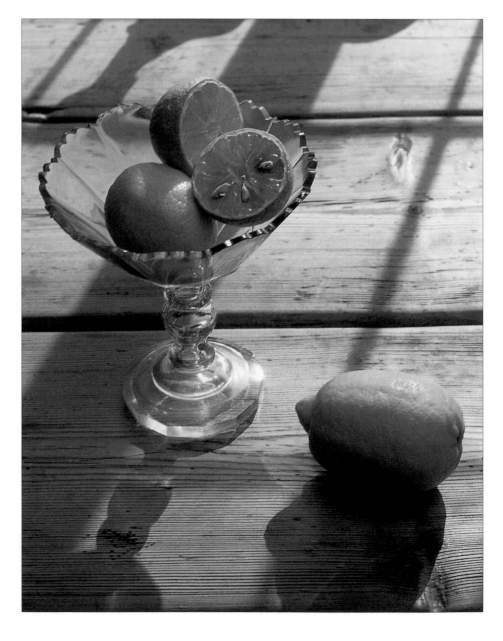

The set-up
Always look for interesting shapes and lines when you're setting up a still life. In this arrangement, the lemons are angled in different directions, which adds interest to the scene. One lemon was also cut in half, which provides the opportunity to explore its internal structure and texture. Although the initial stages of the painting were made in flat lighting conditions, during the second painting session the sun moved round, casting diagonal shadows that form a strong contrast to the horizontal planks of the rough wooden table.

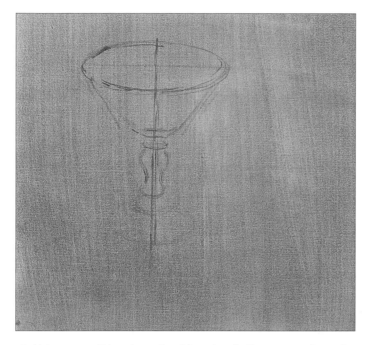

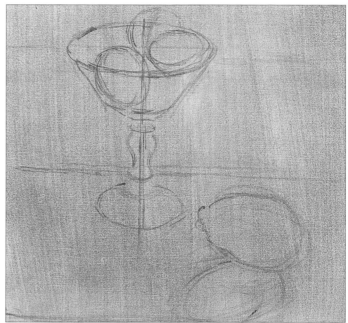

1 Using a small brush and a thin mix of olive green, draw the glass dish. Put in vertical and horizontal guidelines to help you get the shape of the ellipse right and a vertical line as the centre of the stem: these guidelines will be covered up later, but with plain glass it's very obvious if the shape is wrong.

2 Draw the lemons (including the shadow cast by the lemon on the table) and indicate the lines of the planks of wood on the table top. Try to think of the lemons as rounded geometric forms rather than simply drawing an outline, and look at where edges overlap.

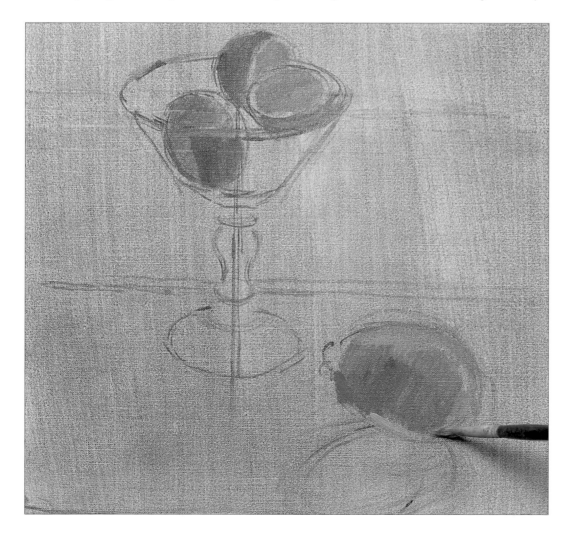

3 Once you are happy with your underdrawing, you can start to apply some paint. Mix a dark olive colour from olive green, lemon yellow and a minute amount of cadmium red and block in the shaded sides of the lemons. Add more lemon yellow to your mixture and paint all the unshaded parts of the lemons, including the cut surfaces. Leave unpainted the ring of pith around the edges of the cut lemons.

> **Tip**: Look carefully at the different yellows within the still life; some areas have a blue-green tinge, while others are much warmer. Look at the relative tones, too; you will probably find that the shaded areas are actually much darker than you expected.

▶

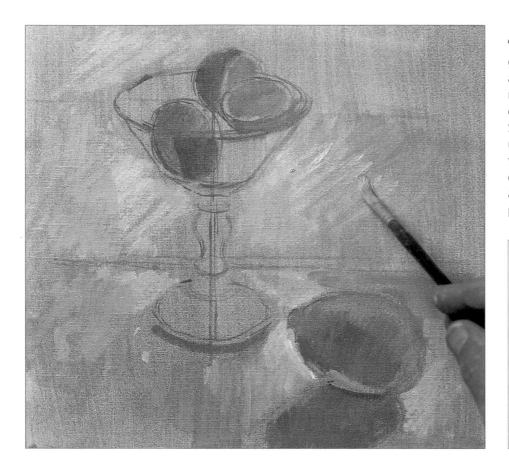

4 Block in the shadow under the lemon on the table using a neutral grey mixture of cobalt blue, raw umber and a touch of alizarin crimson. Mix a neutral grey-brown from raw umber, cobalt blue and titanium white. Scumble this mixture over the table top, using diagonal brushstrokes that echo the direction of the light. Note that the colour is not uniform: there are warm and cool areas within it, so adjust the proportions of your mix accordingly.

Tip: Although the scumbling can be fairly loose, take care not to go over the outlines of the lemons or the glass bowl. One advantage of scumbling is that it allows some of the underlying colour to show through, and this helps to create the texture of the rough wooden table top. The contrast between this texture and that of the more smoothly painted glass bowl and lemons will be important in the final painting.

Assessment time

Clear glass has no colour of its own; it takes its colour from what is around it, so you need to establish the basic tonal framework of the scene first. Once you have done this, you can concentrate on refining the lights and dark, and on making the glass really look like glass.

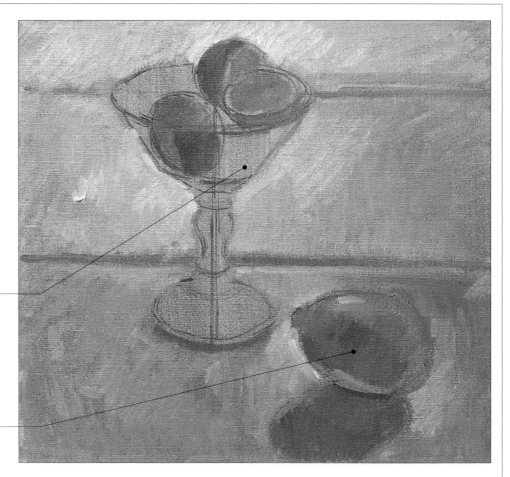

Spend time assessing which colours and tones are reflected in the glass before you apply any more paint.

The lemons are starting to look rounded, but require more work in order to look convincing.

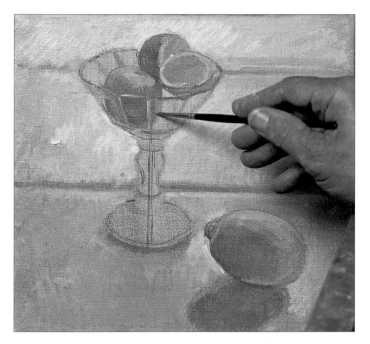

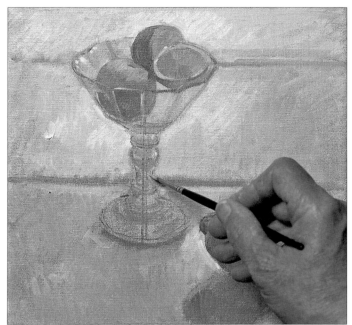

5 Now begin to indicate the different facets of the glass dish by putting in warm (pinky brown) or cool (blue-biased grey) lines as appropriate. Brush a pale blue around the rim of the cut lemons.

6 Continue to paint the stem and the base of the glass dish, using warm- or cool-biased mixes as appropriate. The tone can change quite dramatically within a small area, so take your time and use a small brush.

Tip: Each facet of the glass is a slightly different tone, as it is angled differently towards the light. Look beyond the glass and see what colours you can see through it to assess these tonal changes.

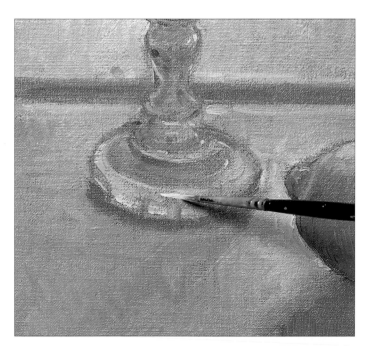

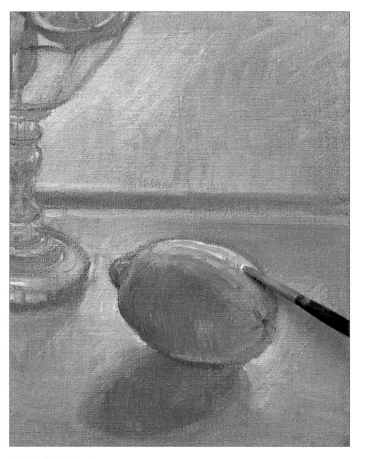

7 Using the same pale blue colour that you used around the rim, lightly touch in the segments on the surfaces of the cut lemons and put in the highlights reflected in the base of the glass dish.

8 Using a pale yellow mixed from lemon yellow and white, draw in the highlights on the foreground lemon. Use slightly uneven, broken strokes to create texture on the surface of the lemon.

▶

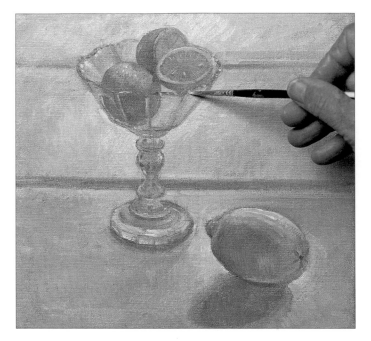

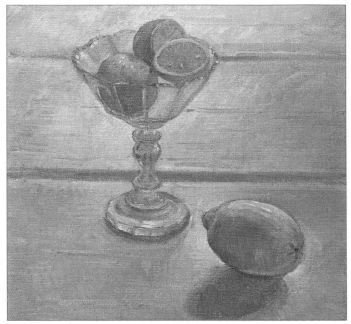

9 Now put in the scalloped edge of the dish. The crisp lines of the cut glass pick up highlights, and you can use these to imply the shapes. Use a small brush and put little touches of blue-grey around the back of the dish, which is largely in shadow, and white tinged with yellow around the front.

10 Using a fine sable brush and almost dry paint, gently stroke fine lines of the grey-brown mixture from Step 4 over the table top to imply the grain of the wooden table. The effect is subtle but it adds much-needed texture to the table top without detracting from the still-life arrangement.

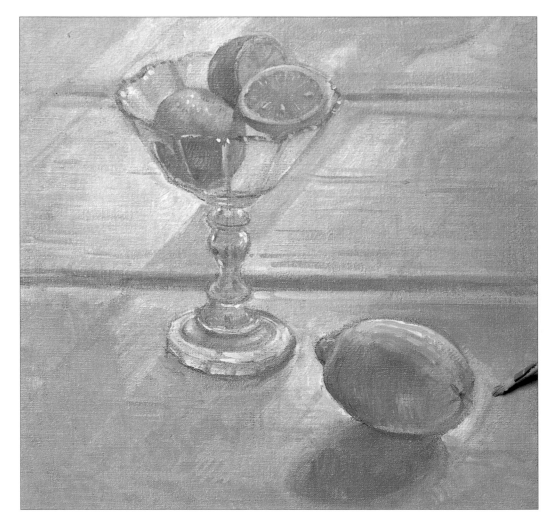

11 Mix a pale blue-grey from cobalt blue, titanium white and a little of the mixture used to paint the table top in Step 10. Block in the diagonal shadows cast on the table by the glazing bars in the window, scumbling the mixture on thinly so that some of the underlying colour comes through. Paint the shadow cast by the glass in the same way. This immediately brings more drama to the scene.

Tip: It's very often the contrast between light and dark areas that gives a painting its impact. If the scene doesn't look as strong as you would like, try darkening the dark areas rather than lightening the light ones. If the scene is allowed to become too high-key, the drama may be lost.

The finished painting

The drama of the lighting enhances this little still life immeasurably, with the strong diagonal shadows giving the scene much more drama and impact. The highlights are not overstated but bring much-needed sparkle to the work. A mix of cool and warm tones in the glass provides information about the strength and direction of the light.

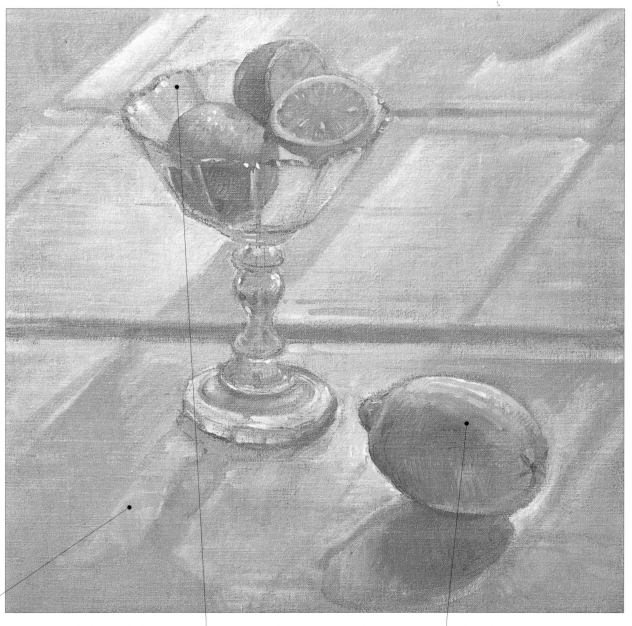

The contrast between light and dark areas is what gives the still life its impact.

Both cool and warm tones can be seen in the glass dish.

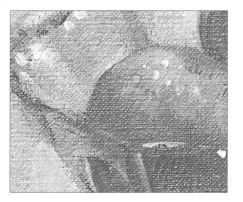

Relatively thick paint captures the texture of the lemon skin beautifully.

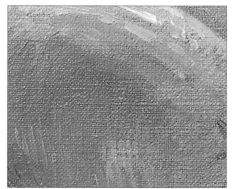

Still life with glass and ceramics

This project is primarily an exercise in observing and painting glass and hard-edged, solid-coloured objects. The technique chosen suits the hard, crisp quality of the objects.

The thing to remember when painting clear glass is that it has no colour of its own: any colour that you can see comes from surrounding objects that are either reflected in the glass or can be seen through it.

Although we know that solid-coloured objects such as the play bricks and pots in this scene are a uniform colour, you cannot paint them as such: their position in relation to the light source means that some areas will be darker or lighter in tone than others, and you must convey these tonal variations in order to make your picture look three-dimensional. There will also be some very bright, almost white, highlights where the lights catches one edge of the object. Although there are relatively few colours in this still life, there is a great deal of tonal variation, which you need to assess very carefully.

Shadows also play an important part in creating a three-dimensional impression. Keep the lighting simple: use just one light, positioned to one side of the objects so that they cast soft shadows both on to other objects within the group and on to the background wall. You can control the size and intensity of the shadows by altering the distance between the light and the objects. If you find that the shadowed side looks too dark, place a sheet of white cardboard or hang a piece of white fabric (a T-shirt will do) on the other side of the still life from the light in order to reflect some light back on to the collection of objects.

Materials
- *MDF (medium density fibreboard) primed with acrylic gesso*
- *B pencil*
- *Acrylic paints: phthalocyanine blue, titanium white, alizarin crimson, burnt umber, yellow ochre, cadmium yellow, phthalocyanine green, purple lake, cadmium red*
- *Matt acrylic medium*
- *Brushes: medium flat*

The set-up
This still life is an eclectic mix of stoneware pots and glass bottles, chosen for the contrast between transparent objects and ones that are solid, and children's play bricks and a wooden ball, selected for their contrasts in shape and colour. Light from a table lamp, positioned out of shot to the right of the set-up, casts interesting shadows on both the objects and the background wall.

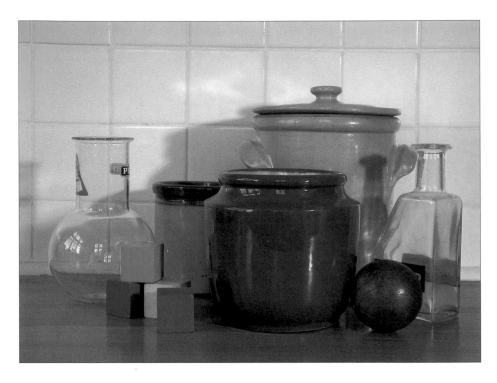

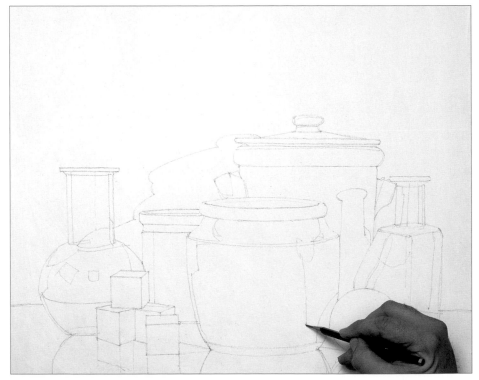

1 Using a B pencil, make a light underdrawing of the still life. Include the highlights and shadows, as these are an integral part of the composition.

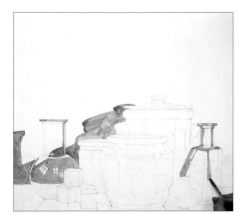

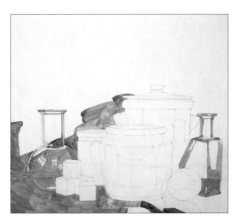

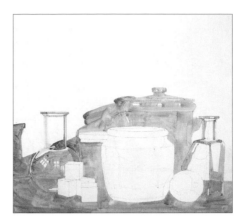

2 Mix a dull grey from phthalocyanine blue, titanium white, a tiny amount of alizarin crimson, and a few drops of matt acrylic medium, which makes the paint transparent and a little smoother. Using a medium flat brush, block in the shadows of the objects on the background, and the shadow that can be seen through the glass bottle on the left, leaving some of the highlights untouched. Use the same grey to outline the glass bottles, which take their colour from surrounding objects and reflections.

3 Add alizarin crimson and burnt umber to the mixture to make a light brown and start to paint the table, working carefully around the objects but remembering to paint the table that can be seen through the glass bottles.

4 Continue until you have completed the table. Use the same light brown to block in the large, lidded ceramic jar in the background and the bottom part of the stoneware jar on the left.

> **Tip**: The brushmarks will remain evident as the paint dries. Do not try to smooth them out or obliterate them, even though the objects you are painting are smooth in texture, as the brush marks give added interest to the painting.

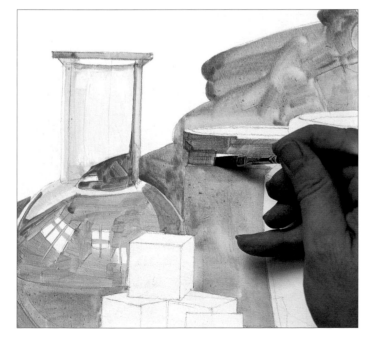

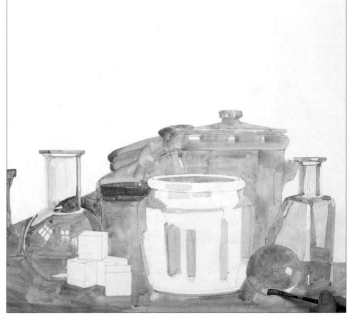

5 Mix a deep brown from burnt umber, yellow ochre and alizarin crimson and paint the dark rim of the stoneware jar. The flat brush makes it easy to paint straight edges such as this. Use a very thin version of the blue-grey mixture from Step 2 to paint the glass bottle on the right.

6 Mix pale brown from yellow ochre and burnt umber and paint the shaded interior of the foreground jar, leaving the highlit rim untouched. Mix a pale, greyish green from the previous pale brown mixture and a little phthalocyanine blue and paint the lightest areas on the green foreground jar with broad, vertical brushstrokes. Add a little alizarin crimson to the mixture used to paint the inside of the foreground jar and paint the ball in the foreground, leaving the highlights white.

▶

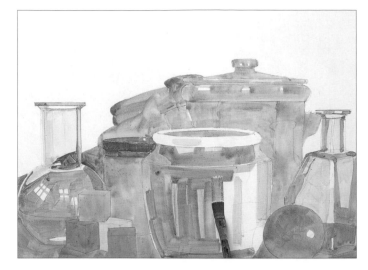

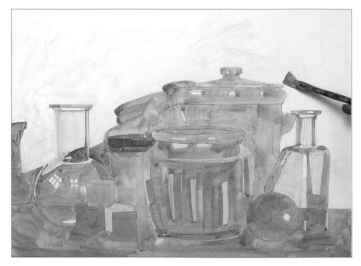

7 Now paint the children's bricks in the foreground, using phthalocyanine blue, cadmium yellow, and a bright green mixed from cadmium yellow and phthalocyanine green. Add some blue to the green mixture and start painting the green jar, working around the dull green highlights that you put down in the previous step.

8 Paint the rim of the green jar, painting around the highlights. Now paint the background. Add more titanium white to the pale brown mixture used in Steps 3 and 4 and brush around the outlines of the objects, feathering the brush strokes upwards, away from the jars. The flat brush makes it easy to work right up to the edge of each object.

Assessment time

The basic shapes and reflections have been put in, and all the objects have been given one layer of colour. You can see, however, that the picture looks rather flat and one-dimensional. You need to work over the whole

painting again, increasing the tonal contrasts and adding more detail, in order to make the image look three-dimensional and make the objects stand out clearly from the background.

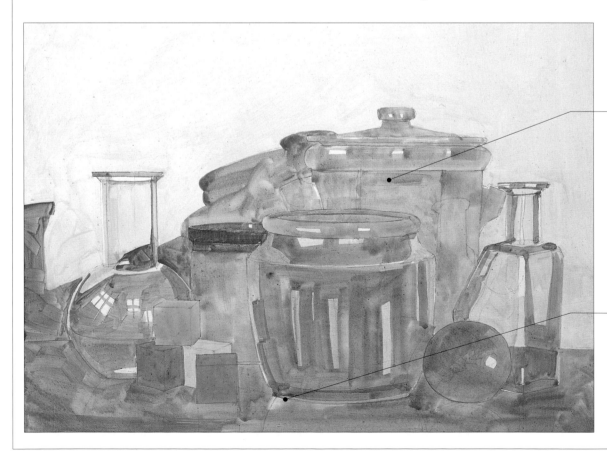

The large brown pot, in particular, lacks form and merges with both the background and the objects in front of it.

The absence of shadow makes it hard to "read" the image and work out the strength and intensity of the light.

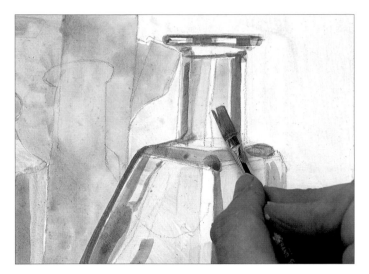

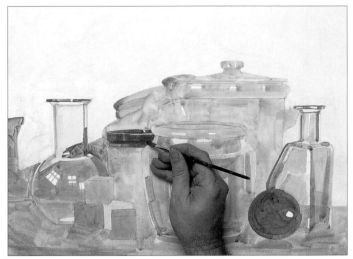

9 Mix a very pale, dilute blue from phthalocyanine blue and titanium white. Paint over the interior of the right-hand glass bottle, working around the highlights and using vertical brushstrokes. Although the glass is clear, it should be slightly darker in tone than the background wall that can be seen through it.

10 Mix a very pale brown from titanium white and burnt umber and fill in the colour in the lower half of the right-hand glass bottle, through which you can see the colour of the wooden table. Mix a rich brown from alizarin crimson, burnt umber and yellow ochre and paint the ball. Add a little purple lake to the mixture and paint the rim of the two-tone stoneware jar.

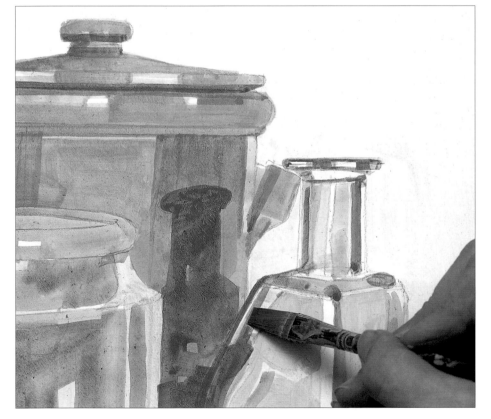

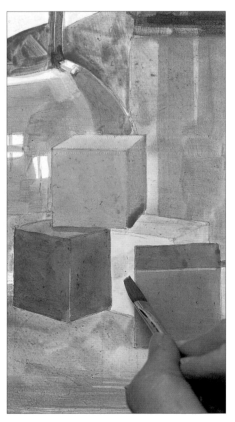

11 Use the same dark brown for the shadow under the lid of the stoneware jar in the background and on the darkest areas of the lid itself, remembering to paint around the highlights. Darken the tone of both stoneware jars, using vertical brushstrokes and reserving the highlights. Add phthalocyanine blue to the brown mixture and paint the shadow of the glass bottle on the large jar. Use the same colour on the left-hand edge of the bottle, which picks up reflected colour from the green jar to its left.

12 Strengthen the colours on the children's play bricks, making the tones slightly darker on the shaded sides. The shape of the brush will help you to keep the edges of the bricks straight.

▶

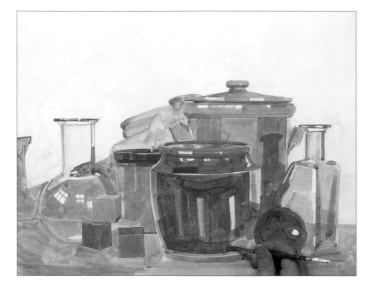

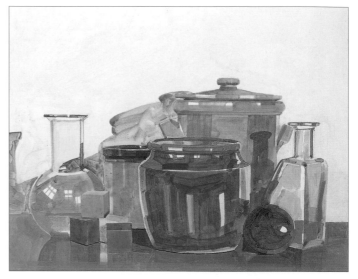

13 Paint over the green jar again, using the same paint mixture as in Step 7, again reserving the highlights. The jar is now beginning to take on more depth and solidity.

14 Add burnt umber to the green mixture used in the previous step and, using the edge of the brush, paint a shadow under the base of the green jar, the ball, and the bricks. This has the effect of giving a crisper edge to the objects and helps to define them more clearly. Add alizarin crimson, yellow ochre and a little purple lake to the shadow mixture and paint the deep shadows between the bricks and the jars, and between the ball and the green jar.

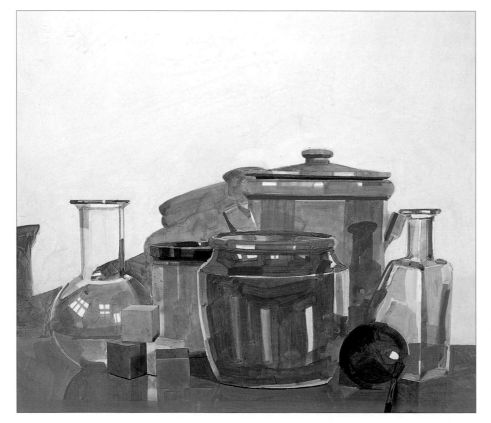

Tip: MDF primed with acrylic gesso is perfect for this subject, which consists of smooth-surfaced, hard-edged objects. You could create a softer image by working on canvas or by adding a retarding medium.

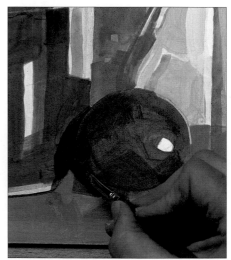

15 Mix a purplish blue from phthalocyanine blue, cadmium red and titanium white and reinforce the shadow colour on the wall. Mix a dark, warm brown from phthalocyanine blue, burnt umber and a little cadmium red and darken the shadow under the lid of the stoneware jar. Add more red to the brown mixture and darken the ball.

16 Add phthalocyanine green to the brown mixture to make a very dark green and paint the very dark shadow cast by the ball on the side of the green jar.

The finished painting

All the surfaces in this still life are very smooth and hard, and so an impasto approach, with lots of textured paint, would be inappropriate. Here the artist has built up the layers gradually, adjusting the tones and colours until he achieved the correct density. He has also paid close attention to the shadows and the way the light casts highlights on the objects, as these things are critical in making the objects look three-dimensional.

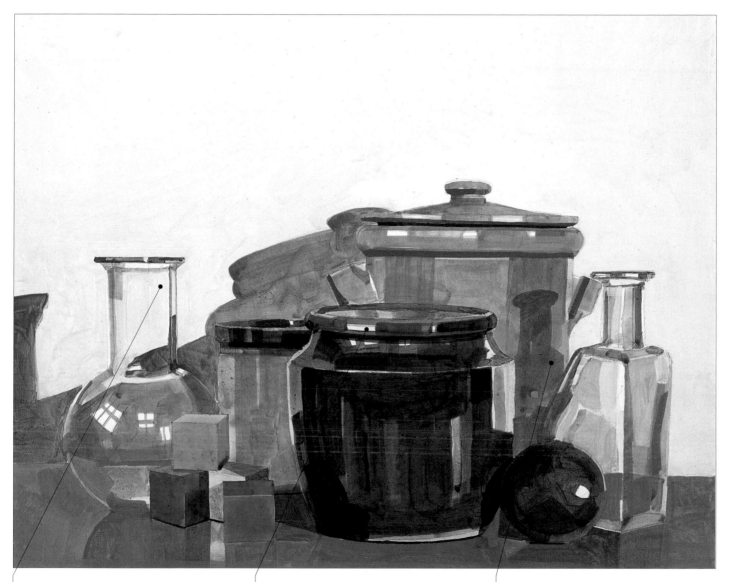

Glass takes its colour from surrounding objects which are either reflected in it or seen through it; here, colour is reflected from the shadows cast on the background.

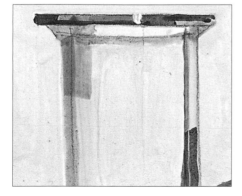

The highlights, which are mostly left white, reveal the intensity and the direction of the light source and show up the different facets of the jars.

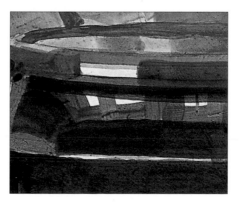

The shadow cast by the bottle is subtly coloured but helps to make the bottle look more three-dimensional.

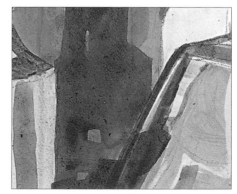

Painting buildings

Although you can get away with shapes and proportions being slightly wrong in some subjects (landscapes, for example), if buildings in your paintings are askew, it will be very noticeable. If you are painting anything other than a head-on view of a façade, therefore, you must give some consideration to perspective. This sounds a lot scarier than it is: in fact, a combination of careful observation and a little basic theory, which you can get from any good book on drawing, will set you on the right track. Just remember that all parallel lines on the same plane recede to the same vanishing point.

Unless you are very confident, start by making a light underdrawing and measuring the different parts of the building. Using a pencil to measure things is a classic method that artists have employed for centuries. Hold the pencil out in front of you at arm's length and align the tip with the top of the building. Then run your thumb down the pencil until it aligns with the base. Transfer this measurement to your canvas, again keeping the pencil at arm's length and holding your arm straight. Look, measure and then check again; in fact, whatever you are painting, you should make a conscious effort to spend more time looking at your subject than you do looking at the canvas.

Buildings are one area where including a lot of detail in your underdrawing can really help you, as establishing the relative sizes and positions of doors, windows, arches and other features is critical. Also remember to count: if there are five arched window on a façade, make sure there are also five in your underdrawing.

It is also important to assess the tones in your subject carefully. The exterior of a building is often comprised of one main material (brick, concrete, stucco, for example) and hence it is largely through differences in tone that we make it look three-dimensional. Remember that both acrylic and gouache paints look slightly darker when dry than when wet; test your mixes on scrap paper, and leave them to dry so that you can judge the real tones before you apply them to your painting. Shadows also play a part in this: even a small shadow cast by a window ledge or a decorative embellishment such as a stone statue or door knocker will contribute to the three-dimensional illusion.

Once you have established the basic form of the building, you can put in decorative details and textures. On worn, weathered buildings and peeling paintwork, scumbling is often a good technique for creating texture. If you are painting in acrylic, you might also consider using one of the many proprietary texture mediums on the market. Drybrush, sgrafitto, spattering and sponging are all useful techniques for creating texture on buildings.

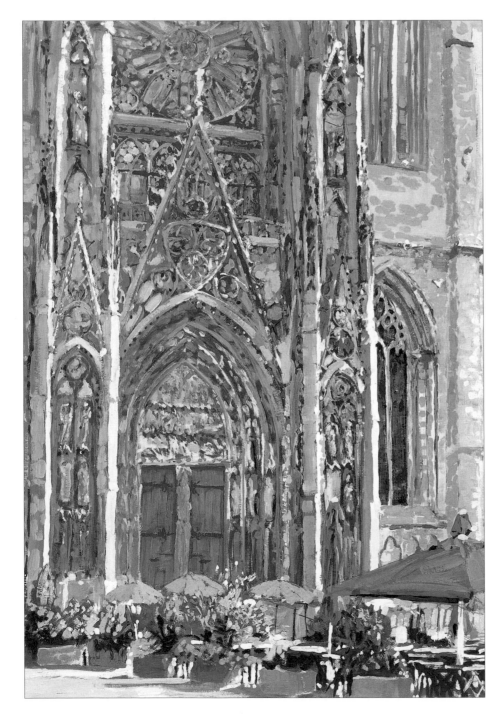

◀ **Rouen Cathedral**
This is a scene that has been painted countless times, most notably by the French Impressionist artist Claude Monet (1840–1926). In this version, the plants and café umbrellas bring a touch of modernity to the scene and hint at the bustling street life that goes on around the cathedral.

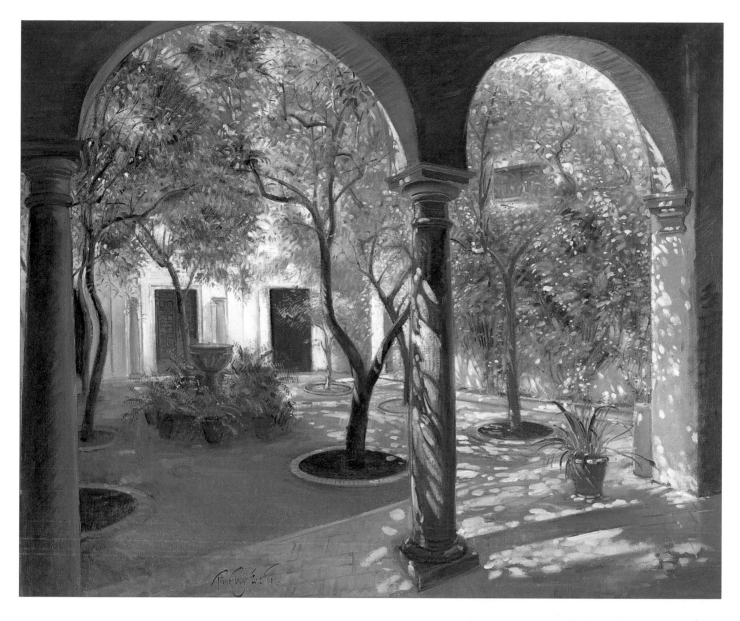

perspective and make a light underdrawing to check that you have got things right; this will ensure that your building does not look as if it is about to fall over.
• Draw and paint your building in the same order that it was built – the main structure first, followed by doors and windows, and finally architectural details such as railings and statues.
• If you are painting the façade of a building, pay particular attention to the direction and length of any shadows: they will help you to create a sense of depth in an otherwise flat subject.

The shaded courtyard ▲
This is a delightful evocation of a shaded courtyard in southern Spain. The shadows cast by the plants and the arches create an intriguing and lively pattern of dappled light on the ground. Note that the shadows are predominantly purple in tone: shadows are rarely, if ever, black.

Midday, Gnomon ▶
Textures and the strong diagonal midday shadows are what make this somewhat dilapidated building look so interesting. Scumbles of oil paint allow the underlying colours to show through – a classic method of conveying the texture of worn, weathered surfaces.

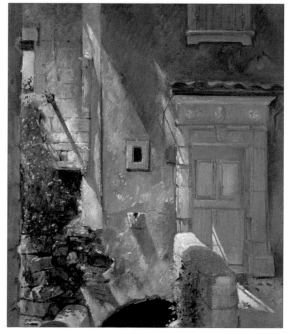

Church in snow

Buildings are an integral part of many landscape paintings. Even when they're not necessarily the prime focus of attention, they add an element of human interest by implying the presence of man; and they also help to give a sense of scale.

In this project, the church in the background brings another dimension to a tranquil rural setting. Its solid form, positioned roughly on the third, contrasts well with the landscape around.

Begin by establishing the basic shape of the building and painting it as a flat area of tone. You can then develop this, creating contrasts of light and shade that reveal the different sides of the building, and finally putting in just enough detailing to tell us about the architectural style and period. The human brain is amazingly adept at interpreting a few generalized indications of shape and texture, and too much information can actually destroy the balance of the painting as a whole – particularly when the building is in the background, as here. The further away something is, the less detail is required.

For this project, the artist began by toning the canvas with dilute olive green oil paint. The cool colour suits the wintry scene and gives a good, neutral mid-tone from which to start painting.

Just like water, snow reflects colour from the sky and objects nearby. Where the sun strikes, the snow may be tinged with warm yellows or even pinks, depending on the time of day, while shadows will contain shades of blue and violet. Resist the temptation to paint everything as a brilliant, monotone white: shadowy areas contrasting with small patches of bright, sunlit snow will have far more impact. The shadows in the snow also reveal the contours of the land beneath.

Materials

- *Stretched and primed canvas*
- *Oil paints: olive green, permanent mauve, titanium white, cobalt blue, raw sienna, viridian, burnt sienna, Indian yellow, cadmium red, lemon yellow*
- *Turpentine*
- *Brushes: selection of small and medium filberts*

The scene

Although the church is far away and relatively indistinct, it is still the main focus of the scene. Along with the trees, it provides a strong vertical element on which the viewer's eye can alight, while the curve of the water leads us around the scene.

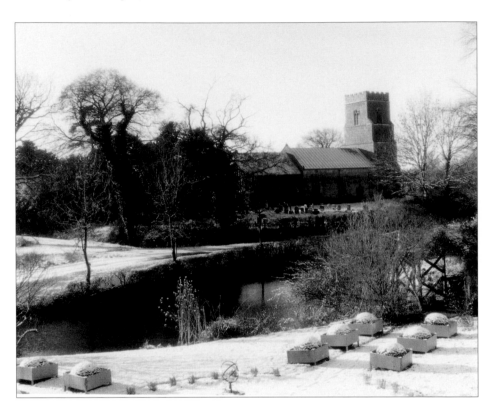

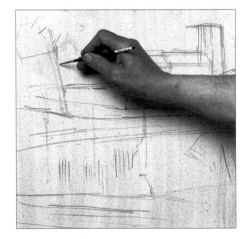

1 Make an underdrawing of the church, main trees and water area, using a small brush and thin olive green paint. When you paint buildings it is particularly important to get the proportions and angles right, so measure carefully and take your time over this stage. Also indicate the shadows on the snow in the foreground and roughly scumble in the largest reflections in the water.

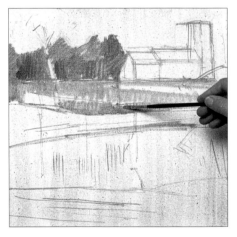

2 Block in the trees on the far bank, using a mid-toned purple mixed from permanent mauve, titanium white, cobalt blue and raw sienna, and a blue-green mixed from olive green, viridian and a tiny amount of burnt sienna. Using a small brush, begin putting in the cool shadows on the snow on the far bank, using a blue-grey mixed from cobalt blue, titanium white and permanent mauve.

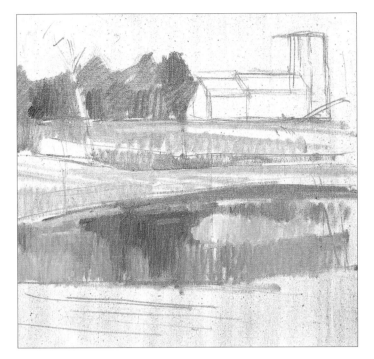

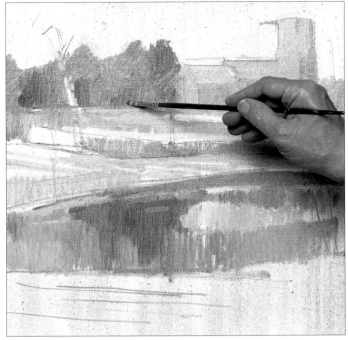

3 Continue putting in the shadows on the snow on the far side of the water. Block in the reflections of the trees in the water, using olive green for the darkest trees and lighter olive green and purple mixes elsewhere, and leaving gaps for the brightest areas of water.

4 Mix a pinkish brown from burnt sienna, titanium white and cobalt blue and paint the walls of the church. Paint the snow-covered roof, which is in shadow, in a cool blue-grey. Overlay some pale blue on the purple trees in the background; this helps to link the trees with the snow.

Assessment time

Lively scumbles are a quick way of establishing basic shapes and tones in the early stages of a painting, and are particularly useful when you are painting outdoors. The underpainting is now virtually complete. For the rest of the painting, concentrate on texture and detailing, checking periodically to ensure that you maintain the tonal balance.

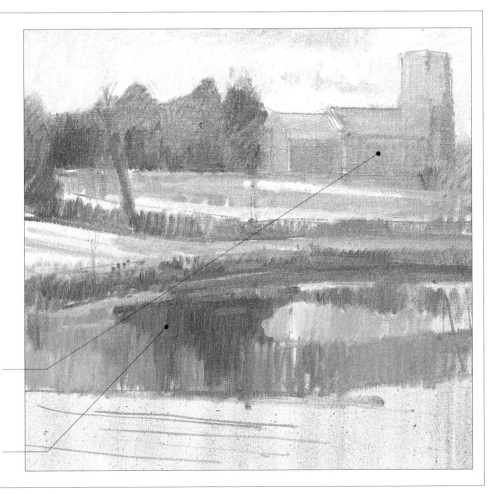

The church, which has been roughly blocked in, adds solidity to the scene.

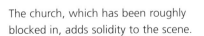

Lively scumbles establish the basic shapes and tones.

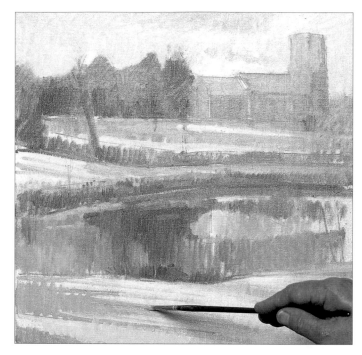

5 Indicate the grasses on the near bank by scumbling on a little of the dark green mixture from the previous step and raw sienna. The warmth of the raw sienna helps to bring them forward in the painting. Brush on more blue for the shadows in the foreground snow, using horizontal strokes that follow the direction of the shadows. For the unshaded areas of snow, use a warm off-white colour mixed from titanium white and a tiny amount of Indian yellow.

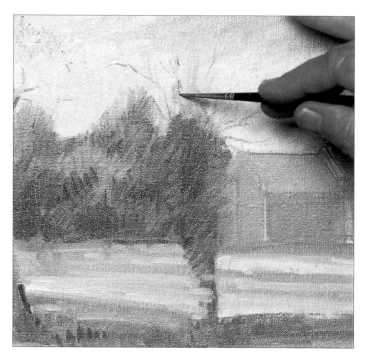

6 Using a fine brush and the purplish-grey mixture from Step 2, put in the bare branches that poke up from the ivy-covered trees in the background. Don't try to put in every single detail or the painting will start to look overworked and fussy; you can create a general impression of the shape and texture of these thin branches by means of a series of short parallel lines. Reserve the main detailing and texture for the foreground of the scene.

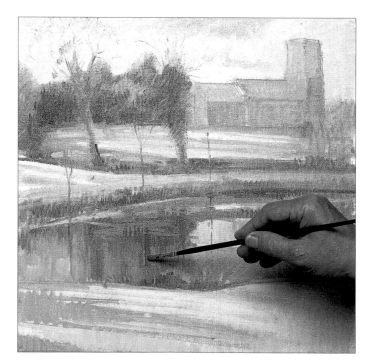

7 Put in the thin saplings along the bank, as well as their reflections. Darken and strengthen the colours of the reflections: once you've established the general area, you can smooth out the brushstrokes, blending the colours together on the canvas.

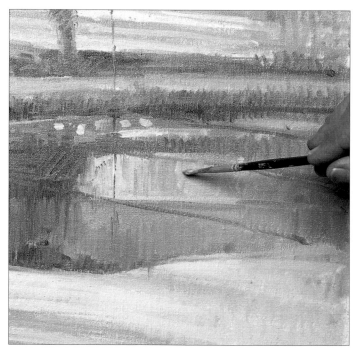

8 There is an overly bright and distracting area of water near the centre of the image, which needs to be toned down in order to blend in with the rest of the painting. Leaving the brightest areas untouched, lightly brush a very pale purple over this area.

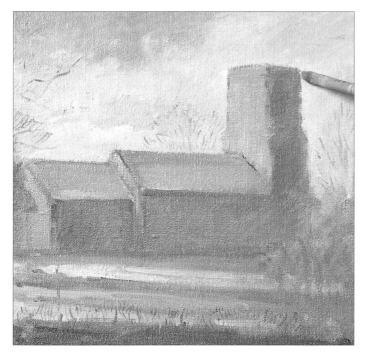

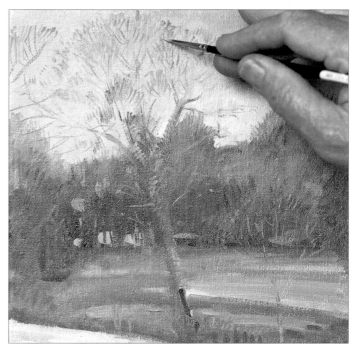

9 Mix a warm but pale yellow from Indian yellow and titanium white. Lightly touch it into the sky, where the winter sun shines through from behind the clouds.

10 Continue with the linear, drybrush detailing on the bare branches of the trees, as in Step 6, again resisting the temptation to put in too much detail.

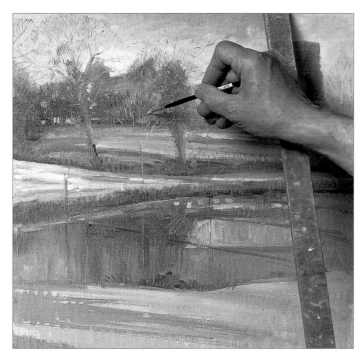

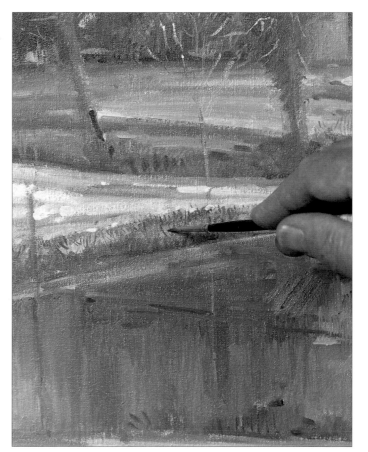

11 Using a fine sable brush and a pale blue-grey mixture, put in the branches of the young saplings on the bank. Adjust the proportions of the colours in your mixture: the shaded branches are bluer in tone, while those branches to which the snow is clinging are whiter.

Tip: If the marks look too sharp, soften them by blending them with your fingers.

12 Strengthen the colours of the low bushes on the far side of the water, using short vertical strokes of reddish browns and dark olive greens. The warm colours help to bring this area forwards in the painting.

▶

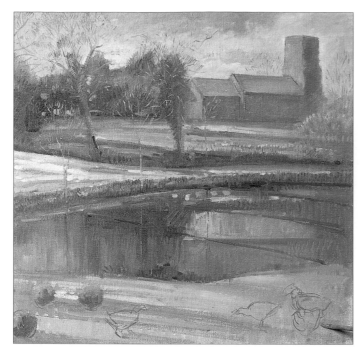

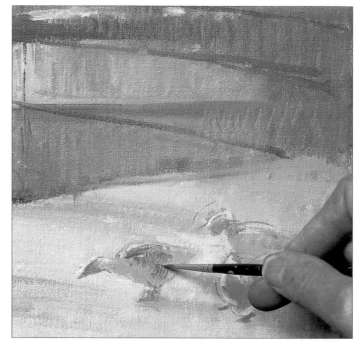

13 Using thin paint, draw the shapes of the box topiary and geese on the near bank. Roughly block in the shapes of the topiary with a pale blue-green mixture, adding more white on the side that catches the light. Using the same colours as before, brush in the shadows cast by the topiary and the geese.

14 Warm up the foreground snow by scumbling the off-white colour from Step 5 over those areas that are not in shadow. Paint the geese in a blue-tinged white, adding more blue to the mixture for the markings on the feathers. Paint their feet, legs and beaks in cadmium red mixed with white and a little lemon yellow.

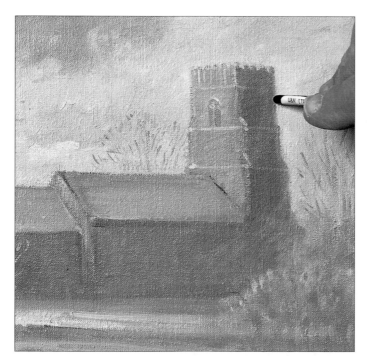

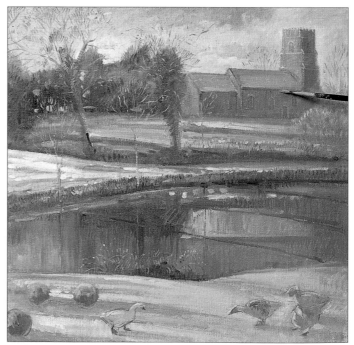

15 Using a paler version of the stone colour from Step 4, paint the sunlit sides of the church so that the building looks three-dimensional. Paint the lines on the tower in a blue-grey, adding more white where the snow clings to the ridges. Paint the castellations on the turret by overpainting some of the sky colour. Use the brush handle to blend colours around the edge of the church and create a crisp outline.

16 Paint the windows of the church in a dark brown, leaving the underlying colour showing through for the stonework.

The finished painting

This is a muted scene that nonetheless captures the feeling of thin, early-morning winter sunlight very well through its use of pale blues and pinks. The church is rendered indistinctly and almost appears to be seen through a haze, but there is enough detail to tell us about the architectural style. The geese in the foreground are painted in more detail and add life to what might otherwise be a rather static scene. Note how many different tones there are within the snow.

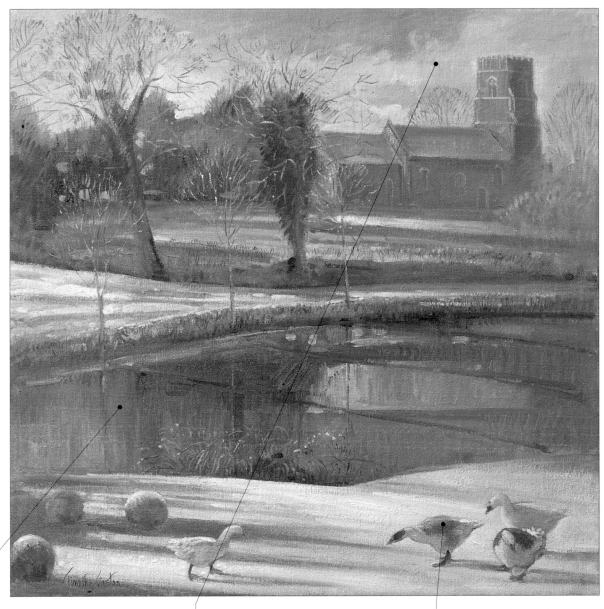

The brushstrokes in the reflections have been softly blended.

Warm but pale yellow in the sky lightens the scene.

The geese and their shadows enliven the foreground.

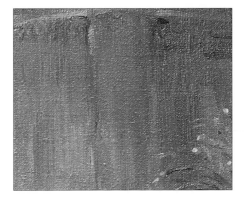

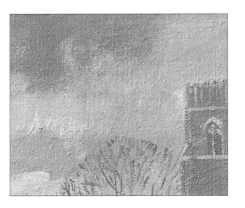

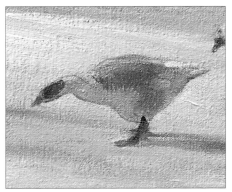

Arch and balcony

In the eighteenth and early nineteenth centuries, it was common practice for members of the aristocracy to undertake a grand tour of the major cities of Europe in order to complete their education. In those days before the advent of picture postcards and easy-to-use cameras, sketches made *in situ* were, for many, the only means of recording the wonders that they saw. As a consequence, watercolour paintings abound of the sites that they visited: great palaces and chateaux, romantic vistas and ruined follies were all captured on paper to show to admiring friends and relations.

In some respects this project, which relies on careful observation and measuring to record the detail of the building, is very much in the same tradition. However, it also goes beyond that, seeking as it does to capture the spirit of the place and the quality of the light. Attempting to create a sense of atmosphere is one of the things that will lift your work above the level of a technical exercise and turn it into a painting. Moreover, whether you are painting close to home or in a land far away, the very act of consciously examining your subject over an extended period of time somehow seems to imprint the scene in your memory in a way that taking a photograph can never do.

The building that features in this project is the Royal Pavilion, in Brighton, in the south of England, commissioned and closely overseen by the then Prince Regent (later King George IV), who confessed that he cried for joy when he contemplated the Pavilion's splendours.

Often when you are painting buildings – particularly ones such as this, which are rendered in stucco or plaster or constructed from smooth stone – you are dealing with very subtle differences in tone. You need to observe your subject and assess the tonal differences very carefully, as this is what conveys the three-dimensional nature of the building.

Remember, too, that gouache paint always looks slightly darker when it is dry than it does when it is wet. Make sure you test your mixtures on a scrap piece of paper or board and allow them to dry thoroughly before you apply them to your painting, as this is the only way to judge whether or not you have got the mix right. Although it is possible to paint over areas if you find you've made them too dark, it is far better to get the tone right first time – particularly when you are using the gouache in the form of thin washes, as here – otherwise your painting may start to look heavy and overworked.

Materials

- *Watercolour paper*
- *Acrylic gesso*
- *HB pencil*
- *Illustration board*
- *Gouache paints: raw umber, zinc white, jet black, ultramarine blue, brilliant yellow*
- *Brushes: small round*

The scene

Many people might have been tempted to select a viewpoint that included the whole of the arch and window, with the arch symmetrically positioned, but this could lead to a very static composition. This viewpoint is much more interesting: it allows us to see the form of the arch, rather than just a flat façade, while the turret on the edge of the balcony is positioned "on the third".

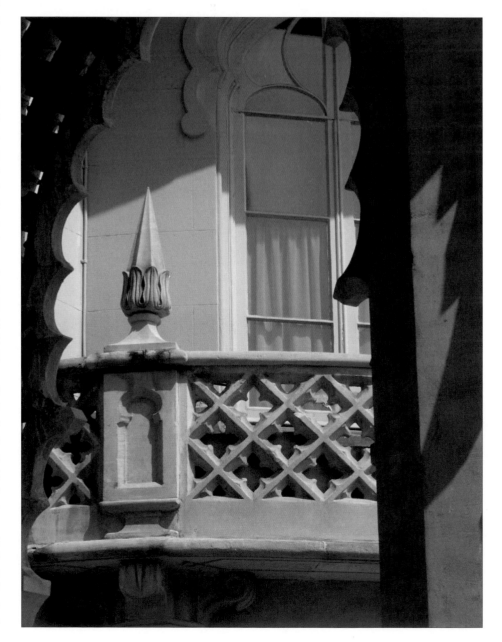

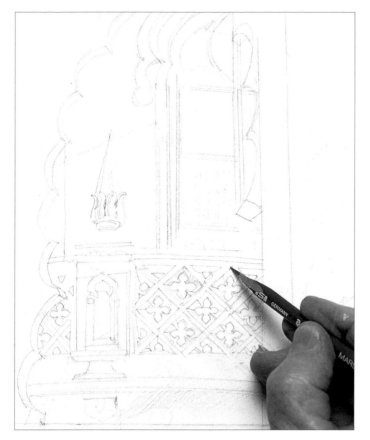

1 Using a sharp HB pencil, make an underdrawing on watercolour paper primed with acrylic gesso. It is important to measure everything carefully. Pay particular attention to the shape, size and number of the quatrefoil shapes in the tracery of the limestone balcony.

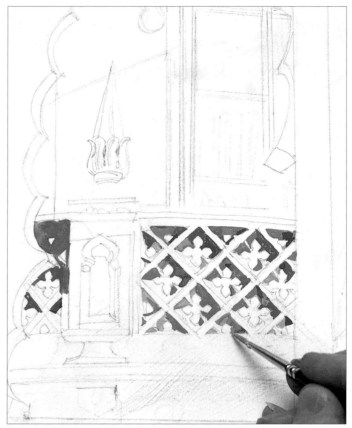

2 Mix a dark brown from raw umber, zinc white and jet black and, using a small round brush, paint the dark spaces around the quatrefoil shapes on the balcony. In some areas light is reflected back: paint these shapes in a blue-grey mixture of zinc white and ultramarine blue.

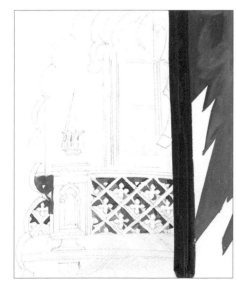

3 Using the dark brown mixture from Step 2, paint the shaded side of the foreground arch. Add more white to the mixture and paint the dark cast shadows on the right-hand side of the scene, making sure you paint them with crisp edges.

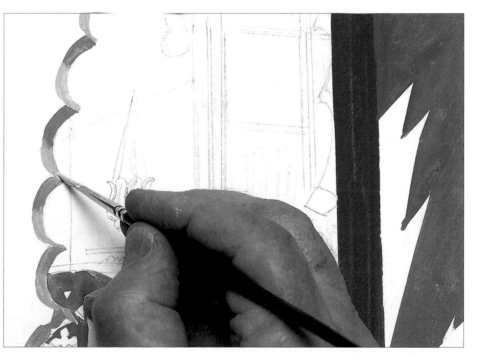

4 Paying careful attention to where the light falls and alternating between the brown and blue-grey mixtures used in the previous steps, paint the scallop shapes on the left-hand side of the foreground arch.

▶

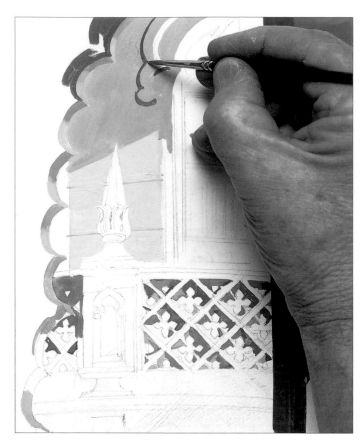

5 Mix a warm stone colour from zinc white, brilliant yellow and a litle raw umber and paint the lightest area of wall behind the balcony. Add ultramarine blue to the dark brown mixture and paint the shaded area above the turret and the edge of the stuccowork to the left of the window.

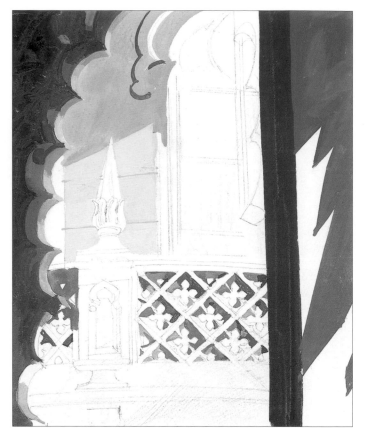

6 Paint the shaded left-hand side of the foreground arch, using the same dark mixtures as before. Although bright highlights are visible through gaps in the stonework, it is too difficult to try to work around them at this stage: you can reinstate them later using pure white gouache.

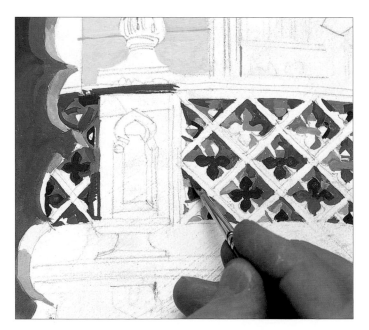

7 The blue sky reflected in the window can be seen behind some of the cut-out shapes in the balcony: paint these in a bright blue mixed from ultramarine blue and zinc white. Complete the dark shadows behind the quatrefoil shapes on the balcony; note that the colour changes should not be uniform in tone.

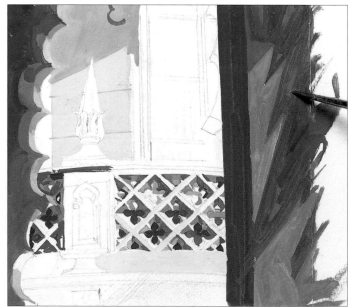

8 Mix a light brown shadow colour from raw umber and zinc white and paint the unpainted stonework on the right of the foreground arch. Scumble a little ultramarine blue over the cast shadows that you painted in Step 3 to make the colour look less flat and create some variety of tone.

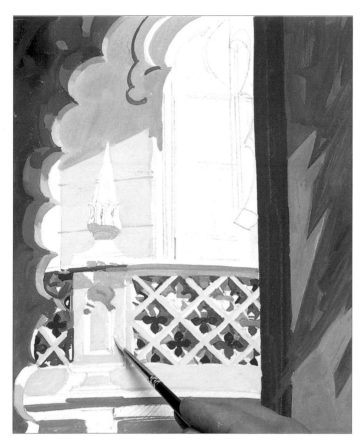

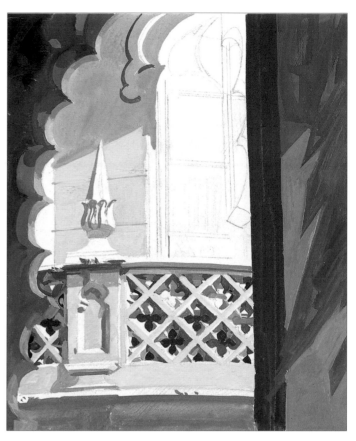

9 Add ultramarine blue to the warm stone colour that you mixed in Step 5 and paint the shadow areas on the balcony. Paint the lightest areas of stone on the balcony in a pale mixture of brilliant yellow and zinc white; you will need to look very carefully to see where the tone changes.

10 Add raw umber to the stone colour and paint the area under the overhang of the balcony, which is in shadow and therefore darker in tone. Using a mid-tone brown, put in some of the dark detailing and the most deeply shaded side of the turret.

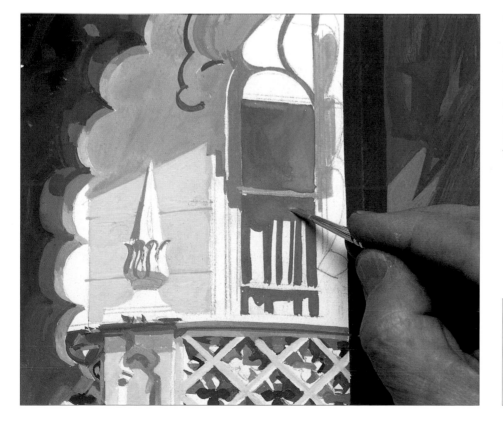

11 Put in the mid-toned areas of the glazing bars on the window, using a slightly paler version of the stone colour used earlier. Mix ultramarine blue, zinc white and a tiny amount of yellow and paint the reflections of the sky in the window, painting around the very lightest areas, where the curtain hangs in folds.

Tip: To avoid dirtying the white on your palette when mixing it with other colours, use a clean brush and add white to the colour you have already mixed rather than vice versa.

Assessment time

Now that the painting is almost complete, spend some time assessing the tonal values. Is the difference in tone between the light and dark areas strong enough? Any adjustments that you make in the final stages will be very slight.

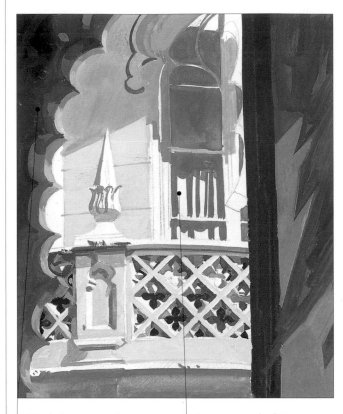

This dark mass tends to overpower the image; the highlights should be reinstated.

The unpainted white areas are too stark; they leap out from the image and demand attention.

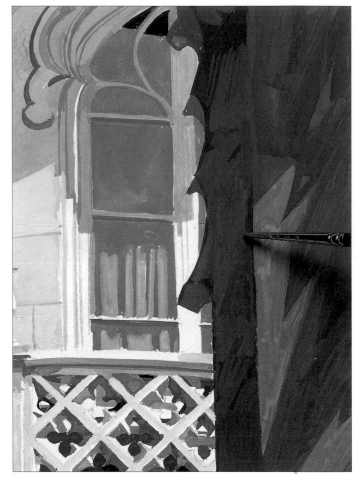

12 Using the stone colour, reinforce the shadows on the underside of the glazing bars. Mix a pale blue from ultramarine blue and lots of zinc white and paint those highlight areas of the curtain that are unpainted. Paint the scalloped edges that jut out from the right-hand side of the arch and scumble a little blue over the darkest part of the arch in order to create some texture and variety of tone in the stonework.

13 Dot in some pure white highlights on the left-hand side of the arch, where light shines through the tracery of the stonework.

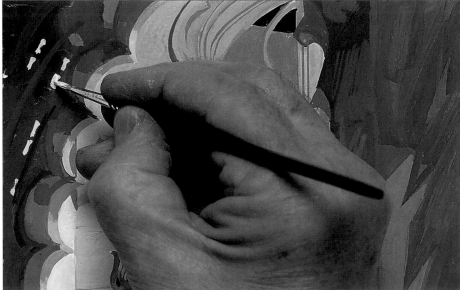

Tip: Keep the paint mix quite thick when you are putting in highlights. If you use very watery paint, it is harder to control and may run. Touch the tip of a fine brush into the paint so that there is very little paint on the fibres, and hold the brush almost vertical to the support so that you can make very small, tightly controlled marks.

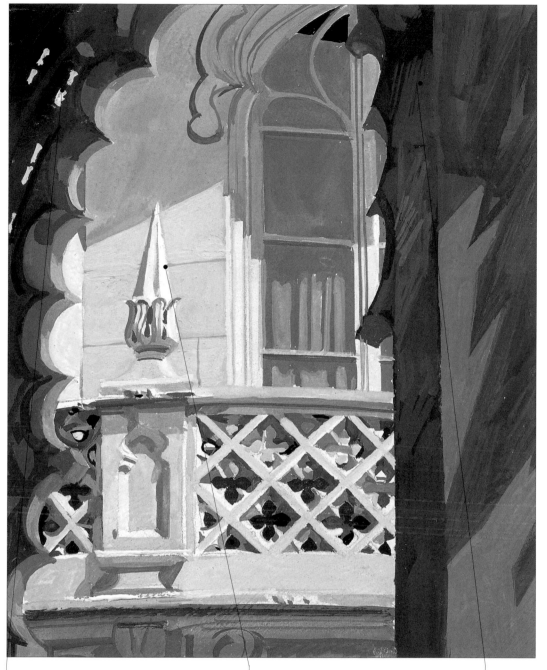

The finished painting
This is a considered painting of an interesting architectural detail. However the bold shadows and sense of light and shade lift it beyond being a mere record of the building. The arch frames the view, but the fact that it is off-centre creates a more dynamic and interesting composition. The colour palette is limited, but the subtle differences in tone have been carefully observed to create a scene that really looks three-dimensional.

Using gouache enables you to paint highlights over dark paint without any of the underlying colour showing through.

Note how the subtle differences in tone convey the feeling of strong sunlight and the form of the turret.

Scumbling different colours over the darkest area prevents it from looking flat and creates texture and variety in the stonework.

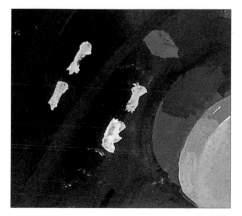

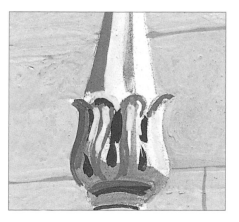

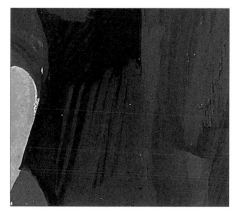

Moorish palace

Small details can often sum up the character of a building far more effectively than a view of the building in its entirety – particularly when, as here, there is an abundance of decorative detail in the form of beautifully shaped arches and mosaic tilework.

This scene shows part of a fourteenth-century Moorish palace in Andalucia, in southern Spain. The view is painted from the central courtyard, which is surrounded by a cool, shaded gallery of the horse-shoe-shaped arches that are so typical of this area and period. An arched doorway on one side of the gallery leads into a beautiful walled garden resplendent with splashing fountains.

Try to respect the architect's intentions when you are painting buildings of any kind. Symmetry was an important consideration in Moorish architecture and a symmetrical composition will help you to capture something of the formality of this particular building. Remember, however, that you are making a painting, not an architectural plan: you also have to take into consideration things like the play of light and shade and the contrast between the heat of the garden and the coolness of the gallery.

Materials
- *Acrylic paper*
- *Acrylic paints: phthalocyanine green, phthalocyanine blue, cadmium red, titanium white, lemon yellow, alizarin crimson, ultramarine blue, brilliant yellow green*
- *Brushes: large round, medium flat, medium round, small flat*
- *Charcoal pencil*

The courtyard and gallery
From this angle, the arch creates a "frame within a frame", leading us through to the garden and fountains. We can also see the gallery surrounding the courtyard, which tells us more about the building as a whole, and there is an interesting and atmospheric contrast between the brightly lit garden and the cool, shaded gallery.

The garden and fountains
Here, you can see the garden and fountains clearly. Architecturally, however, it is not as interesting as the view from the courtyard.

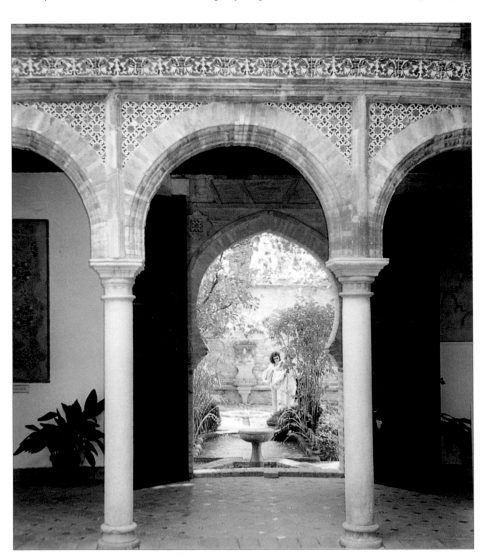

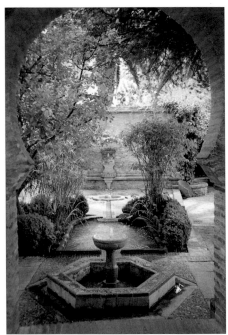

Tip: Always spend time exploring your subject from different viewpoints before you start painting; even a slight adjustment to your position can make a substantial difference. Instead of trying to capture the whole scene, decide what elements appeal to you most – and make quick compositional sketches to decide which viewpoint works best.

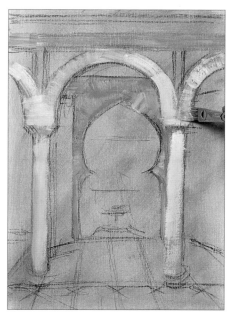

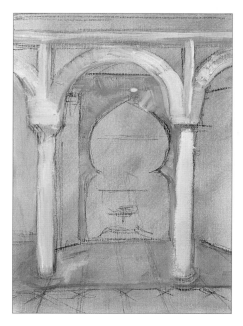

1 Mix a bright blue from phthalocyanine green and phthalocyanine blue. Using a large round brush, lay a flat wash over the paper. Leave to dry. Using a charcoal pencil, sketch the scene, observing the perspective carefully to ensure that all the lines run at the correct angles.

2 Mix a warm, off-white stone colour from cadmium red, titanium white and lemon yellow. Using a medium flat brush, paint the lightest tones of the vertical columns and foreground arch. Add a little more red to the mixture and paint the arch into the garden and the line of bricks above the foreground arch.

3 Add more water to the mixture and paint the shaded tiled area of floor beyond the arch. Because the paint is very dilute, it serves as a glaze, allowing some of the colour of the support to show through.

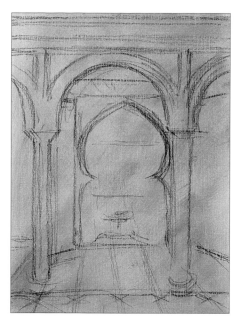

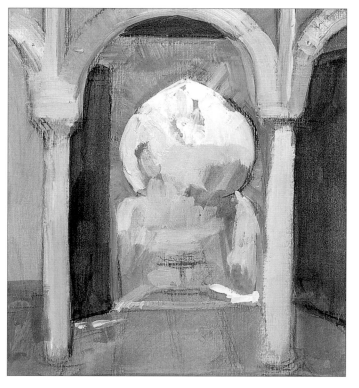

4 Mix a purple shadow colour from alizarin crimson, ultramarine blue and a little lemon yellow and, using a medium round brush, paint the huge wooden doors on each side of the arch leading into the garden. Use a dilute version of the same colour for the tiled courtyard floor.

5 Mix a pale, bright green from brilliant yellow green and titanium white and paint the lightest foliage. Add more brilliant yellow green and a little ultramarine blue and dot in some darker foliage. Paint the pool surround in the stone colour from Step 2, adding more white for the side in sunlight.

▶

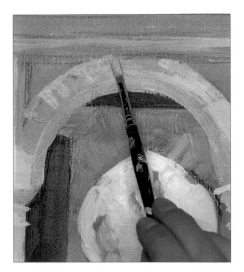

6 Mix a warmer stone colour from cadmium red, lemon yellow and titanium white and, using a small flat brush, paint the darker-toned bricks that run around the top of the arch.

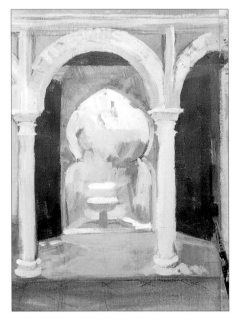

7 Paint the fountain base in the same colour and the interior of the fountain bowl in the initial pale stone colour. Add more water to the pale stone colour and scumble it loosely over the ground inside the archway. Reinforce the shadows at the top and base of the supporting columns. Brush a little very dilute lemon yellow over the wooden doors.

Assessment time

Although the dark wooden doors give some indication of perspective and distance, the image looks very flat and one-dimensional. There is some detailing on the brickwork of the arches, but the garden in the background consists of little more than a few blocks of colour. The next stage is to reinforce the sense of depth. More foreground details, suggesting the intricacy of the carved arches, would help to bring the arches forwards in the scene. Introducing some reflected light into the glazed tiles of the gallery floor would help to connect this area with the sunlit garden that lies beyond.

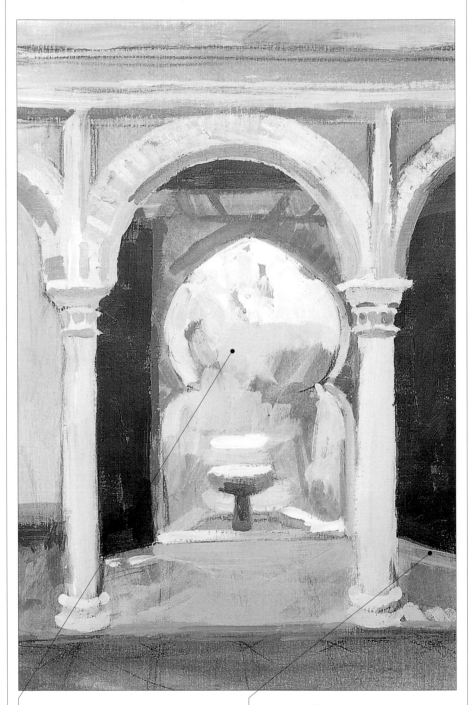

Indistinct masses of green imply the garden beyond, but more definition is needed.

The sloping line of the door gives some indication of depth and perspective.

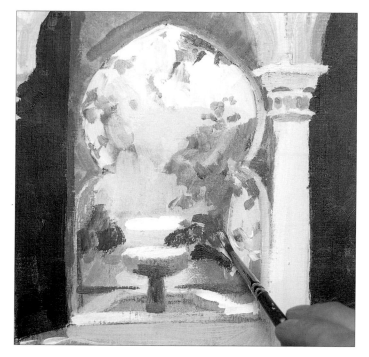

8 Mix a dark green from phthalocyanine green and brilliant yellow green, and a lighter green from brilliant yellow green and lemon yellow. Using a small round brush, dot these two mixtures over the foliage to give it more form, using the lighter colour higher up, where the sun catches the trees.

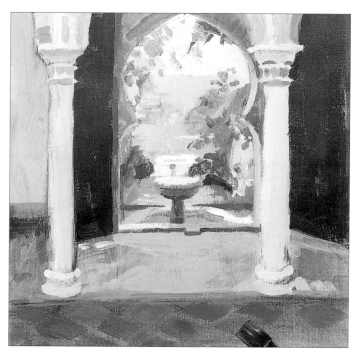

9 Mix a dull red from cadmium red, titanium white and a little phthalocyanine blue. Using a medium flat brush, put in the terracotta tiles of the courtyard, leaving lines of the blue glaze showing through. Darken the shaded edge of the step leading into the garden with the same colour.

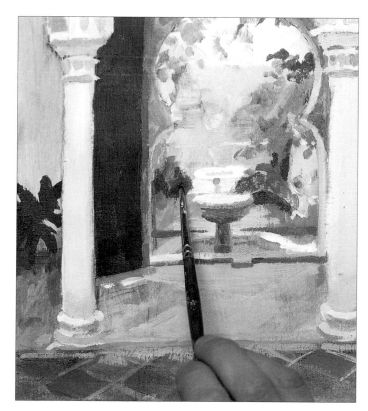

10 Mix a greenish black from phthalocyanine green and a little ultramarine blue. Block in the dark leaves of the potted plant to the left of the foreground arch and dot the same colour into the foliage in the garden; again, this helps to link the inner and outer courtyards.

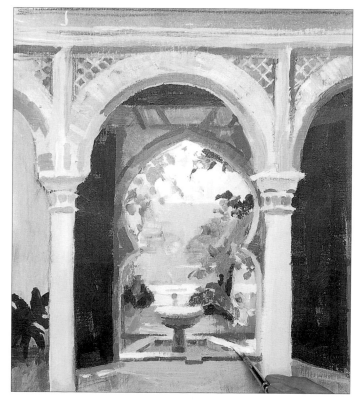

11 Add a little cadmium red and some titanium white to the pale stone colour and, using a small flat brush, put in the pink-coloured tiles around the top of the archway. Paint the small blue tiles in this area in a mixture of phthalocyanine blue and titanium white. Darken the shaded edge of the step.

▶

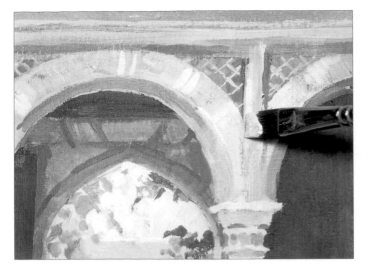

12 Add a little titanium white to the pale stone colour and, using the tip of a small flat brush, paint mortar lines around the top of the arch. Using the same colour, paint the highlit side of the column that separates the central arch from its neighbour.

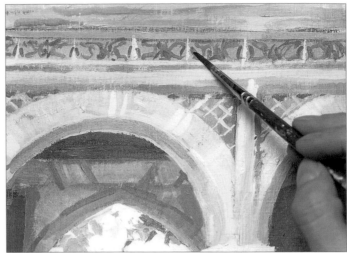

13 Using a small round brush and the terracotta mixture from Step 9, paint the plaster above the tiles. Paint the decorative tiles above the arch using the same colour and phthalocyanine blue. Interpret the pattern loosely. Add the mortar lines that separate the tiles, as you did in Step 12.

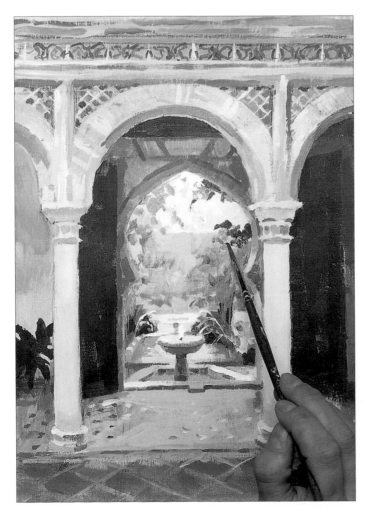

14 Paint the water splashing from the fountain in titanium white. Mix a pale ochre from lemon yellow and brilliant yellow green and paint the back wall of the garden, allowing some of the foliage colour to remain visible.

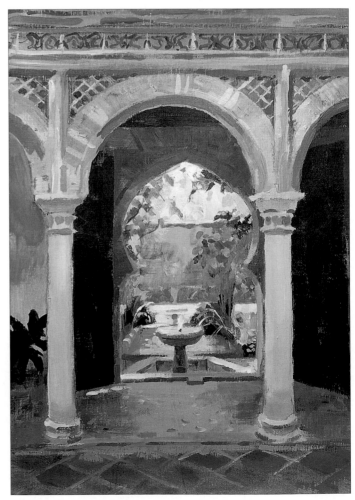

15 Mix a very dilute, dull purple from alizarin crimson and phthalocyanine blue and paint the shadows cast by the heavy wooden doors on the tiled floor with smooth, even brush strokes.

The finished painting

This painting is all about contrasts: contrasts of light and shade and of warmth and coolness. The colour palette is beautifully balanced: the colour of the blue-toned ground is picked up in the tilework and the water, while terracotta and ochre complement the blue and bring added warmth to the scene. The arch in the foreground acts as a frame for the arched doorway and the garden beyond – an established compositional device that draws the viewer's eye through the picture.

The soft colours of the tiles, brickwork and plaster look faded, as befits the age of the building.

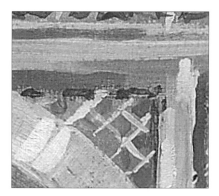

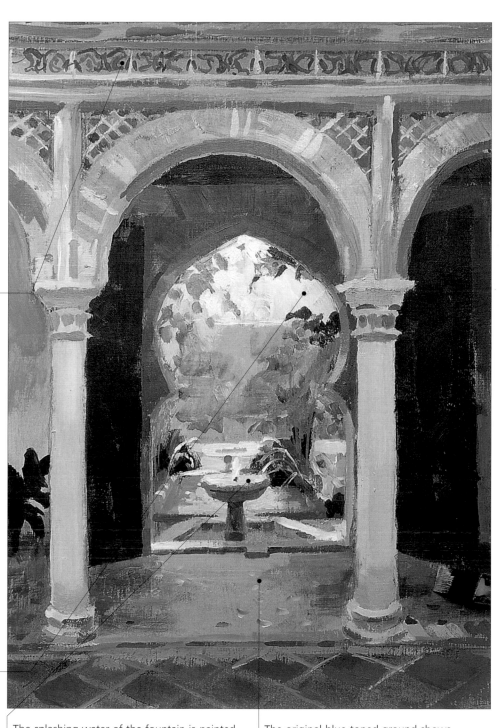

Pale yellows and greens are used to show how strongly the sunlight is hitting the tops of the trees.

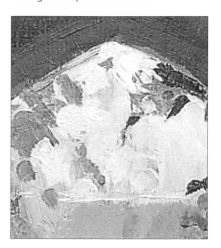

The splashing water of the fountain is painted with energetic, curving brushstrokes.

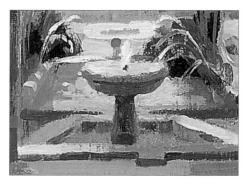

The original blue-toned ground shows through the thin terracotta glaze, creating a feeling of coolness in this shaded area.

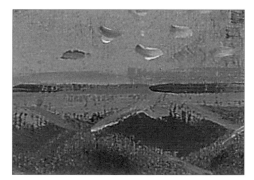

Wisteria-covered archway

Using an archway as a frame for a view is a classic compositional device, drawing the viewer's eye through the scene to linger on what lies beyond. Here, however, the view through the arch is little more than a soft, out-of-focus blur: the main interest lies around the arch itself, in the form of the old and somewhat worn brick wall and the violet-coloured wisteria flowers that cascade over it.

In this project, acrylic paint is used both in thin glazes to build up the colour and more thickly, mixed with white, for the mortar lines in the brickwork and the wisteria flowers.

Contrasts of texture are important in building up the image, and a range of techniques is used to achieve this. Spatters of paint in the foreground convey the gravelly texture of the path; fine texture paste on the wall gives a sense of the worn, crumbling brickwork; and different brushstrokes, from flowing curves to short dabs and dashes, capture the textures and shapes of the foreground plants.

Materials
- *300gsm (140lb) NOT watercolour paper*
- *HB pencil*
- *Painting knife*
- *Fine texture paste*
- *Ruling drawing pen or fine-nibbed steel dip pen*
- *Masking fluid (frisket)*
- *Acrylic paints: light blue violet, vermilion, Hooker's green, yellow ochre, titanium white, violet, burnt sienna, cadmium orange, cadmium yellow, ultramarine blue*
- *Brushes: medium chisel or round*
- *Waterproof sepia ink*

The scene
Although this viewpoint shows the arch and pathway well, there is no real focus of interest and the detail of the flowers is indistinct.

The wisteria flowers
By moving around to the right, the artist was able to see more clearly the colours in the petals and how the flowers hang in clusters. Taking reference photographs or making quick sketches of details such as this will prove invaluable.

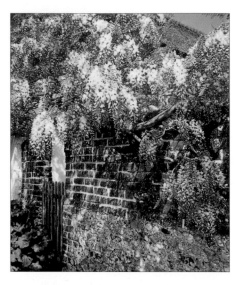

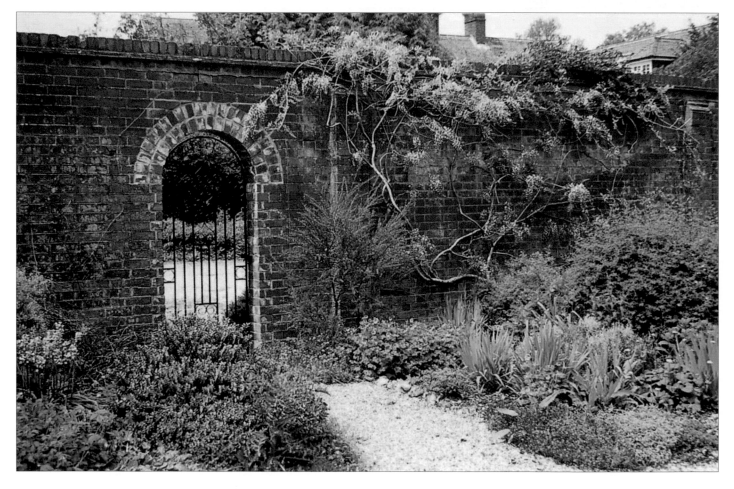

1 Using an HB pencil, lightly sketch the scene. Using the tip of a small painting knife, dab texture paste randomly over the brickwork and the path. Leave to dry. Dip a ruling drawing pen or fine-nibbed steel dip pen in masking fluid (frisket) and mask out the lightest parts of the wisteria and the other foreground flowers, and the mortar lines around the archway and in the brick wall. Leave to dry.

2 Mix a very dilute wash of light blue violet and, using a medium chisel or round brush, apply it over the sliver of sky that is visible at the top of the image and through the archway. Brush dilute Hooker's green over the foliage that can be seen through the arch. Mix yellow ochre with a little vermilion and titatnium white and brush this mixture over the path on the far side of the arch.

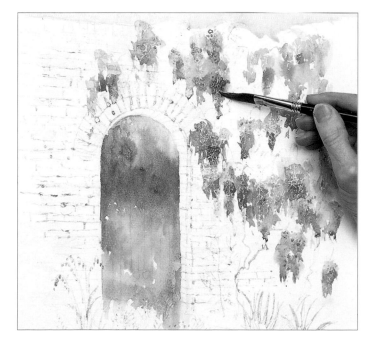

3 Mix separate washes of violet and light blue violet. Alternating between the mixtures, brush these colours over the flowers. For the deepest-coloured flowers, drop more violet, wet into wet, into the first wash. Leave to dry.

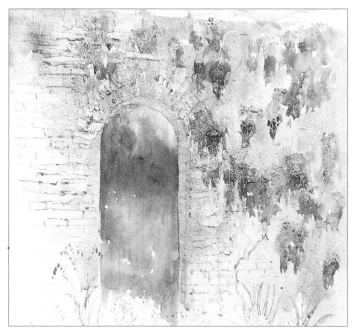

4 Brush a dilute wash of burnt sienna over the brick wall, changing to very pale yellow ochre for the lower part of the wall, and a mixture of burnt sienna and cadmium orange over the archway.

▶

5 Mix a warm brown from burnt sienna, Hooker's green and vermilion and, while the brickwork is still wet, drop this mixture into it in places to deepen the colour. Brush in the general shapes of the wisteria foliage and the foliage above the wall in Hooker's green. Using various mixtures of Hooker's green and Hooker's green plus cadmium yellow, start painting the spiky foliage of the foreground plants.

> **Tip**: When painting the foliage, match your brushstrokes to the shape of the plant – curving, calligraphic strokes for long-leaved plants, short dots and dashes for round-leaved plants.

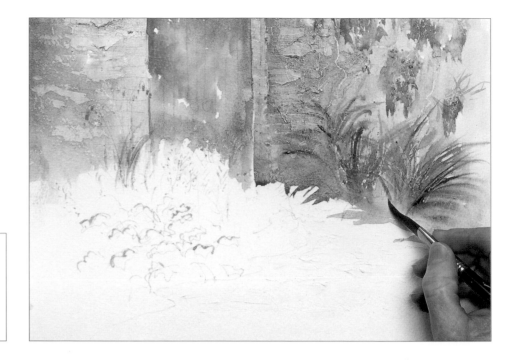

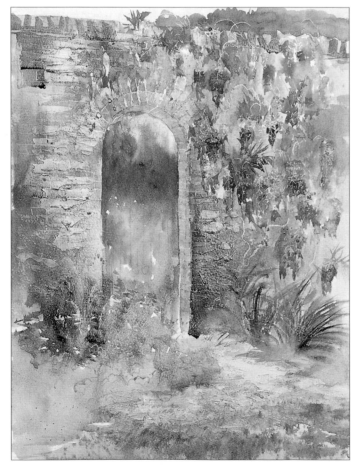

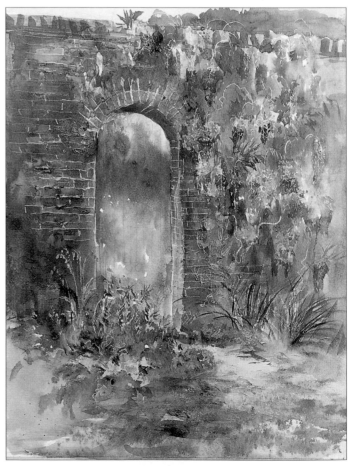

6 Brush the warm brown colour from Step 5 over the foreground and the darkest parts of the wall to build up the colour. While it is still wet, add more burnt sienna to the mixture and spatter it over the first brown. Mix a dark blue-green from Hooker's green and ultramarine blue and paint the foliage to the left of the arch, adding cadmium yellow to the mixture for the grass at the base of the image. Leave to dry.

7 Using the blue-green mixture from the previous step, continue painting the foliage to the left of the arch, noting the spiky shapes of the leaves. Mix a dark brown from violet and burnt sienna and brush this mixture over the wall and path, so that the colour is gradually built up in thin glazes. Apply the colour unevenly to create some tonal variation and texture.

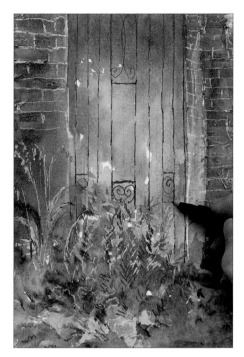

8 Using a technical drawing pen or fine-nibbed steel dip pen loaded with waterproof sepia ink, draw the wrought-iron gateway. (Black ink would look too harsh: sepia is a much more gentle colour.)

Tip: The ink must be waterproof, otherwise it will smudge if any paint is applied on top of it.

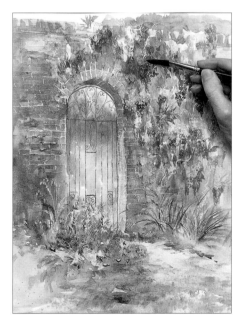

9 The wisteria flowers look a little flat; build them up by brushing on pure violet in the darkest areas. Leave to dry.

Assessment time

Rub off the masking fluid with your fingertips; sometimes it is hard to see whether or not you have removed all the fluid, so run your fingers over the whole painting to make sure no lumps of fluid are left. Blow or shake off any loose, dried fluid before you continue painting.

Although the painting is nearing completion, it needs a little more "punch" and contrast. Take some time at this stage to assess where more work is needed: by glazing selected areas with thin layers of acrylic paint, you can build up the colours to the required density while at the same time adding much-needed texture on areas such as the path and brickwork. The adjustments that you make in these final stages of the painting will be relatively small, but they make an important contribution to the overall effect.

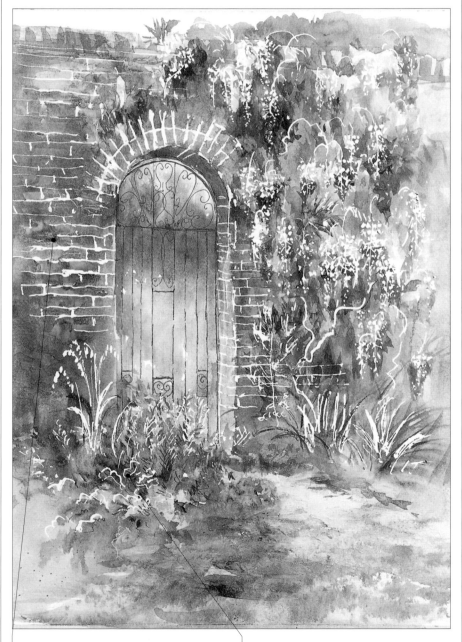

The areas previously covered by the masking fluid are too stark and need to be knocked back.

More detail is required in the foreground foliage.

▶

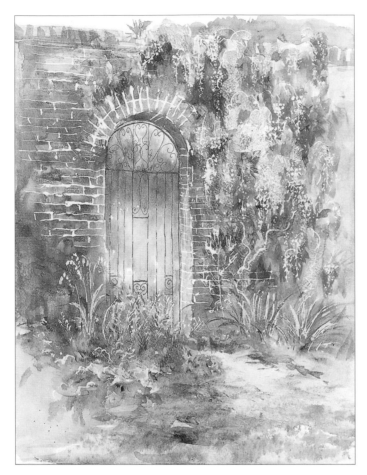

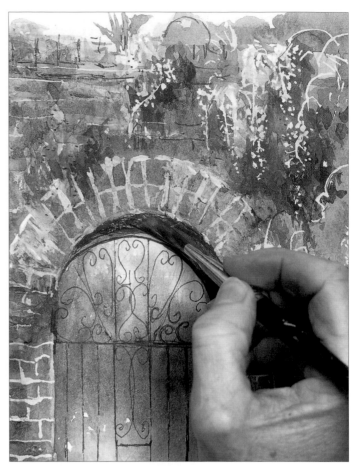

10 Apply a thin glaze of light blue violet over the exposed parts of the wisteria flowers. Mix a dilute yellowy green from Hooker's green and cadmium yellow and brush it over the wisteria trunk and the foliage at the base of the right-hand wall. Mix a blue-green from ultramarine blue and Hooker's green and brush it over the plants to the left of the gate to tint the exposed areas and deepen the foliage colour.

11 Mix a pale, yellowish brown from yellow ochre and green and paint some of the exposed mortar lines in the brickwork. Do not worry if you go outside the mortar lines as it will simply serve as a glaze, enhancing the texture of the crumbling brickwork. Dot violet paint into the wisteria flowers to give more contrast between the light and dark flowers. Paint the shaded interior of the arch in the same colour.

12 Dotting the paint on the tip of the brush, paint the lightest wisteria flowers in a pale, opaque mixture of white and light blue violet. This points up the contrast between the lightest and darkest areas and gives the flowers more depth.

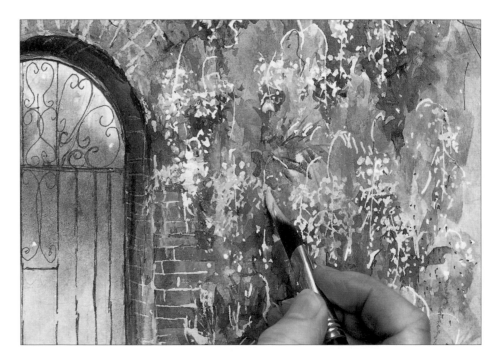

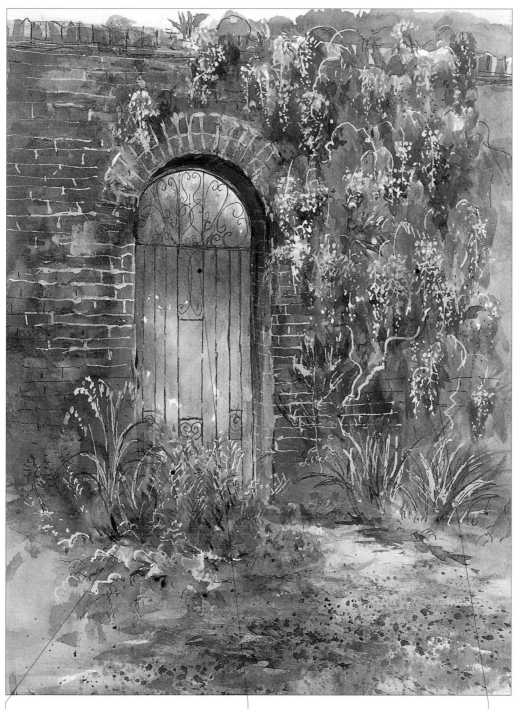

The finished painting
This is a soft, romantic painting of part of an old walled garden. The plants are painted in a fairly loose, impressionistic way rather than as highly resolved botanical studies, but they are nonetheless recognizable from their general shapes and colours. The path draws our eye through the scene to the flower-covered wall and archway; the arch itself is positioned slightly off centre, which adds interest to the composition and prevents it from looking too static.

The blue-green colour of the plants in this area balances the blues and violets of the wisteria.

Although no detail is visible, the garden beyond the archway is implied through the use of soft, muted colours.

The artist has paid careful attention to the different colours within the flowers and to the overall shapes of the flower clusters.

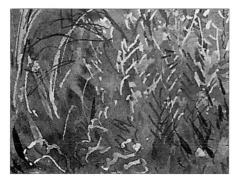

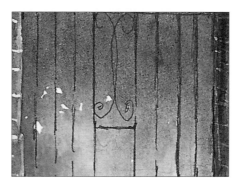

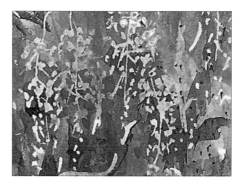

Domestic interior

For this project the artist painted part of his kitchen, with one of his own paintings hanging on the wall. Why not set yourself the challenge of painting a small corner of your own home? It will have relevance and personal associations for you and your family – and you will have the advantage of painting something that you know well already. You can include objects that have special significance for you, such as family heirlooms or holiday souvenirs – but be selective and don't try to include too much, or it will be difficult to establish a centre of interest in the scene.

Choose your viewpoint carefully and remember that it's perfectly all right not to include the whole of an object. Here, for example, the artist decided to include less than half of the table, but did add a tablecloth. This gives an air of informality to the scene, making it seem like a snapshot of family life. The fact that the table is slightly angled, rather than painted square on, also leads the viewer's eye into the scene and makes for a much more dynamic composition.

One of the beauties of working with acrylics is that you can build up several layers of thin glazes. This gives a richness and luminosity to the work, as glazed colours reflect light more readily than opaque colours. This is the approach that is taken in this project and it seems to work particularly well in a scene such as this, which contains many smooth surfaces.

Materials
- *Canvas primed with acrylic gesso*
- *Acrylic paints: cadmium yellow light, raw umber, ultramarine blue, yellow ochre, permanent violet, vermillion, magenta, titanium white, cerulean blue, cadmium red, cadmium yellow deep*
- *Brushes: medium flat, flat wash, small round*
- *Rag*
- *Painting knife*

1 Dot cadmium yellow light acrylic paint over the canvas and wipe over it with a rag to spread the paint over the support. It's better if the coverage is slightly uneven. Leave to dry.

The scene
Fruit and flowers on the table inject colour into a scene that consists largely of wood and brick. The flowers also provide a visual link with the painting on the wall.

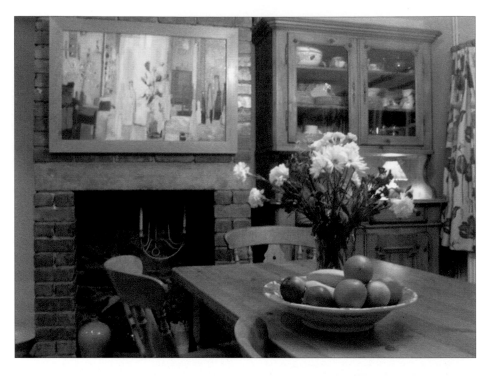

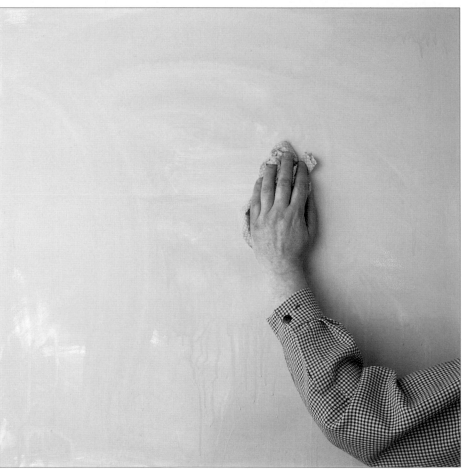

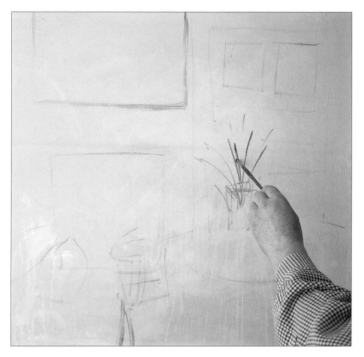

2 Using a medium flat brush, "draw" the frame of the painting on the wall and the fireplace recess in raw umber. Mix a dark green from cadmium yellow light and ultramarine blue and outline the struts of the chair, the panels in the dresser and the flower stems. Leave to dry.

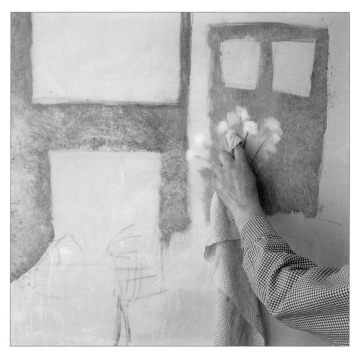

3 Block in the brick-covered chimney breast and the wood of the dresser in yellow ochre, painting around the green flower stems. While the paint is still wet, wet a rag with water and wipe off circular smudges of colour for the flower heads. Although the paint feels dry, it won't be totally immovable for about 24 hours and the yellow will come off if you rub gently.

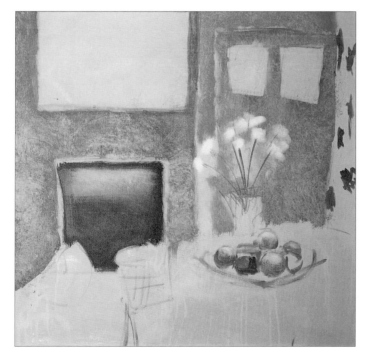

4 Paint the dark recess of the fireplace in permanent violet and the shaded side of the dresser in raw umber. Sketch the outline of the bowl of fruit on the table in yellow ochre and block in the oranges and bananas in the same colour, leaving the highlights untouched. Paint the reddest part of the apples in vermillion and begin putting in the red flowers on the curtains.

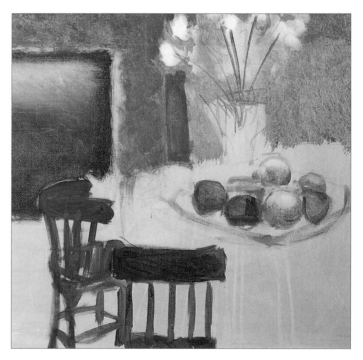

5 Paint the chair in vermillion. Although you are simply blocking in the underlying colour at this stage, without putting in any detailing, it will act as a glaze and establish the warm colour of the wood. At this point the artist decided to include another chair in his composition. He painted it in permanent violet as a chair in this position would be in shade and hence darker in tone than the other chair.

▶

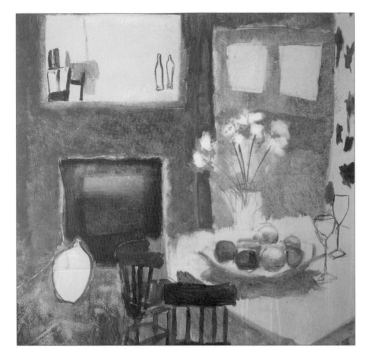

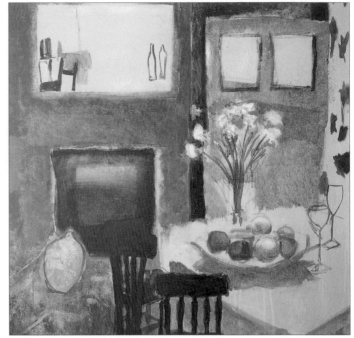

6 Outline the stone jar on the hearth in the green mixture from Step 2. Begin putting in some of the detail of the painting on the wall. Paint the shadow under the fruit bowl in raw umber. Paint the tiled floor and the shaded sides of the table in magenta. Draw the outlines of two stemmed wine glasses on the table in green.

7 Glaze yellow ochre over the stone jar on the hearth. Paint the shaded sides of the chair in a dark, almost black mixture of red and green, leaving the seat red; immediately it begins to look more rounded and three-dimensional.

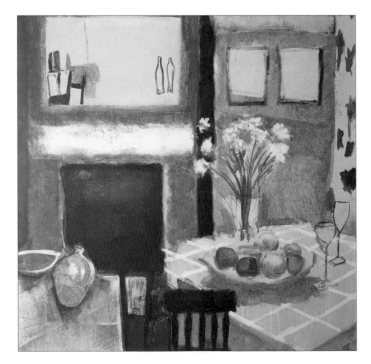

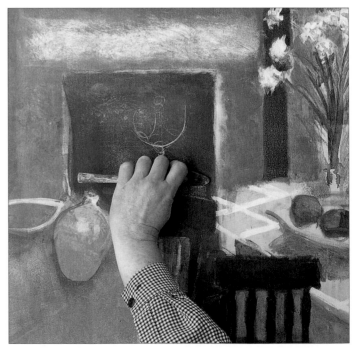

8 Outline a round bowl on the hearth in titanium white and block it in using yellow ochre. Paint the highlights on the stone jar in titanium white. Brush dilute titanium white over the tiled floor and the fireplace lintel. Use a thicker mix of titanium white to paint the checks on the tablecloth. Brush ultramarine blue over the fireplace recess and the shaded side of the dresser. Leave to dry.

9 Using the tip of your painting knife, scratch off paint in the shape of the outline of the candle sconce in the fireplace. Still using the painting knife, scratch off paint to create highlights on the back of the chair. You could equally well paint these elements in white, but sgraffito imparts a lively quality to the work and is an interesting technique to experiment with.

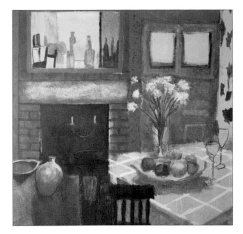

10 Paint the lines of the bricks in vermillion. Mix a dull brown from raw umber and cadmium yellow light and paint the picture frame. Glaze the same colour over the shaded side of the dresser, which you painted blue in Step 8.

Tip: Because the colours in glazes mix optically, rather than physically, the mixes often look more lively.

Assessment time

The overall warm mood of the scene has been set. Although the colours may look unnatural at this stage, they will be modified as the painting progresses. Never be afraid to alter things halfway through if you feel they're not working. At this point the artist decided that the checked tablecloth was overpowering the image and that the chair-back in the immediate foreground blocked the viewer's eye from moving through the picture. Radical changes were needed!

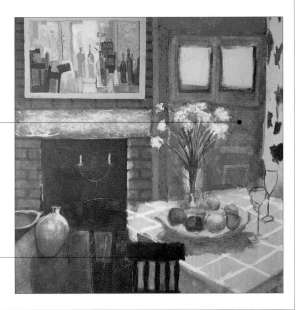

The rich, warm colours look very dominant at this stage, but they provide a warm undertone for the scene.

The chair-back interferes with the composition.

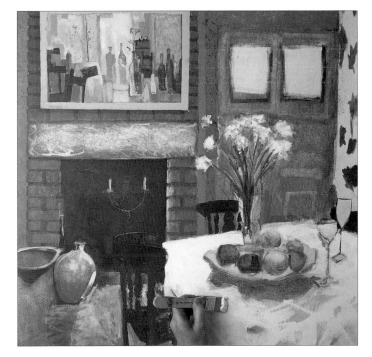

11 Using a large flat wash brush, brush titanium white over the tablecloth and the tiled floor, carefully brushing around the stone jar on the hearth and between the struts on the chair. At this point the artist also painted out the chair in the immediate foreground, which he felt had become too intrusive, and at the same time added another chair-back to the fireplace end of the table.

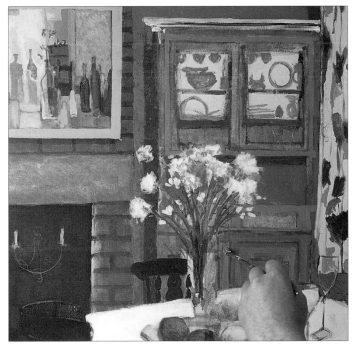

12 Complete the pattern on the curtains using cerulean blue and cadmium red. Using a small round brush, paint the china in the dresser in cerulean blue. Mix a mid-toned brown from cadmium yellow light, raw umber and titanium white and brush this mixture over the dresser. The colour now looks more natural, but it still retains the warm glow of the underlying orange.

▶

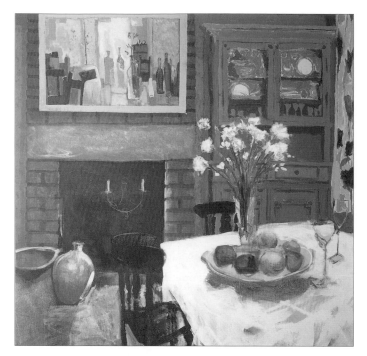

13 Finish painting the china in the dresser. As it is behind glass, which reflects the light, it is hard to see any detail in the china, so a general impression of the shapes will suffice.

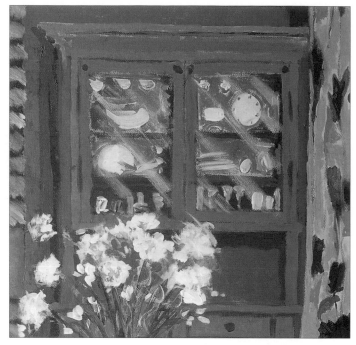

14 Using a small brush, brush thin diagonal strokes of dilute titanium white and white mixed with cerulean blue over the glass doors in the dresser to show how the glass reflects light from the window.

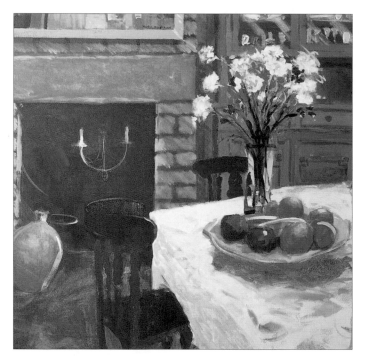

15 Glaze the floor with a mixture of vermillion and titanium white. Paint white highlights on the fruit.

Tip: Allow some of the previous white to show through on the floor, as this creates the impression of light being reflected off the glazed tiles.

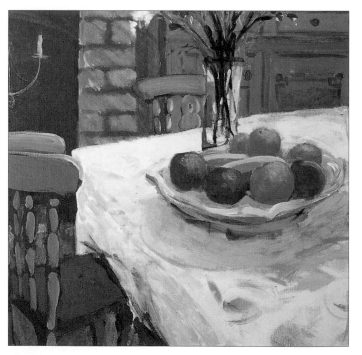

16 Use the mid-toned brown mixture from Step 12 to give the chairs their natural wood colour, leaving the previous purplish tone visible in the most deeply shaded parts. Adjust the tones on the fruits so that they look rounded, using the same colours as before. The bananas, in particular, look too light so paint them again in cadmium yellow deep using permanent violet for the shaded facets.

The finished painting

This is a colourful, contemporary-looking painting. The composition looks informal but has been carefully considered, while the choice of predominantly warm colours creates a cosy and inviting mood. The flowers and fruit contrast well with the solidity of the furniture and fireplace and provide a homely touch that tells us this is a domestic interior.

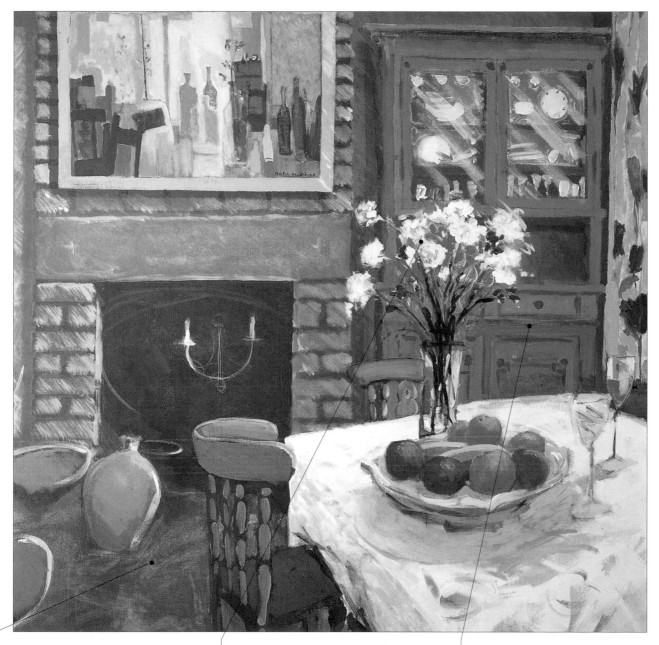

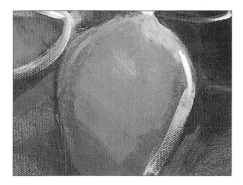

The colour is built up in glazes, creating the effect of light shining on the tiled floor.

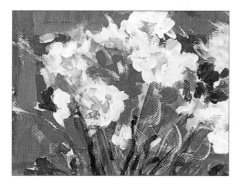

The flowers are loosely painted and enliven the composition.

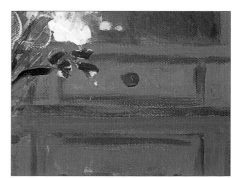

The underlying colours modify subsequent glazes and help to create the wood texture.

Painting people

People are one of the most challenging and rewarding of all subjects to paint and your aim should be to capture not only a good likeness but also something of the sitter's character and personality.

Whether you're painting a head-and-shoulders portrait or a full-length study, it's generally advisable to start by making a reasonably detailed underdrawing. Take careful measurements and concentrate, in particular, on establishing the position of the facial features.

One of the joys of using oils or acrylics for painting people is the ease with which you can blend colours wet into wet on the support, to create almost imperceptible transitions from one tone to another. This

is invaluable when painting flesh tones: the contours of the body are generally soft and rounded, which means that differences in tone can be very subtle – but they are critical in achieving a sense of light and shade and making your subject look three-dimensional. The same technique can be used for painting hair.

If you are new to portrait painting, start with a simple set-up – a plain background and perhaps just one light positioned to one side of your model to cast an obvious shadow. A head-on view, with the model looking directly at you, is the best way to begin. With a profile there are other complications to bear in mind, such as how the nose breaks the line of the cheek.

As you gain more experience and confidence, you can begin to introduce more elements – props that tell us something about the sitter's interests, a domestic interior that reveals something of their lifestyle, even a street scene of people going about their everyday business. Take care not to overcomplicate things, however, or the background will begin to detract from the portrait.

Venice grainseller ▼
In the contre-jour scene such as this, with the light coming from behind the subject, detail is subdued. Nonetheless, the shapes and overall proportions must look right.

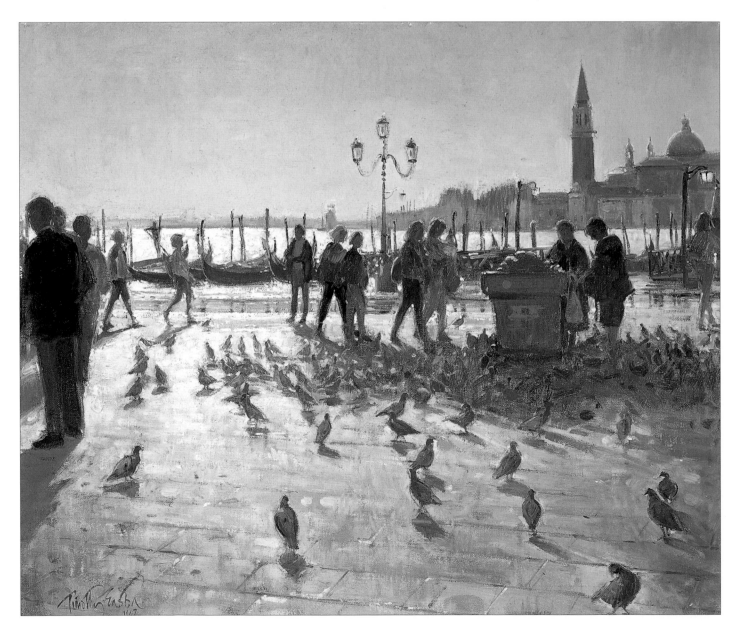

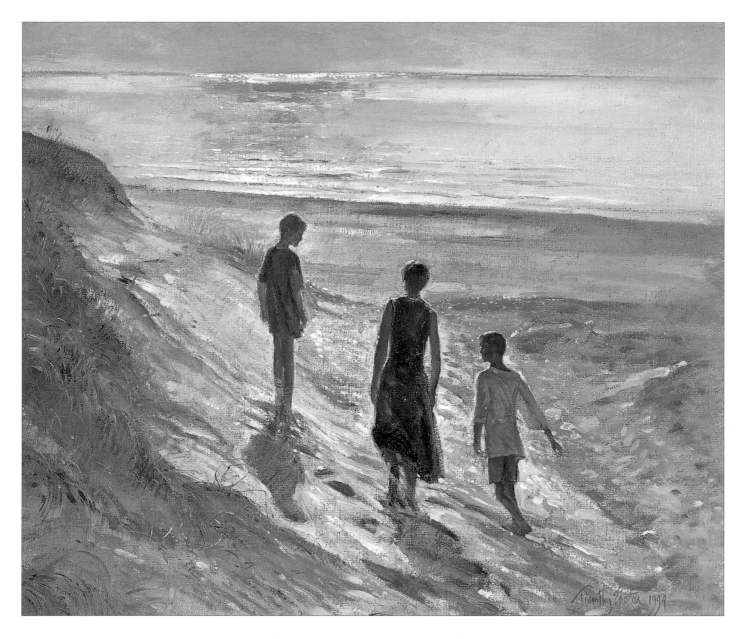

- Treat a portrait in the same way as you would any other subject: plot the facial features systematically, and a likeness will follow.
- Pay attention to things like spectacles and clothes that will give a clue as to what the person is like.
- Assess skin tones carefully. The transitions between one tone and another are subtle, but they help to establish the different planes of the body.

Down to the sea ▲
We cannot see the faces in this delightful painting of a mother and her children walking towards the sea, which imparts a somewhat enigmatic mood to the scene, inviting us to make up our own story about who they are and what they are doing.

Brittany market ▶
The figures are almost incidental to this colourful market scene, as we can see very little of the facial detail, but the stances have been carefully observed and they bring life to the scene.

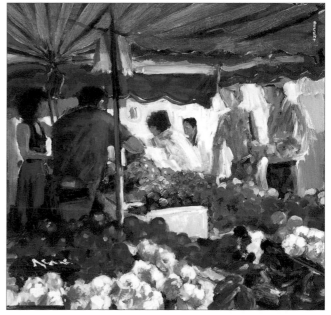

Portrait of a young child

There are several things to remember when you are drawing or painting a portrait of a child. The first is that young children are very active and have a short attention span: you cannot realistically expect them to sit still for hours while you work on your portrait, and for this reason you will probably find it easiest to work from a photograph.

Second, in children the head is much larger in relation to the overall body size than it is in adults. Although the human race is infinitely varied, as a general guideline the head is about one-seventh of the total height of the body in adults – but in babies it may occupy almost as much as one-third of the total. The little girl in this portrait is about two years old: her head represents approximately one-quarter of her total height.

This project starts by toning the support – a classic technique that was much used by some of the great portraitists such as Peter Paul Rubens (1577–1640). This provides the advantage of starting to paint from a mid-tone background, rather than a stark white ground, which makes it easier to judge the subtle flesh tones and the effects of light and shade cast by the sun. It also establishes the overall colour temperature of the portrait from the outset. In this instance, burnt sienna gives the portrait a lovely warm glow, which is particularly appropriate to the dappled sunlight that illuminates the scene.

Materials
- Board primed with acrylic gesso
- Acrylic paints: burnt sienna, ultramarine blue, titanium white, cadmium red, lemon yellow, alizarin crimson, phthalocyanine green
- Brushes: small round, medium flat, small flat
- Rag
- Matt acrylic medium

The pose
Relaxed and informal, this child's attention is occupied by something that we cannot see. Note that she is positioned slightly off centre. If a figure in a portrait is looking off to one side, it is generally better to have more space on that side, as this creates a calmer, more restful mood. Placing a figure close to the edge of the frame creates a feeling of tension.

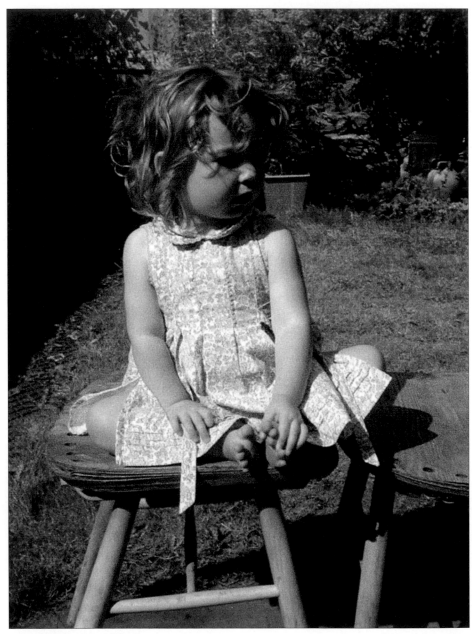

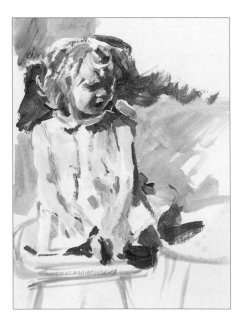

Preliminary sketch
Flesh tones can be tricky, and you may find it useful to make a quick colour sketch experimenting with different mixes, such as the one shown on the left, before you start painting.

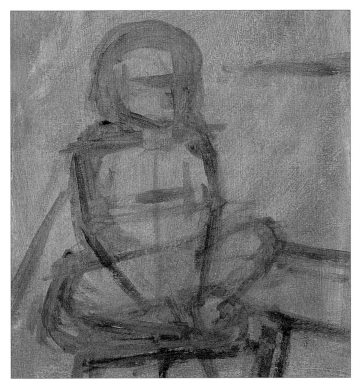

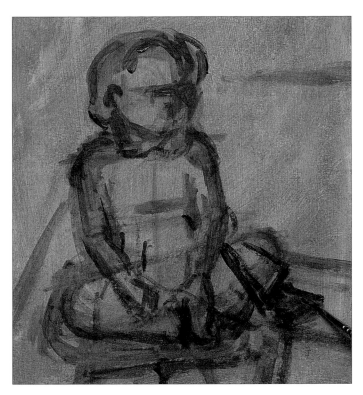

1 Tone the primed board with burnt sienna acrylic paint and leave to dry. Mix a dilute, warm brown from burnt sienna and a little ultramarine blue. Using a small round brush, make a loose underdrawing, concentrating on getting the overall proportions and the angles of the head and limbs correct.

2 Mix a darker, less dilute brown, this time using more ultramarine blue. Using the small round brush, put in the darkest tones of the hair, the shadows on the face and under the collar of the girl's dress, and the main creases in the fabric of the dress. These creases help to convey form.

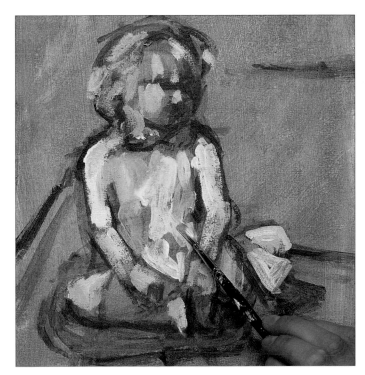

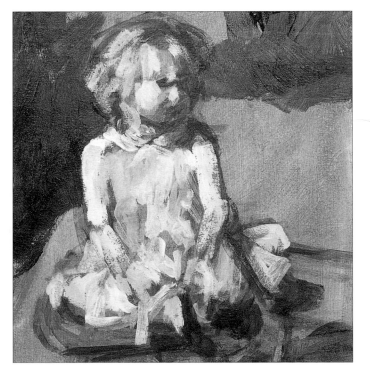

3 Mix a very pale pink from titanium white, cadmium red and a little lemon yellow and paint the palest flesh tones on the face, arms and legs, as well as some highlights in the hair. Add more water and put in the lightest tones of the girl's dress. Note how the colour of the support shows through.

4 Mix a warm purple from ultramarine blue and alizarin crimson. Using a medium flat brush, block in the dark foliage area to the left of the girl. Add more water and ultramarine blue to the mixture and paint the darkest foliage areas to the right of the girl and the shadows under the stool.

▶

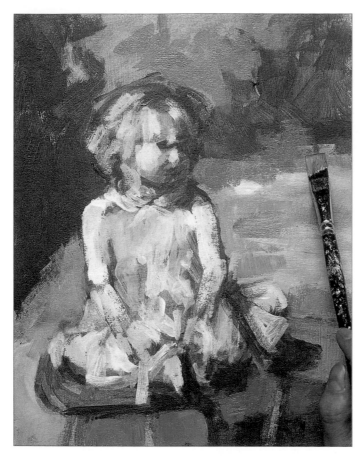

5 Mix a bright green from phthalocyanine green, lemon yellow, titanium white and a little cadmium red. Block in the lawn and background foliage. Use less lemon yellow for the shaded grass and more white for the brightest parts.

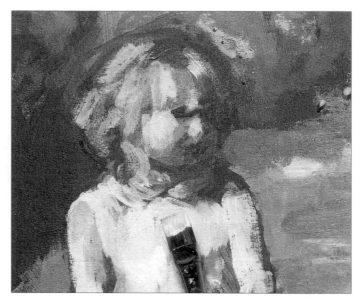

6 Mix a very pale green from titanium white and phthalocyanine green and brush it loosely over the child's sun-bleached cotton dress.

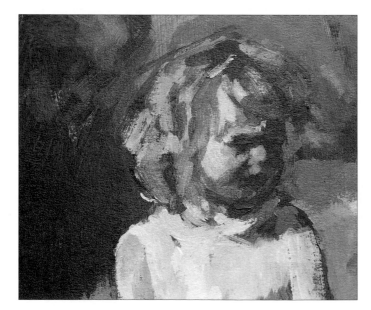

7 Mix a dark brown from burnt sienna and ultramarine blue and start to put some detailing in the hair and on the shadowed side of the face. Mix a warm shadow tone from alizarin crimson and burnt sienna and build up the shadow tones on the left-hand (sunlit) side of the face, alternating between this mixture and the pale pink used in Step 3.

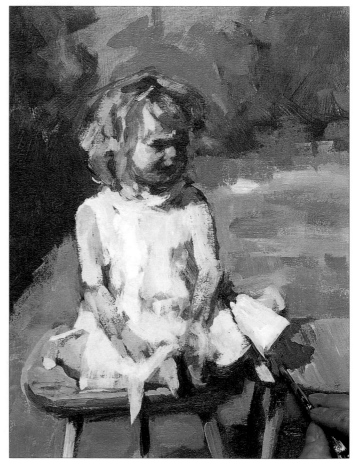

8 Add titanium white to the purple mixture from Step 4 and paint the stool to the right of the child. Paint the stool on which she is sitting in a mixture of brown and titanium white, with brushstrokes that follow the wood grain. Mix a rich brown from burnt sienna and alizarin crimson and, using a small round brush, paint the shadows at the bottom of her dress.

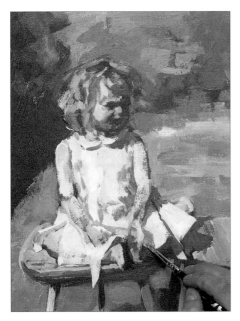

9 Dab some of the purple mixture (the stool colour) over the background foliage. Using the same colour in this area establishes a visual link between foreground and background; the light colour also creates the impression of dappled light in the foliage. Mix a dark, bluish green from ultramarine blue and phthalocyanine green and paint the shadow under the dress collar and any deep creases and shadows in the fabric of the dress.

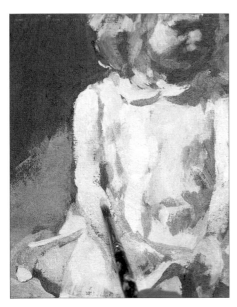

10 Using the pale pink mixture from Step 3 and a round brush, go over the arms and legs again, carefully blending the tones wet into wet on the support in order to convey the roundness of the flesh.

Assessment time
The blocks of colour are now taking on some meaning and form: for the rest of the painting, concentrate on building up the form and detailing.

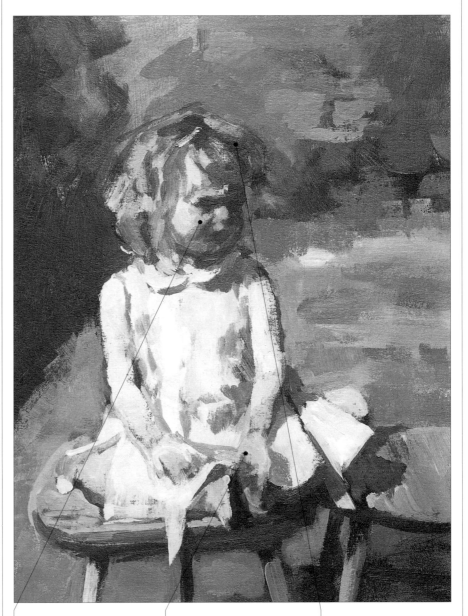

The tonal contrasts on the face are too extreme and need to be blended to make the skin look more life-like.

The hands and feet, in particular, need to be given more definition.

The child is not sufficiently well separated from the background.

Tip: To make flesh look soft and rounded, you need to blend the tones on the support so that they merge almost imperceptibly; it is rare to see a sharp transition from one tone to another. Working wet into wet is the best way to achieve this, gradually darkening the tone as the limb turns away from the light. With acrylic paints, you may find that adding a few drops of flow improver helps matters: flow improver increases the flow of the paint and its absorption into the support surface.

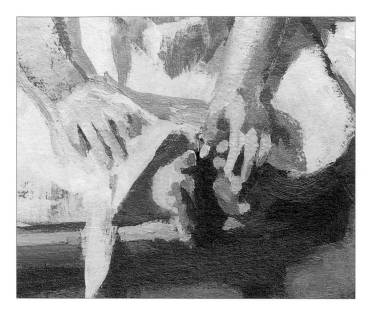

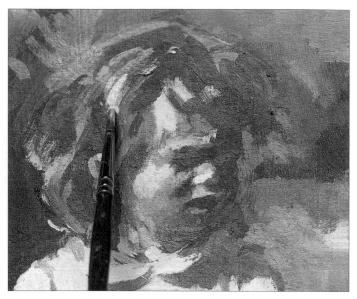

11 Mix burnt sienna with a tiny amount of titanium white. Using a small round brush, paint the dark spaces between the fingers and the shadows between the feet and on the toes. Try to see complicated areas such as these as abstract shapes and blocks of colour: if you start thinking of them as individual toes, the chances are that you will make them bigger than they should be.

12 Refine the facial details, using the same mixes as before. Put in the curve of the ear, which is just visible through the hair, using the pale pink skin tone. Mix a reddish brown from alizarin crimson, ultramarine blue and burnt sienna. Build up the volume of the hair, looking at the general direction of the hair growth and painting clumps rather than individual hairs.

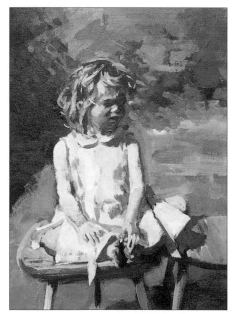

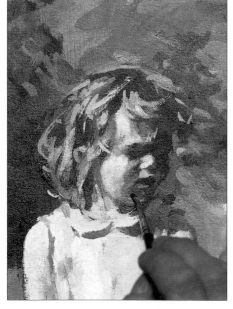

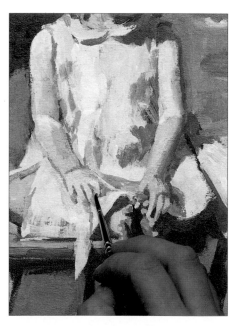

13 Using the purple shadow mixture from Step 4 and a small flat brush, cut in around the head to define the edge and provide better separation between the girl and the background. Mix a dark green from phthalocyanine green and ultramarine blue and loosely dab it over the dark foliage area to provide more texture. Using cool colours here makes this area recede, focusing attention on the little girl.

14 Add a little matt acrylic medium to the pale pink flesh tone and go over the light areas of the face, working the paint in with the brush so that it blends well and covers any areas that are too dark in tone. The matt medium makes the paint more translucent, so that it is more like a glaze. Do the same thing on the arms, adding a little burnt sienna for any areas that are slightly warmer in tone.

15 Make any final adjustments that you deem necessary. Here, the artist felt that the girl's hands were too small, making her look slightly doll-like; using the pale flesh colour from previous steps, she carefully painted over them to make them a little broader and bring them up to the right scale.

The finished painting

This is a charming portrait of a toddler with her slightly chubby face and arms, rounded mouth, big eyes, and unselfconscious pose. There is just enough detail in the background to establish the outdoor setting, but by paying very careful attention to the tones of the highlights and shadows, the artist has captured the dappled sunlight that pervades the scene.

Although no detail is visible in the eyes, we are nonetheless invited to follow the child's gaze.

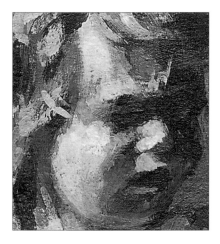

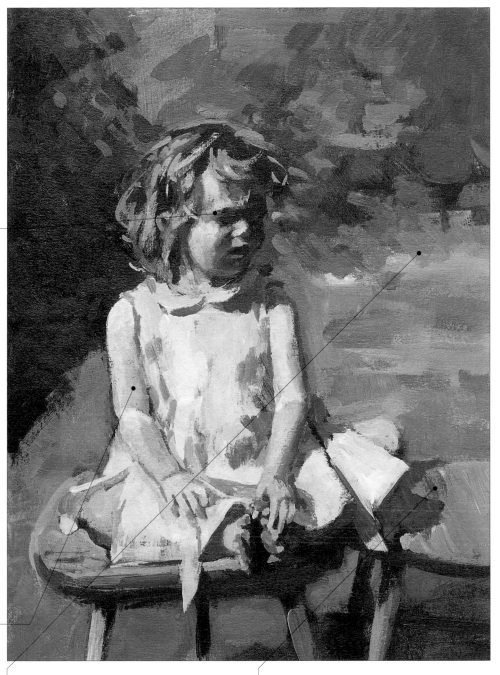

Subtle blending of colour on the child's arms and face makes the flesh look soft and rounded.

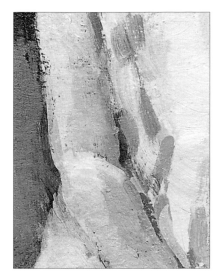

There is just enough background to give the scene a context without distracting from the portrait.

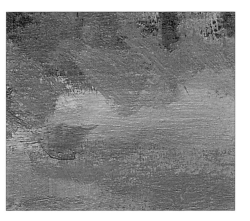

Brushstrokes on the stool follow the direction of the woodgrain – an effective way of conveying both pattern and texture.

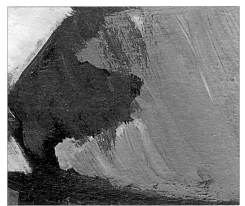

Head-and-shoulders portrait

The surroundings and clothing in this head-and-shoulders portrait have been kept deliberately simple in order to give you an opportunity to practise painting skin tones.

You might think it would make life very simple for artists if there was a ready-mixed skin colour that could be used in all circumstances. However, although you may come across a so-called "flesh tone" in some paint manufacturers' catalogues, it cannot cope with the sheer variety of skin tones that you are likely to encounter.

Even in models with the most flawless of complexions, the skin will not be a uniform colour in all areas. The actual colour (particularly in fair-skinned individuals) can vary dramatically from one part of the subject to another: the cheeks, for example, often look redder than the forehead or chin simply because the blood vessels are closer to the surface. And, just as with any other subject, you need to use different tones in order to make your subject look three-dimensional. To understand this, look at black-and-white magazine photographs of models with good bone structure: note how the cheekbones cast a shadow on the lower part of the face. Even though (thanks to make-up) the skin colour may be virtually the same all over the face, in strong lighting there may be big differences in tone.

You also need to think about colour temperature: using cool colours for the shadows and warmer ones for the lit areas is a good way of showing how the light falls on your model. Although cool blues and purples might seem strange colours to use for painting skin, it is surprising how using them with warmer colours can bring a portrait to life.

The same principles of colour temperature also apply to the light that illuminates your subject. Although we are generally unaware of the differences, the colour of sunlight is not as warm as, say, artificial tungsten lighting. It's hard to be precise about the colours you should use for painting skin tones, as the permutations are almost infinite, so the best advice is simply to paint what you can actually observe rather than what you think is the right colour.

Materials
- Board primed with acrylic gesso
- B pencil
- Acrylic paints: Turner's yellow, cadmium red, titanium white, burnt umber, cadmium yellow, lamp black, phthalocyanine blue, alizarin crimson, yellow ochre
- Brushes: large flat, medium flat, small flat

The pose
A three-quarters pose with the light coming from one side, as here, is generally more interesting to paint than a head-on pose, as it allows you to have one side of the face in shadow, thus creating modelling on the facial features. The lighting also creates highlights in the model's dark eyes, which always helps to bring a portrait to life. Although this model was sitting in front of a very busy background, the artist chose to simplify it to a uniform background colour in the finished portrait to avoid drawing attention away from the face.

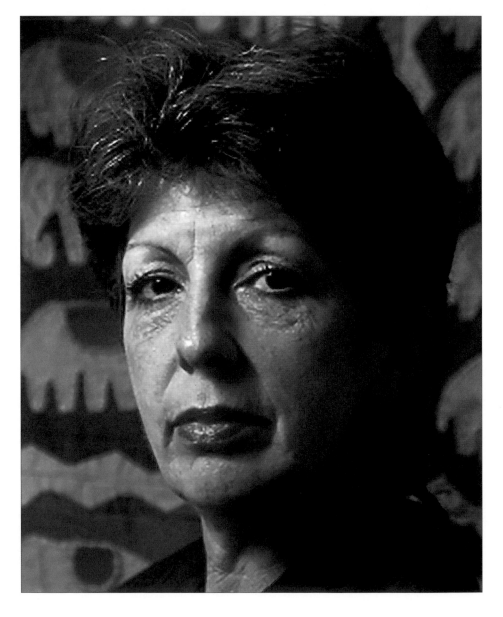

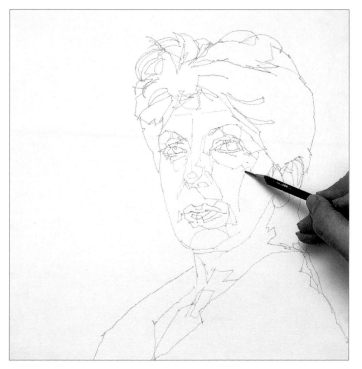

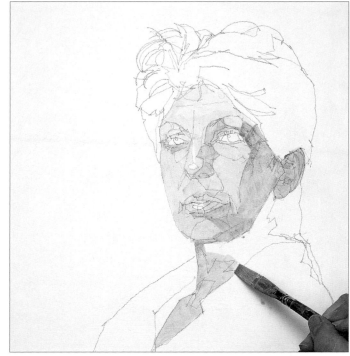

1 Using a B pencil, lightly sketch your subject, indicating the fall of the hair, the facial features and the areas of shadow. Put in as much detail as you wish; it is particularly important to get the size and position of the facial features right.

2 Mix a light flesh tone from Turner's yellow, cadmium red and titanium white. Using a medium flat brush, block in the face and neck, adding a little burnt umber for the shadowed side of the face.

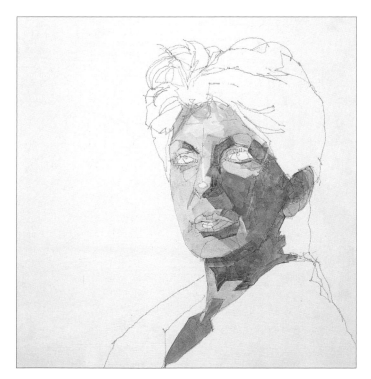

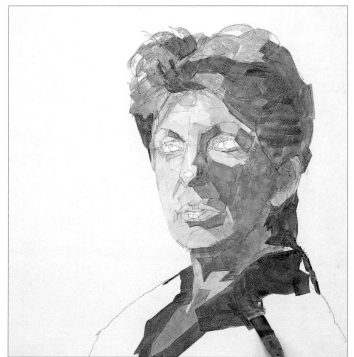

3 Add a little more cadmium red to the flesh-tone mixture and use it to darken the tones on the shadowed side of the face, under the chin and on the neck. Mix a red-biased orangey mix from cadmium red and cadmium yellow and paint the cheek and the shadowed side of the neck and the shaded area that lies immediately under the mouth. Immediately the portrait is taking on a feeling of light and shade.

4 Mix a pale bluish black from lamp black and phthalocyanine blue and begin putting in the lightest tones of the hair, making sure your brushstrokes follow the direction in which the hair grows. When the first tone is dry, add burnt umber to the mixture and paint the darker areas within the hair mass to give the hair volume. Add more phthalocyanine blue to the mixture and paint the model's shirt.

▶

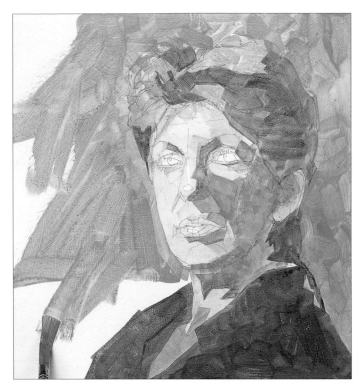

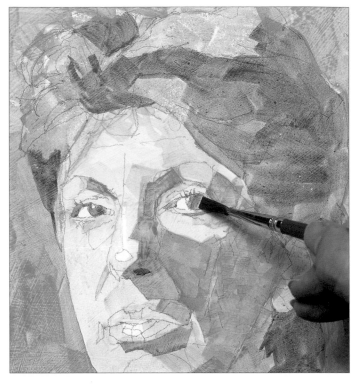

5 Mix a pale brown from cadmium red, burnt umber, Turner's yellow and titanium white and loosely block in the background, painting carefully around the face. You may find it easier to switch to a larger brush for this stage, as it will allow you to cover a wide area more quickly.

6 Mix a rich, dark brown from lamp black, burnt umber, cadmium red and a little of the blue shirt mixture. Using a small flat brush, paint the dark of the eyes and the lashes, taking care to get the shape of the white of the eye right. Use the same colour for the nostril.

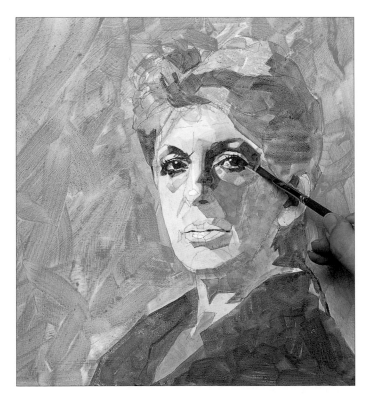

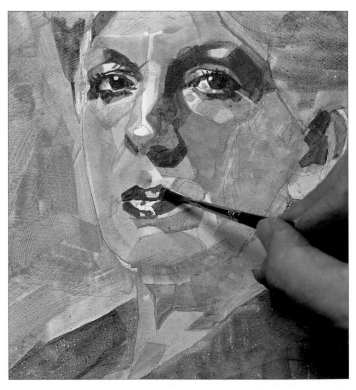

7 Use the same colour to define the line between the upper and lower lips. Mix a reddish brown from burnt umber and phthalocyanine blue and paint the shadows under the eyes and inside the eye sockets.

8 Paint the mouth in varying mixes of alizarin crimson, cadmium red and yellow ochre, leaving the highlights untouched. The highlights will be worked into later, using lighter colours.

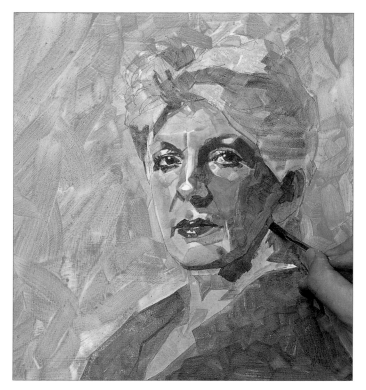

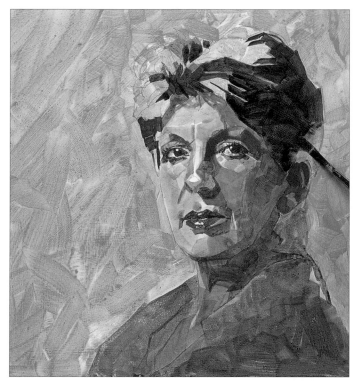

9 Darken the flesh tones on the shaded side of the face where necessary, using a mixture of alizarin crimson, phthalocyanine blue and a little titanium white, adding more blue to the mixture for the shadow under the chin, which is cooler in tone.

10 Mix a dark but warm black from burnt umber and lamp black and paint the darkest sections of the hair, leaving the lightest colour (applied in Step 4) showing through in places. This gives tonal variety and shows how the light falls on the hair.

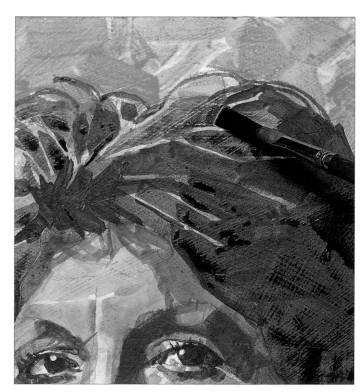

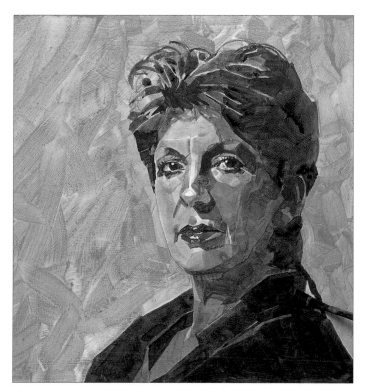

11 Add more water to the mixture to make it more dilute and go over the dark areas of the hair again, this time leaving only a few highlights showing through as relatively fine lines.

12 Mix a dark blue from phthalocyanine blue and lamp black and paint over the shirt again, leaving some of the lighter blue areas applied in Step 4 showing through. Your brushstrokes should follow the direction and fall of the fabric.

▶

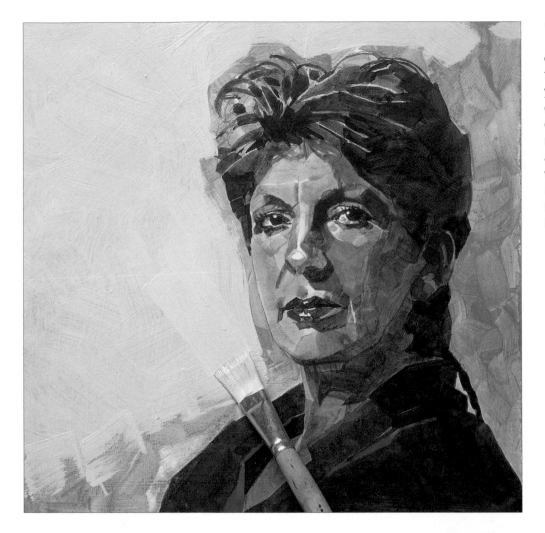

13 The beauty of acrylics is that you can paint a light colour over a dark one, without the first colour being visible. If you think the background is too dark and there is not sufficient differentiation between the model and the background, mix a warm off-white from titanium white, yellow ochre and burnt umber and, using a large flat brush, loosely paint the background again.

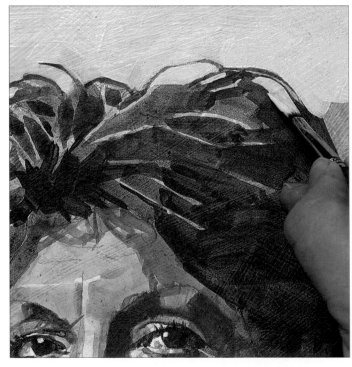

14 Using a small flat brush, cut around individual hairs with the background colour, carefully looking at the "negative shapes".

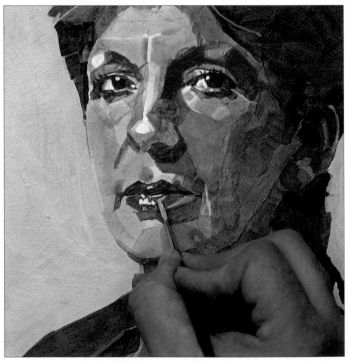

15 Using a fine round brush and titanium white straight from the tube, dot the highlights on to the eyes, nose and lower lip.

The finished painting

This is a relatively simple portrait, with nothing to distract from the sitter's direct gaze. Although the colour palette is limited, the artist has achieved an impressive and realistic range of skin and hair tones. Interest comes from the use of semi-transparent paint layers and allowing the directions of the brush marks to show through.

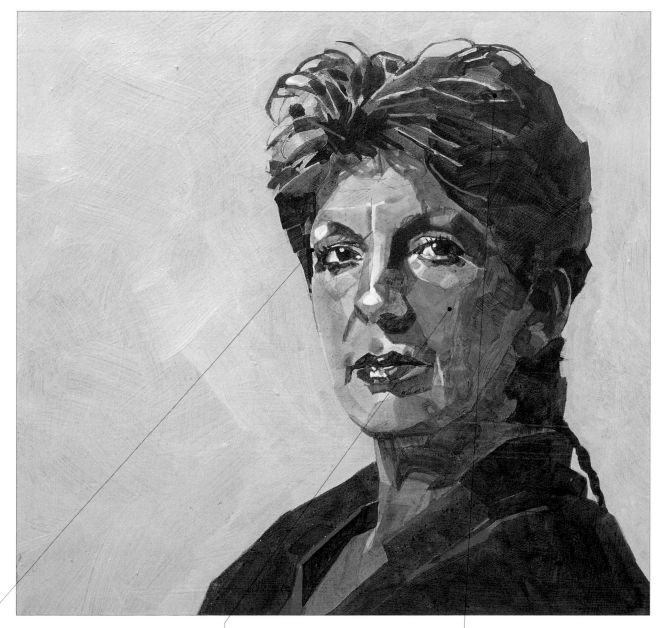

Carefully positioned highlights in the eyes make them sparkle and bring the portrait to life.

Variations in the skin tone, particularly on the shaded side of the face, help to reveal the shape of the face and its underlying bone structure.

The highlights in the hair are created by putting down the lightest tones first and allowing them to show through subsequent applications of paint.

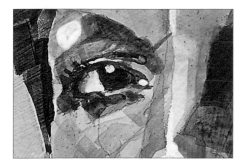

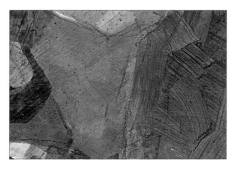

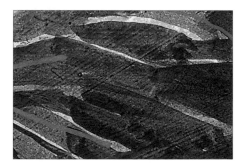

Café scene

At first glance, this café and street scene looks extremely complicated and full of movement, with a complex play of light and shade across the whole scene. You could be forgiven for wondering how on earth you can capture such a wealth of detail in paint.

The trick, at least in the initial stages, is to forget about the detail and to concentrate instead on the overall impression. Look for blocks of colour and tone – and try to see the scene as a series of interconnecting shapes, rather than as individual elements. If you get too caught up in details such as a person's hair or the precise pattern on one of the café umbrellas, the chances are that your painting will become tight and laboured.

Remember, too, that the spaces between objects (which artists describe as "negative" shapes) are as important in a painting as the objects themselves (the "positive" shapes). Although the rational part of your brain may be telling you that a person or a solid object such as a table should take precedence over an apparently empty background, in painting terms the two are equally important: one helps to define the other.

The complex pattern of light and shade requires careful treatment, too. There are many shadows here, both in the open foreground and in the dark, narrow street in the background. Shadows are rarely, if ever, black; instead, they often contain colours that are complementary to the main subject. If buildings are a warm terracotta colour, for example, their shadows may contain a little complementary green.

Sketch
Scenes of people can change quickly, so make a quick preliminary sketch to capture the moment.

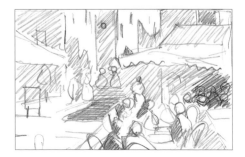

Materials
- *Board primed with acrylic gesso*
- *Willow charcoal*
- *Acrylic paints: cadmium yellow, cadmium red, titanium white, phthalocyanine green, alizarin crimson, lemon yellow, ultramarine blue*
- *Brushes: large round, medium flat, small round*
- *Absorbent paper towel*

The scene
This is one type of subject in which painting from photographs really comes into its own. There is so much going on that you could do little more than put down the bare bones of the scene on the spot – but a quick reference photo or two will "freeze" the action and provide you with plenty of information on which to base your image.

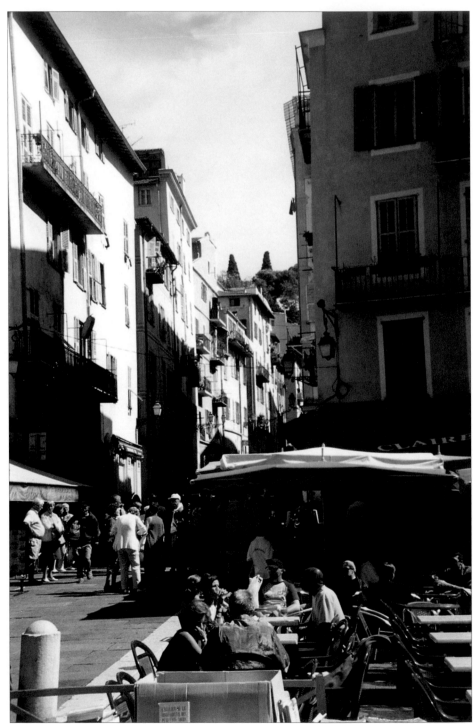

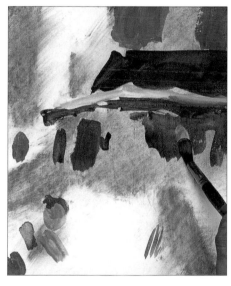

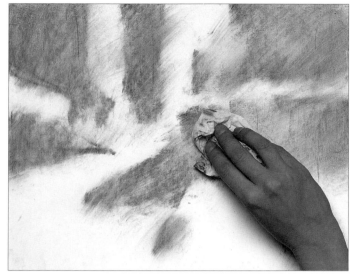

1 Block in the darkest areas of the background buildings and the shadows on the pavement, using the side of a stick of willow charcoal, as this allows you to cover large areas quickly. Although the charcoal will be covered up by subsequent applications of paint, it allows you to establish the structure of the scene at the outset, and makes it easier for you to find your way around the complex mix of colours and tones.

2 To avoid dirtying your colours when you begin applying the paint, gently dust off any excess charcoal powder using a clean piece of paper towel. (Alternatively, you could use a spray fixative.)

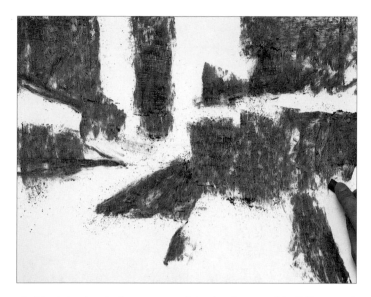

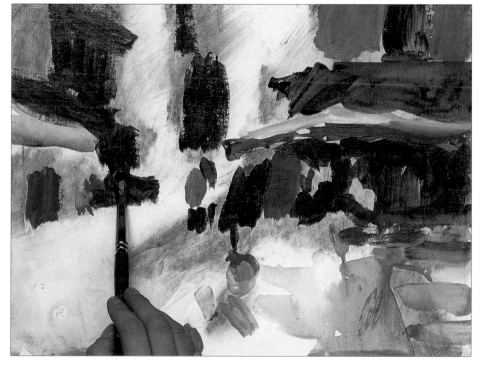

3 Mix a warm orange from cadmium yellow and cadmium red. Using a large round brush, brush in the warm colours of background buildings. Paint the café umbrellas and awning in mixtures of cadmium red and titanium white, varying the proportions of the two colours to get the right tones. Putting in these strong tones in the early stages helps give the scene some structure. The order in which you apply them is not terribly important, but while you have got one colour on the palette try to use it everywhere that it occurs.

4 Loosely indicate the café tables in phthalocyanine green. Mix a very dilute green from phthalocyanine green and titanium white and paint the shadow areas in the foreground. (Note that this green is a cool complementary colour to the reds used on the awning and umbrellas.) Add alizarin crimson to the mixture and paint the very dark colours of the buildings in the background. This gives you the necessary darkness of tone without having to resort to using black, which often tends to look flat and lifeless. It also picks up on colours used elsewhere in the painting, creating one of many colour links that will ultimately help to hold the whole image together.

▶

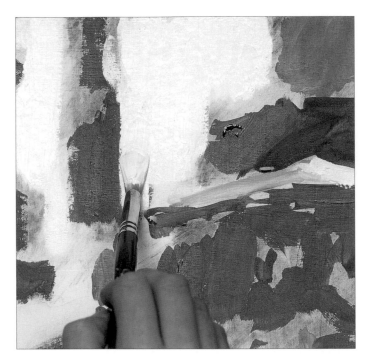

5 Mix a pale yellow from lemon yellow and titanium white and put in the light-coloured buildings in the background. Add more titanium white to the mixtures that you used to paint the umbrellas in Step 3, making the paint fairly thick, and paint the pinkish stripes on the umbrellas.

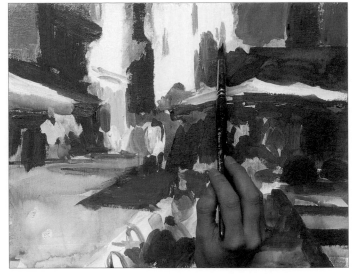

6 Using the dark mixture from Step 4, begin blocking in the figures sitting at the café tables. Do not try to put in substantial detail at this stage: simply look for the overall shapes. Look at the tilt of people's shoulders and heads and concentrate on getting these angles right, as they will help to make the painting look realistic. Brush more of the dilute phthalocyanine green and white mixture over the street area, particularly at the point just beyond the café where the street narrows and is in deeper shade.

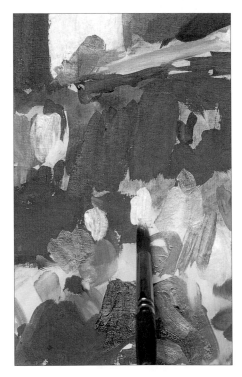

7 Block in the colours of the shirts of the café customers in the foreground, making the colours darker in tone for the creases in the fabric, as this helps to reveal the form of the body and give more of a sense of light and shade.

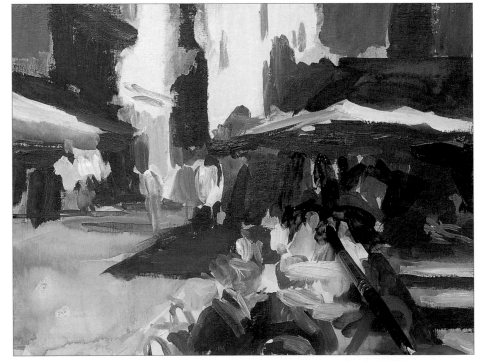

8 Brush over the highlight areas with titanium white, using the paint thickly in order to create some texture. Deepen the tones of the big foreground umbrella where necessary. Using the same dark mixtures as before, carefully brush around the figures sitting at the café tables; although the figures are little more than blocks of colour at this stage, and very little detail has been put in, defining the negative shapes (the spaces between the figures) in this way helps to separate them from the background so that they stand out more clearly.

Assessment time

Using brilliant blue and alizarin crimson, block in more of the shirt and trouser colours of the passers-by on the left. The main elements are now in place, and the rest of the painting will be a gradual process of refinement: although they may look like fairly abstract blocks of colour at this stage, the subjects will soon start to emerge more clearly. Training yourself to look for blocks of colour, rather than attempting to define every element, is a useful exercise.

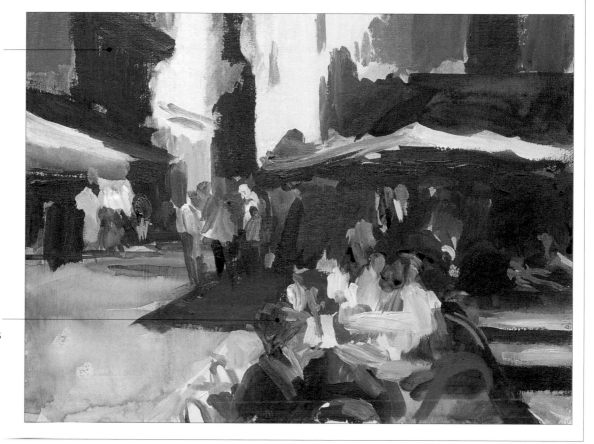

The dark blocks laid down in Step 1 provide the structure for the image.

The people are painted as bold blocks of colour; detail can be added later once the basic shapes and colours are in place.

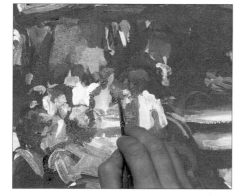

9 Pick out details using a small round brush. Paint the curved chair backs in phthalocyanine green, and the hair of the café customers in various browns mixed from cadmium yellow and cadmium red. Remember to look carefully at the spaces between objects as well as at the objects themselves: going around the figures in a dark tone helps to make them stand out.

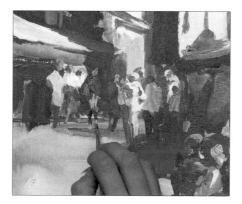

10 Continue adding defining details across the painting, again looking at the negative spaces and looking for identifiable blocks of colour on the clothes of the passers-by. Vertical strokes of green on the background buildings are a quick-and-easy way of implying the dark window recesses; the colour also provides a visual link with the green chairs in the foreground.

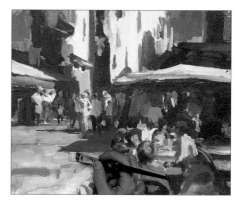

11 Because it is so bright, the eye is drawn to the paved foreground area in the bottom left of the painting, which looks very empty. Using more of the green mixture from Step 6 and a medium flat brush, make broad horizontal strokes across this area. This enhances the feeling of dappled light playing on the ground and creates texture and interest.

▶

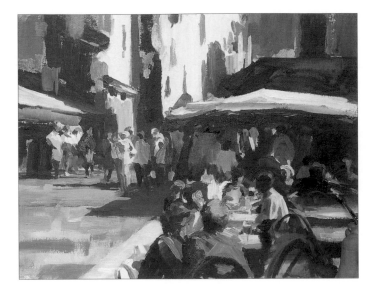

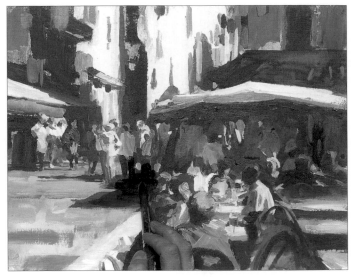

12 Switching to a medium flat brush allows you to shape straight-edged elements, such as the eaves of the roofs (top right) and the table edges (bottom right), more precisely.

13 Using a pale, blue-grey mixture of titanium white and ultramarine blue, loosely indicate the lettering on the café awning. Continue adjusting tones across the whole scene: adding a pale, but opaque yellow to the background buildings reinforces the sense of light and shade, while the shadows on the ground can be made stronger with a bluish-purple mixture as before.

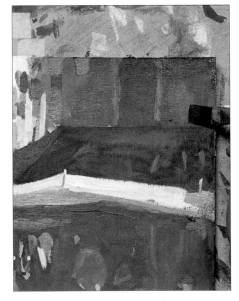

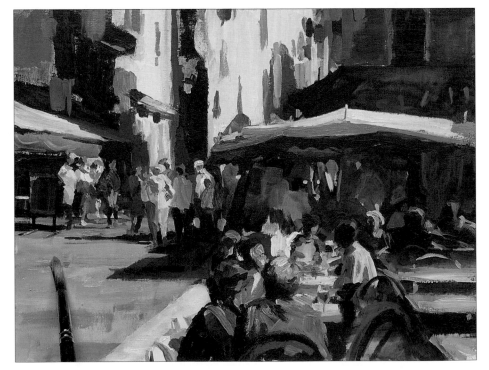

14 Using the flat brush again, block in rectangles of colour on the roofs to define their edges more clearly. The precise colours that you use are not too important: look for the relative lightness and darkness of different areas, as this is what will make the picture look three-dimensional.

15 Using a fine round brush and the same pale blue-grey mixture that you used for the café awning lettering, "draw" in the vertical posts of the awning and the large foreground umbrellas. Adjust the tones on the shaded sides of both awning and umbrellas, if necessary, to reinforce the different planes of the image. If you decide that the bottom left corner is still too bright in relation to the rest of the painting, brush more of the bluey-green shadow mixture across it. Finally, look for any areas that catch the light, such as the edges of the foreground tables and chairs, and lightly touch in the highlights here with a pale mixture of phthalocyanine green and titanium white.

The finished painting

This is a spontaneous-looking painting that belies its careful planning and the meticulous attention to capturing the effects of light and shade. The composition looks informal, like a snapshot of a moment "frozen" in time; in fact, the large, virtually empty space on the left helps to balance the image, while the receding lines of the café tables lead the viewer's eye through the picture to the bustling street and buildings in the background.

Creating the right tonal balance is one of the keys to an image like this; resisting the temptation to put in too much detail, with the consequent risk of overworking the painting, is another. Here, the artist has succeeded on both counts.

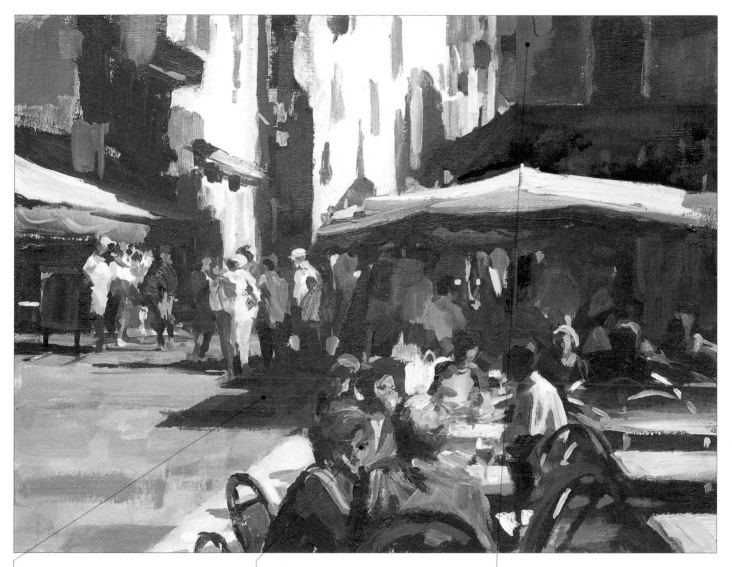

Deep shadows reveal the intensity of the sunlight. They are balanced by the large, brightly lit buildings in the background and help to bring the scene to life.

Although there is relatively little detail on the faces, by concentrating on the tilt of the heads and bodies the artist has conveyed a feeling of animation.

The artist has used some artistic licence in choosing the colours for the building in the background, but they complement and balance the foreground colours well.

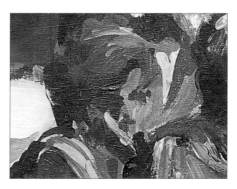

Reclining nude

The reclining nude – more particularly, the reclining female nude – is a classic subject in Western art.

There are a few practical considerations to take into account – particularly if you are painting from life. First, make sure your model is comfortable: provide a sofa, blanket or other soft surface for her to lie on and make sure that the room is warm and free of draughts.

As far as the pose is concerned, it is often better to allow the model to settle into a position that feels natural to her than to tell her what pose to adopt. Although you can obtain interesting and dynamic paintings by directing the model to tense her muscles, such poses are difficult to hold for any length of time.

This particular pose is easy to hold, even for a relatively long period of time. The model's weight is evenly distributed along the whole length of her body and she is able to rest her head on her right forearm, cupping her hand around her head for extra support.

The differences in flesh tone need to be very carefully assessed in this project. Certain areas, such as the hands, the soles of the feet and the lower body, tend to be warmer in colour than others, because the blood vessels run closer to the surface of the skin. The upper body, on the other hand, is usually cooler in tone. However, one of the joys of painting in oils is that the paint remains soft and workable for a long time, so you can blend colours on the support as you work to create subtle transitions from one tone to another as the body curves towards or away from the light source.

Materials
- *Stretched canvas*
- *Rag*
- *Oil paints: cadmium orange, brilliant pink, raw sienna, cadmium red, cadmium yellow, brilliant turquoise, titanium white, ultramarine blue, lamp black, vermilion, cerulean blue*
- *Turpentine (white spirit)*
- *Drying linseed oil*
- *Brushes: selection of small and medium rounds, small or medium flat*

The pose
One of the most interesting things about this particular model is the way in which her upper vertebrae and ribs are so clearly defined. The natural curves of her body create clearly defined areas of light and shade, which add interest to the composition. Note the masking tape on the blanket, outlining the model's pose. This enables the model to get back in the same position if she inadvertently moves during the session or has to take a break.

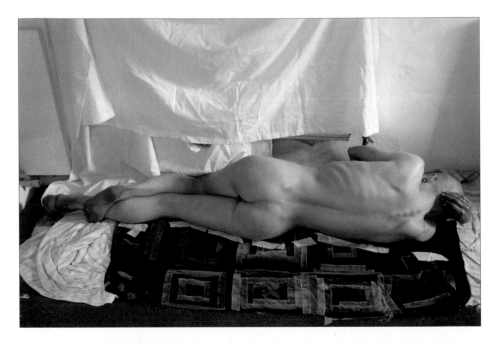

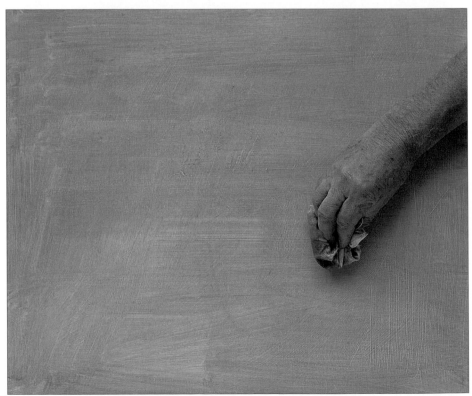

1 With a rag, spread cadmium orange paint evenly over the canvas, changing to brilliant pink in the top left. Leave to dry.

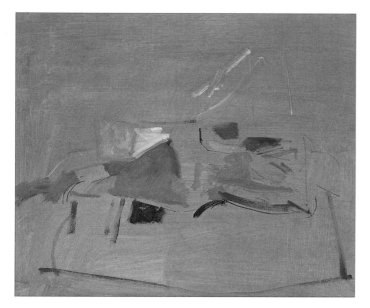

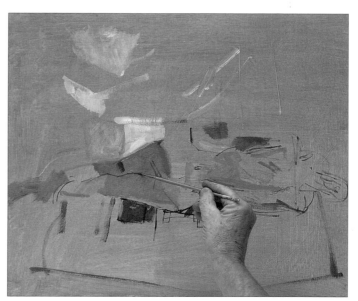

2 Using a medium round brush and raw sienna, "draw" the edges of the blanket on which the model is lying and the dark shadow under her hips. Delineate the head and upper body and the legs in cadmium red. The actual colours are not too important at this stage, as this is merely the underpainting, but warm colours are appropriate to the subject. Mix a range of warm flesh tones from cadmium yellow and cadmium orange and block in the warmest toned areas – the buttocks, the soles of the feet, and the curve of the spine. Start putting in the main folds of the background cloth using mixtures of brilliant turquoise and titanium white.

3 Mix titanium white with a little ultramarine blue and block in some of the dark folds in the background cloth. Using a fine brush and cadmium red, loosely "draw" the head and supporting hand, reinforce the line separating the legs and indicate the angle of the hips.

Tip: It is always important to remember the underlying anatomy of the pose, even when you are painting fleshy parts of the body where the shape of the bones is not visible.

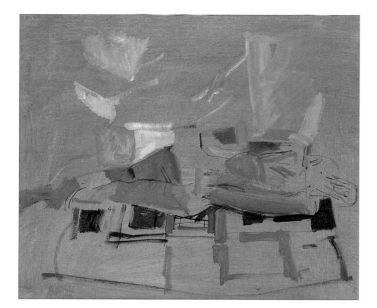

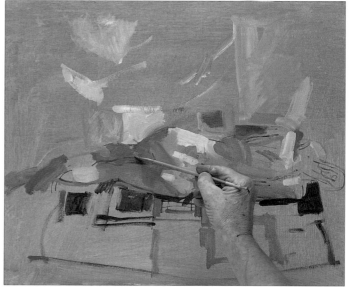

4 Using green (mixed from titanium white, cadmium yellow and ultramarine blue) and a dark grey (mixed from ultramarine blue and raw sienna), start putting in the pattern of the patchwork blanket. Mix a pale blue-green from ultramarine blue and raw sienna and indicate the shadows under the ribs and the shaded part of the back. Note that this mixture is a complementary colour to the first flesh tones: shadow areas often contain a hint of a complementary colour.

5 Mix a pale orange from cadmium red, cadmium yellow and titanium white and begin putting in some of the paler flesh tones. Alternate between all the various flesh tones on your palette, blending them into one another on the support and continually assessing where the light and dark tones fall and whether the colours are warm or cool in temperature. Almost immediately, you will see that the body is starting to look three-dimensional.

▶

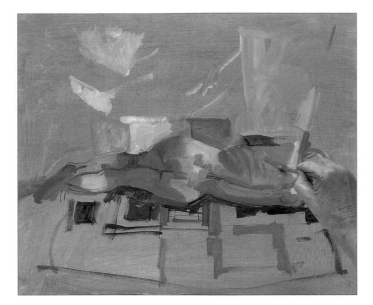

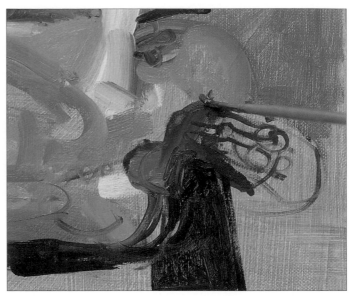

6 Continue working on the flesh tones. The highlights and shadows reveal the curves of the body: the backs of the thighs, for example, are in shadow and are therefore darker in tone than the tops of the buttocks, which are angled towards the light. Note the greenish tones on the upper body: the upper body is often noticeably cooler in tone than the lower body, perhaps because the blood vessels in this area are not so near the surface of the skin.

7 Block in the most deeply shaded areas of the white background cloth with a blue-biased mixture of ultramarine blue and titanium white. Use a slightly lighter version of this colour to paint the model's shaved head, allowing some of the ground to show through in parts as the colour of her scalp. Loosely "draw" the hand and fingers in cadmium red, indicating the joints in the fingers by means of rough circular or elliptical shapes.

Assessment time
Although the areas of warm and cool tone have been established, the figure still looks somewhat flat and one-dimensional. More tonal contrast is needed: spend time working out how you are going to achieve this. Remember to work across the picture as a whole rather than concentrating on one area – otherwise you run the risk of over-emphasizing certain areas and making them too detailed in relation to the rest, thus destroying the balance of the painting.

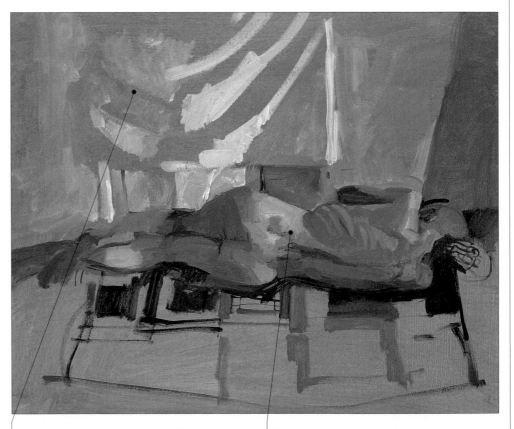

The broad areas of light and shade have been established – now you can refine this area.

There is not enough tonal contrast for the figure to look truly three-dimensional.

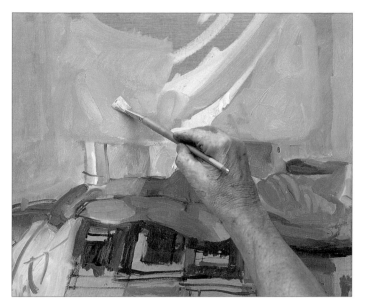

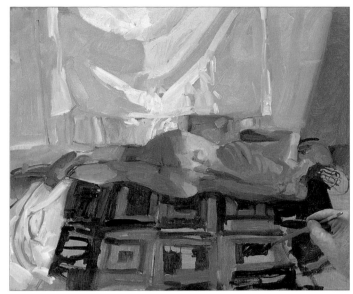

8 The cloth at the model's feet is draped to create interesting folds. Block in its shape loosely in a mixture of ultramarine blue and white, then put dark strokes of a darker grey or brown over the top to indicate the main folds. Begin putting in some of the mid-tones in the background cloth, using mixtures of ultramarine blue and white as before.

9 Loosely paint the pattern of the patchwork blanket on which the model is lying, using broad strokes of the appropriate colour. Do not try to be too precise with the pattern: a loose interpretation will suffice. You should, however, note how the lines of the pattern change direction where the blanket is not perfectly flat.

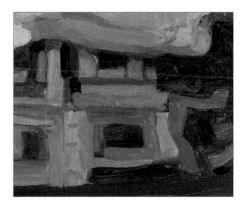

10 Continue working on the blanket, gradually building up and strengthening the colours while keeping them fresh and spontaneous.

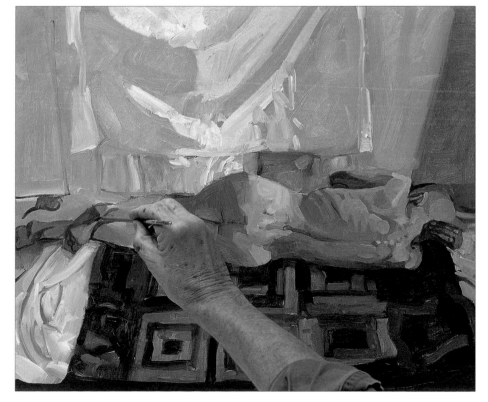

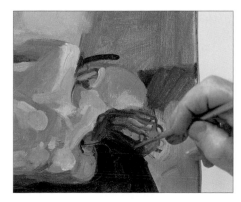

11 Redefine the fingers in cadmium orange and a little brilliant pink.

12 Darken the area around the head with a mixture of ultramarine blue, white and a little lamp black, so that the head stands out from the background. Work on the flesh tones, to improve the tonal contrast: the shoulder blade, for example, is lighter than the tones laid down so far, so paint it in a mixture of cadmium orange and white. Use the same colour to define the highlights on the top cervical vertebrae. The soles of the feet are very warm in colour; paint them in a mixture of cadmium red and vermilion.

▶

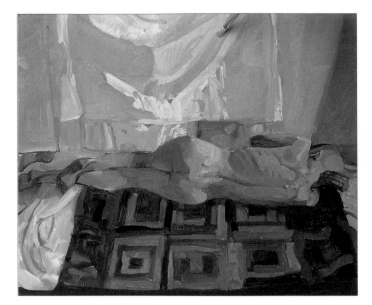

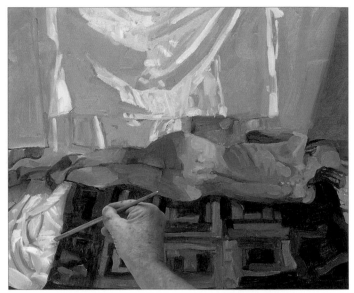

13 Now turn your attention to the background cloth, reinforcing the dark and mid-toned folds with a mixture of ultramarine blue, white and a tiny amount of cerulean blue – all the time assessing the tones of the cloth in relation to the overall scene rather than looking at it in isolation.

14 Use pure white for the brightest areas of the background cloth, changing to a smaller brush for the finest creases. Note how the folds vary in tone depending on how deep they are: use some mid-tones where necessary to convey this.

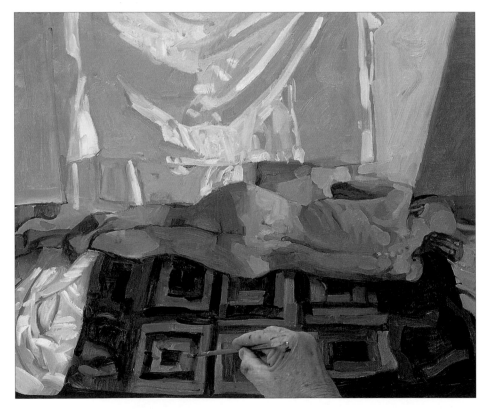

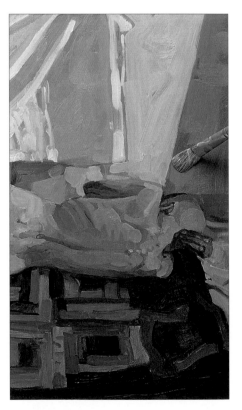

15 Mix a dark green from ultramarine blue and cadmium yellow and reinforce the dark colours in the blanket. Use the same colour to strengthen the shadow under the model and give a sharp edge to the curve of her body. Brighten the light greens and pinks in the blanket; as the patchwork pattern is made up of straight strips of fabric, you may find that it helps to switch to a small or medium flat brush so that the lines of the pattern are straight and crisp-edged.

16 The triangular-shaped wedge of cloth on the right, just above the model's head, is too light and leads the viewer's eye out of the picture. Mix a mid-toned green and block it in, directing your brushstrokes upwards to avoid accidentally brushing paint on to the model's head.

The finished painting

The figure is positioned almost exactly across the centre of the picture – something that artists are often advised to avoid, but in this instance it adds to the calm, restful mood of the painting. The dark colours and sloping lines of the blanket and the folds in the background cloth all help to direct the viewer's eye towards the nude figure. The background cloth is painted slightly darker in tone than it is in reality: overly stark whites would detract from the figure.

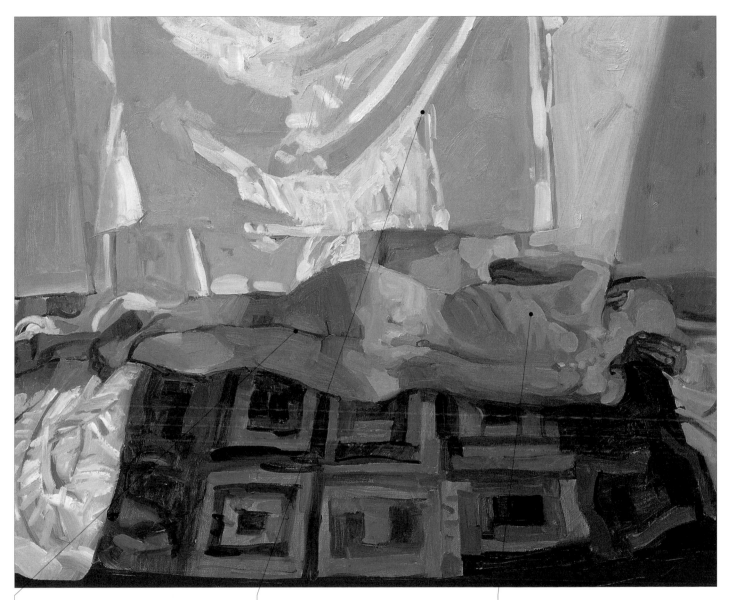

The legs are slightly bent: light and dark flesh tones show how some parts are angled into the light while others are shaded.

Careful assessment of tones is required in order to paint the white backcloth convincingly.

Skin is stretched taut over the ribs and upper vertebrae: subtle shading reveals the shape of the underlying bones.

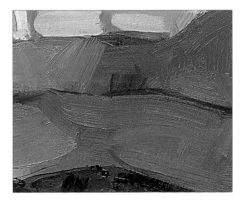

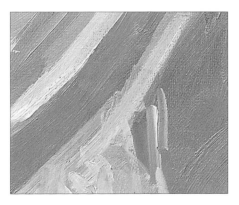

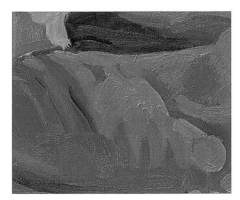

Cupped hands

Hands and gestures are very expressive and can tell you a lot about a person's character and mood. Sadly, many people seem to find it difficult to draw and paint hands – and the reason is usually that they give too much attention to individual elements such as the fingers, rather than trying to see the hand as a whole. You should always try to think of the hand as a complete unit rather than as something made up of four fingers and a thumb. If you paint each finger separately, the chances are that you'll make them too big in relation to the rest of the hand.

This project is a simple pose that gives you the chance to examine the structure of the hand in some detail.

Before you begin the painting, spend time looking your own hands. Some people's fingers are short and stubby, while others have long, elegantly tapering fingers; nonetheless, you will be able to make some general observations that apply to all hands. Look at the number of

joints and see how the fingers widen slightly at these points. Spread your hand out flat: you will see that each finger is a different length and that the joints do not align with one another. Similarly, the knuckles run in a curved line across the back of the hand. Arch your hand, with your fingertips placed on the table top and your wrist elevated, so that you can see the bones and tendons that connect the fingers to the rest of the hand and arm.

Finally, note how the creases in the skin, and subtle changes in tone as each finger turns away from the light, will help you to create a three-dimensional impression.

Materials
- *B pencil*
- *Board primed with acrylic gesso*
- *Acrylic paints: raw umber, ultramarine blue, cadmium red, cadmium lemon, titanium white, quinacridone red*
- *Brushes: medium flat, small flat*

The pose
In this project the sitter's hands are clasped loosely around a cup of coffee – a pose that is easy for the sitter to hold, giving you plenty of time to make your study. The structure of the fingers and the way the joints are articulated can be seen clearly. Light comes from the top left of the scene and causes the cup to cast interestingly shaped shadows on the sitter's left hand.

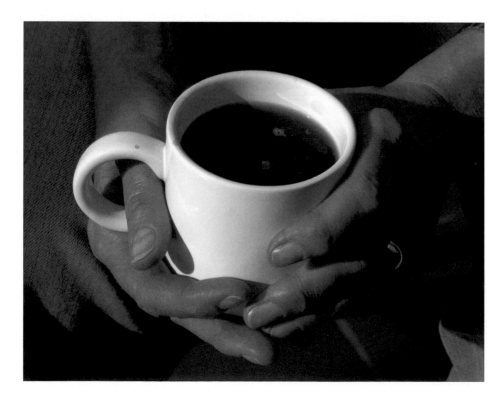

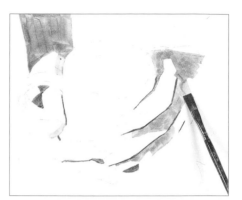

1 Using a B pencil, make a light underdrawing. Mix a dark brown from raw umber and ultramarine blue and, using a flat brush, paint in the shadows above and below the fingers. Add a little cadmium red and block in the shadows on the sitter's left hand.

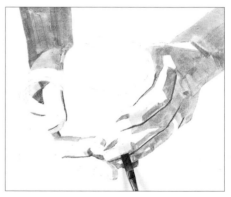

2 Mix in a little more red. Paint the shadow on the finger undersides.

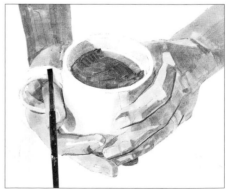

3 Paint the hands in a mix of cadmium red, raw umber and cadmium lemon, and paint the coffee in a mix of raw umber and cadmium red. Mix grey from ultramarine and raw umber and paint the shaded parts of the mug. Lighten the mix and paint the rest of the mug.

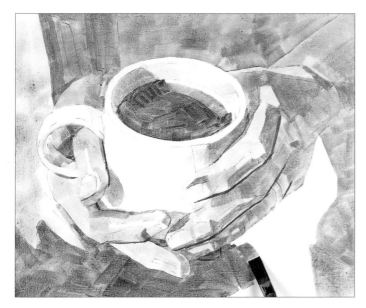

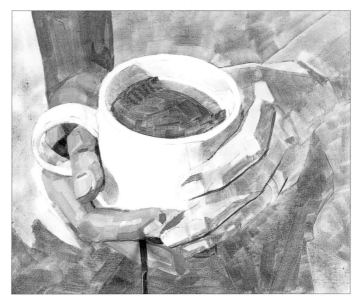

4 Add a little more ultramarine blue to the mixture used for the coffee mug and paint the sitter's trousers. Paint the reddish brown area between the sitter's legs in a mixture of cadmium red and raw umber.

5 Mix cadmium red, raw umber, cadmium lemon and a little titanium white and paint the mid-pink tones on the hands. Note how the changes in tone between the different segments of the fingers define their form.

Assessment time

We are beginning to get some sense of the shape of the hands and how the fingers bend, but the tonal differences are not yet sufficient for them to look fully rounded. The background and the hands are, at this stage, too similar in tone; as a result, the hands do not stand out clearly. Overall, the colours are too pale and need to be strengthened.

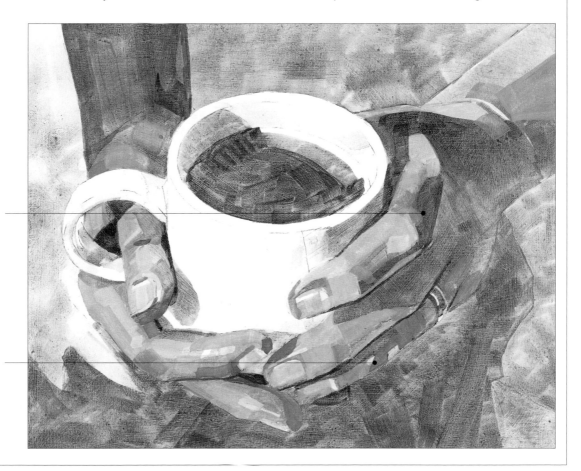

The form of the hands needs to be more fully developed.

The hands merge into the background.

▶

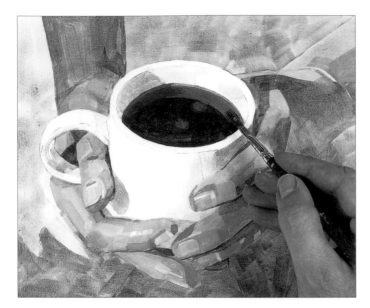

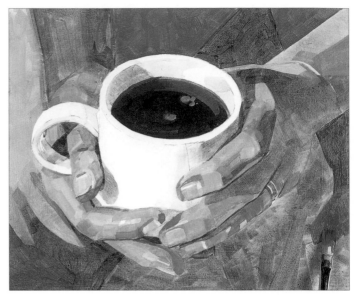

6 Mix a dark brown from raw umber and ultramarine blue and paint over the coffee again, adding a little white to the mixture for areas where the light hits the liquid. It is important to realize that the coffee is not a uniform shade of brown throughout.

7 Mix a neutral grey from ultramarine blue, raw umber and titanium white and put in the shadows on the trousers caused by creases and folds in the fabric. Darken the flesh tone overall, leaving little areas of light tone on the nails, which are shiny and catch the light.

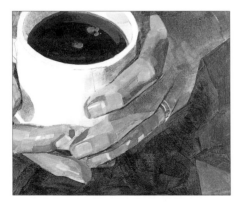

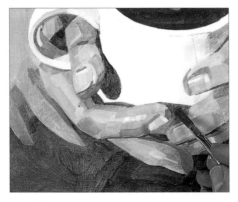

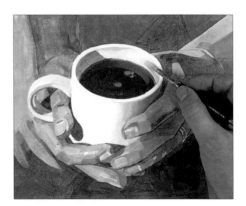

8 Darken the brown between the legs. Immediately, the hands start to stand out from the background.

9 Use a range of dark neutral greys to paint the shadows cast on the mug by the fingers.

10 Using lighter tones of grey and white, tidy up the tones on the coffee mug.

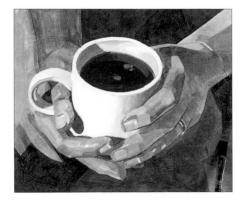

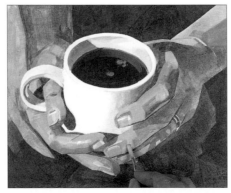

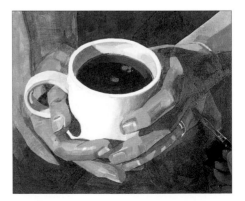

11 Darken the background – the sitter's trousers. This throws the hands forward to become the main focus of the painting.

12 Lighten the flesh tones where necessary and refine the tones on the fingers, making use of the same mixtures as before.

13 Darken the shadows on the left hand using raw umber, quinacridone red and ultramarine blue. This gives depth to the scene.

The finished painting

This is a simple and relaxed pose that has been skilfully painted, with careful attention being paid to the different flesh tones in order to convey the shape of the hands and the way the fingers curl around the coffee mug. The background is a plain colour, which allows the hands (the focal point of the image) to stand out clearly.

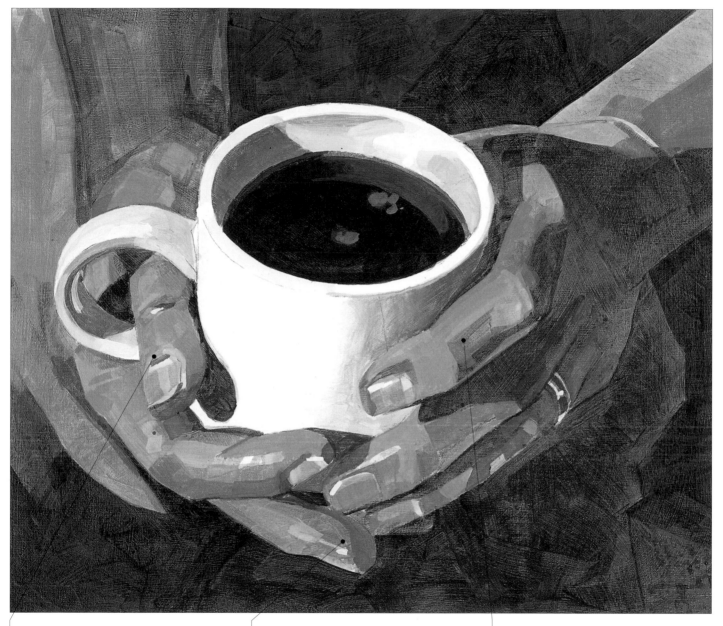

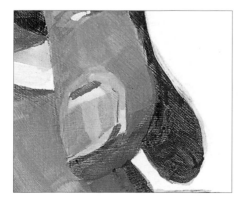

Shadows cast by the fingers reveal both the direction and the intensity of the light.

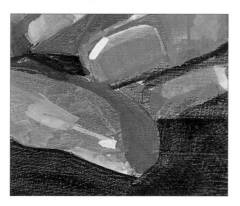

The dark background allows the hands to stand out clearly.

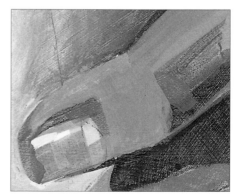

Changes in tone, delineated with a flat brush, reveal the form of the fingers.

Glossary

Alla prima A term used to describe a work (traditionally an oil painting) that is completed in a single session. *Alla prima* means "at the first" in Italian.

Composition The way in which the elements of a painting are arranged within the picture space.

Drybrush The technique of dragging an almost dry brush, loaded with very little paint, across the surface of the support to make textured marks.

Fat over lean A fundamental principle of oil painting. In order to minimize the risk of cracking, oil paints containing a lot of oil ('fat' paints) should never be applied over those that contain less oil ('lean' paints) – although the total oil content of any paint mixture should never exceed 50 per cent.

Glaze A transparent layer of paint that is applied over a layer of dry paint. Light passes through the transparent glaze and is reflected back by the support or any underpainting. Glazing is a form of optical colour mixing as each glaze colour is separate from the next, with the mixing taking place within the eye.

Ground The prepared surface on which an artist works. See also **Support**.

Hue A colour in its pure state, unmixed with any other.

Impasto Impasto techniques involve applying and building oil or acrylic paint into a thick layer. Impasto work retains the mark of any brush or implement used to apply it.

Mahl stick A piece of equipment used in oil painting, consisting of a light rod of wood (often bamboo) with a soft leather ball secured on one end. The mahl stick is held in one hand and rested on the edge of the work, with the painting hand resting on the rod.

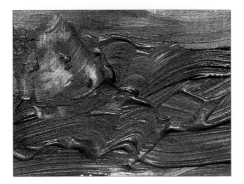

This steadies the painting hand and keeps it clear of any wet paint.

Mask Any substance that is applied to the support to prevent paint from reaching specific areas.

Palette (1) The container or surface on which paint colours are mixed. (2) The range of colours used by an artist.

Perspective A system which creates the illusion of three-dimensional space on a two-dimensional surface.

> **Aerial perspective**: the way the atmosphere, combined with distance, influences the appearance of things. Also known as atmospheric perspective.

> **Linear perspective**: linear perspective exploits the fact that objects appear to be smaller the further away they are from the viewer. The system is based on the fact that all parallel lines, when extended from a receding surface, meet at a point in space known as the vanishing point. When such lines are plotted accurately on the support, the relative sizes of the objects will appear correct in the painting.

Primer A substance that acts as a barrier between the support and the paint, protecting the support from the corrosive agents present in the paint and the solvents. Priming provides a smooth, clean surface on which to work. The traditional primer for use with oil paint is glue size, which is then covered with an oil-based primer such as lead white. Nowadays, acrylic emulsions (often called acrylic gesso) are more commonly used.

Resist A substance that prevents one medium from touching the support beneath it.

Scaling up A method of transferring an image to a larger format. First, a grid of squares is superimposed on the original image. Then a second grid of larger squares in the same proportion is marked out on the new, larger support. Finally, each square of the original is copied on to the corresponding square on the larger format.

Scumble A technique that involves applying dry, semi-opaque paint loosely and roughly over a dry underlayer, leaving some of the underlayer visible to create optical colour mixes on the support. The technique also produces interesting surface textures.

Sgraffito The technique of scratching off paint to reveal either an underlying paint colour or the colour of the support. The word comes from the Italian verb *graffiare*, which means "to scratch".

Size A weak solution of glue used to make canvas impervious prior to applying layers of primer or oil paint.

Solvent See **Thinner**.

Spattering The technique of flicking paint on to the support to create texture.

Support The surface on which a painting is made. See also **Ground**.

Thinner A liquid such as turpentine which is used to dilute oil paint. Also known as Solvent.

Tone The relative lightness or darkness of a colour. Also known as **Value**.

Tonking An technique named after the British artist Henry Tonks (1862–1937), which involves placing a sheet of newspaper over the wet oil or acrylic paint, smoothing it down and peeling it away to remove excess paint.

Underdrawing A preliminary sketch on the canvas or paper, over which a picture is painted. It allows the artist to set down the lines of the subject, and erase and change them if necessary, before committing irrevocably to paint.

Underpainting A painting made to work out the composition and tonal structure of a work before applying colour.

Value See **Tone**.

Wash A thin layer of transparent paint.
> **Flat wash**: an evenly laid wash that exhibits no variation in tone.
> **Gradated wash**: a wash that gradually changes in intensity from dark to light, or vice versa.
> **Variegated wash**: a wash that changes from one colour to another.

Wet into wet The technique of applying paint to a wet surface or on top of an earlier wash that is still damp.

Suppliers

Manufacturers
Daler-Rowney UK Ltd
PO Box 10, Bracknell
Berkshire RG12 8ST
United Kingdom
Tel: (01344) 461000
Website: www.daler-rowney.com

Winsor & Newton
Whitefriars Avenue, Wealdstone
Harrow, Middlesex HA3 5RH
United Kingdom
Tel: (020) 8427 4343
Website: www.winsornewton.com

H. Schmincke & Co.
Otto-Hahn-Strasse 2, D040699 Erkrath
Germany
Tel: (0211) 2509-0
Website: www.schmincke.de

Stockists
UNITED KINGDOM
ABS Brushes
Wetley Abbey, Wetley Rocks
Staffordshire ST9 0PS
Tel: (01782) 551551
Website: www.absbrushes.com

Art Express
Design House, Sizers Court
Yeadon LS19 6DP
Tel: 0113 250 0077
Website: www.artexpress.co.uk

Atlantis Art Materials
7–9 Plumbers Row, London E1 1EQ
Tel: (020) 7377 8855
Website: www.atlantisart.co.uk

Dodgson Fine Arts Ltd
t/a Studio Arts, 50 North Road
Lancaster LA1 1LT
Tel: (01524) 68014
Website: www.studioarts.co.uk
or www.studioartshop.com

Falkiner Fine Papers
76 Southampton Row
London WC1B 4AR
Tel: (020) 7831 1151
E-mail: falkiner@ic24.net

Hobbycraft
Hobbycraft specialize in arts and crafts
materials and own 20 stores around the
UK. Freephone (0800) 027 2387
Website: www.hobbycraft.co.uk

Paintworks
99–101 Kingsland Road
London E2 8AG
Tel: (020) 7729 7451
E-mail: shop@paintworks.biz

Russell & Chapel
Tel: (020) 7836 7521

Stuart Stevenson
68 Clerkenwell Road
London EC1M 5QA
Tel: (020) 7253 1693

Turnham Arts & Crafts
2 Bedford Park Corner
Turnham Green Terrace
London W4 1LS
Tel: (020) 8995 2872
Fax: (020) 8995 2873

UNITED STATES
Art & Frame of Sarasota
1055 South Tamiami Trail
Sarasota, FL 34236
Tel: (941) 366-2301
Website: www.in2art.com

Dick Blick Art Materials
PO Box 1267, Galesburg
IL 61402-1267
Tel: (800) 828-4548
Website: www.dickblick.com

Hobby Lobby
Website: www.hobbylobby.com

Michaels Stores
Michaels.com, 8000 Bent Branch Dr.
Irving, TX 75063
Tel: (1-800) 6432-4235
Website: www.michaels.com

Mister Art
913 Willard Street, Houston,
TX 77006
Tel toll free: (866) 672-7811
Website: www.misterart.com

The Easel Studio
Tel toll free: (800) 916-2278
Website: www.easelstudio.com

CANADA
D.L. Stevenson & Son Ltd
1420 Warden Avenue
Scarborough, Ontario M1R 5A3
Tel: (416) 755-7795
E-mail (US):
customerservice@artpaintonline.com

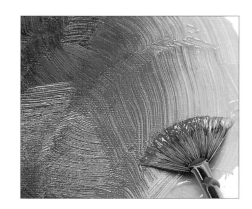

Customized paper and canvas stretchers:
Upper Canada Stretchers Inc.
1750 16th Avenue East
Box 565 Owen Sound
Ontario N4K 5R4
Tel: (1-800) 561-4944
Website: 222.ucsart.com

Colours Artist Suppliers
414 Graham Avenue, Winnipeg
Manitoba R3C 0L8
Tel: (204) 956-5364
(Six stores across western Canada.)

AUSTRALIA
Art Materials
Website: www.artmaterials.com.au

North Shore Art Supplies
10 George Street
Hornsby, NSW 2077
Tel: (02) 9476 0202

Oxford Art Supplies Pty Ltd
221–223 Oxford Street
Darlinghurst, NSW 2010
Tel: (02) 9360 4066
Website: www.oxfordart.com.au or
www.janetsart.com.au

NEW ZEALAND
Draw Art Supplies Ltd
PO Box 24022
5 Mahunga Drive
Mangere Bridge, Auckland
Tel: (09) 636 4989
Website: www.draw-art.co.nz

Fine Art Supplies
PO Box 58018, 38 Neil Park Dr.
Greenmount, Auckland
Tel: 09) 274 8896
Website: www.fineartsupplies.co.nz

Index

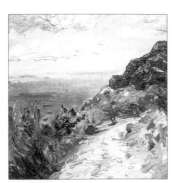
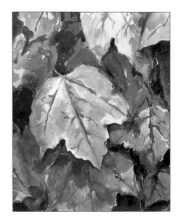

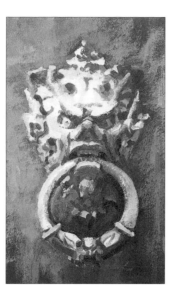

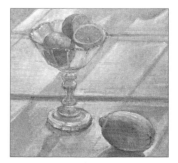

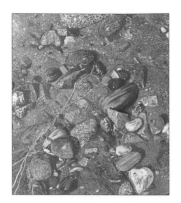
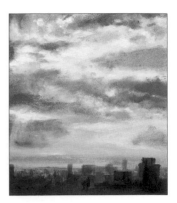
Acknowledgements

The publishers are grateful to the staff at Paintworks, 99–101 Kingsland Road, London E2 8AG for the generous loan of materials and equipment.

Special thanks to the following artists for their demonstrations and step-by-step projects:
Martin Decent: pages 146–51, 158–63, 172–7, 216–221.
Paul Dyson: pages 106–109, 124–9.
Timothy Easton: pages 110–115, 152–7, 178–83, 192–7.
Abigail Edgar: pages 28–9, 46–7, 48–9, 52–3, 57–9, 61 (bottom), 62–3, 69–71, 73–5, 80–81, 83 (bottom right), 84–5, 86 (bottom right), 87, 142-5, 204–9, 224–9, 236–41.
Wendy Jelbert: pages 100–105, 130–135, 166–71, 210–215.

John Raynes: pages 116–121, 136–9, 198–203, 242–7.
Ian Sidaway: pages 9–18, 26, 27, 31, 32–3, 35, 38–41, 42–5, 50–51, 52, 56, 60, 61 (top), 64–67, 68, 72, 76–9, 82, 83 (top), 86 (top), 88–95, 184–9, 230–235, 248–251.

Thanks to the following for their kind permission to reproduce copyright photographs and paintings:
Keith Adams: page 136 (top).
Martin Decent: pages 99 (top), 122, 141 (top), 165 (top), 192, 223 (bottom).
Timothy Easton: pages 98, 99 (bottom), 123 (both), 140, 141 (bottom), 164, 165 (bottom), 193 (both), 222, 223 (top).
Jon Hibberd: pages 61 (bottom left), 83 (bottom left).

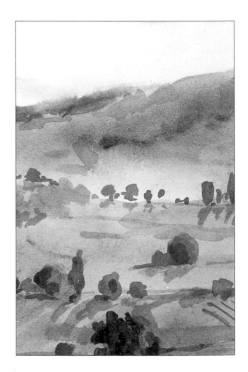